MAMA'S LITTLE BABY

THE BLACK WOMAN'S GUIDE TO PREGNANCY, CHILDBIRTH, AND BABY'S FIRST YEAR

DENNIS BROWN, M.D., AND PAMELA A. TOUSSAINT

Illustrations by
Mona Mark and Gil Ashby

A DUTTON BOOK

DUTTON
Published by the Penguin Group
Penguin Books USA Inc., 375 Hudson Street,
New York, New York 10014, U.S.A.
Penguin Books Ltd, 27 Wrights Lane,
London W8 5TZ, England
Penguin Books Australia Ltd, Ringwood,
Victoria, Australia
Penguin Books Canada Ltd, 10 Alcorn Avenue,
Toronto, Ontario, Canada M4V 3B2
Penguin Books (N.Z.) Ltd, 182–190 Wairau Road,
Auckland 10, New Zealand

Penguin Books Ltd, Registered Offices:
Harmondsworth, Middlesex, England

First published by Dutton, an imprint of Dutton Signet,
a division of Penguin Books USA Inc.
Distributed in Canada by McClelland & Stewart Inc.

First Printing, July, 1997
10 9 8 7 6 5 4 3 2 1

Illustrations in chapters 7 and 12 by Gil Ashby; all other illustrations by Mona Mark.
All scripture references in this book are taken from the New International Version® of the
Bible.

 REGISTERED TRADEMARK—MARCA REGISTRADA

LIBRARY OF CONGRESS CATALOGING-IN-PUBLICATION DATA:

Brown, Dennis, M.D.
    Mama's little baby : the black woman's guide to pregnancy, childbirth, and baby's first
year / Dennis Brown and Pamela Toussaint.
    p.   cm.
Includes bibliographical references and index.
ISBN 0–525–93989–X
1. Pregnancy.   2. Afro-American women.   3. Childbirth.   4. Infants—Care.
I. Toussaint, Pamela.   II. Title.
RG525.B686   1997
618.2'4'08996073—dc21   96–52949
                                                                                      CIP

Printed in the United States of America
Set in Janson Text
Designed by Leonard Telesca

This book is printed on acid-free paper.

This book is dedicated to
Cecil and Aquilla Brown, and Ken and Gloria Toussaint,
who nurtured us all our lives.

Contributing Writers and Researchers

Ann Brown
Holly Favino
Melanie Lee
Julie Levine
Joy L. Rankin
Anita Samuels
Cateena Walker

Special thanks to: Linda Villarosa, for recommending me for this book; my awesome editor, Deb Brody, for giving me the freedom to work; my agents, Madeline Morel and Barbara Lowenstein—the ultimate team; Donna Holt, Gladys Parris, Sue Dalton, Tony Carter, and Lori Hicks, for giving me much-needed feedback while I was writing; Gwen Spears, Armentia Jarrett, Lola Coleman, Melva Nicholson-Brown, C.N.M.s in Los Angeles, for sharing the rich history of midwifery with me; Carol Ambrose, C.N.M., Marcia Jackson, C.N.M., and Jennifer Dohrn, C.N.M., for their kind assistance and dedication to serving women; fitness experts Alicia Villarosa, C.S.W., and Dominique Adair, M.S., for helping me write a realistic exercise chapter; Dr. Meredith Sirmans, for his willingness to share his expertise in obstetrics; dietician Lenea Pollett, for her critical eye and encouraging words on the nutrition chapter; Tonye Allen/Trilobite, for taking great photos on the fly in L.A.; Allford Trotman, for finding me wonderful shots of hard-to-find things; Halley Ganges, our baby-care photographer, for working with us (despite the rash); Cliff and Benilde Little-Virgin and Wilma Almonor, for sharing themselves and their beautiful children, Baldwin and Merault, with our cameras; our painstaking illustrators, Mona Mark and Gil Ashby; Mirtha Lowney, for talking to me about babies ad nauseam; Kimberly Patamia of the American College of Nurse Midwives, for *always* returning my calls; Dr. Brenda Wade, for helping us navigate the emotional waters of parenting; Diane Green and Dorothy McClean, for sharing colorful baby-care anecdotes; Judy Robinson and Sheila Robinson, for their administrative assistance; Bill Green and New Life Fellowship, for lending their facilities, expertise, and support; Fiona Asmah, for her first-hand knowledge of West African culture; all of the mothers who attended our focus groups in New York, Los Angeles, and Virginia, and those who lent information by phone and fax; the wonderful fathers who shared their feelings about becoming daddies, especially "my brother" Ray; Kenneth and Gloria Toussaint, for their love and support; and above all, to Christ, through whom I can do all things.

—Pamela A. Toussaint

Contents

PART THREE: INTRODUCTION TO YOUR BABY

Introduction

Afunny thing happened to me one day during office hours at my practice in Harlem. I was asked to consider co-authoring a book on pregnancy, birth, and infant care from a "black perspective." Interesting, I thought. I began to search myself and ask, How exactly *does* my practice differ from that of my white colleagues? And, What would a "black perspective" be on a natural, everyday occurrence like childbirth? At first, I got an attitude. After all, I offered *all* my patients, blacks and non-blacks, the same state-of-the-art care taught me at the University of Michigan Medical School, Long Island Jewish Hospital, Bellevue Hospital/New York University Medical Center, and now Presbyterian Hospital in New York. What do you mean, "How does my practice *differ*"? My co-author also wrestled with the issue. When she talked about the book project, her white colleagues asked her, "Well, what *is* so unusual about the way blacks have babies?" Some black friends had questions too. She felt as if she was expected to say, "Well, didn't you know we deliver through our noses and raise our babies on Yoo-Hoo?"

While we were convinced that our project was valid and exciting (and thankfully, so were our agents and editor), in our heart of hearts we weren't completely sure what such a book would look or sound like. Would it be angry? Would it be full of statistics about what blacks "suffer disproportionately from"? Would it talk endlessly about the ill-effects of slavery and racism? Would it be full of ominous-sounding African folklore and home remedies? Or would it be an "assimilated" book, one that presented the usual medical information with a few "black thangs" thrown in? Ultimately, we realized that the best people to ask advice from were black parents (you!), who we hoped would find such a book useful.

The parents made a lot of sense. They pointed out that it wasn't the medicine that made my practice different but rather the people. The life experiences brought through my door each day provide the cultural flavor to my practice—a flavor that is so much a part of our doctor-patient interaction it took effort to reveal it. I overlooked our mutual cultural experiences as black people because it's something so natural—like a second skin, if you'll pardon the joke. But in fact, our experience as a people is rather significant. It "colors" our interactions, our thoughts, and our plans, whether we acknowledge it or not.

In our research, we discovered that no pregnancy, birth, or infant care book had yet been compiled specifically for, by, and about black people—not to mention one that covered all three subjects under one roof. Presenting a book on these subjects that featured black faces, black experts, and black babies was our unique endeavor. Exploring our African, Caribbean, and African-American heritage as it pertains to diet, baby names, birthing, infant care, and just "everyday stuff" makes the book relevant in ways other books are not. And providing solid information to black couples about what to expect before, during, and after "that time" comes was our ultimate goal. With this solid understanding, we went to work for three years, with numerous professionals and experts in the areas of pregnancy and birth, to develop the book you know hold in your hands.

As a pediatrician I consider myself a consultant to the parents of my patients. My goal is for parents to understand what's happening with their child. After all, *you* are really the ones doing the administering of medication, care, and love. In planning the content of this book it became clear to my co-author and me how dependent the child is on his family, his relatives, and his environment. Further, we realized that much of a mother-to-be's sense of well-being comes from talks with other mothers, her mate, and friends and family, and from her spiritual life. To that end, we emphasize the importance of the parents' physical, mental, emotional, and financial preparedness to have a child. Giving yourself the best possible prenatal care and being up-to-date on alternative delivery techniques are as important to an infant's good growth as knowing how to feed it and clothe it after it's born.

Sadly, parents are often not being educated and equipped to care for their children. The "black bag" method of medical practice, where the doctor reaches into his bag, pulls out the magic medicine, and says, "Take this," with no explanations, limits parental growth. More parents (and I'm happy to say more black parents) want to be involved in the decision-making process when it comes to childbirth and, subsequently, their child's medical care. The great thing about involving parents is that they begin to ask *you* questions; they begin to learn; *they begin to take more ownership*. It is an empowering process and a wonderful thing. In a health crisis, though, there must be a relationship of trust between parent and doctor. This is why developing a rapport with your caregiver is so important. When you give yourself or your precious child over to a doctor's care you need not only to be informed but also able to rely on his or her judgment.

As we researched cultural information surrounding birth and infant care we discovered that much of the folk medicine in black culture has not been written down but has been passed from generation to generation by word of mouth. We relied often on input from grandmothers, uncles, and family and friends to help flavor the book, and offer tidbits of wonderful black literature written during the days of slavery and post-slavery in this country. The information we discovered tends to have holistic or "whole life" qualities, covering what to eat, think, and do during pregnancy in order to have a healthy baby. Some of this information is at times at variance with current medical recommendations. It has been included in the book for its historic importance and for what we can learn from its essence—or, in a few cases categorically to disapprove of it. We include an overdue tribute to black nurse-midwives, who in biblical times in Africa, during slavery in the United States, and today serve a pivotal role in the care and well-being of black mothers in America. They provide a viable alternative to in-hospital childbirth via freestanding birthing centers and will be of increasing importance to us as we redesign the American health care system. We have melded the old and the new into a blend of value-based information on prenatal care, birthing choices, and infant care, with liberal sprinklings of poetry, lyrics, biblical inspiration, history, instructive photographs and illustrations, and of course, the voices of the many mothers and fathers who have made this book real. Our sincere hope is that this book teaches you, encourages you, makes you feel at home, entertains you, and challenges you to be the best parent you can be.

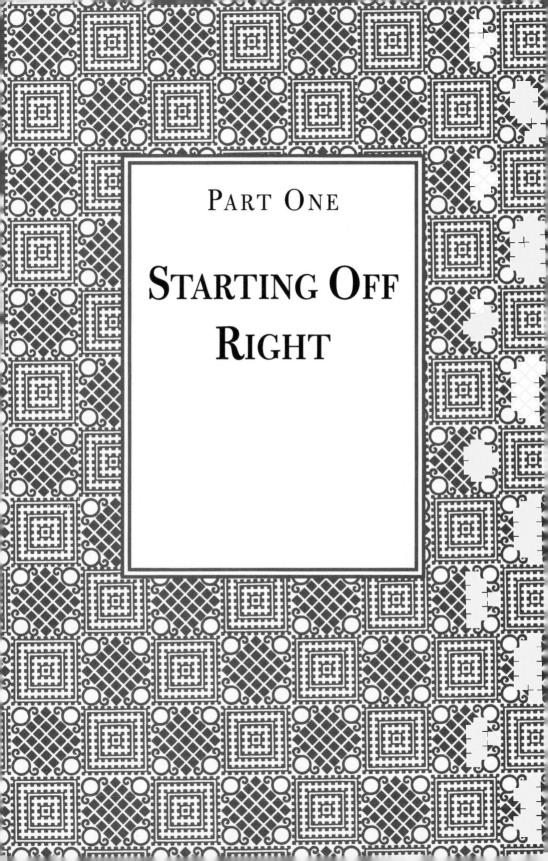

PART ONE

STARTING OFF RIGHT

CHAPTER 1

◇ ◇ ◇ ◇

So You've Decided to Get Pregnant . . .

These days, more and more couples are putting time and thought into their decision to start a family. As a growing number of sisters focus on achieving career satisfaction and finding Mr. Right, many are having their first babies in their mid-thirties and even early forties. Still for others, pregnancy can come as a complete surprise. Even if you're not pregnant, at some point you've probably wondered how a baby would affect your life. For example, you might wonder how having a child would affect your work schedule, your plans to go back to school, or your active social life. If you're thinking seriously about getting pregnant, you need to ask yourself a few tough questions: Is my marriage ready for a baby? How healthy am I *really*? What do I need to put in place in order to bring a healthy baby into the world? Can we afford it? What room will the baby sleep in and who will get up in the middle of the night? Any planning you do before conception will help make pregnancy, birth, and the transition to parenthood smoother. No matter how many wonderful books you read on pregnancy, birth, and parenting, none will be able to predict what your experience will be to a tee—not even ours. However, there are certain factors you *do* have control over that can help ensure a sound pregnancy and a healthy baby. The following is a brief list of steps you can take to prepare your body for pregnancy. (Most of these topics are covered more extensively in other areas of the book. References are noted for your convenience.)

General Health

Visit your doctor for a routine physical and a prepregnancy checkup. During this "prepregnancy planning" appointment, talk to your doctor about going off birth control and discuss how any factors of your personal health history may affect a pregnancy. To prepare, you may need to ask yourself, your mother, and your siblings a few questions. For instance, are you a smoker, or did you recently quit? Are you currently taking any prescription drugs on a regular basis? Are you overweight? Questions to ask your family might include: Did your mother have any miscarriages? Is there any history of cervical cancer, stillbirths, placenta previa, or other medical concern in your family that you should know about? Now is the best time to gather this information and bring your findings with you to your doctor's appointment.

Stop smoking, limit alcohol consumption, and avoid use of over-the-counter medications and prescription drugs. All of these could be harmful to the fetus; your doctor can advise you about which medications are considered safe.

Visit your dentist and clear up any dental work that needs to be done. This will help avoid any exposure to any radiation (X rays), anesthetics, or painkillers during your pregnancy.

Update any vaccines you are due for. Many adults aren't even aware of the fact that they may not have gotten the proper vaccines as babies. And some, such as the tetanus vaccine, need to be renewed every 10 years. It is unsafe to get them done during your pregnancy and it's foolish to risk potential complications from a sickness that could develop if you are not immunized.

Consider any potential health hazards in the environment at work, such as possible exposure to radiation or chemicals and chemical fumes. Not only can these factors possibly prevent you from getting pregnant, but in extreme situations they can cause miscarriage or fetal malformations in the early weeks of pregnancy, before you're even aware you've conceived. See pages 73–74 for more information on occupational health hazards.

Improve your diet, cut down on junk food, and discipline yourself to eat in moderation. This will help you keep off excess weight during your pregnancy and will provide the balanced nutrition you and your baby need. However, you should *not* spend the months before you conceive trying to lose weight in a hurry before you get pregnant. Doing this leaves you at risk for entering your pregnancy undernourished, which can cause complications.

Make time for a regular exercise routine throughout the week. Our fitness experts say that exercising for less than 15 minutes fewer than three times per week will do very little for you physically. Some of the numerous benefits of exercise during pregnancy include the potential to reduce varicose veins and swelling in your legs, the ability to help keep weight gain in check, and increased stamina and flexibility during labor and delivery. Pick an exercise program that you can really enjoy and you'll do it more often.

"I began running three miles a day one year before I became pregnant. I was fanatical about being fit and healthy going into pregnancy."

Choosing a Practitioner and a Birth Place

Start thinking about what kind of pregnancy care and birth setting you want *before* you get pregnant, or as soon as you find out that you are. You may already have an idea of what your caregiver and birth may be like. For example, you may be thinking of using the same doctor a friend or neighbor used simply because he or she is the only "good" one you've heard of, and you may imagine giving birth in a hospital room lying on your back. Be open to learning about all of the choices available so you can choose the one that really suits your desires. As black women take more control of their lives and become more informed about the birthing process, we have become more demanding of our medical providers. This is as it should be. Know that there are a variety of birthing choices available to you. For example, you can choose to use an obstetrician-gynecologist, a general practitioner, or a nurse-midwife and to give birth in a hospital, a birthing center, a birthing pool, or even your own bedroom. Research different options and find out how they can support your own personal and emotional desires.

The benefits of early planning have a domino effect: The more good information you have about what's available, the more time

you have to think about them and come up with your own birthing
"philosophy," the more likely you will be less intimidated and more
outspoken about your desires, and increase your chance of having a
safe and satisfying birth with minimal intervention. For a thorough
discussion of birthing options read Chapter 14, "All About Labor and
Delivery."

Things You May Be Concerned About Now

Previous Abortions

In most cases previous abortions should not affect your ability to
get pregnant or the outcome of a full-term pregnancy. This is particularly true if you've had first-trimester abortions performed in the
United States over the last twenty years. However, if you've had
multiple second trimester abortions (at 14 to 26 weeks of pregnancy)
you may be at increased risk for premature delivery. Also, some
research has found that women who had abortions performed before
1973 had a higher incidence of midtrimester miscarriage in subsequent pregnancies. This seems to be related to the procedures used
at the time, which may cause a woman's cervix to become "incompetent," or unable to stay closed under the weight of the growing fetus.
During your prepregnancy planning visit or your first prenatal
appointment, don't be coy. Tell your doctor or midwife your *complete* pregnancy history, including information about any abortions
or miscarriages you may have had.

Birth Control and Pregnancy Planning

The Pill: If you are on the pill you should stop using it one to two
months before trying to conceive. During that time, switch to con-
doms or another barrier-method of birth control to allow your hormones and your menstrual cycle to readjust. This precaution will
allow your body more transition time between rapid changes in hormone levels. However, there should be no harm to you or your fetus
if you become pregnant immediately after stopping the pill. You
should know that the pill does have a 1 to 2 percent failure rate,
although this may be related to irregular or improper use. If you
become pregnant while on the pill, stop taking it immediately and
discuss it with your doctor or midwife. The risk of fetal harm caused

by brief use of the pill after conception is not definitive, and chances are that your pregnancy should continue normally.

The IUD (Intrauterine Device): Ideally, if you are using an IUD for birth control and you are planning a pregnancy, you should have your doctor remove it. Approximately 1 to 5 women out of 100 will get pregnant while using an IUD. You should know that there is a higher risk of ectopic pregnancy associated with IUD use. Ectopic pregnancy occurs when a fertilized egg implants itself outside the uterus, usually in the fallopian tube. If untreated, the egg soon outgrows the tube, causing it to burst. This can be a life-threatening situation for the mother. Be alert to signs of ectopic pregnancy such as vaginal bleeding, cramping or pain in your lower abdomen, shoulder pain, and faintness or dizziness. (For a thorough list of symptoms and more information about ectopic pregnancy, see Chapter 15, "What-ifs During Pregnancy and Delivery").

If pregnancy has been confirmed while your IUD is in place, there are a few factors to take into consideration. If your removal string is not visible early in the first trimester, you will likely be able to keep the IUD in safely and continue the pregnancy. If the string is visible, your doctor or midwife may advise you to have the device removed. While there's roughly a 20 percent chance of miscarriage during the removal, the risk in this case is greater if your IUD is left in.

Depo-Provera*: If you're ready to stop using Depo-Provera injections, know that it may take an average of 9 or 10 months before you are able to conceive, and can even take up to 24 months. Depo-Provera has a 99 percent success rate of preventing pregnancy, so it's unlikely that many women will get pregnant while using it. The rare instance of fetal exposure to the drug could occur if you become pregnant immediately *before* receiving your first shot (women are advised to abstain from sex two weeks before beginning Depo-Provera). In this instance, there is a concern that a mother with the drug in her bloodstream could have a higher risk of delivering a low-birth-weight baby.

---

*Depo-Provera is not recommended by the National Black Women's Health Project (NBWHP) because of the lack of information available about its long-term effects, according to NBWHP president Julia Scott. She notes that some studies involving young women who took Depo-Provera also showed an increase in breast cancer and that the drug promotes bone loss and osteoporosis.

Depo-Provera can be used by nursing mothers as soon as four weeks after delivery, but research has found that small amounts show up in the breast milk. Although there seems to be no harm to the fetus, long-term effects of the drug on the baby are not known at this time. (For more on resuming birth control postpartum, see Chapter 16, "Postpartum Recovery").

Norplant: If you are considering having your Norplant capsules removed, know that extrication can be painful and difficult, especially if they were deeply implanted. Once they are removed, your fertility should be restored after your first menstrual cycle. Like Depo-Provera, Norplant is more than 99 percent effective in preventing pregnancy. However, according to the Food and Drug Administration, the success rate drops to 92 percent for women who weigh more than 155 pounds.

Sexually Transmitted Diseases and Pregnancy

AIDS and HIV (human immunodeficiency virus, the virus that causes AIDS): A popular AIDS awareness poster tells us that "AIDS *is* a women's issue." Statistics tell us that in the United States, AIDS is a black women's issue. We account for more than half of all cases of women with AIDS—a high statistic considering that blacks comprise only about 12 percent of the entire U.S. population. As more sisters get infected, more of our children suffer with HIV and AIDS than those of any other ethnic group.

An HIV-infected woman can pass the disease on to her child during pregnancy, birth, and through breast-feeding, since bodily fluids are exchanged in each case. About one-third of HIV-positive pregnant women pass the disease on to their unborn babies. Unfortunately, a child who was infected in the womb will usually not live more than one to two years after it is born, although a few rare cases live longer. Once contracted, the AIDS virus invades and destroys cells in the immune system, making the body unable to defend itself against sickness and disease, such as certain types of cancer or pneumonia. When a person with HIV develops one of these illnesses, they are technically considered to have full-blown AIDS.

If you even suspect you may have been infected, arrange to be tested before you get pregnant. If you are already pregnant, you should be tested immediately. Recent studies have found that treatment with a drug called AZT during pregnancy can significantly reduce the risk of a mother passing the virus on to her baby.

Chlamydia and Gonorrhea: Chlamydia and gonorrhea, the most common sexually transmitted diseases in the United States, can have serious effects on pregnancy. Women who have gonorrhea most likely have chlamydia, because these diseases are often found together. Both can lead to pelvic inflammatory disease, which is transmitted to the baby during a vaginal delivery, infecting the baby's eyes and causing blindness if left untreated. Antibiotic ointment, routinely put in a baby's eyes just after birth, can prevent harm. Chlamydia can also cause pneumonia in the baby. In addition, the Centers for Disease Control in Atlanta recently reported a sixfold rise in ectopic pregnancies since 1970 because of the increase of sexually transmitted diseases like chlamydia among women.

Both chlamydia and gonorrhea are spread through vaginal and anal intercourse (gonorrhea can also be spread through oral sex). They can be hard to detect because early symptoms are often mild or completely absent in women, with many women finding out about their infection only when their male partners are diagnosed. Symptoms include unusual or greenish discharge, abdominal pain, and a burning sensation when you urinate. Most doctors and midwives will test for both of these infections at your first office visit. If you are sexually active or suspect you or your partner have been infected, request a chlamydia test before conception to avoid having to be treated with any antibiotics during pregnancy.

Genital Warts (Human Papilloma Virus): Untreated, genital warts can go on to cause inflammation of the cervix and cervical cancer. They can also block delivery of the baby and be transmitted to the baby, causing warts to develop on her vocal cords. Genital warts are caused by the human papilloma virus and are easily passed from person to person through intercourse and during oral and anal sex. The warts look like tiny pink or red swellings in the genital area, and several warts growing close together can have a cauliflowerlike shape. Although they can disappear on their own, they often need treatment prescribed by a physician.

Herpes: Herpes is a sexually transmitted disease that first appears as painful blisters on or around your genitals. A baby can be infected in delivery if it passes through an infected birth canal. While infection at birth is rare, when it does occur it can affect newborns severely, causing brain damage, blindness, and even death. Typically, babies are most at risk when the mother contracts the disease *for the first time* close to her due date, but even then the risk is only about 40 percent. If you have recurring herpes contracted *before* your pregnancy began, there is only a 2 to 3 percent risk of infecting the baby. If there are active herpes blisters present close to labor or during labor the doctor will probably plan for a C-section to reduce the chance of the baby contracting the disease through the vagina. But if you are not having an "outbreak" (no blisters or sores are present in your vagina), your baby can probably be delivered vaginally.

The herpes simplex virus is transmitted through vaginal or anal sex via tiny cuts in the skin or mucous membranes, but a person can also be infected by a contaminated finger coming into contact with the eyes. If you've ever been diagnosed with herpes or have had sexual contact with someone who has, tell your doctor. Since testing is not routine, the only other circumstance that may require testing is if you develop genital blisters. Keep alert to other signs of herpes such as small red bumps around your vagina that develop into blisters that burst and scab over. You may feel pain or tenderness in the genital area until the infection clears. First-time herpes outbreaks often bring on headaches, achiness, lethargy, and fever accompanied by intense itching in your genital area. Schedule an appointment with your doctor if you experience any of these symptoms. A prescription drug called Zovirax, though costly, is widely used for the treatment of herpes, as is L-lysine, an amino acid available over the counter.

Syphilis: Syphilis continues to be an extremely dangerous sexually transmitted disease. Pregnant women can pass the disease to their fetuses through the bloodstream, causing miscarriage or stillbirth. Babies that survive but are born with the infection can suffer bone and tooth deformities, deafness, and damage to their nervous systems.

The first symptom of the disease is a sore that appears around the genitals (on men it's usually found on the penis) about three weeks or so after infection. During this time the sore, also called a chancre, will ooze clear fluid and is highly infectious. If left untreated the sore will heal, but the infection will continue to invade the body, eventually resulting in blindness, heart disease, damage to the nervous system, or death.

Testing for syphilis through a blood sample taken from your arm is routine at your first prenatal visit. If the infection is diagnosed and treated with antibiotics within the first three to four months of pregnancy, before the disease can cross the placenta, there should be no harm to the fetus. If a baby is born with congenital syphilis, treatment can halt further damage to the child.

Being Overweight or Obese

Extremely overweight and obese women often have healthy and safe pregnancies. In fact, most overweight women who eat moderately tend to put on less weight than average-weight or underweight women do during pregnancy (that is, less than the recommended 25 to 35 pounds). But being overweight during pregnancy can put you at a higher risk for gestational diabetes. An ultrasound may be needed to verify your due date since ovulation can be irregular in obese women. Ultrasound may also need to be used to determine the size and position of the baby, which may be obscured by body fat during a regular external exam. However, your key concern if you are overweight or obese is not body weight; it's whether or not you have any other medical conditions such as hypertension or diabetes that could render yours a high-risk pregnancy.

Midlife Pregnancy

If you are in your midthirties or older and are considering getting pregnant, you are not "late." Know that there are many women like you who are having perfectly safe, healthy, and uncomplicated pregnancies at the right time for *them*. Women having babies in their thirties or even forties is no new thing; women having their *first* babies at this age is the relatively new trend. There are many reasons why more sisters are starting families later in life. Some have struggled with infertility, some needed to "get healthy" (smart!), and some had a "surprise" pregnancy, but most women simply waited to have children until they felt ready, which for many meant finding the right husband—first. Whatever your journey, if you have made it to this place, congratulations! Here are some things to be aware of:

◆ You ovulate less often as you get older, so it may take a few months or more before you become pregnant.
◆ The older a woman is, the older the eggs in her ovaries are. The eggs, which are present from birth, have had more time to be exposed to infections, radiation, drugs, or other substances that can affect them. An older woman has a greater risk of having a child with Down's syndrome, although the odds are still relatively low (3 in 1,000 at age 35; 1 in 100 at age forty). Research indicates that this risk may be related to defects in the egg. Some cases have been linked to a defect in the father's sperm, but it's not clear if the

father's age is related to this. Many doctors routinely advise pregnant women at or over age thirty-five to be tested for Down's
syndrome or spinal defects. These tests are amniocentesis, alpha-
feto-protein tests, and chorionic villus testing. Be aware that these
tests are *not* mandatory, and you have the right to decide not to
have them done. Most often, they cannot reverse any defects the
child has, and the relatively high rate of false positives in the
alpha-feto-protein test can cause you weeks of unnecessary worry.
Some couples want the information so they can prepare themselves emotionally and financially to care for a child with a disability; others will make the decision to terminate the pregnancy.
For couples who are certain they would not terminate a pregnancy, these tests may prove to be annoying and intrusive, and can
endanger the fetus (such as in the minor risk involved in the
amniocentesis procedure). See pages 323–24 for an in-depth discussion of testing and more about Down's syndrome.

◆ Some women suffer from high blood pressure (especially if
they are heavy), diabetes, or cardiovascular disease—but all of
these are controllable and treatable, and thus shouldn't interfere with pregnancy.

◆ Some women say they tire more easily being pregnant after
thirty-five, compared to pregnancies they had in their twenties.
On the other hand, many have found that maturity has increased their patience, wisdom, spiritual grounding, and ability
to endure difficulties. Others say the time has helped them
solidify their marriages and has increased their financial security, too. All of these are positive factors that can help provide a
safe, loving environment for a baby.

HISTORICALLY SPEAKING . . .

One Southern granny midwife remembers, "Women felt it was a shock to
have their first baby at 30. Some of
them had *grand*babies at that age!" In
the early 1900s it was typical for women to have frequent
pregnancies and large families—most before the age of 20.
What We Can Learn: Times have changed. Few women are
having ten or twelve children anymore and more of us
are having babies in midlife. Studies show that older women
are more secure in their pregnancies; they *want* the babies

more. This state of mind can have a positive effect on how you prepare yourself for pregnancy and how you treat yourself during pregnancy.

Possible Signs of Pregnancy, and Pregnancy Tests

The first and most obvious signal that a woman is pregnant is a missed period. However, many women experience spotting or a scanty period even after they become pregnant. If your menstrual flow is irregular or light to begin with, you may easily overlook the possibility that you might be pregnant. There are other "typical" signals your body can send, but be aware that your pregnancy, as well as your labor and delivery, are extremely individual. You might experience all of the general "textbook" symptoms, or only one of them. You may even experience one or more of the symptoms but not recognize it—for instance, you may think that your exhaustion is from staying late at work all week, or you may believe the nausea you feel is from a flu going around or from something you ate. The best way of confirming your pregnancy is to pay attention to those physical changes and then confirm them with a pregnancy test and a visit to your doctor or nurse-midwife. They will check for enlargement and softening of your uterus, as well as a change in the texture of your cervix to determine if you are pregnant. In the meantime, you may experience one or more of the following symptoms:

- ◆ A missed menstrual period, a scanty period, or only spotting (Note: It is possible to be pregnant and still have a period, although the period will typically be lighter than usual.)
- ◆ Breast tenderness, tingling, soreness
- ◆ Extreme tiredness, sleepiness
- ◆ Nausea
- ◆ Frequent urination
- ◆ A bloated sensation

HISTORICALLY SPEAKING . . .

 Our sisters from other lands have very creative ways of determining if they are with child. Ugandan women of the Chagga tribe keep count of their "moons" or menstrual cycles by scratching notches on the

bark of trees. When gaps in the notches are discovered . . . voilà. Some Jamaican women look to their dreams to tell them if they are pregnant: Dreams with lots of fish or ripe fruit in them are considered a positive sign of pregnancy. Our Egyptian sisters contend that dreams can also tell you if you're having a boy or a girl: Dream about a *head* kerchief and it's a girl; a *hand*kerchief and it's a boy! *What We Can Learn:* Though we now have highly accurate biochemical techniques to define the onset of pregnancy, many women continue to rely on the calendar, intuition, and supernatural indicators like dreams and visions. As you become more in touch with your body rhythms and gain more knowledge about what to expect when you're pregnant, you can often tell when something is changing or "not right" and you can respond appropriately, and hopefully with less anxiety.

Helping Yourselves Get Pregnant

Fertility Tracking

A great way to help yourselves get pregnant is to keep track of two things: your basal body temperature (BBT) and the changes in your cervical mucus. These are the two major signs of fertility. You will need to check them on a daily basis for at least one month. Use a spare notebook to chart these body changes, making columns like the ones in the example below:

TONI AND MICHAEL'S FERTILITY CHART (Sample)

Date	6/3
Day	Monday
Time	7:30 A.M.
BBT	97.2°
Intercourse	No
Mucus	D
Notes	had cramps

Basal Body Temperature (BBT) is the temperature of your body at rest. Your BBT changes throughout the month and tends to be lower during your period and higher during ovulation (when your ovaries release an egg to be fertilized), though the change may be less than one degree. It's important to use a BBT thermometer or a digital one to track this instead of a common thermometer. These will give you temperature readings in *one-tenths* of a degree, which is what you need to determine your most fertile days. *Goal:* To determine when you are ovulating and to identify your most fertile or "peak" days, when your BBT is *steadily* high. (Generally, women ovulate 14 to 16 days before the start of their next period.) *Tracking It:* Starting with the first day of your period, take your BBT each morning as soon as you wake up, preferably while you are still in bed. It's important that you do this at about the same time every morning. To do this, place the BBT thermometer under your tongue as you would an ordinary thermometer, hold it in your mouth for about five minutes, and record the temperature in the column marked "BBT." Make note of any unusual circumstances that might alter your temperature reading, such as "overslept" or "had the flu." This will help you account for abnormal patterns in your BBT. If you observe abnormalities that you cannot explain, it's best to see your doctor.

Cervical mucus is the mucus emitted from the cervix, the bottom part of your uterus, which opens into the vagina. Cervical mucus is not present while you are having your period but begins to show just after your period ends or one to three days after it ends. It changes consistency from sticky and pasty to wet and elastic. The rule when trying to get pregnant is "The wetter the better." Mucus that is similar to the consistency of a raw egg white provides optimal swimming conditions for sperm. This type of "fertile" mucus will appear around the time of ovulation. *Goal:* To determine when your cervical mucus is at its best consistency for fertilization to occur. *Tracking It:* Every evening, *before* you urinate, wipe your vagina with a tissue to check for the presence and consistency of the mucus. Touch the mucus and note "B" for bleeding, "S" for spotty bleeding, "D" for dry or no mucus, "M" for mucus that's moist but not wet, and a circled "M" for wet, elastic mucus. Enter the appropriate letter in your notebook in the "Mucus" column. Again, if you notice strange patterns in your mucus chart after a few months, tell your doctor.

Helpful Notes

◆ If you miss a day, just put a question mark in that day's space and continue.

◆ Make sure to include your mate in the charting process. Just talking (and hopefully laughing) about the fact that you're trying so hard to get pregnant will bring you closer.

◆ Avoid testing mucus after intercourse; sperm fluid and cervical mucus have similar consistencies and can be easily confused.

◆ Don't get all stressed out attempting to always make love *on* the day of ovulation. A few days before may be just as effective, as sperm can stay alive and able to fertilize an egg for two to five days.

◆ Only 25 percent of couples get pregnant in their first month of trying, while 60 percent of couples conceive by the sixth month of trying—and that's with *no* strategy at all. You are one up on them if you decide to use the fertility chart. You may want to see your doctor together if you have been faithfully charting your fertility (and making love, of course!) for several months with no results. Be encouraged. To quote King Solomon in the book of Ecclesiastes, "There is a time for everything, and a season for every activity under heaven."

Pregnancy Tests

The Home Pregnancy Test

Every time you turn around there seems to be a new do-it-yourself pregnancy test appearing on your drugstore shelf. What all the tests have in common is that they check your urine for the presence of the human chorionic gonadotropin (HCG), a hormone produced by the placenta as it develops. The benefit of home tests is that they allow you both privacy and immediacy. Some tests can even give you a result the first day after you miss your period. If you are careful to read the instructions and perform the test correctly, most home tests are almost 100 percent accurate when positive. Occasionally a medical condition or certain drugs can give you a false positive, or a false negative can occur if you are pregnant but your body hasn't yet produced enough HCG. If the indicator of the test seems hazy or if your bodily signals seem to tell you otherwise, wait a week and test yourself again.

Lab Test or In-Office Urine Test

Your doctor's office or a local lab can perform this test for you, although a lab may want to phone your doctor (not you) with the results. Like the home pregnancy test, this test also checks for the presence of HCG in your urine, but it can detect it with the same accuracy at only seven to ten days after conception. At this point, most women will not have even missed their period yet.

Blood Test

Aside from possible lab error, this test is considered to be the most accurate and can detect pregnancy one week after conception. It also has the advantage of dating your pregnancy by measuring the approximate amount of HCG in your blood.

Most tests, particularly in-home ones, are more likely to be accurate if you wait a week after you miss your period to use them, when the hormone levels in your body will be higher. However, if you are feeling unusual symptoms such as painful cramping, tenderness in your abdomen, dizziness, or unusual or irregular spotting, you may have an ectopic pregnancy, and should be tested immediately. See Chapter 15, "What-ifs During Pregnancy and Delivery," for more information on ectopic pregnancies. It's important to remember to follow any positive test with a visit to the doctor.

HISTORICALLY SPEAKING . . .

"It never failed. I just get my line and tackle together, bought ten cents worth o' worms from the shop down the corner and set myself in my favorite fishing spot, when some man comes a rennin' t'ward me with his arms flailin' all excited talkin' 'bout 'Miss Annie, you gotta come right now, the baby's gettin' born!' Now, don't get me wrong, I love catchin' babies. I just couldn't never understand why they always had to decide to get born on my fishin' day."—A granny midwife anecdote. *What We Can Learn:* Even though we're given due dates (that are often off by as much as three weeks), babies come when they're good and ready, so start preparing yourself for birth early on.

How Does It Happen?

Though millions of women get pregnant and have babies each year, few could tell you how the process of "getting pregnant" actually occurs. We believe that the more you understand your body and what's going on inside it, the better equipped you'll be to handle pregnancy and birth. Hopefully, your appreciation for your spouse will deepen as you begin to realize the miraculous way our bodies function together to produce life.

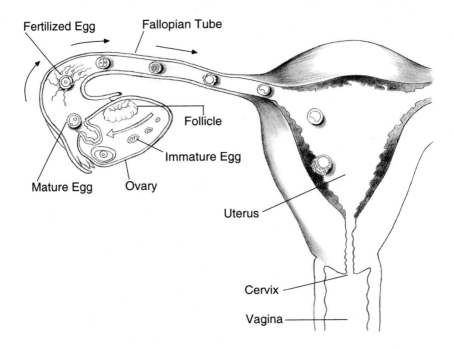

Understanding Ovulation

Your two ovaries, connected to the uterus by the fallopian tubes, are your primary reproductive organs. Each almond-shaped ovary contains approximately 400 follicles or pods that can each produce one mature egg every month. Ovulation occurs when a mature ovum is released into the fallopian tubes to ripen fully and ready itself for fertilization by a sperm cell. (See table on page 21.) The egg is only capable of being fertilized for about 24 hours.

At the start of ovulation your body gives off subtle indicators such as a quick drop, then rise, in your body temperature, and a change in the consistency of the cervical mucus blocking the entrance to the uterus. This cervical mucus, emitted in vaginal discharge, becomes clear, thin, and elastic during ovulation, providing the favorable conditions we discussed above, which allow sperm to pass through the cervix more easily and swim their way to the egg.

Each egg is about the size of a grain of sand, each sperm head only six-hundredths of a millimeter long, and the channel in the fallopian tube they travel through is roughly twice as thick as a human hair! Out of the millions of sperm that flood the vagina during ejaculation, only about one hundred will ever get near the egg. Your vaginal environment is extremely acidic, causing almost a quarter of the sperm to die as soon as they enter it. Many others are defective, or get sidetracked somewhere in the nooks and crannies of the cervical canal or uterus. Those that make it to the entrance of the fallopian tube containing the egg still have a battle on their hands. They must swim against the current of the beating cilia (microscopic hairs that line the uterus, cervix, and fallopian tube), and fight against white blood cells in the woman's immune system that are trying to kill them. However, once a man's sperm enters a woman, it has the ability to stay alive for about two to five days. The sperm that have survived thus far make their way to the fallopian tube, where they get energized by various substances and hang out there until the egg is released. This is why many couples who are trying to get pregnant time their lovemaking to coincide with ovulation or the release of the egg. For the "average" sperm, the process of swimming up to the fallopian tube from the vagina takes a few hours. In optimal conditions, a champion sperm may make the journey from ejaculation to fertilization in as little as thirty minutes.

DID YOU KNOW ...

Scientists report that X sperm cells, which are female, survive longer in the vagina. Y sperm cells, the male counterparts, are more plentiful and swim faster due to their longer tails.

Understanding Fertilization

Typically, fertilization occurs somewhere inside the beginning of the 6-inch fallopian tube. The sperm finalists use their "heads" to drill through the hard shell of protective nutrient cells surrounding the egg. The sperm compete feverishly to be the first to fertilize the egg by releasing its genetic material. Once the winner is established, the ovum immediately sends out chemicals that prohibit any other sperm from getting in. The winning sperm will determine the baby's sex and will contribute the other half of its genes or inherited traits. Like lovesick puppies, the losing sperm hang around the ovum for several days. Experts speculate that the swimming action of their tails may actually help the fertilized ovum continue its journey through the fallopian tube.

Once the egg is fertilized, it begins the process of rapidly dividing into many cells over the next several days. If the fertilized egg divides into two separate but equal parts before it divides further, the result is identical same-sex twins; if two eggs are released from the ovaries and are fertilized by two sperm, fraternal twins (nonidentical, can be different sexes) result. Usually within six to eight days the fertilizes egg has made its way down the tube and implants itself into the rich lining of the uterus, where it will be fed by your blood supply and continue its growth from blastocyst to embryo to fetus to baby. Approximately 280 days after fertilization, your baby will be born!

How to Determine Your Estimated Date of Delivery (Due Date)

Your calculated due date is only an estimate—most women give birth at anywhere from 37 to 42 weeks of pregnancy, with only about 5 percent of all women giving birth on their due date. However, it's important to try to determine it as accurately as possible for several reasons. Many tests you may need during pregnancy, such as a genetic test or blood test, are most accurate when done at a certain point in the pregnancy. If complications arise, the doctor or midwife can determine if the baby is mature enough to induce delivery. It's also easier for them to gauge the healthy growth of the baby, or determine if the baby is late.

Generally, unless you carefully monitor your exact date of ovulation, your estimated date of delivery (EDD) assumes that conception occurs 14 days after the first day of your last period. The average EDD is 40 weeks, or 280 days after the first day of your last period.

Jan	**1**	**2**	**3**	**4**	**5**	**6**	**7**	**8**	**9**	**10**	**11**	**12**	**13**	**14**	**15**	**16**	**17**	**18**	**19**	**20**	**21**	**22**	**23**	**24**	**25**	**26**	**27**	**28**	**29**	**30**	**31**	Jan
Oct	8	9	10	11	12	13	14	15	16	17	18	19	20	21	22	23	24	25	26	27	28	29	30	31	1	2	3	4	5	6	7	Nov
Feb	**1**	**2**	**3**	**4**	**5**	**6**	**7**	**8**	**9**	**10**	**11**	**12**	**13**	**14**	**15**	**16**	**17**	**18**	**19**	**20**	**21**	**22**	**23**	**24**	**25**	**26**	**27**	**28**				Feb
Nov	8	9	10	11	12	13	14	15	16	17	18	19	20	21	22	23	24	25	26	27	28	29	30	1	2	3	4	5				Dec
Mar	**1**	**2**	**3**	**4**	**5**	**6**	**7**	**8**	**9**	**10**	**11**	**12**	**13**	**14**	**15**	**16**	**17**	**18**	**19**	**20**	**21**	**22**	**23**	**24**	**25**	**26**	**27**	**28**	**29**	**30**	**31**	Mar
Dec	6	7	8	9	10	11	12	13	14	15	16	17	18	19	20	21	22	23	24	25	26	27	28	29	30	31	1	2	3	4	5	Jan
Apr	**1**	**2**	**3**	**4**	**5**	**6**	**7**	**8**	**9**	**10**	**11**	**12**	**13**	**14**	**15**	**16**	**17**	**18**	**19**	**20**	**21**	**22**	**23**	**24**	**25**	**26**	**27**	**28**	**29**	**30**		Apr
Jan	6	7	8	9	10	11	12	13	14	15	16	17	18	19	20	21	22	23	24	25	26	27	28	29	30	31	1	2	3	4		Feb
May	**1**	**2**	**3**	**4**	**5**	**6**	**7**	**8**	**9**	**10**	**11**	**12**	**13**	**14**	**15**	**16**	**17**	**18**	**19**	**20**	**21**	**22**	**23**	**24**	**25**	**26**	**27**	**28**	**29**	**30**	**31**	May
Feb	5	6	7	8	9	10	11	12	13	14	15	16	17	18	19	20	21	22	23	24	25	26	27	28	1	2	3	4	5	6	7	Mar
Jun	**1**	**2**	**3**	**4**	**5**	**6**	**7**	**8**	**9**	**10**	**11**	**12**	**13**	**14**	**15**	**16**	**17**	**18**	**19**	**20**	**21**	**22**	**23**	**24**	**25**	**26**	**27**	**28**	**29**	**30**		Jun
Mar	8	9	10	11	12	13	14	15	16	17	18	19	20	21	22	23	24	25	26	27	28	29	30	31	1	2	3	4	5	6		Apr
Jul	**1**	**2**	**3**	**4**	**5**	**6**	**7**	**8**	**9**	**10**	**11**	**12**	**13**	**14**	**15**	**16**	**17**	**18**	**19**	**20**	**21**	**22**	**23**	**24**	**25**	**26**	**27**	**28**	**29**	**30**	**31**	Jul
Apr	7	8	9	10	11	12	13	14	15	16	17	18	19	20	21	22	23	24	25	26	27	28	29	30	1	2	3	4	5	6	7	May
Aug	**1**	**2**	**3**	**4**	**5**	**6**	**7**	**8**	**9**	**10**	**11**	**12**	**13**	**14**	**15**	**16**	**17**	**18**	**19**	**20**	**21**	**22**	**23**	**24**	**25**	**26**	**27**	**28**	**29**	**30**	**31**	Aug
May	8	9	10	11	12	13	14	15	16	17	18	19	20	21	22	23	24	25	26	27	28	29	30	31	1	2	3	4	5	6	7	Jun
Sep	**1**	**2**	**3**	**4**	**5**	**6**	**7**	**8**	**9**	**10**	**11**	**12**	**13**	**14**	**15**	**16**	**17**	**18**	**19**	**20**	**21**	**22**	**23**	**24**	**25**	**26**	**27**	**28**	**29**	**30**		Sep
Jun	8	9	10	11	12	13	14	15	16	17	18	19	20	21	22	23	24	25	26	27	28	29	30	1	2	3	4	5	6	7		Jul
Oct	**1**	**2**	**3**	**4**	**5**	**6**	**7**	**8**	**9**	**10**	**11**	**12**	**13**	**14**	**15**	**16**	**17**	**18**	**19**	**20**	**21**	**22**	**23**	**24**	**25**	**26**	**27**	**28**	**29**	**30**	**31**	Oct
Jul	8	9	10	11	12	13	14	15	16	17	18	19	20	21	22	23	24	25	26	27	28	29	30	31	1	2	3	4	5	6	7	Aug
Nov	**1**	**2**	**3**	**4**	**5**	**6**	**7**	**8**	**9**	**10**	**11**	**12**	**13**	**14**	**15**	**16**	**17**	**18**	**19**	**20**	**21**	**22**	**23**	**24**	**25**	**26**	**27**	**28**	**29**	**30**		Nov
Aug	8	9	10	11	12	13	14	15	16	17	18	19	20	21	22	23	24	25	26	27	28	29	30	31	1	2	3	4	5	6		Sep
Dec	**1**	**2**	**3**	**4**	**5**	**6**	**7**	**8**	**9**	**10**	**11**	**12**	**13**	**14**	**15**	**16**	**17**	**18**	**19**	**20**	**21**	**22**	**23**	**24**	**25**	**26**	**27**	**28**	**29**	**30**	**31**	Dec
Sep	7	8	9	10	11	12	13	14	15	16	17	18	19	20	21	22	23	24	25	26	27	28	29	30	1	2	3	4	5	6	7	Oct

Locate the **boldface** number that represents the first day of your last period. The number below it will be your expected delivery date. Reprinted with permission from the American College of Obstetricians and Gynecologists, ACOG Guide to Planning for Pregnancy, Birth, and Beyond. ACOG, Washington, DC © 1990

WHEN ARE YOU DUE?

One way to find this precious date is to take the first day of your last period, add 7 days to it, then count back 3 months. For example, if your last period began on June 13, add 7 days to get June 20, and then count back 3 months to reach a due date of March 20. Use the chart on page 21 to check your accuracy.

If you aren't sure of the exact day your last period began, your doctor or nurse-midwife can help you estimate a due date. An ultrasound performed in the first trimester can place the EDD within a 7-to-10-day margin. Your abdomen can be measured at each appointment to evaluate the size of the growing uterus.

CHAPTER 2

You and Your Baby: Month-by-Month

First Month (Conception through 4¹/₂ weeks)

Your Baby: By the end of the first month, size—about ¹/₂ inch long (like a grain of rice); weight—less than an ounce. Even after the first few weeks, your baby (technically called an embryo) has a head, a trunk, and its central nervous system and lungs begin to develop. By the end of the month the heart has formed and is steadily beating. Tiny buds that will soon become arms and legs begin to appear.

You: Although many women do not feel or recognize any bodily changes during the first month of pregnancy (counted from the first day of your last period), others will begin to feel some changes. You may feel fatigue, drowsiness, nausea, your breasts may be enlarged and tender (some say "itchy"), and you may need to urinate more. You may feel like you're on an emotional roller coaster as your ovaries increase production of the hormones progesterone and estrogen. The lining of your uterus begins to thicken with blood.

Second Month (4¹/₂ to 9 Weeks)

Your Baby: Size—slightly over 1 inch; weight—still less than 1 ounce. By the end of this month the spinal cord is already well formed and the baby's head alone measures approximately one-third of its entire length. The complex design of your baby's eyes is underway and eyelids begin to form. Ankles and wrists begin to take shape, and distinct divisions of fingers and toes are formed. Fingerprints are already present on the budlike fingers.

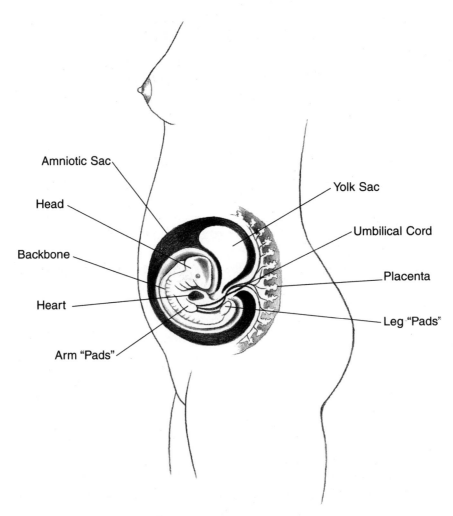

Human characteristics—head, eyes, neck, arms, legs, backbone, and even heart—are already apparent on this month-old embryo. The many "arms" of the placenta grab the nutrients from your blood and funnel them to the embryo through the blood vessels in the umbilical cord. Waste is efficiently removed from the embryo via the same method. The embryo sits in its protective shell, the amniotic sac. The yolk sac's purpose is to create blood cells that build the baby's immune system.

You: If you haven't "felt pregnant" yet, you probably will now. You may experience constipation, heartburn, food aversions or cravings, particularly as your body copes with nausea and "morning sickness," which some women may have had for several weeks now—morning, noon, and night. These discomforts are likely to continue well into the third or midway through the fourth month. The volume of your body's blood increases to accommodate the growing fetus. As the threat of miscarriage decreases your pregnancy becomes more stabilized.

Where a few weeks ago we saw only arm "buds," now even the fingers are distinct. This is a 7-week-old embryo's graduation portrait as it upgrades to fetus.

Third Month (9 to 13¹/₂ weeks)

Your Baby: Size—2¹/₂ to 4 inches long; weight—¹/₂ to 1 ounce. Hair begins to appear on the baby's head, its ears are visible, and inside the mouth are 20 small buds that will later become teeth. The beginning stages of all the organs are recognizable now. The kidneys begin to produce urine, which is excreted and becomes part of the amniotic fluid, the protective swimming pool that the baby floats in during pregnancy. If you are feeling warmer than usual, it is because the amniotic fluid in your womb is a warm 99.5°F. You really do have a "baby in the oven"! The gender of the fetus is still difficult to determine through a regular sonogram. Internally, if the baby is a boy, sperm are already present in his testicles, and a girl's ovaries contain ova (eggs). The baby's heartbeat may be audible during the tenth to twelfth weeks if your doctor uses a special ultrasound stethoscope called a Doppler. Don't panic if you can't hear it yet—the baby's position, your body fat, or a miscalculated due date may be the problem.

You: Your waistline will probably begin to thicken now, and your bra may begin to feel tight now that your breasts have enlarged. Though you still may be able to wear your "normal" clothes, you might need to start looking for roomier items that can take you through the rest of the pregnancy and postpartum months. You will probably continue to feel many of the discomforts common to the first trimester, although for most women, hope is just around the corner.

Fourth Month (13½ to 18 Weeks)

Your Baby: Size—6 to 7 inches long; weight—4 to 5 ounces. You will say goodbye to your waist this month (don't worry—it should come back again later). The length of the fetus increases rapidly, with body growth beginning to outstrip the growth of its head. Its life-support system, the placenta, is now completely formed. The fetus will sleep periodically throughout the day, and moves around when it is awake. During this month its face has developed and it has the ability to suck its thumb, swallow, and hear (though it's not yet able to hear sounds outside the womb). A thin, pinkish skin covers its body, and eyebrows and soft lashes are forming. The eyelids have closed over the eyes and won't open until about the sixth month. Although it looks very much like a little person, it cannot yet survive outside of your womb.

You: Most women can expect to enter the "golden months" of pregnancy during this second trimester. This is the time when the early "blahs" of pregnancy such as nausea, frequent urination, otherwise inexplicable drowsiness, and extreme breast tenderness will either fade or disappear completely (although for some women, these discomforts may carry on). Your belly is beginning to show, yet your energy level is up and you can still move around pretty easily. Maternity clothes fit loosely and comfortably. If it's not your first pregnancy or if you are very slim, you may finally be able to feel fluttering fetal movements, called "quickening." Be sure to let your doctor or midwife know when you feel these movements, because this can help confirm your estimated date of delivery. Also, you may begin to notice changes in your skin pigmentation during this month—your nipples and the area around them may darken, and the linea nigra, a dark line running from your pubic hair to your naval, may become more distinct.

Fifth Month (18 to 22½ Weeks)

Your Baby: Size—8 to 12 inches long; weight—½ to 1 pound. The baby has a real growth spurt this month. The internal organs are maturing and the fingernails have grown to the tips of the fingers. Its lips and mouth are fully formed. White eyelashes appear, and fine, soft hair called lanugo covers the baby's body. A protective, creamy coating called the vernix caseosa, which is sometimes visible even after delivery, is present on the skin. Made up of dead skin cells combined with fatty oils from the sebaceous glands, this creamy covering

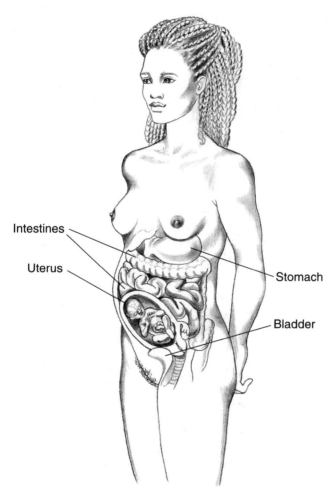

Woman at 20 weeks pregnant.

keeps the fetus's skin lubricated throughout the pregnancy, and may also help the baby pass more smoothly through the birth canal. The baby is very active now, and can turn from side to side and upside-down. The fetus's ears are developing and it hears all of the internal workings of your body and can react to external sounds, like music or singing. The heartbeat should be able to be heard with a specialized fetoscope by the seventeenth or eighteenth week.

You: It's during this month that most mothers first feel fetal movements. If you felt them very faintly last month, you may feel them more distinctly now. Your uterus has expanded to reach all the way to your navel, and the skin of your abdomen is stretching to accommodate this growth. You have probably noticed that your belly button has begun to stretch out and may even be everted (turned inside out) already, particularly if your stomach muscles are weak. Patches of lighter skin may appear on your face. You may feel Braxton Hicks contractions (false labor contractions your body uses to practice for the main event), but these will be more likely to occur during the last few months of your pregnancy.

Sixth Month (22^1/$_2$ to 27 Weeks)

Your Baby: Size—11 to 14 inches long; weight—approximately 1^1/$_2$ to 2 pounds. Your baby is still growing rapidly. The skin is wrinkled, red, thin, and shiny, with no underlying fat. The finger-prints and toe prints are visible, the eyelids begin to part, and the eyes open. This is typically the baby's period of most active move-ment. With plenty of room still available in the womb, it can regu-larly change its position—turning itself upside down, rightside up, even perpendicular to your body. Though the baby's lungs and other organs are not completely developed it has a slim chance of survival if born now.

You: You will probably see the biggest jumps on your bathroom scale during the next several weeks, as your pregnancy enters the final stretch and the baby continues its growth. A common discom-fort during this time are pains on the side of your abdomen as the uterine muscle stretches. It will have to grow to about one thousand times its normal volume to accommodate the growing fetus. You will probably feel the fetus kicking sporadically throughout the day. The twenty-fourth through the twenty-eighth weeks are the baby's period of greatest activity, although you may not always feel it.

Seventh Month (27 to 31^1/$_2$ Weeks)

Your Baby: Size—about 15 inches long; weight—roughly 3 pounds. The baby can suck its thumb, open and close its eyes, react to light and dark, cry, hiccup, and exercise by kicking and stretching. By the end of the month the fetus can respond to stimuli such as pain and light, and can hear sound outside the womb wall. The bones are hardening as calcium is stored.

You: The increased growth of your baby is gradually causing you more discomfort. If you feel radiant and energetic during the second

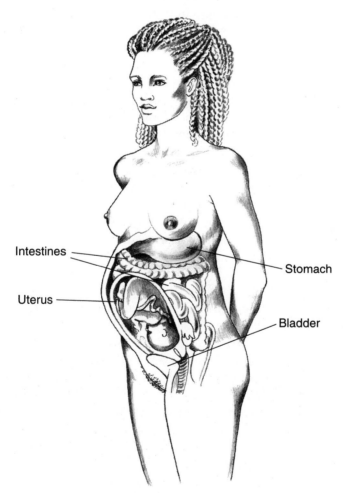

Woman at 27 to 31^1/$_2$ weeks pregnant.

trimester, as each week passes you may begin to feel eager to have that baby *out*. It may become more difficult for you to find a comfortable sleeping position, and you may briefly feel tingling and numbness in your hands and feet as the growing uterus puts increased pressure on your circulatory system. If you haven't already, you may start noticing stretch marks on or around your breasts, hips, and particularly the lower abdomen. You may also suffer from varicose veins and hemorrhoids as the uterus presses against your veins, causing them to swell. Keeping physically active will help you a great deal. Braxton Hicks contractions may be occurring on and off. This is simply the uterine muscles "exercising," which promotes good blood circulation and aids in uterine growth. You may also feel the baby hiccup as it swallows the amniotic fluid, giving its new digestive system some practice. These hiccups usually feel like brief, gentle kicks that occur at short, evenly spaced intervals.

Eighth Month (31¹/₂ to 36 Weeks)

Your Baby: Size—about 18 inches long; weight—roughly 5 pounds. With the fetus still growing larger and fatter and your uterus stretched to its limit, the baby is unable to move around much. The bones of its head are soft and flexible, which will help it squeeze through the birth canal during delivery. Although the lungs may still be immature, most of the baby's bodily systems are well developed and it has an excellent chance of survival if born now. If the baby has been in a breech (upright) position the last few weeks, chances are it will turn itself head-down now, although 3 to 10 percent of babies do not (see Chapter 15, "What-ifs During Pregnancy and Childbirth").

You: It's an extremely tight fit in your uterus now and as the baby gets stronger its kicks will be more forceful. Occasionally the bulge of its buttocks or its elbow may be visible through your abdomen. At other times a foot may seem to get "stuck" underneath your rib cage. Your uterus has grown so that the top lies just underneath your diaphragm. Braxton Hicks contractions, which have actually been occurring throughout the pregnancy, will be stronger now. You will also feel more aches, pains, and discomforts, such as heartburn and shortness of breath, as your uterus rises, crowding out your ribs, stomach and intestines and pressing down on your bladder. Many women find that their breasts occasionally leak "colostrum," the rich, clear or yellow fluid that precedes breast milk. Your prenatal caretaker will probably have you coming in for visits every two weeks rather than once a month.

Ninth Month (36 to 40 Weeks)

Your Baby: Size and weight—during this month the baby will gain roughly a half pound per week. At 40 weeks most babies weigh anywhere between 6 and 9 pounds, with the average baby weighing 7½ pounds and being 20 inches long. During this month the baby will drop farther into the pelvis as its head, now smaller, engages in the birth position. It may seem less active as it becomes more confined in the pelvis. Most practitioners consider a pregnancy to have reached "full term" at anywhere from 37 to 42 weeks.

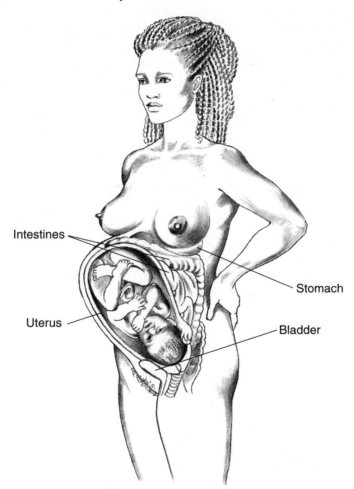

Woman at 36 to 40 weeks pregnant. You're almost there! Look how your organs have shifted to accomodate the baby's growth.

You: This is the home stretch. At this point even some of your maternity clothes may feel tight. Shortness of breath may lessen as the baby drops farther into your pelvis (this process is called "lightening"). However, this can also be uncomfortable, particularly as the heavy uterus presses on your bladder, causing you to urinate frequently. Swelling may be much more noticeable around your ankles and feet this month and you may experience back pain, especially if your baby is in the posterior position (facing front). Your cervix will soften (or "ripen"), and Braxton Hicks contractions are strong and frequent. You can tell Braxton Hicks contractions from the real thing by timing them. They should be irregular, unlike in real labor where contractions come regularly and closer together as time passes. False labor contractions are short, do not get very strong, and often stop if you change your body position—the real ones won't. Be alert to unusual vaginal discharge and other signs of impending labor (see Chapter 14, "All About Labor and Delivery").

CHAPTER 3

Your Changing Body:
What to Expect

During pregnancy your body will undergo a host of changes to accommodate and protect the baby growing in your womb. Some changes fulfill a specific purpose, while others are merely a result of hormonal changes. Most changes are mild and harmless; some can be extreme and need treatment. Emotional changes affect your attitude during pregnancy, and they are often intertwined with your physical changes.

The following is a comprehensive, alphabetical list of the most common bodily changes or effects of pregnancy. Although at first glance they may seem overwhelming, it's important to realize one of the first rules of pregnancy: No two pregnancies are exactly alike. You may experience all of these symptoms or only a few. While your best friend has never had a pregnancy where she didn't vomit daily in the first trimester, your sister may have never felt even a passing wave of nausea or morning sickness while carrying all four of her children. Yet both women are normal, and both had normal pregnancies. Throughout your pregnancy, understand these changes for what they represent—the miracle of life growing inside of you.

Backache

When: Usually during the fifth through ninth months.
Why: This is one of the most common complaints of pregnancy as

your body's weight, shape, and balance change. To compensate for the growing awkwardness and seeming imbalance in your body, you may change your posture, slumping your shoulders, arching your neck, or standing with your stomach thrust forward, all of which put unnecessary strain on your back. Also, during pregnancy your ligaments become more elastic so your pelvis can expand during the baby's birth. However, this also leaves you more vulnerable to strain and injury.

What You Can Do: You'll be better off if you enter your pregnancy with strong abdominal muscles and good posture. If your back has been injured or you have a history of back problems, you will need to take special care. Here are some suggestions to lessen back pain and help prevent it:

◆ Keep your weight gain at reasonable levels. The more excess weight you put on, the more your back must carry. (See Chapter 7, "You (and Your Baby) Are What You Eat.")

◆ Don't wear high-heeled shoes or very flat shoes. Some doctors recommend a wide-based, low-heeled shoe.

◆ Lift heavy objects by bending your knees, squatting, and lifting with your legs and arms rather than your back, but if possible, try to avoid lifting heavy objects or children. When you must carry a child for a short distance, carry the child on your hip.

◆ If you have to stand for a long time, keep one foot resting on a low stool or box, which prevents strain on your lower back.

◆ Although your plush, overstuffed sofa might have been your favorite place to relax, you may find sitting in it more uncomfortable as you get bigger. Choose to sit in chairs that offer firm support, particularly straight-backed chairs. Whenever possible, sit with your legs slightly elevated on a footstool.

◆ Try to keep the things you need off the floor so you don't have to bend down or stretch too much. Stretching to reach over your head also puts a strain on your back.

◆ If your back is sore when you wake up in the morning, your mattress may be too soft. Place a board between the mattress and box spring or switch to a more firm matress. Also try sleeping on your side with one knee bent and your upper leg supported by a pillow (see "Insomnia," this chapter, for illustration).

◆ Some women find that using a pregnancy girdle or belly sling helps support the weight of the abdomen, keeping pressure off back muscles. Ask your doctor or midwife about these options and where to find one.

◆ Do pregnancy exercises such as the Pelvic Rock to relieve back soreness and strengthen your abdominal muscles (see Chapter 9, "Your Physical Tank").

◆ To ease sore back muscles, soak in a warm (not hot) bath or apply a heating pad wrapped in a towel to the sore area.

◆ Ask your husband to give you a warm oil back massage. (See Chapter 9, "Your Physical Tank," for how-tos.)

"My husband and I were making love before we knew I was pregnant. He reached around to caress my breasts and I almost screamed it was so painful. I was terrified that I might have developed breast cancer."

"My breasts went from a 34B to a 34D to a 34DD with each successive baby. People would ask, 'Girl, you had those done?' I'd say, 'Yep, baby-done!' "

Breast Changes (Size and Appearance)

When: Throughout the pregnancy. You will notice the greatest changes taking place in the first trimester and in the eighth and ninth months.

Why: The enlargement and sensitive tingling in your breasts may be one of your first signs of pregnancy. When you are pregnant your breasts increase in size as your milk glands enlarge and the fat layer around your breasts thickens to prepare for breast-feeding. By six to eight weeks your breasts should be noticeably larger. This size difference is typically greater in small-breasted women and less noticeable in women with large breasts (your ability to breast-feed successfully and provide adequate nourishment to your baby has *nothing* to do with the size of your breasts).

Early in your first trimester your breasts may also feel swollen and tender, because of the increased supply of the hormones estrogen and progesterone your body is producing. Some women describe their breasts as feeling "tingling" or "itchy," while others say their breasts are just plain sore and painful to the touch, similar to the way some women feel before their periods. Thankfully, the soreness and tingling soon leave and are typically strongest in first pregnancies.

Your nipples may also protrude more and the veins on your breasts will become more pronounced (veins tend to be more distinct on lighter-skinned sisters). The veins enlarge in order to transport the rich nutrients that make your breast milk. Your nipples and areolae, the dark area around your nipples, will become even darker, gradually fading after you give birth. Lastly, you may see small bumps appear on and around your areolae. These bumps are sweat glands, called Montgomery tubercles, which produce an oily substance to lubricate the nipple area and keep it from drying out.

What You Can Do

◆ Sagging breasts and stretch marks are not caused by breast-feeding but by the added weight the breasts bear in pregnancy. To minimize sagging always wear bras with adequate support. This will lessen the stretching of breast tissue and ease the strain on your back if your breasts are heavy. You can also wear a cotton "sleep bra" at night, made especially for pregnant women. Cotton bras are preferable throughout pregnancy and during the breast-feeding period because they allow your skin to breathe.

◆ Don't wash your breasts with soap, which can leave the area around your nipples dry and flaky. Wash only with warm water and don't use heavy lotions or lubricants on them.

Braxton Hicks Contractions

When: Usually not until the seventh or eighth month, especially in first pregnancies, although in some women and in subsequent pregnancies they are felt earlier, even as early as 20 weeks.

Why: "It felt like the baby had grown too big to fit in my body—my belly became so tight and heavy I could hardly walk straight. But a minute or so later I noticed that feeling was gone," said one woman as she described the first time she felt a Braxton Hicks contraction. These "false" contractions (as opposed to real labor contractions; see pages 301–302 for comparison of false and true contractions) are your body's way of practicing for the big event. Unlike real contractions, these usually last roughly 30 seconds and gradually disappear when you shift positions, walk around, or sit down. Your abdomen may harden and may make walking uncomfortable or tiring. As these contractions become more frequent in the last month and a half, they may become more intense and painful. Some women say theirs felt like menstrual cramps.

What You Can Do: Unlike real contractions, which come at certain intervals that can be timed, you may not always be able to feel exactly when a Braxton Hicks contraction is coming on or determine when it will end. But you'll definitely feel it when it's there.

◆ If it's not very uncomfortable you can simply ignore it and wait it out. Some women feel these contractions while resting and may need to get up and walk around to help the feeling disappear. Others feel these contractions more frequently when they are particularly active, or lifting heavy things. If this is the case, try sitting down and relaxing to help relieve discomfort. If you are getting more than four contractions per hour, this may be a strong signal that you are doing too much and need to stop. This could also be a sign of premature labor.

◆ Drink plenty of water and other fluids. Dehydration can intensify your contractions or cause them to occur more frequently.

◆ Keep your prenatal caretaker informed about the occurrence and frequency of your Braxton Hicks contractions, especially if they are accompanied by pain or an unusual vaginal discharge. This information will help them determine how close you are to your due date and whether you are in danger of premature delivery.

Colostrum (Leaking Breasts)

When: From the fifth month and on, although typically not until the eighth and ninth months, and not until after delivery in some women.

Why: Colostrum is a thin yellow or clear fluid that precedes your regular breast milk. This special kind of breast milk, low in fat and rich in protein and antibodies, is perfectly designed to nourish your baby adequately for the first three or four days after delivery until your milk comes in. (And don't let anyone tell you otherwise.)

What You Can Do: Don't be alarmed to find wet spots on your blouse. Although leaking from colostrum tends to be minimal, once it appears you can wear gauze or cotton breast pads to catch any leakage.

Constipation

When: Mid to late pregnancy.

Why: Constipation seems to be a problem associated with at least half of all pregnant women. Increased levels of hormones during pregnancy cause your bowel muscles to relax, and later in your pregnancy, the growing pressure your uterus places on your rectum can interfere with its proper functioning. In some cases, the iron or vitamin supplements you may be taking can contribute to constipation.

What You Can Do

◆ Drink at least 8 to 10 cups of fluid a day. Water and fruit and vegetable juices are best. For persistent cases, prune juice has long had a reputation for moving stubborn stools.

◆ Eat plenty of fiber. Raw fruit with the skins and raw or lightly cooked vegetables are excellent, as are whole-grain breads and cereals, dried beans and lentils, and dried fruit such as raisins, prunes, dried apricots, and dates. Add a spoonful of wheat germ or wheat bran to your diet (sprinkled over cereal or in a shake), gradually working up to a few tablespoons daily. However, don't overdose on roughage. It's possible to compound the problem by clogging your digestive system with an overload of difficult-to-digest foods. A moderate amount of grains, fruits, and vegetables each day should be fine.

◆ Exercise for at least a half hour daily.

◆ Avoid using mineral oil, which can prevent absorption of vitamins A and D from your body. If nothing works and you absolutely need a laxative, consult your doctor or midwife.

Faintness and Dizziness

When: Early in your pregnancy and in the last trimester.

Why: Actual fainting is not a common symptom of pregnancy, although it's well reinforced on TV shows and in old movies. Only a few women actually experience it. Dizziness, however, is more common, and can be caused by low blood pressure, low blood sugar, or too little iron in your blood. In the first trimester, faintness can be caused by a blood supply that has not yet caught up with your quickly expanding circulatory system.

What You Can Do

◆ If you must stand for a long period (more than an hour), move around frequently to stimulate circulation.

◆ Don't let yourself get overheated and don't stand up suddenly from a sitting position, which can cause faintness from the rapid drop in blood pressure.

◆ Wear loose clothing, particularly around the waist and neck, to encourage good circulation.

◆ Keep a small, nutritious snack handy (raisins, a few slices of bread and cheese, whole-wheat pretzels or crackers) in between meals to keep your blood sugar up.

◆ Get plenty of rest and sit down frequently if you feel a tendency toward dizziness. If the feeling is strong, lie down or sit down quickly with your head between your knees. If you faint standing up there's more risk of injury.

◆ Be sure to tell your doctor of any incidence of fainting. Fainting can be symptomatic of a more serious problem such as anemia or an ectopic pregnancy.

Fetal Movement

When: Can be first felt anywhere from 14 to 26 weeks, though most women feel the first movements between weeks 18 and 22 (within the fifth month).

Why: Many women don't feel "officially" pregnant until they feel their baby move or kick, giving them confirmation that there really is a life growing in there. Although the fetus can move itself around as early as the seventh week, these movements are generally too mild to feel until the fifth month. Women who have been pregnant before may feel movement earlier because they know what the sensation feels like. If you're in your first pregnancy you may initially ignore the movements or attribute them to something else. These first felt movements, called quickening, may feel like fluttering, a twitch, or similar to (but not quite the same as) an upset stomach. Don't worry if it seems like a few days go by between kicks when you first feel them. The baby is most active between the twenty-fourth and the twenty-eighth week, and it's at this time you will probably begin feeling movement more often throughout the day. Unfortunately, the fetus is often lulled to sleep by your movements and wakes as you sit still. This explains why women often notice the kicks more when they are resting, or feel the baby moving when they go to bed or before they get up in the morning. However, the baby may be more restful on some days and have more energy on others. Watch closely: you will be able to see the little jabs and pushes moving the surface of your abdomen.

As your pregnancy progresses, the baby grows larger and has less room to move around. The baby is also getting stronger, and the movements may get more uncomfortable as its feet lodge under your ribs or the baby moves itself perpendicular to your abdomen.

BY THE WAY ...

One mother says that she casually asked her two-year-old if she remembered being in the womb. Her daughter looked at her, smiled, and said, "Yup, I remember I used to tickle you with my feet!"

What You Can Do: Just relax and enjoy the excitement of your baby's movement. Familiarize yourself with the variation and frequency of kicks, stretches and turns. Some doctors suggest that after 28 weeks you test the fetal movement twice a day. You can do this each morning and evening by sitting down, eating a snack (to stimulate the baby with glucose), and timing how long it takes you to feel 10 separate movements, whether they are kicks, stretches, turns, or flutters. Generally this will take less than an hour, and at most two hours. If you feel a sudden absence of movement after a few weeks of feeling the baby moving throughout the day, be sure to call your doctor or midwife.

If the baby is simply lodged in a position that is uncomfortable for you, the most you can do is try switching positions or getting up and moving around. Usually the baby will adjust itself and give you some relief.

Frequent Urination and Incontinence

When: The first trimester and last two months.

Why: It may seem like you and your toilet are attached at the hip during the first weeks after you get pregnant. Some women even wake once or twice a night to make a trip to the bathroom. The main reason for this is your growing uterus, which begins to press up against your bladder. Even though your bladder may be nearly empty, the pressure causes it to feel full. The added fluids you'll be drinking throughout your pregnancy will also increase your need to urinate. Thankfully, this feeling usually lessens after the first trimester as your uterus grows and rises in your abdomen. However, the need to urinate more often returns near the last month or so of pregnancy as the baby grows to full term and drops deeper into your pelvis, once again pressing against your bladder. Some women find themselves leaking urine at this time, particularly when they cough, sneeze, or laugh. This occasional inability to hold back your urine is called stress incontinence. Incontinence can also occur postpartum, as your perineal muscles recover from the stress of giving birth vaginally.

What You Can Do: Use the bathroom every time you feel the need. Don't try to hold it back; this is uncomfortable and could cause a bladder infection. If you feel a burning sensation when you urinate, call your doctor. This could also be a sign of infection. Do your Kegel exercises. These "squeezes" firm up your perineal muscles, prepare you for pushing the baby out during delivery, and can also help diminish postpartum incontinence. (See Chapter 9, "Your Physical Tank," for details and illustrations.)

Gums (Bleeding and Swelling)

When: Mid to late pregnancy.

Why: The hormones of pregnancy can cause your gums to become puffy and bleed when you brush. A lack of vitamin C can also agitate the problem.

What You Can Do: Although they may be tender, be sure you brush and floss regularly, paying special attention to your gums. (This is a great time to begin flossing your teeth, if it's not already a habit.) Also:

- ◆ Schedule a dental appointment for a cleaning and checkup after the first trimester and again once after you give birth. Be sure to request to not have X rays taken while you are pregnant unless it is absolutely necessary (see Chapter 4, "Your Habits and Your Lifestyle: Being Careful"). Unless there's a critical problem, wait until after you give birth to have routine repair work done.
- ◆ Vitamin C helps strengthen gums. Eat a healthy diet, including an adequate amount of vitamin C as well as calcium, needed for your teeth as well as bones.

Don't be surprised to see your pubic hair growing up to two inches longer than usual!

Hair and Nail Growth

When: Throughout your pregnancy, but most noticeable after the first trimester.

Why: For many sisters, one great benefit of pregnancy is that their hair and nails grow faster and their hair seems thicker than ever before. To the surprise of many, this may also include your pubic hair, which can grow up to an inch or two longer at its area of longest growth. This is again caused by those pregnancy hormones.

What You Can Do: In this case, there's nothing you need to do but enjoy the benefits while you can. If longer pubic hair bothers you and you cut it, it will only continue to grow back, perhaps faster. Besides, all of these changes will return to normal shortly after you give birth. In fact, many women experience what seems to be an excessive hair loss a few months after delivery, as the volume of the hair returns to normal. (Remember, avoid chemically treating your hair during pregnancy as the chemicals can penetrate the scalp and enter the bloodstream. Why not braid your hair instead?)

Headaches

When: Throughout your pregnancy.

Why: Both women who were prone to headaches and migraines and those who rarely have them may find them frequent once they become pregnant. They are most commonly caused by hormonal changes, but can also be brought on by stress, hunger, exhaustion, nasal congestion, or eyestrain.

What You Can Do: If you find yourself prone to headaches during pregnancy, prevention may literally be your best, and sometimes only, medicine. Do not take aspirin, which can complicate your labor and affect the fetus, particularly in the third trimester, unless prescribed. Although your doctor may OK occasional use of acetaminophen (such as Tylenol), it should only be used when absolutely necessary (see Chapter 4, "Your Habits and Your Lifestyle: Being Careful," for acceptable use of medications in pregnancy). Instead, try these preventative measures.

- ◆ Take time out to relax each day, even if you don't have a headache. Try a soothing warm bath, lying down in a dark and quiet room, listening to relaxing music, or taking a slow walk outside. Be sure to get plenty of sleep, and take naps when you can.
- ◆ Eat regularly to prevent hunger headaches, and keep a snack handy for those unexpected times when you may be eating late.
- ◆ Keep the rooms in your house or apartment as ventilated as possible to avoid sinus headaches. Don't overheat the rooms in the winter, keep a humidifier running if the air is dry, and get out of rooms with secondhand smoke. If you get a sinus headache, try lying down and pressing a hot, moist towel over your forehead and eyes.
- ◆ To avoid vision-related headaches, wait until after the pregnancy, if possible, to be fitted for new glasses or contact lenses. Changes in vision may also be related to hormonal changes, which will only last during the pregnancy.

Heart Pounding

When: Mid to late pregnancy.

Why: Although it may startle you, brief instances of heart pounding are only a result of your body's need to increase its own circulation and meet the baby's needs.

What You Can Do

♦ Relax and breathe deeply. Getting up and moving or getting tense will only prolong a fast heart rate.

♦ If it continues or happens frequently, call your doctor or midwife.

Hemorrhoids

When: Mid to late pregnancy. Particularly in the last two months and shortly after baby's birth.

Why: Hemorrhoids are varicose or swollen veins of the rectum. They are fairly common during pregnancy, caused by pressure of the growing uterus and increased circulation, which can cause dilation of your rectal veins. They are often caused or worsened by constipation (see constipation reference in this chapter). Besides causing itching and burning pain, hemorrhoids can also cause rectal bleeding.

What You Can Do

♦ Constipation and hemorrhoids go hand in hand. If you can prevent constipation from the very start of your pregnancy, you are very likely to prevent hemorrhoids. Take all precautions mentioned for constipation (eating fiber, drinking fluids, etc., see page 38).

♦ If you get hemorrhoids, take sitz baths (sitting in a warm bath) twice a day.

♦ Apply witch-hazel soaks or pads (available in drugstores or health-food stores) to the hemorrhoids.

♦ Do Kegel exercises throughout the day (See Chapter 9, "Your Physical Tank"). These improve circulation to the area.

♦ Keep your rectal and vaginal areas extremely clean, wiping from front to back with toilet tissue moistened with warm water.

♦ Avoid sitting down for long periods of time; lie or recline on your side whenever possible. When you sleep at night, lie on your side instead of your back to avoid putting added pressure on the rectal veins.

◆ Only if necessary, let your prenatal caretaker prescribe topical medications or suppositories.

Heartburn and Flatulence (Gas)

When: Throughout your pregnancy, though more often in the second half.

Why: Pregnancy often causes your digestive tract to work more slowly, as the hormones estrogen and progesterone cause muscles throughout your body to relax. Heartburn is caused when the muscles that separate the esophagus from the stomach relax, and acidic digestive fluid rises and causes a burning feeling on the sensitive throat lining. Later in pregnancy, your stomach and intestines increasingly feel the encroaching pressure of the uterus. This can cause heartburn and intestinal gas. Gas can also be a result of constipation.

What You Can Do: Follow the tips for constipation and—

◆ Eat six small meals a day instead of three large ones, easing the workload on your digestive tract.
◆ Relax and take your time while eating; avoid gulping your food, and chew thoroughly before you take the next bite.
◆ Don't lie down directly after eating.
◆ Limit gas-producing foods such as broccoli, cabbage, brussel sprouts, fried foods, carbonated drinks, and beans. Spicy foods may increase heartburn. (See Chapter 7, "You (and Your Baby) Are What You Eat.")

Insomnia

When: Throughout your pregnancy, though more typical during the last trimester.

Why: "My emotions were running up and down. I was excited about being pregnant and made plans as I lay in bed at night, but at the same time I worried a lot. There were many nights I just couldn't sleep at all," said one sister as she described her insomnia. Insomnia in pregnancy can be caused by a variety of emotional and physical factors. In the beginning the sheer amount of emotional and physical changes, as well as worries or major decisions to be made, can keep you up. The need to urinate may also be waking you at night. Toward the end of your pregnancy it will be uncomfortable trying to sleep with both your growing abdomen and your growing excitement about the impending birth.

What You Can Do

- ◆ Get plenty of exercise and activity during the day to increase your chance of feeling tired at night. Have a soothing light snack before going to bed, like warm milk, whole-wheat bread and butter, or fruit (avoid sugar at dinner and after). If you're getting up to go to the bathroom at night, try limiting fluids after 4 P.M.
- ◆ If decisions or worries are keeping you up, try to find some resolve to them during the day, and empty your mind of serious or important thoughts before going to bed by reading a light novel, writing your thoughts down in a journal, spending time in silent prayer, or playing some instrumental music.
- ◆ Getting yourself comfortable is probably the best way to ensure a good night's rest, especially in your third trimester. Sleeping on your left side may be best. Try putting a pillow between your legs or under your knee (see illustration). Sleeping on your back

A favorite sleeping position for women in mid to late pregnancy.

after the fifth month can decrease oxygen flow and blood circulation to the baby, and can irritate hemorrhoids and your digestive tract. Some women also prefer to have two pillows under their head, use another behind their back to give support, or have one to "hug" in between their arms to support their chest. Experiment to see which is most comfortable for you.

Leg Cramps

When: In the second and third trimesters.

Why: These painful cramps most often hit at night when you are sleeping or when you stretch in bed with your toes pointed. The attack often feels like a clamp is squeezing your calf muscle. No one is quite sure what causes these cramps. In the past there was concern that they might be caused by a calcium deficiency, but this diagnosis is not considered accurate.

What You Can Do: If you get a cramp in your calf, resist the urge to bend over and grab the painful spot with your hand. This will cause you to bend your knee and only worsen the pain. Instead, straighten your leg and flex your ankle and toes toward your nose (the opposite of pointing your toes). As the immediate pain begins to disappear, you can then reach over and massage the sore spot.

Morning Sickness (Nausea and Vomiting)

When: Typically in the first trimester.

Why: Surprisingly, morning sickness does not always result in the pregnant woman rushing off to the bathroom to vomit. Many women never actually vomit, but feel nauseous or simply have a bad taste in their mouths. Another myth about morning sickness is the name itself. Although many women feel it more often when they first wake up, many others also feel it in the afternoon, at night, or on and off throughout the day. Some days the feeling may be more frequent, and on others you may hardly feel it at all. Some studies show that morning sickness is only experienced by about half of all pregnant women. These feelings of nausea and vomiting typically leave after the first trimester, although for some women it drags on into the second, and a very few women may feel it throughout the entire pregnancy.

No one really knows the actual cause of morning sickness, but it seems to be a combination of both physical and psychological reasons. Many doctors suggest that the most likely reason is the high level of the hormone HCG in pregnancy. Other theories believe it may be caused by the relaxed state of muscle tissue in the digestive tract and the rapid stretching of your uterine muscle during early pregnancy. Emotional factors may influence morning sickness as well. Many women experience it more frequently in times of stress from physical or emotional fatigue. The triggers can vary from woman to woman. Although some may feel waves of nausea suddenly hit them for no discernible reason, many feel morning sickness most often when their stomach is empty (such as after a full night's sleep, hence the name). Many sisters said that their nausea was triggered by strong smells or tastes. For example, some say that the smell of raw meat would send them running, while others said that the smell of Chinese food (even though some loved eating it during pregnancy), onions, or even the taste of toothpaste made them ill. If you have other children in diapers while you are pregnant it may become difficult to change a messy diaper without holding your nose and looking the other way. Even the sight or thought of something foul can produce nauseous feelings. Although there is no specific cure or medication to take for morning sickness, there are many ways you can help alleviate it or even lessen its occurrence.

What You Can Do

- Eat small meals throughout the day to prevent your stomach from being completely empty. Foods high in protein (meats, dairy products) and complex carbohydrates (pastas, legumes) help reduce nausea. Avoid coffee or acidic drinks such as orange juice on an empty stomach. Carry a snack to nibble on or a juice box to sip to prevent feeling nauseous while you're driving or on the go.
- Have a snack of crackers or a banana and a drink such as apple juice waiting by your bedside to eat before you get out of bed in the morning. Don't get up out of bed quickly, but sit up for a few minutes, allowing the food to digest.
- As much as possible, avoid strong or foul smells or tastes.
- Relax. Being exhausted or stressed can only leave you vulnerable to nausea and too tired to suppress the desire to vomit.
- If you do find a wave of nausea coming on, some women find that they are able to "think the feeling away" by finding something else to focus on—a tree, picture, or object in their peri-

phery—and concentrating on it, taking deep breaths until the feeling passes.

◆ Try Sea-Bands, a product for motion sickness that puts pressure on your inner wrists to alleviate queasiness. These are available at many pharmacies and through maternity catalogs.

◆ Though some women may end up losing a few pounds after the first trimester from frequent vomiting or a loss of appetite, a modest weight loss is not likely to interfere with you or the baby's nutrition. However, don't view your morning sickness as an opportunity to lose weight, scrimping on the daily nutrition. Try to make the calories that you do hold down count by eating as nutritiously as possible and taking prenatal vitamin supplements during the time of day you are least likely to feel queasy (see Chapter 7, "You (and Your Baby) Are What You Eat," for more on a healthy diet during pregnancy and more morning-sickness remedies).

◆ Very few women may need medical treatment for extreme nausea and vomiting. Consult your doctor if you suspect this is a severe problem.

Nasal Congestion and Nosebleeds

When: Throughout your pregnancy.

Why: While nasal stuffiness is a fairly common complaint of pregnancy, the symptoms may be mild enough for you to brush it off as a minor cold. It's believed to be caused by those good old pregnancy hormones, which increase blood circulation in the mucous membranes of your nose, and can cause the membranes to swell. Nosebleeds often accompany nasal stuffiness, and both can be more frequent in winter, when heaters fill your house with hot, dry air.

What You Can Do

◆ Use a humidifier in winter to help moisten the air.

◆ Try not to blow your nose with force, which can put pressure on nasal blood vessels.

◆ If you get a nosebleed, lean forward (don't lie down) and squeeze your nostrils together with your thumb and forefinger, breathing through your mouth and holding this position for 5 minutes. If this fails to stop the bleeding after a few tries, call your doctor.

Numbness and Tingling (in Legs, Toes, Arms)

When: Typically after the fifth month.

Why: As your abdomen grows bigger you may occasionally feel numbness and tingling in your arms, hands, and particularly in your legs and feet. This is generally associated with the weight gain and water retention needed for pregnancy. It could also be caused by your growing uterus, which begins to place its added weight on your nerves. Although it may be briefly uncomfortable until you begin moving around and restoring circulation to the area, the condition is harmless and will likely subside after delivery. If you are experiencing numbness in the hands only, you may have carpal tunnel syndrome. This syndrome is common in pregnant women and can be exacerbated if you spend a lot of time typing at a computer terminal or performing jobs that require continual, repetitive hand motions, such as assembly line work. Ask your doctor about it if this numbness persists.

What You Can Do: Shake the affected part of the body.

Overheating

When: Throughout your pregnancy.

Why: Pregnancy increases the rate at which your body expends energy, making you feel warm even in winter. This can cause you to sweat more easily.

What You Can Do

◆ Dress in thin, cotton layers whenever possible. The natural cotton fabric allows your skin to breathe more easily and the layers allow you to take off or put on easily, depending on how you feel.
◆ Drink plenty of fluids to replace those lost through perspiration.

Pelvic Discomfort and Abdominal Pain

When: Mid to late pregnancy, but most frequent during the eighteenth through twenty-fourth weeks.

Why: Sharp pains along your abdomen or sides of your pelvis are typically caused by the ligaments around the uterus that are pulled and stretched as it grows. This kind of pain is most commonly felt when you are getting up from a bed or chair, or are coughing.

What You Can Do

◆ Get up slowly from a sitting or reclining position. Avoid quick changes in position, especially when you're turning at the waist.

◆ If you feel a sharp pain, bend forward to relieve it rather than stretching.

Salivation (Excessive)

When: First and second trimesters.

Why: No one seems to know the reason why, nor is there a cure for it, but excessive salivation seems to be a common but harmless symptom of pregnancy for some women.

What You Can Do: There's not much you can do, but chewing gum (which causes you to swallow frequently) can help. Or, during the night, put a dry washcloth between your head and your pillowcase to absorb any saliva.

Shortness of Breath

When: Mid to late pregnancy.

Why: Just as your bulging uterus presses upon your stomach, it also compresses part of the area in your chest used for expanding your lungs. In the ninth month, after the baby drops into your pelvis, you may find it easier to breathe.

What You Can Do: Stretch by holding your arms up over your head to shift the baby's position and give yourself temporary relief. Be sure to sleep on your left side and use pillows to prop yourself up as needed.

Skin Changes (Discoloration, Pigmentation, and Pimples)

When: Mid to late pregnancy.

Why: The same pregnancy hormones that caused the darkening of your nipples and areolae can also cause changes in the pigmentation of your skin. A faint line that runs down the center of your abdomen darkens to become the linea nigra or "black line." Lighter-skinned black women are more susceptible to developing what is called the "mask" of pregnancy, technically known as chloasma—dark coloring over the cheeks, nose, and forehead, though some dark-skinned sisters may develop light patches. Moles, freckles, and any blemishes may also darken. Hormonal changes can also cause some women's skin to become oily and break out during pregnancy (similar to what may happen to your skin before and during your period), though others say their skin was more supple and healthy-looking than ever during pregnancy.

What You Can Do

◆ Avoid staying out excessively in the sun, wear a hat or visor, or use a sunblock of at least SPF 15 when outdoors (yes, even black women need sunscreen). Even a light tan can intensify the discoloration.

◆ Use a cover stick or light makeup to disguise or even out irregular pigmentation.

◆ If you're fighting acne, wash your face more often during the day, avoiding using heavy foundation makeup (use a good powder instead) and heavy creams. *Do not use* the prescription drugs Accutane or Retin-A, which can have harmful effects on the baby. Also, drink as much water as you can stand *every* day.

Stretch Marks

When: Mid to late pregnancy.

Why: The stretch marks many sisters dread acquiring are light streaks that can appear on the breasts, hips, thighs, and abdomen during pregnancy. They are caused by the rapid stretching your skin undergoes as your body increases in weight and size. While 90 percent of all pregnant women experience some stretch marks, this degree may vary, depending on how much weight you gain and your skin's natural elasticity. Despite an abundance of creams and oils that claim to reduce stretch marks, unfortunately, none of them can prevent or change the lines on your body. Although they may seem frighteningly obvious, especially in the last two months as your baby nears its peak weight, most stretch marks gradually fade after delivery, sometimes becoming barely noticeable except by close inspection.

Swelling of Feet

When: Mid to late pregnancy, but most noticeable in last two months.

Why: Mild swelling, especially in the feet and ankles, is a common occurrence in pregnancy, particularly in the last trimester, as your body increases its need for fluids. At times, particularly at the end of the day or after you've been sitting or standing for a long period of time, you may notice that your feet look fatter, or that lines are left on the skin where the elastic of your socks gripped your ankle. At its worst, swelling (also called edema) may be slightly uncomfortable. However, be alert to swelling in the hands and face, particularly if it's sudden or severe. This can be a symptom of preeclampsia, a much more serious problem (see page 330–31).

What You Can Do

◆ Whenever possible, raise or prop up your feet while sitting, or lie down when you can. This relieves the strain that gravity places upon the circulation in your legs.

◆ Wear comfortable shoes with low heels and avoid tight elastic-topped socks or stockings that can restrict circulation.

◆ Special maternity support hose or knee-highs can help reduce swelling if it's very uncomfortable or persistent. Ask your doctor or midwife about them.

Tiredness (Fatigue)

When: Throughout your pregnancy, although greatest during the first and last trimester.

Why: In the first trimester your body is changing at lightning speed. Your hormones are increasing, bringing a host of physical and emotional changes. The placenta, the life-support system that brings oxygen and nutrients to the baby in the uterus, is being formed and won't be completed until the fourth month. Your energy generally returns in the second trimester after your body adjusts to the changes and morning sickness leaves. Most women can enjoy this period as the golden months of pregnancy. However, fatigue usually returns in the last trimester. This is because your body is reaching its peak weight and is growing increasingly cumbersome. You will probably be feeling Braxton Hicks contractions as well, which can limit your activity.

What You Can Do: Your tiredness is *not* all in your mind. It's a legitimate signal from your body that you need rest to compensate for the added work it's doing. Don't push yourself to get in extra hours at work or keep the house clean when you feel like falling asleep at your desk or the kitchen table. Listen to your body, and go home or go to bed.

◆ Get rest when you feel the need for it, whenever possible. Go to bed an hour earlier if you can, especially if you cannot nap during the day.

◆ If this is your first pregnancy and there are no other children at home, enjoy this opportunity to rest when you feel like it. If you do have small children in the house, nap when they nap. Arrange for your husband or a relative to take other children for a few hours to give you a rest.

◆ If you're working, you may have trouble taking a break when you want it, so use your scheduled free time to your advantage. At lunch, if there's no place to recline try putting your feet up, or go outside and relax on a park bench.

Vaginal Discharge

When: Throughout your pregnancy.

Why: Increased vaginal discharge is typical during pregnancy. A healthy discharge should be milky in color and have a mild odor to it, similar to the increased discharge that appears right before your menstrual period. The only cause for concern is if the discharge is yellow, greenish, or thick and clotted, or is accompanied by a burning or itching feeling. If this is the case you may have developed an infection. Although it can be treated, a vaginitis infection may return on and off throughout the pregnancy. Fortunately, this cannot affect the baby.

What You Can Do: If your discharge is excessive wear sanitary pads or panty liners. *Never* use tampons during pregnancy, which can introduce germs into your vagina. Do not use a douche either, unless prescribed by your doctor with proper instructions on the way to douche safely during pregnancy. When you're pregnant it's possible to force air into your circulatory system from the pressure of the douche solution. This can cause severe complications or death. Late in pregnancy it's also possible that you could break your bag of waters while douching.

◆ Keep your vaginal area clean and dry. Wear cotton or cotton-lined underwear to allow air to circulate better. Avoid wearing pants that are tight in the crotch.
◆ Avoid using heavily scented bubble baths or deodorant soaps and perfumes around your vaginal area, as they can make the problem worse.

Varicose Veins

When: Mid to late pregnancy.

Why: Another thing no one looks forward to is varicose veins. These swollen veins appear most often in your legs, but often can also show up around your vagina. Most women notice them later in pregnancy as the uterus puts added pressure on veins, allowing blood to pool in the veins as flow is restricted. The problem is aggravated by standing or sitting for long periods of time, when the valves in your veins must work harder to defy gravity and move blood up your legs. The symptoms of these veins can vary greatly. Although some women may know they are there simply by seeing them, other women may have pain, achiness, or a feeling of heaviness. The veins are more common in obese women, but are also inherited in families. If the women in your family have a history of varicose veins you may already have them or you may notice them first appearing in pregnancy. It's best to start prevention measures as soon as possible.

What You Can Do

◆ Avoid long periods of standing and sitting. If you must sit, get up and move around frequently to help stimulate circulation. When it's possible, try to elevate your legs above your hip level while sitting. When you lie down, prop a pillow underneath your legs or sleep on your side.
◆ Exercise regularly.

- ◆ Avoid tight, elastic clothing, particularly stockings and socks with elastic tops.
- ◆ Don't gain excessive weight.
- ◆ Don't strain during bowel movements (which can also cause hemorrhoids).
- ◆ Avoid lifting or carrying heavy objects as much as possible.
- ◆ Try wearing support pantyhose, putting them on early in the day and taking them off before you go to bed.
- ◆ Use a leg cover creme, like Dermablend, to camouflage the veins if you're planning to wear a short outfit.
- ◆ You can ask your practitioner about possible cosmetic surgery after your pregnancy.

Weight Gain

When: Throughout pregnancy, though most women typically gain the most weight during the second trimester, as the baby reaches its peak size.

Why: Gaining weight is an unavoidable and necessary part of pregnancy. It will help if you begin to understand that there are good reasons for it, while keeping in mind that pregnancy should never be an excuse to gorge and eat sweets and fats excessively because you're "eating for two."

Most women put on an average of 25 to 30 pounds during pregnancy, which varies depending on your body type, metabolism, the size of the baby, and your prepregnancy weight. An obese woman may put on only 17 to 20 pounds during pregnancy, while an extremely thin woman may need to gain as much as 35 to 40 pounds. And this weight gain does not always rise steadily. Although some women gain in similar steady increments each month following the first trimester, others vary widely from month to month depending on different factors. For example, most women put on an average of 3 to 4 pounds during the first trimester. However, a woman dealing with heavy bouts of morning sickness may actually lose a pound or two, while a thin, underweight woman may gain 8 pounds because her body needed to catch up to reach a healthy pregnancy weight. In general, petite, small-boned women tend to gain less overall weight than tall, large-boned women.

During the second trimester you should gain approximately 12 to 14 pounds, and be gaining a pound a week in the seventh and eighth months. In the ninth month you may gain nothing at all or even lose a pound or two—a total of roughly 8 to 10 pounds for the last tri-mester. Again, factors may cause your weight to vary—over the holi-days you may eat richer foods than normal or if you get sick you may gain less weight. In general, you should try to keep a moderately steady weight gain, but don't panic if you vary slightly. Most impor-tantly, don't diet during pregnancy. Some studies seem to indicate that the more excess weight the mother puts on during pregnancy, the greater the likelihood is of delivering a larger baby (which can cause a more difficult vaginal delivery). However, this is not conclu-sive, and should not be used as a reason to diet during pregnancy. Your baby cannot thrive on your fat stores, which provide calories but no nutrients. The only time for concern and when you should call your doctor is if you notice a sudden, sharp increase or loss of weight.

If you eat carefully and keep a healthy weight gain during preg-nancy, you'll be less likely to drop your guard postpartum. Dealing with the demands of a newborn, an increased appetite from breast-feeding, and possibly coping with postpartum stress has caused many women to overeat and become overweight only *after* their baby was born.

What You Can Do

- ◆ Eat nutritiously, limiting sweets and fatty foods. Avoid over-eating. (See Chapter 7, "You (and Your Baby) Are What You Eat," for more.)
- ◆ Exercise regularly. Keep an active lifestyle by taking a flight of stairs rather than an elevator, walking to a neighbor's rather than driving, and taking a brisk walk when you feel up to it, rather than saunter-ing. Don't let yourself overheat and stop if you become exhausted. (See Chapter 9 for more about exercising during pregnancy.)

Your Changing Emotions

Pregnancy is a time not only of physical changes, but of emotional changes, too. It's important that you and those around you (especially your mate) acknowledge and understand this. The rapid hormonal changes in your body can account for many of the mood swings you may have during pregnancy, such as a quick temper, or a feeling of extreme joy only an hour after you were crying your heart out over a sad TV show. In some women hormonal changes also increase forget-fulness. Other factors can contribute to the emotional changes that come during pregnancy. You may have anxiety about financial pressures, a strained marriage, or worries about leaving work and having to decide whether or not to stay home with the baby after it's born. If you must return to work shortly after the birth you may feel guilty about putting your baby in someone else's hands. Or maybe you're thinking about all the things you may never get to do now that you're becoming a parent. These are all very legitimate and normal concerns. It helps if you begin planning early in pregnancy for the hurdles that may be ahead so you have less to stress about. (See Chapter 6, "Getting Your House in Order.") Some problems will take more time to sort out than others. But don't spend your pregnancy worrying. Worrying leads to frustration and depression—and that's the last thing you need now. Concentrate on taking good care of yourself during your pregnancy and preparing for the birth. Focus your energies on how you can welcome your new baby with as much love and good care as you can give. In the long run, this is what counts.

Your ever-changing body size can be yet another source of frustration. As you watch your waistline disappear, see stretch marks appear, witness your protruding navel, and watch your breasts and butt grow out to *there*, I think it's safe to say you'll probably feel a bit un-sexy. You may also hate the way you "carry" the baby, looking large and round all over, while your girlfriend who is as far along as you are hardly looks pregnant, carrying her baby small and low. Feelings of clumsiness or awkwardness in the last trimester, when you may waddle like a duck, may make you look as cool and together as the Nutty Professor. Despite all of the outward changes that conspire to get you down, we want to remind you that God don't make ugly. *You are beautiful when you are pregnant*, and the changes in your body represent the miracle it holds inside of it. If the physical changes burden you, consider that the baby is working hard too, trying to grow healthy and strong in what is probably the smallest living space in the world—your womb. Remind yourself that if you eat well and get regular exercise, you'll be back to that Coke-bottle shape in no time. Make sure you get lots of hugs, kisses and whispers of affirmation from your mate. Surround yourself with folks who are as excited as you are about your pregnancy, and together, you can send those ugly blues packing.

CHAPTER 4

Your Habits and Your Lifestyle: Being Careful

In African-American folklore, everything a pregnant woman did, who she talked to, what she looked at, and what she ate while she was pregnant was very carefully guarded, lest she cause some harm to come to her baby. Though we live in a modern world, we have also created modern risks to pregnancy (radiation, chemical substances) to go along with it. Throughout your pregnancy there are going to be many things in the air outside, in your own home, and on your plate, that can harm you and your baby. Most of these can be classified as "teratogens." A teratogen is a substance that can harm the fetus or cause birth defects when a woman is exposed to it during her pregnancy. New research has also found more information about some old risks (such as the effects of alcohol and smoking on pregnancy). Sexually transmitted diseases, more widespread than they were a hundred years ago, are also teratogens and pose a threat to a greater number of women today.

Not all teratogens are proven to cause harm 100 percent of the time, nor do they do the same degree of damage. For example, a woman infected with the disease toxoplasmosis during pregnancy will pass the disease on to her child in 1 out of 3 cases. On the other hand, only 2 to 3 infants out of 1,000 born with group B streptococcal bacteria will develop an infection. However, toxoplasmosis can cause a baby to be born prematurely, or cause fever or jaundice, while a group B strep infection in an infant can cause severe meningitis (a deadly brain infection) or death.

Much of the potential risk depends on what point in the fetus's growth it was exposed to the teratogen. For instance, many medications can do their greatest damage early in the pregnancy, while aspirin can pose a threat mostly in the last trimester. It's also important to consider how much or how large a dose the mother was exposed to, or how frequent the exposure was. Finally, the mother and child's individual sensitivity to certain substances can vary widely—which is a factor that's difficult to assess until the damage has already been done.

The number of harmful agents you can expose yourself to in everyday life may seem overwhelming and impossible to control. So how can you keep track of everything you should or shouldn't use, eat, or expose yourself to during pregnancy? Start by reading the chapter and simply getting yourself acquainted with the information. Most of it involves common sense. The decision of how you want to respond to the information is left to you, but it can empower you to do all you can to increase your odds of having a healthy baby.

Cigarettes, Alcohol, Illicit Drugs, and Medications

"When I was four months pregnant with my second child I was still living in Zimbabwe. I had just begun to read about how to care for yourself during pregnancy, while I was sitting outside smoking a cigarette. Then I came to the part that described how smoking affects the baby, and how the baby is almost coughing and choking inside of you from the nicotine. I took the cigarette out of my mouth, ground it out, and never picked one up again."

SMOKING . . .

increases the risk of sudden infant death syndrome (SIDS), in which apparently healthy infants are found dead in their cribs. Almost a third of infant deaths attributed to smoking during pregnancy (1,900 babies a year) occurred due to SIDS.

Smoking and Pregnancy

Smoking can hurt your baby before, during, and after the birth. When you smoke during pregnancy, carbon monoxide travels to the fetus's blood, lowering the amount of oxygen that gets to both mother and fetus. The nicotine crosses the placenta, causing the fetal blood vessels to constrict. This reduces the amount of oxygen and nutrients that reach the fetus, making it difficult for the baby to grow and thrive. You can compare it to allowing the baby to do its most vital growth in a small, smoke-filled room. In a recent study, researchers compiled data from nearly 100 studies conducted over the last forty years and found that smoking by pregnant women causes the deaths of 5,600 babies and 115,000 miscarriages in the United States each year.

Most of these deaths are the result of complications that arise when the baby is born prematurely or at a low birth weight (smoking by pregnant women is the cause of 53,000 low-birth-weight babies born each year in the United States). Smoking also increases the risk of sudden infant death syndrome (SIDS), in which apparently healthy infants are found dead in their cribs. In fact, almost a third of infant deaths attributed to smoking during pregnancy (1,900 babies a year) died from SIDS (see box on page 428—for more about SIDS). And although in some rare instances a baby may have a healthy delivery and birth weight despite smoking, damage may be done that is either unmeasurable at birth or unapparent until years down the road. Physical and mental capabilities may be impaired, which can result in learning disabilities as the child grows older. If you have any understanding of the hardships children with learning disabilities face getting through school, you'll do everything you can to avoid inflicting this on your baby.

Smoking also increases your risk of complications during pregnancy. Women who smoke are more likely to have vaginal bleeding during pregnancy, suffer miscarriage, risk abnormal placental implantation, premature placental detachment, premature rupture of membranes, preterm delivery, and stillbirth.

So what's the good news? If you stop smoking in the early months of pregnancy, particularly before the fourth month, your odds of having a low-birth-weight baby are almost the same as a nonsmoker, no matter how long you've been smoking before your pregnancy. Take this step now to improve your health and your baby's health—for life.

DRINKING

Each year in the United States 55,000 infants are born with fetal alcohol syndrome (FAS). Babies born with this syndrome have behavioral problems, are shorter, and weigh less than normal babies—and they do not catch up.

Alcohol

Alcohol use during pregnancy is the leading cause of mental retardation and a leading cause of birth defects in the United States. Yet we all probably know someone, or even a couple of people, who had occasional drinks throughout their pregnancies and still gave birth to healthy children. So what is the danger in drinking while you are pregnant, and is there a level that's safe?

When you drink, the alcohol quickly reaches the fetus through the bloodstream. The same level of alcohol that goes through the mother's bloodstream also goes through the fetus's. Yet it takes the baby twice as long as the mother to eliminate alcohol from its system. Each year in the United States 55,000 infants are born with fetal alcohol syndrome (FAS). FAS can be the result of heavy or binge drinking during pregnancy (heavy drinking is considered five or more drinks of alcohol a day). Babies born with this syndrome are shorter and weigh less than normal babies, and do not catch up. Most are mentally retarded and may have multiple behavioral problems, including hyperactivity, nervousness, and a poor attention span. Other symptoms include abnormal features of the face, head, and limbs; central nervous system problems; and heart defects. And although fetal alcohol syndrome is completely preventable, many babies are still diagnosed with it. A recent study found that the percentage of babies born with health problems because their mothers drank alcohol during pregnancy rose sixfold from 1979 to 1993, from 1 per 10,000 births in 1979 to 6.7 per 10,000 in 1993. The study also found that despite a growing awareness that avoiding alcohol prevents FAS, about one-fifth of the pregnant women studied continued to drink even after they learned they were pregnant.

Is there a safe level of alcohol intake? The answer is no. The more a mother drinks during pregnancy, the greater the risk for the baby. Although many researchers believe that the few glasses of wine or the beer you had *before* you knew you were pregnant are not likely to damage the developing embryo, consistent use (and particularly heavy abuse) can be harmful. The truth is that no one knows exactly how much alcohol it takes to harm a fetus. Hereditary, individual, and physical factors may play a role in why each fetus may be affected differently. The best and safest advice is to cut alcohol out of your diet entirely during pregnancy. If you struggle with alcoholism, it is important to discuss this with your doctor or midwife, who can help you identify and hopefully alleviate the underlying causes for the abuse.

Marijuana, Cocaine, and Other Drugs

Besides harming yourself, using illicit drugs during pregnancy can cause mild to severe damage to your developing baby, depending on the drug, the frequency of use, you and your baby's individual sensitivity to the drug, as well as the lifestyle factors that often accompany drug use. Risk is particularly high in the first trimester, when the baby's vital organs and body systems are forming. However, any time you quit using drugs during pregnancy can increase your baby's chances at a better outcome.

Marijuana is one of the most commonly used drugs. Women who are moderate or heavy users during pregnancy (two to five "joints" per week) tend to have preterm deliveries with babies that have low birth weights. Marijuana remains in the body for a long period of time, increasing the risk and length of exposure to the baby. It also contains carbon monoxide, which can limit the amount of oxygen the baby receives.

Cocaine, the second most often used illicit drug, is particularly dangerous during your pregnancy. Cocaine can damage the function of the placenta, shorting the flow of nutrients and oxygen to the baby, and can retard fetal growth. Women who use cocaine during pregnancy have a 25 percent chance of premature labor and are also at risk for miscarriage and stillbirth. Babies who survive can suffer multiple long-term effects. These include chronic diarrhea, irritability, and abnormal brain and breathing patterns. Like many other drugs or toxic substances that may enter your body during pregnancy, there is no specific threshold of cocaine that a fetus can safely tolerate.

Every known illicit drug (including LSD, PCP, heroin, crack, etc.) can cause serious harm to the fetus. Be honest with your doctor or midwife about any drugs you may have taken intentionally or accidentally while you were pregnant so that they will have a full knowledge of your medical history and can begin giving you and your baby the best care possible. If you have an addiction, seek help immediately—give both yourself and your baby a fighting chance.

Over-the-Counter Medications and Prescription Drugs

If you are on a prescription medication, discuss your desire to become pregnant with your practitioner prior to conception and immediately if you become pregnant. Most women are bound to get a mild illness—a cold, a flu—at some point in their pregnancy. However, the typical pain relievers in your medicine cabinet may not be safe to take now that you're pregnant. Since almost everything you inhale or ingest can cross the placenta, a dose that may be safe for an adult can cause havoc in the baby's small and immature system. And some common over-the-counter drugs are simply dangerous to the fetus's development and to your pregnancy.

So how can you know what's safe and what's not? Start here:

◆ Discontinue use of any prescription medications (narcotics, antidepressants, diet pills, tranquilizers, and sedatives) or over-the-counter drugs, even nasal sprays, until you get clearance from your doctor or midwife. This includes topical medicines (for external use only), since the harmful agents in them can enter your circulation when absorbed through the skin.

◆ Keep your doctor or midwife informed about any medications you may have been taking up until you found out you were pregnant. The risk of these harming the baby at this point is very low, but it's important for your caregiver to have as much information as possible.

◆ Read labels. The labels of many common medications you'll find in your medicine cabinet contain warnings for pregnant women. These may change as new products come on the market, or as medicines that were previously thought to be risky are now found to be safe.

◆ Take nothing except natural, noninvasive remedies whenever possible. For example, try easing a cold with a humidifier, lots of rest, and drinking plenty of fluids. Drink some chicken soup, which scientists have found to contain natural ingredients that actually help soothe a cold.

There are certain circumstances that may warrant taking a medication with slight or little risk to the fetus to prevent greater harm if your condition is left untreated. For example, a fever of 102° can cause birth defects if it continues for two or more days. Harm is more likely if the fever is left untreated and is allowed to rise to 104° for a day or more, particularly during the first trimester. In this case, your doctor will OK moderate use of acetaminophen (Tylenol, Datril, and Anacin III) to bring down the fever.

Occasional use of acetaminophen seems to have little effect on the fetus, and it may even be used to treat a severe headache, but only with the approval of your caretaker. Aspirin is not recommended during pregnancy. If you've taken one occasionally in the first two trimesters, damage is not likely. However, it is most risky during the third trimester, when it may cause prolonged pregnancy and labor, and lead to complications during delivery. Aspirin also interferes with the clotting of blood. If it is taken two weeks before delivery it can increase the risk of hemorrhage during delivery and bleeding problems in the baby. Ibuprofin (Advil, Nuprin, and Medipren) are fairly new on the market and not fully tested for long-term effects and widespread use. Their risk seems to also be associated with the last trimester. Again, even if you use Tylenol, never take it without the approval of your doctor or midwife.

Avoid the use of antibiotics during the first trimester, when the risk of harming the developing fetus is greatest. However, particularly after the first three months, if you develop an infection or come down with bronchitis, use of antibiotics prescribed by your doctor is generally considered a safe way to treat your illness.

Accutane

While many sisters love to see their bumps and pimples miraculously clear up as they develop the "glow" of pregnancy, a few women actually find their faces breaking out, especially during the first trimester, when hormones are rapidly fluctuating. It's tempting to use some strong acne treatment to clear it up. However, Accutane, a prescription medication used to treat severe cystic acne, should *never be used* during pregnancy. Accutane has been known to cause serious birth defects when used by pregnant women, including abnormalities of the brain, ears, face, and thymus gland, and possibly mental retardation. However, if you used Accutane before you became pregnant, this should pose no risk to the fetus.

THE GOLDEN RULE

If a substance is generally considered unhealthy for adults to be ingesting or inhaling, it is probably more unhealthy for the unborn baby to ingest or inhale.

A Healthy Lifestyle at Home: Common Household and Yard Hazards

Yes, there is a growing list of things found in the air, home, water, and other common places that can possibly harm your baby. But you don't need to live in a bubble or walk around with a checklist in order to guard against these elements. Most can be remembered with this simple rule: If a substance is generally considered unhealthy for adults to be ingesting or inhaling, it is probably more unhealthy for your unborn baby to ingest or inhale. If you don't take precautions to avoid or minimize your exposure to these things already, now is a good time to become aware of them for your own long-term health as well as your baby's.

Lead in Paint and Water

Lead found in crumbling paint, soil, and water not only can reduce the IQ of children who ingest it, but can affect pregnant women and their fetuses as well. Heavy exposure to lead can put you at increased risk for pregnancy-induced hypertension and even miscarriage. In the baby it can cause a wide range of behavioral and neurological problems, and varying degrees of birth defects.

◆ Lead is commonly found in tap water, particularly in old homes whose deteriorating pipes may be made of lead. If you suspect this, call your local Environmental Protection Agency (EPA) for information on where the water can be tested. In the meantime, and if you are unable to have your pipes changed, run the cold water for 5 minutes when the tap hasn't been used for 6 hours or more. This will flush out the water that has stood in the pipes and absorbed greater amounts of lead. Also, never use hot tap water for cooking or drinking. Hot water leaches off greater amounts of lead than cold water.

◆ If you live in an old house, particularly those built before 1955, and are having layers of paint removed, stay away while the work is being done. If you notice areas in your house where the paint is deteriorating or flaking off, have it removed and painted over. If you suspect that the flaking paint may be old, have it tested or removed by a professional.

◆ Lead can also be leached and ingested into your body from earthenware, pottery, or china. Food and drink, particularly those that are hot or acidic, can react with the surface of the plates or containers, drawing out lead that old ceramics contained to make them more durable. Federal standards were not set on lead levels in dishes until 1971. Avoid using old, imported, or home-crafted dishware; save it for display.

◆ If you live directly next to a major highway, lead from car emissions may be found in your soil. If you're fortunate enough to have a yard, and spend a lot of time gardening or playing there with your other children, consider having a soil sample tested. Your local EPA can advise you as to how this can be done.

Household Chemicals and Toxic Substances

Household Cleaning Products Inhaling chemical fumes isn't good for you or your growing baby, whose developing systems may be more sensitive and easily affected by them. Although no studies have shown a direct correlation between light, ordinary use of household cleaning products and fetal abnormality, no studies have proven their use completely safe. Use your nose as a guide, and take these precautionary measures:

◆ Read labels carefully, and quit using cleaning agents with warning labels about inhalation or skin contact. Also avoid products with a strong odor, and if you must use them, use only in well-ventilated areas. Avoid using aerosol sprays altogether if possible. You can usually find pump-spray alternatives for aerosol products. Have your husband or a friend or family member do the big jobs that require use of very toxic products such as oven or tile cleaning. Stay out of the area while it's being done.

◆ Use rubber gloves when using chemical cleaners. Toxic chemicals can be absorbed through the skin, and you will also protect your hands from the harsh products.

Paint, Furniture Finishes, and Paint and Finish Removers Although you may be eager to refinish the baby furniture your sister gave you or paint the walls in the nursery lime green, you should know that paint or varnish removers typically contain very toxic and strong-smelling chemicals, as do many paints and furniture finishes. Although you can sometimes find milder product alternatives (such as using latex-based rather than oil-based paint), it may be best to put off the work until after you give birth, or, better yet, let someone else do it.

Pesticides and Chemical Weed Killers

Avoid using chemical insecticides, pesticides, and weed killers while you are pregnant, and stay away from areas where they are being used as much as possible. Try using natural or nontoxic alternatives to get rid of pests. And consider paying some neighborhood kids to pull up your weeds by hand. If a neighbor is spraying their yard, stay away from the area for a day or two if possible, and tightly shut all windows and doors in your house or apartment. If you must have your house fumigated for a pest such as fleas or termites, make sure that all cabinets and drawers are firmly shut and that all the food in them is tightly sealed. After you return and the chemicals have settled, wash countertops thoroughly.

Lyme Disease

Lyme disease is carried by infected ticks, particularly deer ticks, who pass the bacteria on to humans when they bite. Symptoms of the disease include a reddish, bull's eye–like rash around the bite site, fatigue, and flu-like symptoms such as fever and achiness. In pregnant women the disease may be passed on to the fetus. Although it's not proven yet, researchers suspect that Lyme disease may be a cause of birth defects or miscarriage.

Now before you say you don't have any ticks in your neck of the woods, know that ticks have been found not only in fields and wooded rural areas, but in lawns and gardens too. The best way to avoid getting the disease is to wear long-sleeved shirts, pants, and socks that cover your ankles when in woodsy or grassy areas, and wear a mild or natural insect repellent effective for Lyme ticks on your clothing, but not on your skin. When you come back indoors, examine yourself for ticks and take a shower. If the ticks are removed soon after they attach to your skin, you greatly reduce your chances of getting infected. If you suspect you've been infected, call your doctor or midwife immediately, and he or she can begin prescribing an antibiotic treatment that may prevent severe illness and possibly passing the disease on to your baby.

Unless you are allergic, other minor outdoor annoyances such as poison ivy, insect bites, or bee stings should pose no problem to your pregnancy.

Chemicals, Food Additives, and Bacteria in Food

While you are pregnant, keep remembering that you are nourishing both yourself and your baby. Not only is it important for you to eat nutritiously (see Chapter 7, "You (And Your Baby) Are What You Eat"), but also for you to pay closer-than-usual attention to the kinds of foods you eat and what ingredients they contain. Food that's full of artificial ingredients and preservatives is a bad idea even when you are not pregnant. Here are some tips that are helpful for a healthy diet during pregnancy and beyond:

◆ Know what you're eating: Read food labels carefully as you shop and pay particular attention to expiration dates.

◆ Wash fruits and vegetables well before eating or cooking them (except fruits such as bananas or oranges, which are peeled). This removes residue from pesticides and other chemical sprays.

◆ Use common sense and avoid dairy products or meats that may have spoiled or stayed out too long.

◆ Food contains the most nutrition and least amounts of fat, excess sugar, additives, and salt when eaten closest to its natural state. Try to buy most of your food in the first, last, and back aisles of the grocery store, where the fresh produce, meat, and dairy products are displayed. Avoid canned, boxed, processed, and ready-to-eat frozen foods whenever possible. (For more specific information on this topic, turn to Chapter 7, "You (and Your Baby) Are What You Eat").

Caffeine

While an occasional Coke or cup of coffee during the day is not likely to harm the fetus, there are other reasons to cut back on or eliminate caffeine from your diet during pregnancy. Caffeine is a stimulant and crosses the placenta, which means it enters the baby's blood. When it's absorbed by your body it increases urination, which draws needed fluids out of your body more quickly (during pregnancy, you should be trying to *increase* your fluid intake). Recent studies have found that caffeine depletes calcium in your body. Also, beverages that use caffeine (colas, coffee, tea) often include food additives, artificial ingredients, and excess sugars, which aren't recommended during pregnancy.

Kitty Litter and Toxoplasmosis

Toxoplasmosis is a sickness caused by a parasite that lives in some mammals, such as cats, one of our favorite house pets. Fortunately, it is rarely found in domestic cats who have not had to hunt and kill for their food. It is possible though, for people to become infected by eating raw or undercooked meat, or drinking unpasteurized milk, and by coming in contact with cat feces. Toxoplasmosis causes only a mild sickness in adults, and many people who get it may have no symptoms at all. It's estimated that about half the people in the United States have already been infected. If you've lived with cats for a while it's likely you've already been infected and are immune to the disease. However, if you are *first* infected when you are pregnant, there can be risk to the fetus, particularly if the infection occurred in the first trimester. The disease is not always transmitted to the fetus—generally in only about one-third of all cases. If the fetus does become infected, the disease can cause the baby to be born prematurely or to be born too small, or can cause fever, jaundice, and other long-term problems.

If you have not been tested for toxoplasmosis before conception or in early pregnancy you can take the following precautions:

- ◆ Avoid eating raw or undercooked meat, and unpasteurized milk.
- ◆ If you have a cat, it's best to have someone else change the litter box while you're pregnant. If you must do it yourself, wear gloves and wash your hands thoroughly when you finish. Change the litter box daily, because the feces are generally not infectious for the first 24 hours. If you garden in the soil, make sure you wear gloves because cats often bury their feces. If you grow and eat any of your own fruits or vegetables, make sure you wash and rinse them thoroughly before eating them.
- ◆ Avoid holding your cat's body close to your face or having it sleep in or on your sheets or pillowcases.

Baths, Hot Tubs, and Saunas

Years ago, doctors believed that dirty bathwater could enter the vagina during or immediately after pregnancy and cause an infection.

But it is now generally understood that water will not enter the vagina unless it is forced, such as with a douche. Throughout your pregnancy, bathing can be a great way to relax and can also be used during labor as a way to relax during contractions. Water birth is an alternative for some couples and their doctors or midwives, although its safety depends on the methods used and the skill and knowledge of the delivery attendants. Unless you plan to have your baby delivered by a professional experienced in water birth (see Chapter 5, "Delivering Your Baby: You *Do* Have a Choice"), using a bath up until your water has broken is probably the best course to follow.

The most common concern about baths while you are pregnant is the temperature of the water. You may have enjoyed a steamy, hot bath before you got pregnant, but you should know that raising your body temperature to 102°F (38.9°C) or higher during pregnancy and keeping it there for several minutes can harm the developing baby, particularly during the first trimester. Doctors recommend that your bathwater be no hotter than 100°F. Generally, you can judge this by keeping your bathwater lukewarm rather than hot, or by testing it with a toe or wrist. If your skin feels an initial stinging sensation, or if it takes a submerged foot or hand a little while to "get used to" the temperature, it's probably too hot.

Hot tubs and saunas, which are typically made to be enjoyed for longer periods of time, should also be avoided during pregnancy. Dangling your feet or legs in a hot tub shouldn't pose a problem and will still let you enjoy the fun if you are out relaxing with friends.

Hygiene, Tampons, and Douching

Good hygiene is always an important part of a healthy lifestyle. When you are pregnant you have even more reason to take good care of yourself. For example, you should always make sure you wash your hands before eating and after using the bathroom. This is especially true for those who work in public areas such as day-care centers or schools, where viruses are quickly passed. The common cold is typically passed from casual contact. Since pregnancy limits the amount of medication you can use, taking preventative measures can save you days of suffering through the full effects of clogged sinuses and a runny nose.

Never use tampons or douches while you are pregnant. Douching may occasionally be prescribed by your doctor, but only as treatment for a specific problem, accompanied with clear instructions on how to douche safely while pregnant. During pregnancy, unlike any other time, it's possible to introduce air into your circulatory system under pressure from the douche solution, which could endanger your life. Tampons should also not be used because they can introduce foreign bacteria in your vagina and risk infection.

Electric Blankets and Heating Pads

Although research is not definitive, use of electric blankets and heating pads during pregnancy may raise your body temperature and harm the fetus in the same way that overly hot baths, hot tubs, and strenuous exercise can. If you find your sheets icy cold at night, use the electric blanket or heating pad to warm up the bed, and then turn it off when you climb in. If treatment with a heating pad has been recommended by your doctor or midwife, wrap it in a towel and limit its use to 15 minutes at a time.

There is also some research that suggests that there may be risk of fetal damage or miscarriage from the electromagnetic field created by electrically heated water beds. If you sleep on this kind of water bed, investigate replacing your heater with a shielded heater, which has the electromagnetic field built into it, minimizing the danger. If this is too expensive an option, it may be wise to switch beds until the pregnancy is over.

Radiation and X Rays

There are some kinds of radiation that can be hazardous during pregnancy and others that pose minimal risk. Radiation from television sets, video display terminals (VDTs—see "Occupational Hazards", this chapter), and microwave ovens is a very low level radiation, and is not considered harmful. At most, avoid standing or sitting closer than an arm's length away from the screen or oven.

X rays involve ionizing radiation, a strong form of radiation that can damage the fetus and its central nervous system in early pregnancy, particularly in the third and fourth weeks. For this reason, it's generally wise to avoid having X rays taken during pregnancy. However, there are many factors that can determine if X-ray radiation poses a risk to the baby, and in many cases, the risk can be minimal. Severe damage to the baby typically occurs at high doses that measure from 50 to 250 rads, but no risk appears evident at doses lower than 10 rads. Most X rays performed today are very site specific, and only expose the area that needs to be viewed. Also, a typical diagnostic X ray measures only 5 rads, eliminating most risk.

Again, despite the low risk, it's best to avoid taking chances. If you absolutely need to have an X ray (such as a dental X ray) taken while you're pregnant, always be sure to tell the doctor and the technician about your pregnancy. They will cover your abdomen and pelvis with a lead apron (some use two) that can protect the fetus from any exposure.

Occupational Hazards

Nowadays there are more women in the workforce. Recent studies have shown that in the United States, the current earning power of black women is more than that of black men. Computers, faxes, and telephones allow many women to have greater flexibility to choose where they want to work. And a rising number of sisters are choosing to run small businesses out of their homes or remain part of a larger business or company from a home office. Whether you are employed at home or outside of it during pregnancy, there are certain precautions you can take while on the job:

◆ Try not to stand for long periods of time, which can increase fatigue and aggravate varicose veins or swelling.

◆ Physically strenuous work, heavy lifting, and extensive standing can cause strain to your body and may put you at risk for early and late miscarriage. This can be a problem particularly in mid to late pregnancy. Many doctors recommend that you leave your duties at 20 weeks if you continually lift weights of 50 pounds or more, and at 34 weeks if you lift 25 pounds or more. If your work is physically demanding consider taking a disability leave or temporarily switching your duties.

◆ Avoid sitting for extended periods of time (an hour and a half or more). While a desk job is the least taxing on your body and can probably be continued up until you're ready to deliver, sitting in one place can cause or worsen hemorrhoids, varicose veins, and swelling in your feet and legs. Make sure to get up and walk around periodically. Although it may not be possible to elevate your legs above hip level while at your desk, try using a footstool or prop your feet upon a stack of telephone books to keep yourself more comfortable.

◆ In the 1980s, reports about miscarriage from video display terminal (VDTs) radiation stirred up controversy. However, a recent 6-year study from the National Institute for Occupational Safety and Health (NIOSH) found no evidence to support this. The radiation emitted from VDTs, color television sets, and microwave ovens is a low-level radiation called non-ionizing radiation, and is not considered dangerous. In addition, more radiation is emitted from the back of a computer terminal—rather than the front—and there has never been a risk associated with exposure to VDT radiation for 20 hours a week or less. More studies are currently being conducted, which researchers hope will settle the matter. In the meantime, if you want to be careful, sit 3 feet away from the back and sides of your co-workers' terminals and an arm's length away from your own. If you want to eliminate any suspected risk, consider spending 20 hours or less a week in front of your terminal.

◆ One recent study has found that pregnant women working on the night shift are $2\frac{1}{2}$ times more likely to suffer miscarriage than women working in the day. Scientists attribute this to possible interference with our bodies' natural rhythms, although the study did not examine the kind of work night-shift workers did compared to their daytime counterparts. Discuss this with your caretaker.

◆ There are many fields that are associated with exposure to certain teratogens that can be hazardous to your pregnancy. For example, two chemicals involved in the production of silicon microchips have been associated with miscarriage in pregnant women. Health-care workers face a risk of exposing themselves to viruses, bacteria, infections, and certain chemicals. Tollbooth attendants may be exposed to high levels of lead and air pollution emitted from exhaust pipes.

If you are concerned about any possible hazards in your workplace, contact the National Institute for Occupational Safety and Health (NIOSH), Clearing House for Occupational Safety and Health Information, 4676 Columbia Parkway, Cincinnati, OH 45226, telephone 1(800)356-4674 or the Occupational Safety and Health Administration (OSHA), 200 Constitution Avenue NW, Washington, D.C., 20210, telephone (202) 219-8148. Whether you are pregnant or not, it is your right to know what chemicals or hazards your job exposes you to.

Travel

Despite what our mothers might have been told when they were pregnant, travel is fine at most times during your pregnancy—you don't want to turn down the chance at a romantic, prebaby getway with your husband or going off to visit all the people who "want to see you while you're pregnant." Always let your doctors or midwife know in advance, and make sure they give their OK—if you have high blood pressure, diabetes, or other medical problems you may be told to skip the trip. Also, some doctors may advise not traveling during the first trimester because of the possibility of miscarriage (particularly if the trip involves stress, excessive physical activity, or a hectic pace). During the last trimester long-distance travel may put you out of reach of their care in the event of an early labor. Since both babies and travel are never completely predictable, use these traveling tips to prepare for unexpected circumstances:

◆ Jot down your blood type, allergies, medications you're currently taking, and any other vital information about yourself on a card and carry it in your wallet. If you're currently on a prescription medication, carry it on you during travel, rather than in your luggage.

◆ Have the name of a local obstetrician handy. Usually your doctor or midwife can give you a recommendation for one in the area, if it's in the United States. Some insurance companies can provide a list of physicians who are in their plan in any state or county you may travel to. If you are traveling internationally, the International Association for Medical Assistance to Travelers, Suite 5620, Empire State Building, 350 Fifth Avenue, New York, NY 10001, can provide you with a directory of English-speaking physicians throughout the world for a small donation.

◆ Avoid traveling to areas of high altitude during pregnancy because adjusting to the decrease in oxygen may be a strain for both you and your baby. If your doctor or midwife does allow you to go, take it easy the first few days and avoid heavy exercise or activity.

◆ Keep a bottle of water handy, particularly in hot weather, to keep yourself hydrated. Take along a few snacks as well, in case the food you like isn't available or you get sudden pangs of hunger.

◆ Go to the bathroom frequently, or as often as you feel the need. Holding it in will only make you feel uncomfortable and risk getting a urinary tract infection.
◆ However you travel, make sure that en route you get plenty of opportunity to stretch your legs and avoid sitting for long periods of time, which can increase swelling, varicose veins, backache, and constipation.

Travel by Cars, Buses, and Trains: Always make sure to wear your seat belt with the lower strap across you below your belly and the upper strap between your breasts. The fetus is well cushioned in its amniotic sac and should come out of most car accidents unharmed if you are belted in. Keep your car seat pushed back as far as possible to give your legs room to stretch. If you have airbags in your car, this is even more reason to keep your seat belt on and your seat pushed back. Without the restraint of a seat belt, airbags inflating with excessive force can harm your body. For long-distance drives try to take a rest stop every hour and a half to stretch, walk around, and use the bathroom if you need to. Traveling by bus may be cramped and rest stops may be less frequent, so a train may be a better option.

Travel by Airplane: Flying is considered to be a safe option during pregnancy. However, most airlines in the United States allow pregnant women to fly only until 36 weeks of pregnancy (yes, they *will* ask you questions at the check-in gate if they think you look late-term); call your carrier for specifics when booking the tickets. Never fly in an unpressurized cabin. Commercial airplanes are pressurized, but many small, private planes are not. Pressure changes at high altitudes, particularly above 7,000 to 9,000 feet, can quickly reduce the available oxygen. Otherwise, try to sit in an aisle seat to allow you room to stretch your legs as well as to give you the freedom to get up and use the bathroom or walk up and down the aisle. You may be able to reserve the seat right behind the plane's emergency door, which offers the most leg room, if you tell the reservation agent that you're pregnant. Other things to remember: Special meals are available on planes if you order in advance, and the metal detectors used for airport security checks are not harmful to your baby.

Travel by Boat: Cruises are usually a slow and easy way to travel. However, whether you're on a large ship or small boat, you may be prone to motion sickness. Use either Sea-Bands or motion sickness medicine that's cleared by your doctor or midwife. Also, for trips longer than a day or so, make sure you have access to a physician.

Foreign Travel: Beware of the drinking water when you travel to a foreign country, unless you're sure it is safe. Otherwise, drink bottled water or juices. In some countries the bacteria on raw or unpeeled vegetables or in the milk may cause you intestinal upset. For country-specific information of such hazards and on immunizations for travel, you can contact the American College of Obstetricians and Gynecologists, One East Wacker Drive, Chicago, IL 60601, telephone (312) 263-7150.

Lovemaking

The good news: For most couples, making love can still be a safe and satisfying part of life during pregnancy, even in the last trimester. The not-so-great news: As you may have found out already, even in the first trimester, your physical and emotional changes, combined with both you and your partner's attitudes and fears about the future with baby, can make lovemaking a major deal. Most couples can continue making love up until their date of delivery, but whether you'll *want* to is another story. It's hard to feel sexy when you're fighting back the nausea of morning sickness and even tongue-kissing may make you want to gag! And worries about feeling fat or unattractive during pregnancy can also inhibit your pleasure. Fatigue may leave you groggy or exhausted in the early morning and evening hours, when you and your partner normally made love. Your breasts may be tender in the early months, and later in pregnancy, and although you both may enjoy their larger size and firmness, you may find them leaking colostrum (early breast milk) when they become stimulated. An increase in vaginal secretions may make your sex life a slightly messier affair than it was before, and the change in its odor may be unattractive to either or both of you. And omnipresent throughout the second and third trimester is your ever-growing abdomen, which will constantly get in the way. Experiment with sexual positions that may feel more comfortable than the traditional, man-on-top position: Lying on your sides fitted in a spoon shape is one option.

Emotional changes that may interfere with lovemaking are also plentiful. With hormones changing, you may find your moods swinging. Worries about work, finances, giving birth, and the changing relationship and responsibilities you and your partner are about to acquire may put a damper on your sex life. Although fears of hurting the baby during sex are common, this is a needless worry. The baby is cushioned and protected in the bag of waters, and most likely is lulled to sleep by the rhythmic motion.

◇ ◇ ◇ ◇ ◇ ◇ ◇ ◇ ◇ ◇ ◇ ◇ ◇ ◇ ◇ ◇ ◇ ◇

"I was in my ninth month with our second child and my husband and I were just a goin' and a goin' at it on the couch when suddenly, there was all this water. He said, 'Baby, did you pee on me?' We discovered my water had broken. It was time for labor!"

◇ ◇ ◇ ◇ ◇ ◇ ◇ ◇ ◇ ◇ ◇ ◇ ◇ ◇ ◇ ◇ ◇ ◇

Despite all of these normal bodily changes and very natural reasons for worry, not every couple will be affected by all of these physical changes nor will everyone have the same degree of emotional worries. Much of your love life has to do with you and your partner's attitudes about these changes. Keeping a sense of humor is always a benefit, as is allowing yourself time to relax and be romantic. Use this time to explore the pleasures of touch and caressing one another, as well as experimenting with different positions. If you have worries or conflicts over upcoming responsibilities, try to keep them out of the bed. Laugh about something together to get those home fires burning.

If you are "overdue," your doctor or midwife may actually prescribe sex as a way to help bring on labor (which worked just fine for the sister quoted above). Uterine contractions triggered by orgasm can become stronger in the last six months of pregnancy, but they don't usually bring on real labor unless your cervix is ready to begin dilating as well. If you have a tendency toward preterm delivery though, having sex is usually not recommended in the last six weeks.

In certain circumstances, your doctor or midwife may advise you to stop making love during pregnancy. These can include the following :

◆ If you have a history of miscarriage or show signs of potentially miscarrying, you may be advised not to have sex in the first trimester.

◆ If you show signs of unexplained bleeding in the last few weeks before you are ready to deliver. Slight spotting may be caused by intercourse or an internal exam you had at your doctor's or midwife's. While you should notify them immediately if the blood is red, if it is brownish red it is generally not a cause for concern.

◆ If you have a history of premature labor or show signs that threaten a premature labor in the last eight to twelve weeks.

◆ If your bag of waters has ruptured.

◆ If you are known to have placenta previa (a low-lying placenta, usually near or over the cervix, where it could be dislodged by deep penetration).

◆ If you are carrying multiple fetuses.

◆ If you have been confined to strict bed rest for a medical condition.

If none of the above apply to you, and you *both* enjoy some form of lovemaking during pregnancy—indulge! Research done on the state of marriages during and after pregnancy suggests that couples who have satisfying love lives during pregnancy and baby's first year are more likely to stay together.

CHAPTER 5

Delivering Your Baby: You *Do* Have Choices

When asked about her latest birth experience, one sister who just had her fourth baby told us, "I knew what I needed to do and when I needed to do it—and I did just that!" The timidity and fear that she had during her first two pregnancies was replaced by empowerment and confidence. By the fourth time, this sister ran the show. Birthing became something *she* did, not something others did *to* her. In this chapter, we hope to help you develop that kind of confidence the *first* time, by informing you about your birthing options.

As you read books, magazine articles, pamphlets, and brochures about pregnancy and birth, you have probably learned that there are several places where you can give birth and several positions in which you can do so. Birth-place choices include: hospital delivery rooms, special birthing rooms within hospitals, freestanding birthing centers, birthing pools, and home. Birthing positions include: sitting, squatting, kneeling, standing, and even floating. Read about the advantages and disadvantages of each place and position. Visit those that seem interesting to you, even though they may not be traditional settings, and then make an informed choice that's best for you and your baby.

Hospital Births

History: Until the late 1800s, giving birth in a maternity ward meant literally taking your life into your own hands. Infection and infant death were rampant and your chances of coming out of the hospital alive and with a healthy baby were much lower than they are today. Poor hygiene, crude instruments, and lack of knowledge and skill on the part of male doctors who were new to the whole idea of childbirth were also major contributors to the negative publicity that surrounded hospital births. It was so bad, in fact, that some say churches advised pregnant women to repent and get right with God before they left for the hospital—or else!

By the 1940s, though, hospital birth became all the rage when middle- and upper-class whites decided that birth at home with a midwife was "gauche," something reserved only for the poor of pocket (that would be us). But as most trends eventually trickle down to the masses, this one did too. Before long, low-income whites and the few black families who could scrape up enough to afford a trip to the hospital followed suit. After a while, it became a status symbol for us to go to the hospital, even though we were treated poorly—if at all—when we got there.

At the same time, new license requirements threatened to force the granny midwives who served most of our women out of business in many states, though they continued to attend women in home births in much of the rural South. Hospitals were now required to provide better care for women because folks expected to get more for their money. (Granny midwives, on the other hand, often received chickens, eggs, and IOU slips for their "labors.") Conditions at hospitals continued to improve and doctors began to dominate the childbirthing process. The woman, unfortunately, became a passive, strapped-down patient who was treated as if she had a terrible illness that she had no idea how to help cure.

Birth also became more "medicalized." Most women perceived this as a good thing, particularly because of the availability of the much-desired pain medications that could now make childbirth "painless." Chloroform and ether, which were poured on a handkerchief and given to women in labor to inhale with each contraction, were succeeded by "twilight sleep," a combination of hallucinogens and morphine injected every hour. Women were so excited about the prospect of no pain that they traveled far and wide to go to hospitals that offered the drugs. It was later discovered that fetal brain damage and death were too often the result of these "miracle medicines."

It was not until the speak-out sixties that some women began vocalizing their dissatisfaction with the minor-league role they were allowed to play in the birth of their own babies. Women wanted control of their birth experience back somehow, but alternatives to hospital birth were slim to none. In one mother's letter to the *Ladies' Home Journal* decades ago, she shared her own experience with hospital birth: "Hospitals seem to assume that just because a woman is about to give birth she becomes a nitwit, an incompetent, reduced to the status of a cow (and not too valuable a cow, at that). . . ."

Until about twenty years ago, a woman who showed up at a hospital to give birth would be moved to three different rooms before it was all over: a labor room to labor in, a delivery room to deliver in, and a recovery room to recover in. The baby, meanwhile, was far away in the hospital nursery being "properly handled" by the neonatal nursing staff. Holding your baby immediately after birth was unheard of.

Today, the number of rooms has been cut down to two: one for you to labor and give birth in and one for your immediate recovery and hospital stay. Often, a woman may be jammed into one ward with two or three other laboring women, separated only by a thin curtain. Though you may think that a large hospital will provide you the best care, that isn't always the case. Smaller, community hospitals that are well run can sometimes offer a more intimate birthing experience and personal care. Your best option in a hospital is to choose one that has a birthing room.

"When I heard that my friend gave birth with two women screaming their heads off on either side of her in a hospital ward, I said no way am I going through that."

Birthing Rooms in Hospitals

History: As women became more vocal in the late sixties and early seventies, a growing opinion began to form that natural birth was better than a scientifically managed birth experienced in most hospitals. Finally, fearful that women might decide to return to home

A HISTORY OF BIRTH
1500 B.C.–1840

In *The American Way of Birth*, Jessica Mitford chronicles the cyclical journey birth has taken from the most natural, unhurried process a woman can experience to one dominated by physicians, drugs, and high-tech equipment. A brief look at the history of birth suggests that the pendulum is swinging back to birth becoming a more personal, woman-led experience.

■ **1500** B.C.—Shiprah and Puah, midwives in Egypt, are ordered by Pharaoh to kill all Hebrew baby boys. The courageous women refused the king's orders because they feared God and saved many lives at the risk of their own.

■ **A.D. 1400**—European midwives, who were often poor, illiterate peasant women, are accused of witchcraft by church leaders; thousands are burned at the stake. Called the "women's holocaust" by some.

■ **1500**—University-trained physicians begin to attend women in childbirth for the first time. Farmer Jacob Nufer of Switzerland saves his wife's and baby's lives by performing the first known cesarean section with the tools used to castrate or neuter the animals he tended. Interestingly, his wife went on to bear four more children vaginally, disproving the rule that once a woman has a cesarean there is little chance that she can deliver vaginally the next time.

■ **1588**—Peter Chamberlain introduced forceps, the first piece of technology used in childbirth; Chamberlain was a barber-surgeon, one of many untrained, unlicensed men who cut hair *and* practiced as doctors on the side!

■ **1839**—Lady Flora Hastings of England dies of what may have been the first fibroid tumor. Although she was an unmarried virgin, she was thought to be pregnant due to the swelling of her abdomen.

■ **1840s**—Many mothers die after hospital birth of a mysterious disease known as "childbed fever." Dr. Ignaz Semmelweis of Vienna discovers the cause: Doctors were not washing their hands between handling the dead women's bodies and delivering the new mothers' babies. Despite opposition from the medical community, Dr. Oliver Wendell Holmes of Boston proves that this was indeed the cause of the deadly purpural fever. Due to fear and poor conditions, most babies are still birthed at home.

birthing, hospitals began to listen to customer complaints and some began to provide special rooms for women in labor that simulated home settings.

Today, women who are seeking a more relaxed yet medically staffed environment in which to give birth are choosing to deliver their babies in birthing rooms, now available in most city hospitals in the United States. Instead of the antiseptic, crowded hospital room you'll now find a decorated, bedroomlike setting, sometimes called the LDR (for labor, delivery, recovery) room, designed to give you a homey feeling, with the availability of high-tech equipment, nurses, and doctors right on the premises if you need them.

Advantages

◆ Best environment for women who have had pregnancy complications during this or previous pregnancies and who are considered "high risk"
◆ Less antiseptic setting than a regular hospital room
◆ You will stay in that room for the labor and recovery, until you check out of the hospital
◆ One mother per room
◆ Your mate and family members can stay in the room with you, possibly even overnight. Note: Birth coaches and other attendees are often required by the hospital to complete a childbirth class in order to be allowed at the birth. Plan early so you aren't disappointed.
◆ Doctors, nurses, anestheticians, equipment, and an operating room are readily available should you need more involved medical assistance during childbirth.

Disadvantages

◆ Birthing rooms are often given out on a first come, first served basis as there are many fewer birthing rooms in a hospital than there are wards.
◆ If you have a nurse-midwife attending you, she may be required to adhere to the hospital's rules, even though they may conflict with her—and your—wishes.

■ **1845–1849**—Dr. James Sims of Alabama experiments on enslaved black women who suffered with torn perineums (the area between the vagina and the rectum) after childbirth, often operating on them more than thirty times without anesthesia. He continued this horrifying experimentation in New York on destitute Irish immigrants.

■ **1847**—Dr. James Young Simpson of Scotland discovers that chloroform can be given to mothers during childbirth (still done at home) as an anesthesia. The first user was so pleased she named her daughter Anaesthesia. The idea takes a while to catch on in America.

■ **1863**—A committee is formed to study the psychological effects associated with the use of chloroform.

■ **1882**—First modern cesarean performed in Germany by Dr. Max Sanger using silk threads to suture the uterine and abdominal walls. A 12-inch cut was made and the baby was removed feet first. Today, the cut is made just wide enough to deliver the baby's head (about five inches).

■ **1904**—Mary McLeod Bethune opens her own school—the Daytona Industrial Institute for the Training of Negro Girls—in Florida, with $1.50 and five students. It later became an important community resource and evolved into Bethune-Cookman College.

■ **1900–1930**—The Age of Technology. Birth leaves the home, and hospitals become much more accepted by the upper class as places to deliver babies, mostly due to the prospect of receiving anesthesia. Dr. William A. Hinton develops the test for the detection of syphilis and, in 1950, becomes the first professor at Harvard Medical School.

■ **1913–1940**—Dr. Joseph deLee promotes the idea that women in labor should *always* (a) lie flat on their backs with their legs open and strapped into stirrups; (b) be sedated from the first stage of labor; (c) have an episiotomy; (d) have forceps used.

The pleasant, unsterile atmosphere of a birthing center labor and birth room is becoming an appealing choice for more pregnant women. This is one of the rooms at the Childbearing Center in New York. Photo courtesy of Maternity Center Association, N.Y.; by Vanessa Saullo.

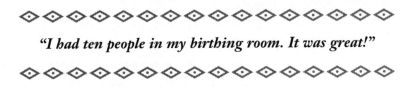

"I had ten people in my birthing room. It was great!"

Freestanding Birthing Centers/Maternity Centers

History: Many women became dissatisfied with hospital birth and the slow pace at which the medical establishment was responding to women's desire to have involved, "active" labors. Certified nurse-midwives and obstetricians stepped in to fill this need by establishing birthing and maternity centers that cater to the woman seeking personal care, a natural birth, and a noninterventionist (the avoidance of drugs, monitors, or surgery unless absolutely necessary) philosophy. Birthing and maternity centers differ from birthing rooms in hospitals because they are separate buildings "free" from the constraints of hospital policies and the often sterile hospital setting. In fact, you do not have to drive up to a medical building at all,

A HISTORY OF BIRTH
1918–1960s

■ **1918**—The Maternity Center Association is established in New York to promote the health of mothers and infants via neighborhood clinics staffed by public-health nurses and physicians. Poor and middle-class black women learned prenatal care and nutrition and infant care at the center.

■ **1930s**—About 50 percent of all "city" women in the United States choose to have their babies in hospitals. Twilight sleep, a combination of hallucinogens and morphine, becomes the popular anesthetic for childbirth despite its effects, which included wild tossing and turning, screaming, and an amnesia-like stupor afterward. After it was rejected by the elite, it was used in rural areas on low-income clinic patients, who were likely to include black women.

Mary McLeod Bethune founds the National Council for Negro Women and later becomes an adviser to President Franklin D. Roosevelt and Eleanor Roosevelt.

■ **1933–1950**—Dr. Grantly Dick-Read of England and, later, Dr. Ferdinand Lamaze popularize the ideas of childbirth without fear and labor without pain, respectively. The view was that pains in childbirth were caused largely by fear and tension and advocated physical and mental relaxation exercises and prenatal education.

■ **1941**—Historically black college, Tuskeegee University, is one of the first institutions to offer a certificate program in midwifery.

■ **1951**—The American College of Obstetricians and Gynecologists is formed to unite practitioners to advocate for quality

health care for women, maintain high clinical standards, promote patient education, and monitor the changing issues facing women's health care. Ninety percent of American OB/GYNs are affiliated with ACOG.

■ **1955**—The American College of Nurse Midwives (ACNM) is founded to develop and support the profession in order to promote the health and well-being of women and infants. Approximately 5,500 CNMs are currently affiliated with the organization.

■ **1960s**—Mothers struggle to reclaim birth as a natural process. Women want to be awake during labor, yet modern obstetrics practices continue to flourish.

Certified Nurse-Midwife Armentia Tripp Jarrett innovates the Madera Project in Madera County, California. It was the first to demonstrate a significant reduction in maternal-child morbidity and mortality by the use of a nonphysician. Its success paved the way for the passage of a California Assembly bill that allowed for more of such projects to be done using CNMs.

as often regular homes or apartments have been converted into birthing suites.

Today, there are hundreds of birthing centers across the country bringing thousands of healthy babies safely into the world. According to the *New England Journal of Medicine*, freestanding birthing centers offer a safe and acceptable alternative to hospital confinement for selected (low-risk) pregnant women. Women, once they visit the centers, talk to others who have given birth there, and are personally educated about the benefits, often find birthing centers a great alternative, though there is still some skepticism. It is still ingrained in many of us that "hospital" and "high-tech" equal better care. But sisters are finding out through negative hospital birth experiences that this ain't necessarily so.

Advantages

◆ Truly a homelike atmosphere, some offer a bedroom suite, full bath, living room, television (even cable), music, and facilities to store or cook your own food.

◆ Most often, as many family members or friends can attend the birth as you want and designated family members can usually stay overnight.

◆ Staffed by board-certified nurse midwives (CNMs) who are well trained and scrupulous about caring for mother and baby's physical and emotional well-being during labor and after the birth.

◆ Drugs and routine use of technology are avoided; women are coached into natural, more gentle childbearing.

◆ CNMs have relationships with "backup" obstetricians who are on call to offer advice or arrange for a transfer to an affiliate hospital if necessary.

◆ Your baby stays with you after birth so you can bond and begin breast-feeding sooner.

◆ A CNM will visit you in your home in the days after the birth to check on you and baby.

◆ Birth in a maternity or birthing center is about half the cost of a hospital birth.

Disadvantages

◆ Birthing rooms are usually only available for women who are unlikely to experience any complications during childbirth (low risk). "High-risk" patients cannot give birth in a center.

A HISTORY OF BIRTH
1966–1975

■ **1966**—In the wake of the civil unrest in Watts, the people of South Central Los Angeles helped create the Charles R. Drew University of Medicine and Science, dedicated to training primary health-care providers to serve underserved communities.

■ **1970**—The few remaining granny midwives in the South are prohibited from practicing.

In response to the growing women's movement, natural childbirth or Lamaze classes begin to be offered in upscale U.S. hospitals. The electronic fetal monitor (EFM) becomes widely used to record the fetal heart rate during labor. The American College of Obstetricians and Gynecologists issues a report indicating that use of the EFM may "not be worthwhile."

Ultrasound, used to estimate due dates and anticipate fetal complications, becomes routinely used. There is controversy over its necessity and its yet-undetermined effects on the fetus.

■ **1972**—Pearline Gilpin begins the nurse midwifery program at Meharry Medical College; later a master's degree program in midwifery is added. These were some of the first such programs to be offered at a historically black college.

■ **1975**—Frederick Leboyer of France popularizes the "gentle birth" concept in which the baby is lowered into warm water at birth and given a massage to ease its transition into the world.

About the same time Dr. Robert Bradley of Colorado espouses husband-coached childbirth, in which the spouse is a full participant in the birthing process.

The Maternity Center Association establishes the Childbearing Center in New York City. This facility served as the model for most of the 140 freestanding birthing centers now operating throughout the country.

◆ If complications develop during pregnancy, and you *become* "high risk," you would have to forge a new relationship with their backup obstetrician and may have to change your plan to give birth in a center.

◆ If necessary, you will need to be transported to a hospital for further care, which could be anxiety-inducing.

◆ Many popular health-insurance plans still don't cover delivery in a birthing center, though aggressive inquiry and insistence has paid off for many mothers-to-be.

HISTORICALLY SPEAKING . . .

 In a West African birthing room you might find 8 or 10 people supporting the expectant mother as she prepares for birth. Mothers, fathers, siblings, and other elders all gather and chant affirmations led by the medicine man. "You will have a safe delivery. Sheep have no midwives, yet they are delivered safely. So will you be!" he says. And all in the room agree, "So be it!" The group is there to talk, laugh, tell stories, and otherwise attempt to divert the expectant mother from the pain that is before her. It is not uncommon for them all to stay in the birth room for up to 24 hours of the mother's labor! *What We Can Learn:* Though it might be hard to imagine going through labor in a room filled with siblings and relatives telling stories and chanting encouragement, the idea of folks who love you turning out to "labor" with you is a great picture. Think about the people in your life who you'd like to have around helping *you* labor, and make sure they're there.

"I planned to have a home birth but I didn't plan to give birth in my bathtub—the baby did! So my midwife delivered her right there in the tub. I had a 'water birth,' of sorts. It was wonderful! The water really helps."

A HISTORY OF BIRTH
1980–the present

■ **1980s**—Mark the emergence of all sorts of inventions to help the birthing process, including birthing stools and cushions. African-American physician Alfred Goldson of Washington, D.C., invents and markets the Baby Bonder, plastic breasts that can be filled with milk and slung over a man's shoulders so he can experience "breast"-feeding.

The Sympathy Belly is introduced, a heavy plastic womb and breasts to be worn by men so they can feel what it's like to be pregnant.

Cesarean rates increase rapidly; Obstetricians' malpractice insurance continues to skyrocket, though few patients who wage lawsuits actually go to trial and even fewer plaintiffs win.

■ **1988**—The first baby is delivered at the Childbearing Center at Morris Heights, Bronx, NY. The center was established to provide pre-natal and postnatal midwifery care to low-income women and has successfully impacted the high infant mortality rate in that area.

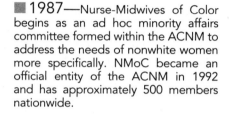

■ **1987**—Nurse-Midwives of Color begins as an ad hoc minority affairs committee formed within the ACNM to address the needs of nonwhite women more specifically. NMoC became an official entity of the ACNM in 1992 and has approximately 500 members nationwide.

■ **1988**—The Gift of Life program, begun by Dr. John Porter, begins delivering babies in Montgomery, Alabama, and becomes an outstandingly successful model for how to give low-cost, personal care to pregnant women.

■ **1990s**—Women become more empowered and demand more personalized care during pregnancy and childbirth. The use of certified nurse-midwives increases each year. Some experts predict that sweeping political, social, and financial changes will occur by the year 2000, causing the childbirth experience to return to being the natural, woman-led experience it once was.

Water Birth

History: The idea of underwater birth was first introduced in Russia in the sixties and then spread to France and the United States when the idea of natural childbirth became popular. French physician Frederick Leboyer, author of *Birth Without Violence*, promoted a theory that to help ease the trauma of the baby's transition from the dim, swishy, wet world of the womb to the cold, bright outside world, the baby needed soft lights, no noise, and a warm bath immediately after birth. Medical authorities dispute the idea that newborns treated this way benefit any more than those who were not, but many women still like the idea behind it.

Today, water birth is a fairly new and exciting practice that has enjoyed only limited success here in the United States, mostly because actual birthing pools are so few and far between (the most noted is the Family Birthing Center in Upland, California). Birth centers overseas who perform water births report excellent results. Though it has only been used by a handful of black couples, the overall results are encouraging. There is some concern among many physicians and hospitals that infection may enter the cervix after the bag of waters has ruptured or the protective mucus plug has been expelled. The concept has so far not received wide acceptance from either the medical community or from pregnant women, but some of Leboyer's ideas on treating the baby as gently as possible in its transitional phases have been incorporated into normal birth procedures. Many midwives encourage women to take warm baths during the stages of labor to ease contractions, and birthing centers offer dimmer switches and tubs as part of their "gentle birth" offerings.

Advantages

◆ Warm-water baths have proven soothing effects for women in labor.
◆ Women who have had successful water births say it was wonderful.
◆ Birthing in shallow water allows for more freedom of movement than on a bed.
◆ This type of birth has been performed most often in France and in California with few complications.
◆ The baby has been accustomed to a watery environment throughout pregnancy.

Disadvantages

◆ Not formally accepted by the medical establishment.
◆ Hospitals with birthing pools are virtually nonexistent in the United States.
◆ There is a small risk of the baby drowning if kept underwater too long.

"I've been somewhat afraid of hospitals ever since I was a child. I talked to a lot of people, including women at my church who had home births, and they educated and encouraged me. Now, I wouldn't have any other kind of birth."

"I don't like to use the term home birthing*," says one nurse midwife who practices in Harlem and attends sisters in home births. "Doctors prey on it and to women it sounds too much like home cookin'."*

Home Births

History: In parts of Africa, it is still expected that a woman will return to the home of her parents to give birth. Being surrounded by familiar sights, sounds, smells, and faces, especially your mother's, was considered key to having a successful birth. Many black southern women will also tell you that the idea of having a baby in familiar surroundings is no new thing. In the early 1900s, tireless black midwives in Louisiana, Mississippi, Alabama, Georgia, Florida, and other states traveled great distances—often on foot—to perform in-home deliveries. There was a tremendous amount of caring and nurturing going on between a midwife and her laboring woman during those home births. The freedom of movement and the relaxed environment you can enjoy only in your own home will help you have a more efficient labor with less need for intervention.

Today, since natural birth has become popular again, more women are choosing home births, birthing rooms, and birthing centers, out of a desire for these very benefits. Sisters who tried home birth once told us they wouldn't do it any other way. They rave about how much giving birth in your own home in your own bed can positively affect your childbirth experience. Still, the trend has a way to go before most women consider it "normal." Many of us, influenced by parents and grandparents who worked hard to give us a better life, still consider giving birth at home "going backward."

Advantages

◆ You will be able to relax and move around freely in your own home.

◆ You do not have to pack a bag or travel anywhere while you're in labor.

◆ Your children, husband, and other family or friends can easily attend the birth if you desire or they can be entertained in the next room.

◆ No extra hospital or birthing center fees to pay.

◆ You can be cared for by a certified nurse-midwife with a backup obstetrician.

◆ You will avoid acquiring any infections from other mothers or babies.

◆ Breast-feeding has been shown to be easier when it is begun in a home setting.

Disadvantages

◆ Only for women with low-risk pregnancies.

◆ You will have to be transported to a hospital if an emergency cesarean must be performed.

◆ You will need to prepare the room for the birth, usually including the purchase of a birth kit containing a bed pad, gauze pads, cord clamp, tape measure, lubricant, waterproof sheeting, sanitary napkins, and other supplies.

◆ You may not receive the same "perks" you would receive at most hospitals, such as a free dinner for you and your partner, a diaper bag (at some hospitals), a receiving blanket, etc.

HISTORICALLY SPEAKING ...

 In Botswana, tribal women go alone into the woods a little way off from their village to deliver their babies. They tell themselves not to be frightened and simply arrange a blanket of leaves for the baby to fall onto. Similarly, women of the Baganda tribe give birth in their gardens, hanging on to a plantain tree and supported by a woman friend. The woman receives the baby, places her on a plantain leaf, and cuts the umbilical cord with a sharp reed. Women from rural Zaire exemplify the importance of natural surroundings by giving birth in a forest or in a wooded area, as the baby in the womb has grown familiar to the sounds of the forest while the mother lived and worked there. In West Africa when a woman is about to give birth, her midwife takes her into the birthing chamber and has her kneel down on padded cushions as she supports her back and leads her in rhythmic deep breathing. Then, in one awesome push, the baby is born. *What We Can Learn:* Take advantage of the fact that you have choices. Some experts feel that medical science has taken the normalcy out of childbirth and has taken over the birth experience so much that women have become merely passive participants. Exercise your ability to choose. If you fear hospitals, consider a birthing center or home-birthing with a midwife. If you've read about water birthing and found it interesting, go visit a center and make an informed decision.

Practitioners: Who's Who

Family Doctor: Provides medical care for the whole family. Trained in obstetrics and gynecology.

Obstetrician Gynecologist: Specializes in obstetric and gynecological care. Able to handle any and all complications that can arise during pregnancy, labor, delivery, and postpartum.

Certified Nurse-Midwives (CNMs): Licensed in all 50 states, certified nurse-midwives are registered nurses with additional graduate education in nurse-midwifery. They are medical professionals who work with, and are under the guidance of, obstetricians.

Certified Midwives (CMs): Women trained and certified in midwifery who are not registered nurses.

Direct-Entry Midwives (DEMs): Self-taught lay midwives who learn the trade by watching and assisting at a number of births, some with certified nurse-midwives, some with obstetricians. Some are nurses and some have informal midwifery education.

Birth Positions

Hand in hand with exploring where to give birth and who will assist you in labor is thinking about *how* you'd like to give birth, barring any complications. Though it may be difficult for you to decide now, it will be helpful for you to know that sitting, squatting, kneeling, and supported standing positions help you to make full use of gravity to facilitate the baby coming down and out. They are also the predominant methods of birth still used in many African countries. The old style, lie-down-flat, legs-up-in-a-stirrup position that many of our mothers may have been told to assume for birth is considered old hat. It does not take advantage of gravity to help the baby's delivery and, in fact, it was designed to help the doctor have easier access to the vaginal area, not to help a woman's labor progress.

Stop here and think: If you could have any kind of birth experience (short of having the stork bring the baby to your door), what would it be? What would the atmosphere be like? Who would be there? Hold that picture in your mind as you begin to write your birthing plan.

Developing Your Birthing Plan

It just makes good sense that after you labor over the decision of what type of birth setting you desire, who will attend you during birth, and what positions you might like to give birth in, you would put your desires on paper to help ensure that your wishes are carried out. Remember that during childbirth your focus will be on giving birth and you will not be able to do too much directing or arguing with medical staff.

Oscar-winning actress Butterfly McQueen from *Gone with the Wind* told Scarlett O'Hara she "didn't know nothin' 'bout birthin' no babies!" But midwives have known for centuries how to help us safely deliver our babies without intervention—at home, in a birthing center, or in the hospital. © 1939 Turner Entertainment Co. All Rights Reserved.

More and more parents are using birth plans before they deliver as a way of being proactive about decisions and circumstances surrounding the birth of their child. Your practitioner may have you fill out a preprepared birth plan with the option of adding more requests to it. If this is not the case, tell your practitioner that you would like her help to create your own birth plan from scratch. The birth plan shouldn't be presented as a list of nonnegotiable demands, but rather as a list of your wishes with the understanding that it may be modified according to what the hospital or practitioner finds allowable, and according to your circumstances. Understand that a birth plan is not a formal contract, but an understanding between you and your doctor or midwife that can help you experience your ideal birth. If there are issues you disagree on, seek to understand your practitioner's point of view and discuss reasons for your wishes as well as a possible compromise. Following are topics to include in your birthing plan.

During Labor

◆ Who you would like present with you at your birth (family, children, friends, a labor assistant, etc.) and whether they need any training in order to be allowed to attend the birth

◆ How long you will labor at home, and the possibility of returning home if you are checked at the hospital and are more than 5 centimeters dilated

◆ Whether you want your water to be broken if labor is not progressing

◆ Whether you want to be otherwise induced if your labor is not progressing

◆ The opportunity to use a labor-delivery-recovery (LDR) room or birthing room if you are delivering in a hospital and they have these rooms available

◆ The option to walk around as much as you feel is necessary during labor

◆ The use of pain medication, induction, and electronic fetal monitoring (continuous or intermittent) during labor and the possibility of using alternatives

◆ Use of cameras or videotape during labor or delivery

◆ The use of an IV, and whether you can forgo having a routine IV to allow you freedom of movement during labor, or use of a saline lock or heparin—which allow you to move around easily as an alternative

◆ The ability to drink and eat light, easily digestible snacks during active labor if you choose

◆ The birth environment in your labor and delivery room, including the use of music, soft lighting, etc.

◆ Using a bath or shower to relax in active labor

During Delivery

◆ Your option to try different birthing positions (see page 307–17)

◆ Having a full-length mirror (many hospitals and birthing cen-

ters have these specifically for birth) brought in so you can see the baby come out
◆ The opportunity to reach down and touch your baby's head as it emerges
◆ The ability to participate in the decision to use forceps or vacuum extraction to bring the baby out (see page 288)
◆ The option of having a bikini-line cut if you must have a cesarean section
◆ General anesthesia versus epidural anesthesia during a C-section

After Delivery

◆ The possibility of having your partner cut the umbilical cord or help bathe baby after birth
◆ The opportunity to hold the baby and breast-feed *directly* after the birth
◆ Your consent on any medication, shots, or eyedrops given to the baby after it is born and postponing these until you have first held the baby
◆ Your preference of having baby room-in with you, or sleep in your room at night so you can nurse (or bottle-feed, if you choose) when the baby is hungry
◆ If baby needs to be fed and you are planning to breast-feed, ask that no formula be given unless with your consent
◆ Whether or not you would like the baby circumcised if he is a boy
◆ The length of your hospital or birthing-center stay

A Tribute to Our Midwives: Yesterday and Today

Even though the number of midwife-attended deliveries had declined sharply in the United States by the 1940s, midwives continued to attend more than 75 percent of births in the southern states of Mississippi, Alabama, Louisiana, South Carolina, Florida, and Georgia. Grannies, as they were affectionately called, were much more than women who came to "catch" babies. They were dieticians, psychologists, loan officers, sex therapists, prayer partners, marriage counselors, and friends to the women they attended.

Segregation, economic climate, and rural isolation influenced a southern black woman's choice of the midwife for her birth attendant, even as recently as 1950. Few white doctors were willing to venture into the thickly populated, muddy, rural areas in the South where many black families lived. This same medical establishment that was reluctant to serve the black community was quick to characterize granny midwives as "ignorant" and "untrained," although a tradition of apprenticeships with experienced midwives had served to teach grannies the knowledge and skills necessary for safe delivery.

Federal and state-funded programs that provided training and supervision of grannies began with the Sheppard-Towner programs in the 1920s. Since many of the grannies were illiterate, the rigorous written exam proved too much for the majority and they were unable to fulfill the requirements for licensure. Many of the younger, more formally educated midwives did pass inspection and became certified. The not-so-hidden agenda in many of these "training" programs was to phase the midwives out of practice entirely and substitute the medical model for care. Sadly, the planned abolition of grannies did not consider the impact of the loss of a central female figure in the black community.

Trained nurse-midwives emerged on the scene in 1918 with the founding of the Maternity Center Association in New York, whose purpose was to promote the health of mothers and infants through the initiatives of neighborhood clinics staffed by public-health nurses and physicians. In 1931, the Lobenstine Midwifery Clinic was opened as a facility for provision of care to women during pregnancy and childbirth and for teaching midwifery to public-health nurses so that they could supervise granny and other lay midwives still in practice. Physicians in the medical community staunchly opposed this. This opposition accounts for why the role of the nurse-midwife was developed in a way that implied close medical supervision.

In 1992, CNMs attended more than 185,000 births in the United States, in hospitals, birthing centers, and in homes, and the numbers continue to grow. At the same time, the number of physicians who are attending hospital births is steadily declining. As health insurance becomes dominated by managed care companies (HMOs), there is pressure on physicians to see twice as many patients in half as much time. On the patient side, women are becoming more educated about childbirth and are demanding more time from their practitioners. Thus, more obstetricians are choosing to work in tandem with CNMs and are delegating more of the obstetric part of their practice to the CNM. This team approach provides women with the personalized care they desire along with the backup of a physician who can step in in case of complications. Lay midwives (also called direct-entry midwives) may soon formalize their affiliations with CNMs in order to standardize training, licensing, and regulation. Should this occur, experts predict that more women will choose a midwife as the primary birth attendant with an obstetrician playing a consulting role.

Maude Callan, one of the first formally educated black nurse-midwives, routinely waded down rivers like this one to get to her car after attending women during home births in rural South Carolina where she practiced. Many of the folks she called on were so poor they "didn't know the use of forks and spoons." Often, Maude would provide a makeshift crib for the newborns, who otherwise might be put into a bed with several older children due to lack of space. She served 10,000 people in a thickly populated rural area full of muddy, unpaved roads and functioned as dietician, psychologist, bail-goer, and friend.

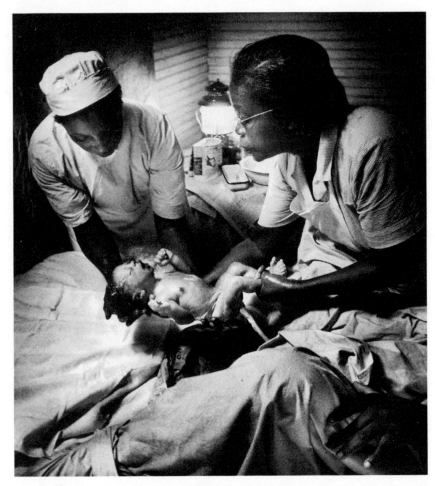

Ms. Callan and her assistant check a minutes-old baby after a home delivery. Midwives often brought along trainees to the birth in hopes of keeping the craft alive among black women. Ms. Callan would hold monthly refresher classes for new midwives that usually opened and closed with a song of praise and a prayer. Midwives were also trained for two weeks at the state midwife institute. Photos of Maude Callan by W. Eugene Smith, *Life* magazine; © Time Inc.

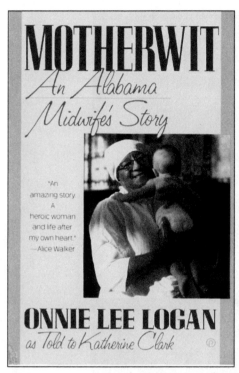

Onnie Lee Logan, a tireless midwife who delivered many black and white babies throughout Alabama, served women at a time when the white medical establishment fiercely sought to put Negro midwives out of business. Ms. Logan's wonderfully inspirational journal-book, *Motherwit* (E. P. Dutton, New York, 1989) chronicles her life and times from 1910 to 1950. Only one or two doctors covered the vast area that Ms. Logan served—and those would often flatly refuse to come attend a black woman in labor. Ms. Logan, who learned the craft from assisting her mother, who was also a midwife, has seen and done extraordinary things in her forty-year practice. She resuscitated a three-pound baby that was given up for dead at birth, she has turned breech babies around in the womb so they would deliver normally, she has delivered a baby behind a fruit stand in the rain, and she helped many a woman who wouldn't dilate (a problem that today would easily make a woman a C-section candidate). In contrast to today's statistics, only one of Onnie's women ever got "torn" (vaginally) during childbirth.

Ms. Logan was a proponent of a husband and wife enjoying the first stage of labor together in a calm, relaxed environment. She'd say, "It was you and yo' husband in the beginnin' [conception] and it was fine. It's you and yo' husband should be in the beginnin' a the birth a the baby, quiet and easy, talkin' and lovin' and happy with one another." Onnie's sterile bag was always preprepared so she could be "ready to just shoot out" on short notice. Ms. Logan was a youth counselor at her church, a part-time social worker and community activist, a philanthropist, and a friend to those in need. Onnie Lee Logan passed away in 1995 at age 85. *Motherwit* concludes with her inspirational words: "I believe God pulled out all of His blessin's on me and I appreciate em and put em to good work . . . I was a good midwife."

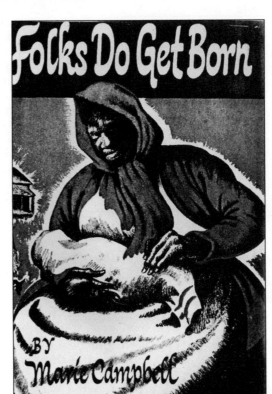

Marie Campbell served women in pregnancy and childbirth in rural Georgia. She tells about her experiences and those of other Negro midwives in her chronicle, *Folks Do Get Born* (Rinehart & Company, Inc., 1946). Ms. Campbell is quick to clarify the misconception that granny midwives were just old, unschooled women who delivered babies on a wing and a prayer. In fact, most midwives traveled great distances on foot to attend midwifery classes given by Board of Health nurses and, sometimes, doctors. The midwives were also fastidious about keeping their "midwife bags" full of clean, sterilized items and did their part to deliver babies under aseptic conditions—often quite a task in the run-down shacks that were home to most black and poor white southern families. Consequently, it was hard to get paid. Ms. Campbell writes, "One . . . favorite story concerns a midwife who was given a pig in payment for her services. She carried the pig home with her and put it into a pen. But in the night the pig broke out of the pen and returned to its former place of abode. The man then refused to give it back to the midwife, because, he said, he had discharged his obligations when he gave her the pig the first time!"

Midwives like these in Clinton, Louisiana, delivered 75 percent of babies in the early 1900s. Midwives continued to attend births well into the 1950s in several southern states, though elsewhere in the United States hospitals became the "in" place to deliver. Often, black women were treated poorly, if at all, at hospitals and were very wary of going to a white doctor for care. Southern midwives would often bring hand-sewn baby clothes, food, and household supplies for the new mothers and their families, many of whom were very poor. The philosophy and tradition of midwifery is to provide holistic care for women during pregnancy, at childbirth, and postpartum, caring for mother, baby, and often the family, too. Photo, circa 1931, reprinted with permission from the College of Nurse-Midwives Archives/National Library of Medicine.

Armentia Tripp Jarrett (*left*), the first certified nurse-midwife of any color to be licensed in the state of California, was the innovator of the groundbreaking Madera Project in Madera County, California. The project demonstrated a significant reduction in maternal-child morbidity and mortality rates by the use of a nonphysician (i.e. nurse-midwife). The success of her efforts are largely responsible for changing legislation that helped improve the way poor women and babies were treated in California. Ms. Jarrett has also served as director of nursing for the International Red Cross in Stuttgart, Germany, and was director of nurse-midwifery at Martin Luther King Jr. General Hospital in South Central Los Angeles. She has graced the halls of institutions such as Johns Hopkins University and Yale University, obtaining degrees in public-health nursing, maternal-child health, and nurse-midwifery. Ms. Jarrett continues to serve as a faculty associate for the nurse-midwifery education program at the Charles R. Drew University of Medicine in the Watts area of Los Angeles. "There are two kinds of patients: one will read up on an illness and be able to participate intelligently in a discussion about her treatment, and others who walk in feeling powerless and 'unable,' relying solely on the doctor's opinion. The latter group will probably never choose a midwife to attend them during birth. In my experience, the people who *are* choosing midwives are some of the most educated and informed black women in the country."

Lola Coleman (*right*), opened the doors of her home in 1978 to establish the Natural Way Midwifery Service, arguably the first private midwifery practice started by anyone—black, white, or otherwise—in the United States. Ms. Coleman integrated her 1948 class at Union University School of Nursing in Albany and, after receiving her nursing degree, went on to study midwifery in England. She became a certified nurse-midwife after studying at Meharry Medical College in Tennessee, the school noted for turning out the most black nurse-midwives in the country. Throughout her career, Ms. Coleman "nursed" a dream to return to the Motherland to live and work. In 1993, she put wings on this dream and purchased a plot of land in Ghana on which to build a home and possibly an office to act as a consultant to African nurse-midwives. "I once stopped a doctor that was unsupportive of nurse midwives doing home births and asked him, 'Why are you so against us?' He finally admitted, 'Well, if I had to go into a woman's house to deliver her baby without any medical equipment, I'd be scared to death!' Meanwhile, of the 4 million babies born each year, only 15 percent are classified as 'complicated.' We need to stop gearing our beliefs about birth to the *ab*normality rather than the norm."

Under the careful direction of **Gwendolyn Spears** *(front, left)* Charles Drew University's nurse-midwifery degree program in Los Angeles has graduated more underrepresented ethnic minorities than any other such program in the country. Graduates are strongly encouraged to give back to their community—and an astounding 80 percent do just that, providing vital care to women and babies in vulnerable populations. Ms. Spears is also chief of nurse midwifery-services at the King/Drew Medical Center, where she directs and oversees the quality of care provided to women who come to the center for pre- and postnatal care and childbirth. "Certified nurse-midwives have the opportunity to redefine health care services to women as we are the experts. We have proven our ability to give low-cost, low-tech, and high-touch care to women of all age groups." **Dr. Ezra C. Davidson, Jr.,** *(front, right)* has come a long way from the small Mississippi town of Water Valley, where he was born and raised. He is now chairman of obstetrics and gynecology at Drew University and chief-of-service at the same department at King/Drew Medical Center. Educated at Atlanta's Morehouse College and a top graduate of Meharry Medical School, Dr. Davidson has trained at Harlem Hospital Center and the Columbia University College of Physicians and Surgeons in New York. He has also served as health adviser to Senator Bill Bradley of New Jersey and has worked with numerous government and private organizations regarding issues of national health policy, particularly those pertaining to maternal and child health. Dr. Davidson contributed to the development of the technology of fetoscopy and fetal blood sampling, two highly sophisticated procedures that help to determine the condition of the baby while she is still in the womb. "It is time that we developed a model that will identify and categorize all major factors that contribute to fetal, neonatal, and infant mortality. We have to do this in a way that will guide society in targeting resources at local, state, and regional levels to improve maternity and infant care and outcome." *Photos pp. 106, 107: Tonye Allen/Trilobite*

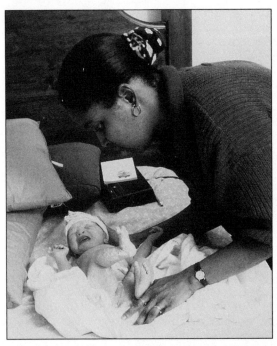

Marsha E. Jackson, C.N.M., gives a newborn her first physical exam after an in-home delivery, which is her specialty. She and partner Alice Bailes, also a certified nurse-midwife, are the codirectors and co-owners of BirthCare & Women's Health, which provides home birth services in Washington, D.C., Virginia, and Maryland. The practice, established in 1987, recently expanded to include the first freestanding birth center in Virginia. Jackson received her undergraduate education from Howard University College of Nursing and went on to earn her master's in nurse-midwifery at Georgetown University. She has also worked as a neonatal staff nurse and childbirth educator and spent six years working with Cities-In-Schools, a program that provided hospital births for pregnant teenagers. "Birth is a very empowering experience for a woman and it's important that she has support throughout her pregnancy so she can have the type of birthing experience she wants. Often, women come to us late in their pregnancies, deciding that they want midwifery services. What happens is that after they start reading and learning about their birthing choices, they ask themselves, 'What am I doing? This is not going to give me the birth experience I want.' " *Photo courtesy Marsha E. Jackson, CNM*

Carol Ambrose, C.N.M., M.P.H. *(not pictured)* is president of Nurse-Midwives of Color, an association that represents more than 400 African-American, West Indian, Asian, and Hispanic certified nurse-midwives across the country. She is also associate midwife in a private OB/GYN practice in Brooklyn, New York. Ms. Ambrose has enjoyed a long career serving pregnant women and their families in the New York area, including a two-year stay as executive director of the Brooklyn Teen Pregnancy Network, Inc. "I need more dark folks in my practice! Sisters need to know that you don't have to leave technology behind if you choose a midwife to attend your birth. If you want your epidural you can still get it with a midwife. We will always try to have you use your inner reserves first before we choose intervention. . . . When women are ready to reclaim their birth options, we'll be here."

CHAPTER 6

◇ ◇ ◇ ◇

Getting Your "House" in Order

Beneath the excitement and anticipation of the new arrival lies a pervasive truth: Having a baby can create a lot of extra work and anxiety if you don't take time to plan ahead. Getting your "house" in order means thinking through the details of what it means to have a new baby in your lives. Take the time early in your pregnancy to get prepared—it will take the stress off you and your husband later. In this chapter we will cover the following topics:

Preparing Your Mate and Other Children for the Baby
Making Lifestyle Decisions
   Money Matters
   Negotiating Your Maternity Leave
   After-the-Birth Decisions to Make Now
   Who Will Care for My Baby?
   A Baby's Needs
   Making Your Home Safe
Choosing a Childbirth Class
Your Baby's Space
Your Appearance

Preparing Your Mate

Many men are admittedly afraid of their newborn babies. "It's like holding an expensive piece of glass," said one father. "You're always afraid you're gonna break it." Most men haven't had much experience holding newborns, far less caring for their needs. *One very effective way to help your husband become more comfortable with the baby when it comes is to encourage and support his involvement in the pregnancy steadfastly.* Invite him to be by your side at your prenatal appointments, encourage him to ask questions about things that may concern him, discuss all the "baby plans" with him and listen to his input, encourage him to talk to or sing to the baby and to feel her movements. Remember that he isn't carrying the baby inside his body the way you are. He cannot feel the flutters you feel in the early months; he cannot sense that your hormones are out of whack today and you need to rest. Involving him in intimate ways will bond him to the baby and make him feel more confident about his role as supporter and father-to-be. Just for fun, fill a knapsack with 20 pounds of potatoes (or whatever you have in the house) and ask him to wear it backwards for an evening. He should be brimming with new-found appreciation for you after one night! (For more ways to help your mate, see Chapter 12, "Becoming Daddy.")

Preparing Your Older Children

If you have other children, use the same methods with them as you used to involve your husband in the pregnancy. There's a tremendous amount of teaching you can do along the way, even with a child who's only one year old. Teach children to be gentle with the new baby by repeating the word *gentle* whenever you are allowing them to touch and explore your belly. You may want to get an older child a baby doll so he or she can practice what you're saying with a real object. An older child may be fascinated by what goes on at a routine prenatal checkup, such as measuring your belly or seeing the fetus on an ultrasound screen. If your visits are in a hospital, make a quick trip upstairs to the neonatal room and show your child the newborns. If you have friends who have new babies, plan a visit with your husband and your child and encourage them to hold and play with the newborn. Preplan the visit so you can arrange to arrive when the baby is awake. If it's okay with your friends, arrange to have your husband give the baby a bottle or change a diaper, if needed. Your child can watch and assist.

Children often feel all sorts of conflicting emotions when they realize they will no longer be the "new baby" in the house. Some ways to soothe these feelings are to show your child his own newborn pictures and speak lovingly about how happy you were when he arrived. Tell stories about what he was like as a newborn and relive humorous things he did. Reinforce your older child's good points by talking about what a great big brother he will make, because he's so smart, creative, loving, protective, or good at sharing. All of these things will make a child feel loved and important, will help him have an easier time adjusting to the new center of attraction, and will build up his self-esteem. However, if your older child did not feel secure in your love already, these methods of reinforcement will have a lesser effect. You will have to do double duty to make up for the deficit in your older child's emotional tank while you welcome your new baby into the fold. Make your husband aware of the importance of this issue if he is not already. It's a great opportunity for him to focus more attention on your older child when you are tending to the baby, or vice versa. Let's wage war against "father hunger"! (See Chapter 12, "Becoming Daddy," for more on how dads can bond.) *Those Baby Blues: A Guide for Parents of New Siblings* is a video that features African-American family psychologist Dr. Brenda Wade and shows actual footage of the new baby's arrival home and depicts the range of emotions older siblings go through because of it. Wade and colleague Dr. Glen Aylward offer insight into what needs are prompting which behaviors and how you can meet the needs of older children without going crazy!

MOTHER TO MOTHER

I was pregnant with my fourth child, and my youngest daughter, Gabrielle, was curious about where babies come from. Not wanting to be too graphic (she was only three), I told her that there is a very special hole that the baby comes out of and it only opens when God says the baby is ready to be born. She was satisfied. I was relieved. Then one night at the dinner table, Gabrielle asked if she could say the grace. She began, "Thank you God for this food and for my brother and sister and my mom and dad, and thank you most of all for Mommy's special hole where the baby is going to come out of!" All I can say is I'm so glad we didn't have any folks over for dinner that night!

Making Lifestyle Decisions

You and your partner should have a serious talk about both of your expectations for your growing family and how those hopes will be affected by your careers. If you work outside the home, as 64 percent of black mothers with infants do, here are some of the questions you need to discuss concerning your work schedules:

◆ Is it best for your family that you return to work soon after the baby's born? If not, how long a maternity leave you will take, and when will it begin and end? Will it be paid or unpaid? Can you afford to take additional unpaid time off?

◆ If you could have the exact type of birth setting you want, what would it be? If you and your mate both work outside the home, whose medical plan offers better coverage for that type of pre-natal care and childbirth? Can you pay out-of-pocket for the things you want that aren't covered?

◆ How do you look financially? This is a perfect time to create or review your budget and financial goals so you can make any adjustments that may be necessary.

◆ If anything happened to you or your husband after the birth, are you covered with enough life insurance to take care of yourself and the needs of a child?

Money Matters

All of these somewhat tedious details are very important to sift through if you are going to have a sense of security when the baby comes. But surprisingly, when it comes to discussing budgeting, life insurance, and managing their money, many black couples are reluctant even to look at the future. They shy away from having to stare their financial futures in the face by saying, "Well, we're leaving it all up to God. He'll provide." But before we drop everything conveniently in God's lap, let's remember that he also expects us to be good stewards of the money he entrusts to us. Walking blindly into the future with a new baby and no financial road map is *not* being a good steward.

The budget sheet (or spending plan) below, adapted from *The Financial Planner Workbook* by Larry Burkett (Moody Press, Chicago), is one that has been used to help countless numbers of people get a handle on their finances. It compares your income to your expenses, and includes the things you will probably buy for the baby's first year, along with suggested cost. Once completed, the sheet will give you a realistic picture of your financial state—which is something you want! (You do, you do.) A budget, or spending plan, if you prefer, is not a jail cell, nor is it only for "people with money." It is an invaluable tool to help you achieve your hopes and dreams.

After you've completed the sheet it's a good idea to sit down with a financial counselor or a friend you trust who handles his or her money well to help you make sound decisions that are right for your growing family. This person can also hold you accountable to stick to your budget. You'll never regret doing it! But even a nicely com-piled budget plan does little good if it sits in the drawer. Commit to the plan for at least one year, reviewing how you did each month, and it will benefit you and your family for years. The International Association for Certified Financial Planners may be able to hook you up with a counselor in your area who can sit down with you and your husband to discuss the best route for you; call 1-800-282-PLAN.

Other helpful budgeting and investing resources include: *The Black Woman's Guide to Financial Independence* by Cheryl Broussard, which speaks to the issues black women face when trying to manage their money; *The Financial Planner Workbook* mentioned earlier offers a bib-lical, value-centered perspective on money, saving, and investing for the future. *The Wall Street Journal Guide to Understanding Money and Investing* and the very popular *Personal Finance for Dummies* (don't be offended by the title, the book simply talks in easy-to-understand lan-guage) can help you figure out where and how to invest your money once you've decided to make saving a part of your lifestyle.

MONTHLY INCOME AND EXPENSES

Gross Household Income
per Month _____
Salary You _____ Spouse _____
Interest (from bank
accounts, etc.) _____
Dividends (from stocks,
etc., if any) _____
Other income (odd jobs,
regular gifts from
relatives, etc.) _____

MINUS:
1. Church Tithe or
Offering _____

2. Taxes (include federal,
state, FICA) _____

3. Savings (current) _____

= **NET SPENDABLE
INCOME** _____

4. HOUSING
Mortgage or rent _____
Home insurance _____
Taxes (divide annual amt.
by 12) _____
Electricity _____
Gas _____
Water _____
Sanitation _____
Telephone (local and
long distance) _____
Maintenance (estimate
average cost) _____
Total _____

5. CAR(S)
Payments _____
Insurance _____
Gas _____
Parking fees _____

License renewals/taxes _____
Maintenance/Repair
(base on an average
year; include oil) _____
Total _____

6. OTHER TRANSPORTATION
Total _____

7. INSURANCE
Health _____
Life _____
Other _____

8. DEBTS
Credit Card(s) _____
Loans (excluding
car note) _____
Other _____
Total _____

9. FOOD
Groceries _____
Breakfasts/lunches
at work _____
Total _____

10. FUN
Eating out _____
Weekend/short trips _____
Vacation _____
Hobbies (incl. lessons,
equipment) _____
Other things you do
for fun _____
Total _____

11. CLOTHING
Adults _____
Children (other) _____
Laundry/cleaning _____
Total _____

12. MEDICAL EXPENSES
   Doctor(s) _____
   Dentist _____
   Prescription drugs _____
        Total _____

13. EDUCATION
   Tuition: You & Spouse _____
   Tuition: Other Children _____
   Books, subscriptions _____
        Total _____

14. CHILD CARE
   Baby-sitter or nanny fees

   _____
   Day care _____
        Total _____

15. HOUSEHOLD ITEMS
   Furnishings (appliances, furniture, decorative items) _____
        Total _____

16. MISCELLANEOUS
   Drugstore items (toiletries, cosmetics, etc.) _____
   Haircuts/beauty _____
   Gifts (occasions, charity, etc.) _____
        Total _____

*17. BABY-RELATED NEEDS
   Diapers _____
   Toiletries _____
   Baby Food _____
   Clothes/Shoes _____
        Total _____
   Breast pump $10–$200 _____
   Washer/drier $600–$1000 _____

Humidifier $30–$80 _____
Blender $30 _____
Car seat $60–$90 _____
High chair $20–$50 _____
Infant swing $50–$120 _____
Portable crib $80–$100 _____
Regular crib $50–$400 _____
Bedding, decorations $50–$200 _____
Changing table $100–$200 _____
Diaper bag $20–$50 _____
Baby tub $10–$20 _____
Maternity clothes $500 _____
Nursing bras (3) $60–$80 _____
Childbirth classes, books, tapes $200 _____
Baby's first photos $30 _____
Other Items _____
Extra life insurance (varies) _____
Savings account $50 _____
Stroller $20–$200 _____
Carriage $200 _____
Infant Carrier $40 _____
Baby Sling $40 _____
Booster seat (toddler) $30–$60 _____
        Total _____

TOTAL EXPENSES _____
1. **NET SPENDABLE INCOME** _____
2. **TOTAL EXPENSES** _____
3. Subtract line 2 from line 1 _____

Line 3 is your surplus income. If it is a negative number, your expenses have exceeded your income.

*Estimates are conservative.

Notes About Your Budget Sheet

◆ Have pay stubs and any other financial information at hand when you sit down to fill out the budget sheet. Couples should do this sheet together, using both salaries if you each generate income. Use a pencil, as there will probably be a lot of erasing.

◆ Insert your monthly expenses for each category (except "Baby-Related Needs"), not the amount spent each *year*. For items purchased only once during the year, simply divide the total amount by 12 to come up with a monthly expense figure. For example, if you spend $700 per year on car insurance, divide $700 by 12 and enter the monthly figure. For bimonthly expenses, divide by 6, and so on.

◆ The "Baby-Related Needs" category should give you an idea of how much you'll need to spend in total during baby's first year. Of course, you may not need or want all of the items listed and may have your own preferences for things like diapers and baby food. Try to determine which items you will need when so you can add those expenses to your basic monthy budget.

◆ If the category doesn't apply to you, also enter "0."

◆ Logically, you cannot spend more than you bring in, so your total expenses should not exceed your spendable income. If they do, there must be a source of income you are leaving out. Remember to include any money that you may be borrowing regularly from friends or relatives.

Best Investment Choices for Baby

The best time to save for your baby's future is now. Here are your best options:

Stocks: More black couples than ever are investing in the stock market and many are seeing solid results. If you are savvy about saving, have extra money to set aside, and are willing to spend some time tracking the market, investing in stocks may be for you. There is also the satisfaction of knowing that you own a small piece of the companies whose products you may use. The first step is to ask a financial planner to help you determine your tolerance for risk. One popular beginner strategy is to purchase a group of stocks called Beating the Dow, which are prepicked blue-chip stocks that have outperformed the market. You are advised to invest for at least one year; most brokerage houses require a $1,000 investment in order to open an account.

INSIDER TIP

Prudential Securities notes that the average cost for tuition, fees, and room and board *for one year* at a public college or university in the year 2011 will be about $87,000 if the current rate of increase prevails. Don't panic—prepare. Here's how to work it, adapted from *Personal Finance for Dummies*. First, do the following calculation:

College tuition for four years
(use *today's* figures)   _____
Amount you'd like to help your child pay   _____ divided by
Number of months until your child
goes to college (216 months from 0–18 yrs)
                                                                _____ equals

Amount needed to save monthly until then   _____

SAVING FOR COLLEGE—NOW

Open an individual retirement account (IRA) and choose to invest in some fairly aggressive mutual funds that expect a return of about 10 percent; the interest will take care of the tuition increase, with some money to spare; invest the amount from the equation above in the IRA each month. When your child is ready for college and fills out her financial aid form, she will be given aid based on your income. All the money you've accumulated in your IRA is exempt from inclusion (under current laws) as income. This way, your child will qualify for more aid and you will keep the money in your IRA. If you need to, you can help your child make up the balance of the tuition by taking a loan against your IRA at a lower rate of interest than you are earning, so you're still ahead. Scholarships, grants, part-time jobs, and help from your relatives and your church community can help make up the rest.

Joining an investment club is one way to invest in the stock market without the feeling that you're going it alone. Typically done with about 10 to 20 people you know and trust, individuals make regular contributions to the "club pot" or account and agreed-upon stocks are purchased by the group on a monthly basis. Each member is responsible for researching and reporting to the group on a certain industry, for example, health care. Many clubs enjoy a higher rate of return with their group investments than the average mutual fund and the highest CD rate. One well-known women's club, the Beardstown Ladies, has reported a return of more than 20 percent annually! And they had little or no experience in investing before they started. Contact the National Association of Investors Corporation at 1-810-583-NAIC if you've gotten a group of people together and are ready to start a club.

If you own a personal computer and modem, electronic trading now also makes it easier to get in on stock market investments and information. The Motley Fools are a group of savvy investors who share valuable advice, strategies for all investment levels, and stock analysis in layperson's terms through America Online (Keyword: Motley Fool). Remember, money traded in stocks is not backed or insured by the federal government.

Mutual Funds: Mutual funds invest in a variety of companies at once. For instance a fund may invest in only midsized companies in the technology industry. There are thousands of funds to choose from, and most require a minimum $500 investment. However some companies, like T. Rowe Price, allow new investors to start with as little as $50 per month. Others, who want to attract investors 35 years of age and younger, may offer even lower initial investments. Some mutual funds are low risk, some moderate, some high. Since you would invest in funds over the long term (18 years) if you are saving for your child's education, you can invest in higher-risk, more volatile funds until your child begins high school, then switch some of the money into lower-risk, more conservative funds and CDs as college approaches. Higher returns are normally associated with higher risk, but mutual funds can often return 10 percent or more. (Think of the relatively low interest rate you're getting at the local bank.) One clear benefit is that mutual funds come complete with professional, full-time portfolio managers, most of whom provide you with periodic reports on how your fund is doing. Between statements, you can track the performance of your funds by checking the *New York Times* or the *Wall Street Journal*, which list all the funds each day. Look for funds with "no-loads," which means that no commissions will be paid out of your money to the salesperson who sold you the fund. Also, choose funds that have performed in the top 15 percent of the funds in their category. Major fund categories include: aggressive, growth, growth and income, balanced, income, global, and foreign.

Bonds: According to *The Wall Street Journal Guide to Understanding Money & Investing,* Americans have more money invested in bonds than in stocks, mutual funds, or other types of securities. Buying bonds is generally considered a low-risk investment. When you buy a bond you are really lending your money to a corporation or government for a specified term. During that term, you will be paid a set amount of interest regularly until the bond reaches maturity (when the "loan" must be repaid to you). U.S. Savings Bonds are bought at any bank at a discount from their face value (for instance, a $1,000 bond might cost you $600) and are available in denominations as small as $25 and as large as $10,000. Savings bonds are backed by the U.S. government and have fixed maturity dates. Depending on your financial goal, you can buy short-term bonds that mature in a year or less, or longer-term bonds that can mature in anywhere from 2 to 30 years. U.S. savings bonds can be cashed in at any bank. Zero-coupon bonds, also called Treasury Strips, are another type of bond that pay a higher interest rate and cost less to buy. They are more risky since they are not backed by the government and are traded on the open market. One drawback to buying bonds to help pay for your child's education 18 years from now is that they may not keep up with the rising inflation rate (about 3 percent per year) or rising college education costs (about 6 percent per year). Choosing bonds that are free of city, state, or federal taxes can help keep more of the return in your pocket and out of Uncle Sam's, though these are generally more appropriate for people in higher-income tax brackets.

Certificates of Deposit (CDs): CDs are debt instruments used by banks that pay depositors a fixed rate of interest on their money after a fixed amount of time. The term can be as short as 3 or 6 months or as long as 5 years. CDs are FDIC insured up to $100,000 and are considered very safe investments, though they are low yielding during times of low inflation and low interest rates. CDs are okay for general savings for your child, but not so great to save for college. For that purpose, you will do better in a more aggressive, higher-yielding investment, such as a mutual fund.

Negotiating Your Maternity Leave

According to a 1993 study done by the Bureau of Labor Statistics, 64.8 percent of married black women with babies under 1 year old work outside the home, either part time or full time. With this many mothers at work (2 million working mothers altogether, black and white) you would think that most employers have their acts together as far as maternity leave policy is concerned, right? Wrong. In fact, the United States is noted for lagging behind most other countries— even those considered "less developed countries"—in terms of offer-ing employees paid maternity leave and subsidized day care. The National Family Leave law (see outline below) was voted down twice before it finally was passed. Though many presidential administra-tions have emphasized their committment to "family values" over the years, sometimes you may wonder just whose families are being valued and exactly how that value is being demonstrated. More than half of the employees at midsized companies in America receive no paid maternity leave. And since so many employers work out mater-nity leave on a case-by-case basis, many pregnant women find them-selves having to learn how to negotiate their own deals.

Successful negotiating requires reading and researching ahead of time and being able to articulate your desires and back up your requests. A poorly negotiated maternity leave can result in you, your mate, and your baby suffering the consequences: not enough recovery time, not enough time spent home with your baby, and not enough money coming in. And your employer gets a disgruntled, miserable employee who may begin shopping her résumé around at the first opportunity. This is a lose-lose situation. It behooves you to check out your company's maternity leave policy (or lack thereof) as soon as you confirm your pregnancy, so you'll know what steps to take to achieve a win-win situation.

One bit of good news for pregnant employees and their husbands arrived in 1993 when the Family and Medical Leave Act was signed into law by President Bill Clinton. Basically, this act gives employees the right to up to 3 months of unpaid leave for any family health crisis or the birth of a child, without the danger of losing their jobs. However, 3 months of *unpaid* leave may not seem like that attractive an option when you've got a new baby. But it's good to know that the law exists in case you need to use it.

The Civil Rights Act of 1991 allows women to receive compensa-tion for damages as well as back pay if they can prove they were discriminated against. This may be one reason why the number of complaints by pregnant employees to the Equal Employment Opportunity Commission is steadily rising. Know your rights and avail yourself of their protections if you feel you are being treated unfairly or being discriminated against. But first, do your best to lobby for the maternity leave plan you want by presenting a solid case. Here are the steps to take to prepare for a negotiation session with your supervisor.

BY THE WAY

According to a study on pregnancy discrimination, women who take maternity leave are 10 times more likely to lose their jobs than employees who take other types of medical leave. Women in the study indicated that their supervisor or human resource administrator was usually the one who showed discrimination toward them, even when that person was a woman. Be on your guard as you negotiate!

How To Begin

◆ Discuss your ideas about working and parenting with your mate *first*. Both of you should candidly discuss your thoughts about family life. Share your values, hopes, and dreams for your growing family. Talk about what you liked and disliked about your own growing-up years. Discuss your feelings about your jobs and career paths. What are your financial goals? How can you get on the road to achieving them? We encourage you to consider thoughtfully the advantages of either parent staying home with your baby, at least part time, until she is of school age. There are many ways to make such an arrangement work. (See "Leaving the Workforce Entirely" in this chapter, for more details.) Should you choose to continue working outside the home, be sure to talk about what type of child care you are both comfortable with and are able to afford. (See "Help! Who Will Care for My Baby?" later in this chapter for more detail.)

◆ Look at your company's employee handbook or human resources brochure (usually given to new employees during the first weeks of employment), and read carefully the parts on maternity and disability leave. Most companies treat maternity as a disability and offer the same benefits to women for childbirth as they would if you had a car accident—commonly 6 to 8 weeks of paid leave. Usually, you'll get all or most of your salary for the first part of your leave and a percentage of your salary for the remainder of the time. If you plan to negotiate additional unpaid leave, make sure you and your mate make *clear* allowances on your budget sheet to account for the loss of income.

♦ Talk with mothers you trust at your company and ask how they structured their maternity leaves. Ask them to help explain the parts of the policy that you may not fully understand. Be discreet in this detective work, though. Your supervisor should *not* learn about your pregnancy through the door of a bathroom stall! Friends who have had babies and work at other companies can also provide valuable information on maternity leave policies in general, letting you in on what's possible, what's usual, and what's unacceptable.

♦ Know the contents of the Family and Medical Leave Act (see synopsis in "Three Acts to Remember," this chapter) if you find that no maternity leave policy exists at your company, so you'll know your legal rights. Call or write your state's employment office or labor board to find out what state laws are in place, if any, regarding maternity leave. Your employer must provide you with whichever leave policy is more generous, the company's or the state's. Many of the state laws are vaguely worded, however, leaving lots of room for debate as to what they are "really" saying. Note: Sadly, several states with high black populations have *no* maternity leave laws on the books (see "Sad States of Affairs").

♦ Wait until you are equipped with all the information you need to begin negotiating your leave before you tell your supervisor you are pregnant. He or she may be surprised about your news and may need time to think through the changes that have to be made to accommodate your absence. Make a date to hash things out as soon as possible after the initial talk, so the details of your plan are fresh in your mind.

The Art of the Deal

Unfortunately, the world of upper management is still dominated by white males. Some men have chauvanistic attitudes toward women executives—especially when they announce they're pregnant. You must negotiate on the offensive, not the defensive. Many supervisors will try to confuse or coerce you with their use of language in hopes that you will be too intimidated to stand your ground. Here are some strategies to help you get what you need out of a negotiation meeting:

◆ Have a brief initial meeting in which you tell your boss that you are pregnant and schedule another time in a neutral setting like a conference room, if possible, to discuss the details.

◆ At the second meeting, present your plan verbally and have a printed outline of your request to give to your supervisor and anyone else who may need a copy after the meeting.

◆ Know your boss's disposition and personal style and use that knowledge to guide the meeting. If he is laid back, be laid back too, but always be professional. Listen to what he has to say and keep calm, even if he is saying things you object to. If you have prepared a good case, you can challenge these objections successfully when he is finished.

◆ Establish that you value your job and reiterate the fact that you are an asset to the company. If you feel it's necessary, remind your boss of your best assets: years of service to the company, special skills or abilities, experience in your field, and successful projects where you played a major role. It usually takes too much time and money to retrain a new person, and your boss knows it. Accentuate the positive.

◆ Offer viable suggestions about how your work can be divided while you're gone, as this will probably be at the top of your boss's list of concerns. Some women maintained their job security by hiring a student intern or former employee (full-time mother, retiree) to fill in part time while they are gone. Just make sure you're convinced that neither candidate may have designs on your job!

◆ Ask for more time than you think you need. You won't regret the extra time home with your baby, and if you get restless, you can always arrange to come back a few weeks earlier. Though policies vary from company to company, the average disability plan allows just six paid weeks off for a vaginal birth and eight weeks for a cesarean section. Some well-known medical experts recommend *at least* four months of maternity leave to get to know your baby and see her get settled into a routine before you leave her. Many sisters said they regretted going back to work too soon, even though it meant more money. The heartache of missing your baby all day may not be worth the cash.

◆ Stop yourself from nodding your head to anything that you haven't had time to think through. Nodding implies agreement. It may come back to haunt you.

◆ End the meeting by asking, "So, are you comfortable with this?" Savvy negotiators have found that most people will answer yes to this question.

Extras You May Want to Ask For

◆ Half-days for the last few weeks of your pregnancy and the first few weeks back on the job after the birth; this way you can ease yourself out and in again.

◆ No overnight trips for the first three or four months after your return, if you're breast-feeding.

◆ Continuance of sales commissions during your leave, if you are in that field.

◆ Substitution of any earned sick time or personal days during the last few weeks of disability leave. By making this substitution, you will receive your full pay instead of the reduced pay usually offered by most companies during the last weeks of your leave.

◆ The possibility of a job-sharing arrangement. Make sure you have this well thought out before you ask, including the specific person who you are suggesting to be your "other half." It's even better if you've gotten that person's positive response to the idea beforehand.

◆ The possibility of telecommuting (working from home). Millions of folks have discovered the wonders of working at home, and statistics show that millions more people will do so each year. These days, companies may be more inclined to consider telecommuting because studies show that productivity increases and employee turnover decreases—two big employer costs. However, you must have a well-designed proposal for how it can work. Writers, editors, artists, researchers, secretaries, and salespeople are some of the most successful at telecommuting because the nature of their work is often more flexible. You may want to suggest a trial period of, say, three months, gradually going from two days home, three in the office, until you graduate to full-time telecommuting. Essential to the long-range success of any telecommuting arrangement is that you demonstrate your ability to be disciplined and productive while working at home.

THREE ACTS TO REMEMBER

The Family and Medical Leave Act of 1993 states that a person who has been employed with a company with fifty or more employees for at least one year has the right to take up to twelve weeks of unpaid leave for a family health crisis or the birth or adoption of a child, without the danger of losing his or her job. During your maternity leave you must receive the same health insurance you were provided with before the leave, and you must be restored to your original position or an equivalent position (this is where it can get funky) at the same pay level.

The Civil Rights Act of 1991 allows women to get compensatory and punitive damages for discrimination, as well as back pay.

The Pregnancy Discrimination Act of 1978 states that if your employer provides health insurance and disability plans to employees who are sick or have an accident, the same coverage must be offered to you for childbirth and related medical conditions. This law makes it illegal for an employer to fire, refuse to hire, or deny a promotion to a woman simply because she is pregnant (though it could easily be said that there were "other reasons").

Paternity Leave: An Option?

It may sound strange to your ears, but paternity leave is a buzz phrase in the world of employee benefits. Several progressive American companies, such as Hallmark Cards in Kansas City, Apple Computer in California, IBM in New York, and Johnson & Johnson in New Jersey, offer family-friendly leave policies, such as paternity leave and job-sharing as well as other "perks" that support dual-career families. When you consider that so many black children—and adults—suffer from emotional scars due to "father hunger," having your mate request time off is an idea worth considering. The Family Leave Act also allows fathers-to-be to take unpaid leave time to be with their wives during labor, childbirth, and recovery without risking their jobs. Paid paternity leave may be something your husband can nudge his boss about, especially if he's got some seniority with the company. Having your mate with you during the first week after the birth is a wonderful way for you to bond with the baby together, from the start. And it will be comforting to know that if the baby is sick or has a doctor's appointment, you and your husband can alternate who stays home to take care of her and who goes to work.

SAD STATES OF AFFAIRS

States with no maternity leave laws (latest available figures are from 1995). If you live in any of these states, write your state representative.

*Alabama
Arkansas
*Georgia
Indiana
*Michigan
*Mississippi
Nebraska
Nevada
New Mexico
*North Carolina
*Ohio
South Dakota
*Texas
Utah
Wyoming

*Denotes states with more than 600,000 black women, according to the Census Bureau

---

Pregnant and Working

Once you've successfully negotiated your maternity leave package, it's time to focus on wrapping things up at the office and preparing yourself for birth. Here is a list of things to think about now:

◆ Avoid complaining to co-workers about your pregnancy woes. Word travels fast, and you may develop a reputation as being grumbly and unprofessional. This is not a good note on which to leave. Keeping your inner and outer tanks in top shape even when you're at work will give you less to complain about. Take walks or naps on your lunch hour, sit at your desk with your feet elevated on a stool, keep fruit and whole-grain crackers on your desk to munch on, and drink lots of water. (See chapters 7, 8, and 9 for more detail on staying well during pregnancy.)

◆ Maintain a professional look throughout your pregnancy. As it is, it will be hard for people at work to take you as seriously since the woman they know as Thelma Johnson, director of marketing, is about to turn into "Mrs. Mommy." Well-tailored clothing and proper demeanor will count for a lot more now that you're pregnant, especially if you are heavyset. Unless you work in a very relaxed, uncorporate atmosphere, save the leggings and sweatshirts for after work and weekends.

◆ Tell as many business contacts as possible when you will be leaving for maternity leave and whom they should contact in your absence. Sending a formal notice to special clients or business associates, or even just a note jotted on the back of your business card, shows that you value your contacts and presents you as an organized professional. Change your voice mail message to inform people that you will be out. Give only an approximate date for your return in case you end up taking more time off than you planned.

◆ Prepare a detailed memo for your boss and the colleagues who will be handling your job responsibilities while you're away. Include a status report of each project at the time you leave, and be sure to include phone numbers for anyone who may need to be contacted in your absence.

After-the-Birth Decisions to Make Now

It's perfectly normal to feel divided the day you return to work outside of the home, even when you've gone over why you're doing it a thousand times. Sisters are in love with their babies, and the thought of leaving them in anyone else's care, no matter how excellent it may be, can break a new mother's heart. Take a good look at all your options. There may be a way you can work part time or at home if you plan it well, though it may require some sacrificing from you and your mate.

Going Back to Work Full Time: The most stressful alternative for new mothers, but a reality for two-thirds of all American women with children.

WORKING MOTHERS

- An Ethiopian mother may work 126 hours per week
- A mother in Mali may work 112 hours per week
- A mother in Haiti may work 55 hours per week

From *Material World: A Global Family Portrait*

"Initially I felt horrible for leaving my child. I felt fat, none of my clothes fit. Using the breast pump at work was a hassle; there was no place to do it privately. It took weeks to adjust, but I knew that half the house payments were coming from my salary. The decision was not about me loving my job."

"I cried all day long on my first day back to work. Even the tollbooth operator on the highway felt sorry for me. He said, 'Miss, you need to go back home and be with your baby.' I looked at him sadly and said, 'Yeah, I wish.' "

Advantages: The return of your full salary
Health insurance coverage
The feeling of being back in pace with the work world
A sense of accomplishment
Knowledge that you can resume your career goals
Interaction with colleagues

Concerns: Feeling guilty for leaving the baby with someone else
Missing your baby
Leaking breast milk at work when you think about the baby
Having to pump and store breast milk at work
Feeling rushed, like there's never enough time
Feeling less committed to the job than you were before

Working Part Time: Studies show this schedule is the "dream-desire" of most women who work full time, even nonmothers.

"I never feel like I get anything completely done. I'm half a parent and half a career woman; neither one is fully satisfying. Most of the income goes to pay the sitter and for my commute to work."

"My part-timing works out well for us because we need the extra income. I work three hours a day, five mornings a week at an unchallenging yet unstressful job. It's nice to have that break away from the baby, and she gets to build her social skills with the other children at the sitter's each day."

◇ ◇ ◇ ◇ ◇ ◇ ◇ ◇ ◇ ◇ ◇ ◇ ◇ ◇ ◇ ◇ ◇ ◇

Advantages: Some income
Lower child-care costs
More time spent with baby than with full-time job
Nice to be home when your husband gets home
Ability to keep your foot in the work world
Easier transition back to work after the birth
Ability to spend more time with your mate, friends

Concerns: Loss of income if you formerly worked full time
Often no medical benefits are offered
Commuting costs
May not feel a deep sense of job satisfaction
May not be viewed by colleagues as a full team member
May feel like you aren't doing either job well
Have to express milk and bottle-feed baby (if you are nursing)
May have jealous feelings toward the caregiver

Working from Home: According to LINK Resources, about 10 million people moonlight at home or at another job, and about the same number are self-employed. The Census Bureau reports that 54 percent

Whether you are telecommuting or running your own business, working from home can be extremely satisfying if you count the cost and plan ahead. Chris Corsmeier.

of African-American entrepreneurs surveyed said they operated their businesses from home. Could this be for you?

"Working at home is good, but it really depends on what day you ask me. I get more work done here than if I were in an office. But since I work for myself, I have to constantly harass people to get paid. My husband thinks I can get much more done at home than I actually can, and my mother, who takes care of the baby in our home for free, is getting burnt out."

Advantages: Flexibility of work schedule

Home to see baby's growth, bond with baby, take trips to the park, etc.

Nanny or sitter can come to your home part time

You may eventually make more money than you would at a nine-to-five job

You can work late without worrying

Possibility of feeling more fulfilled than at an office job

No commuting costs or hassles

You can nap during the day (at least when the baby naps)

You may enjoy some tax advantages

Concerns: Requires tremendous discipline to juggle baby and work schedule

There may be many days when no work gets done and you fall behind

No secretary or assistant to help with administrative tasks

You may not be able to afford part-time help with the baby

Your income will probably be erratic, making it hard to budget

People may perceive you as not really working

You may often feel lonely and "out of it"

You must have the space and the money to set up a well-equipped home office (computer, fax machine or modem, printer, telephone answering machine)

Leaving the Workforce Entirely: Many sister-mothers are fed up with their high-pressure day jobs and confessed that they would like to be at home with their families, but who can afford to quit? And furthermore, who can withstand the pressure? The answer seems to be, "Those who want it bad enough." New mothers note that in many black communities the idea of becoming a "home engineer" doesn't sit so well, particularly among older folks. Some remind us of how much they suffered so we could go to work and don't place as high a value on "staying home." Historically, black mothers *had* to work due to the job discrimination their husbands suffered—and still suffer. Be strong in your convictions if you choose this route. As one Chicago mother says, "The question is, Can we make this decision and be guilt free?" Determining what your deeply held values are will make the decision easier. "I feel obligated to do my part to raise up a different generation of black kids that can positively impact society," she explains, "and quitting my job may be what I have to do to achieve it."

*"I had my baby, went back to work for a few months, and real-
ized one day, This is crazy! My husband and I discussed it,
prayed about it, and argued about it, but four months and a lot
of budgeting later, I was able to quit. We've never regretted it."*

*"As a stay-at-home mother, people will often say to me, 'Why
don't you go back to school or get a job to help your husband pay
the bills?' Being there for my children isn't seen as a valuable
thing in society, though we give it a lot of lip service."*

Advantages: Being at home to guide your baby's growth
Ability to bond well with the baby and establish a
    routine
No added stresses from outside work responsibilities
Ability to maintain your home more readily
No commuting, lunch, or work-clothing costs

Concerns: May feel isolated and "out of it"
May feel stuck in a monotonous daily routine
May feel unappreciated
Loss of potential income

Help! Who Will Care for My Baby?

Though we would love to encourage every working sister-mother
to become a telecommuter or a work-at-home entrepreneur, the
reality is that most women will go back to work full time after maternity leave and will have to make arrangements for child care.

Deciding whether you'd like your child care provider to be
Grandma, a live-in nanny, or a day-care-center worker is one of the
biggest choices you will make for your baby—you are giving her over
to someone else's care for many hours a day! Know your options and
what they entail before you make a choice, and have a backup plan
just in case. As always, even with relatives, it is best to put your
arrangement in writing so both parties are clear. Here's some advice
for whichever option you choose.

In-Home Child Care: Best if it's a relative or trusted friend. Your baby will be most comfortable in the familiar surroundings of her own home and will receive individualized care. This eliminates the need for you to pack a bag, wake and dress baby, or transport her to and from the sitter. Some in-home caregivers will do light housekeeping, too. Make sure you are totally comfortable with whom you choose to leave in your house with your baby. Also, remember that you are liable for employment taxes for household employees paid more than $50 per quarter. And to claim a child care tax credit you *must* give the IRS your caregivers name, address, and social security number. Don't become a "Nanny-gate" victim! Talk to an accountant about your options or call the IRS for tax information at 1-800-829-1040.

Live-in Nannies: If you have a spare room in your house, this may be a very feasible option for you. It requires zero packing or travel time and you can be sure that your caregiver will always be on time (important when you have "x" number of minutes to get to work). Many black couples have hired Caribbean and African nannies to be their live-in caregivers and have been pleased with the arrangement. Since room and board factors into the nanny's pay, this can make it more manageable for you financially. Clearly outline your expectations on paper and discuss when the nanny is to be considered on and off duty. You cannot assume that just because she's home, she's available to watch the baby. Many arrangements of this type have been ruined due to such a misunderstanding!

Share-Care: This is an arrangement that you would make with other working mothers or fathers who live close by and with whom you have a close relationship. One home serves as the day-care site and all of the babies are cared for together by a person everyone elects. The costs are split by the number of people in the network (usually about three). The home setting will be more comforting for your baby than an institutional setting.

Day Care comes in three forms: licensed day-care centers; informal family day care, usually done in someone's home; and on-site day care at your company. Licensed centers can be attached to schools, churches, or community agencies, and, though the quality of care may be good, they are often overcrowded. Staff members typically "love kids" but may not be educationally qualified. Family day care, done by a woman in her home, is by far the most popular option. There are typically four to five children of all ages being taken care of at a time (six should be the limit). This can be a convenient option because she may live in your neighborhood and may not mind if you are late dropping your baby off or picking her up. Before your maternity leave ends, pay her a visit during the day to spot-check the following: Does the house look clean and safe for your baby? What living habits does the sitter have that might negatively affect your child? Do the other children seem well cared for? Is it licensed? Many are not. The Health and Human Services Agency in your state can tell you for sure.

Ways to Relieve Separation Stress

Regardless of who you choose as your caregiver, there are some things you can do to make the separation less painful for you and your baby:

◆ Spend quality time. When the child, even a toddler, knows he's the most important person in your life at this time, you're giving him quality time. So when you come home from work, don't rush to make dinner, put away groceries, or make a phone call; go over and hug him first and spend some time catching up. The child will find it hard to adjust to another delay for your time after missing you all day.

◆ Create a nightly ritual in which you "wind down" your baby and put her to bed. You and your baby will look forward to this time. Your husband may do the ritual nighttime bath or story time.

◆ Exude confidence in your caregiver to your child. If you are ambivalent about your decision to go back to work, even a small child will pick up on this and be confused and angry. Feel confident about whatever decision you make and exude that feeling.

◆ Don't worry that your baby will get so attached to your caregiver that she forgets you're the Mommy. Research indicates that your child will not confuse you and your caregiver. A baby as young as ten days old can distinguish you from other females and has a bond with you that's innate.

◆ Don't worry if you miss your baby's first step or first word. It's only a significant event to her when you are there to share it. So the second word or step, with you and your husband there to enjoy it, should be just as satisfying.

A new mom at Detroit's Hutzel hospital discovers firsthand the vital importance of a baby car seat through Chrysler Corporation's Family Road program. The simulator shown here helps new mothers experience how difficult it would be to hold on to a baby in a crash at 20 miles per hour. Too many mothers still believe that they can hold their babies in their laps with a seat belt and be safe (you can't), and most don't know how to use a car seat properly. A baby one year or younger must be in a car seat, preferably placed in the middle of the backseat, *and always strapped in facing the rear.* For more help or information, call the National Highway Traffic Safety Administration's Auto Safety Hotline, 1-800-424-9393. Alice Belton-Thomas/Family Road

What a Baby Needs

You, your mate, and your baby will spend most of your time together at home. There are certain items a baby needs and some things you can live without. Here is a checklist of things for you and your spouse to consider purchasing, some notes from mothers on how you can save money doing it, and a list of adjustments to make in your house or apartment so it's baby-safe.

Baby Items	*Notes for the Frugal*
Portable crib, regular crib	Baby is perfectly fine in a Portacrib, bassinet, playpen, or basket until she attempts to sit up; all should have firm bottoms and unfluffy bedding.

Baby Items

Notes for the Frugal

Cribs should *not* have any of the following: rough edges, exposed bolts, paint with lead, more than 2³⁄₈ inches of space between the bars, a too-small mattress (should fit tightly along sides of crib), less than 22 inches from the mattress to the top of the rail and less than 4 inches from same when sides are lowered.

Crib bumpers

These are only cloth-covered foam rectangles, but can sell for as much as $75. If you sew or know someone who does, you can save lots of money by making them yourself or having them made. You may want to use a Kente cloth print or other ethnic pattern that matches the color schemes in the rest of your home or in the baby's nursery.

Clothes

Try to get at least half of your baby's clothes from friends with older babies; you can get many of the new clothes you want by giving a list of specific items to whomever is coordinating your baby shower.

Diapers

If you can do it, use cloth diapers. They are about one-third cheaper than disposables and much less of a pain to use than they were thirty years ago—no more pins, just Velcro and go. After changing, swish the diaper in the toilet and drop it in a diaper pail (full of detergent and water or vinegar and water, if you'd like them to soak) for later washing. Diaper services still exist and can launder and deliver clean diapers to your door, though it will add to the cost. Weekly cost (NY): about $14 for 80 diapers.

Baby Items	*Notes for the Frugal*
Diaper bag	May be given to you free at the hospital; indispensable if you use a lot of baby toiletries when you change her; when baby gets older, an extra diaper, bottle, and travel wipes thrown into your handbag will do fine.
Diaper pail	Better than a plastic pail is a sturdy, step-on garbage can with a tight-fitting lid; can become a nice trash can after it's no longer needed as a diaper pail; essential for cloth diaper users (keeps the smell in check).
Car seat	Required by law; worth spending on, but find one that's made for newborn to 40 pounds (not 20 or 30), then go straight to a booster seat for a 40-to-60-pound child. For a newborn, pad the seat and sides of the head with blankets. For older babies, make sure the seat has cushioned, bent sides to protect a sleeping baby's head and neck from flopping. Bonus: Many double as infant seats.
Infant seat	Convenient in the early months to have baby recline in while you do other things (you should still be within eyesight). Car seat models can be cumbersome to carry, though; a wicker basket with large handles can serve the same purpose and is more portable. A front or back baby carrier may be more efficient and cost-effective if you don't mind the baby being "on" you most of the time.
High chair	Won't need this until baby is about 6 months old and can hold her head up. It must have the following: a safety strap attached to the chair (not the table); an adjustable table with strong latches on both sides; sturdy, widespread legs.

Baby Items	*Notes for the Frugal*
Baby carrier	One made of strong fabric with good head support for baby is indispensable until about 6 months. Get a carrier that allows baby to face forward or face you. Check for padding at leg holes and on shoulder straps. If you take public tranportation often you'll avoid having to constantly fold and unfold strollers. Later, invest in a sturdier backpack-type carrier that will make you feel more balanced and still give baby a good view.
Sarong	"Wearing" your baby is terriffic for bonding and has been proven to keep babies happier. Requirement: a piece of cotton cloth about 2 yards by 3 yards, or big enough to knot about you and baby; it's best to "wear" babies under 6 months old in front sling or at hip; older, in back.
Stroller	Great for long trips when you don't want to carry baby; forgo light patterns for dark ones since they stain easily; get a sturdy one with a canopy high enough to allow for baby's growth; go for a midrange-priced stroller with good wheels and sturdy parts.
Carriage	Only recommended if you live in suburban or rural areas, rarely drive, do not have staircases, and have storage space for it.
Baby tub	Necessary for baby until he can sit up in a big tub. Look for ones with back support and nonskid bottoms.
Baby wipes	Again, expensive, but convenient; consider thin, white washcloths instead and throw them into the diaper pail with dirty diapers; cotton balls are also an inexpensive option for newborns.

How to Tie a Sarong: A mother from Kouakourou, Mali, in West Africa "wears" her older baby on her back as she does chores. Sarong-style carriers like hers are gaining popularity in the West as black mothers seek to reclaim the valuable traditions of our African heritage. Here is one way to tie a hip sarong for your newborn: (1) The cloth is knotted around the waist like a skirt; (2) then, holding the baby on your hip, bring up one side of the cloth and wrap it around the baby; (3) hold the baby and cloth with one hand and bring the other side of the cloth up and over your shoulder with your other hand; (4) tie the two corners of the cloth together at your shoulder. The top of a newborn baby's head should be visible. © 1993 Peter D. Menzel/Material World

Baby Items
Changing table

Notes for the Frugal
Save money by emptying out a medium-height dresser and putting a wipeable changing pad on top or doing the same with a waist-level table.

Other Items You May Need
Breast pump

Indispensable if you are breast-feeding and returning to work; note that many women say commercial pumps with their stronger suction work best and are worth the cost of renting from your birthing center or hospital, or purchasing.

Books on infant care

Good to have at hand for reference; get some medical, some homeopathic, and compare.

Nice to Have
Washer/Drier

Great to have in your home for constantly dirty baby clothes, especially indispensable if you are cloth diapering and have no nearby washing facilities.

Humidifier

Great when baby catches a cold or has croup.

Electric baby monitor

Wonderful way to hear the baby when you are in another room or outside; most models offer very clear reception.

Baby swings/Harness

Fun for baby and keeps her entertained with little help from you, though it requires supervision; make sure baby can't slip off or injure her fingers on hinges. Sit your baby in the swing at the store before you purchase to make sure that harness swings (ones that attach to the ceiling and let baby bounce) are very well secured; place swing away from reachable objects and out of high-traffic areas in your home. Note: If you notice your baby looking dizzy after using a swing or harness, this may not be the right entertainment for her.

Baby Items	*Notes for the Frugal*
Playpen	Think of it as a mini indoor playground for baby (if she'll stay in it and be happy—some won't); great for naps. Avoid buying wooden ones with slats; holes in mesh playpens should not be large enough that baby can stick her arms or legs through; should have a firm floor.
Rocking chair	Great for lulling baby to sleep, feeding. Look for sturdy construction and comfort; forgo the ones with weaved seats and backs; they tend to be less durable.

Getting Baby Stuff at Low Cost

If you are in a close-knit church or community group, you may find that everything you need for your baby is sitting in the closets of your fellow worshipers and neighbors. Sometimes mothers with older children will volunteer the items, but there's no harm in asking. Many sisters will be glad to unload good-quality clothing that their children have outgrown. And what's wrong with shopping at a thrift shop to find some baby goodies dirt cheap? If either of you is creative, you can do wonderful things with a can of nontoxic paint, some swatches of African fabric, and old pieces of furniture. For instance, an old (but sturdy) TV stand makes a great changing table with some minor alterations. Think thrift, and remember, you'll probably receive shower gifts, naming-ceremony gifts, and other congratulatory gifts that may save you the cost of buying items yourself. There will be many, many opportunities to spend money on your child when it really counts over the next thirty years!

Making Your Home Safe

From a crawling infant's viewpoint the world below your knees is a very interesting place. Hanging cords, plugs, and pennies that fell on the rug are all things your baby will want to grab, chew on, or eat. This is where your parenting skills will begin to get their first bit of real exercise. Baby should be taught the meaning of "No" and

A crawling baby, anxious to try out her new motor skills, can easily get into dangerous situations. Stay close! Diane Allford, Allford/Trotman Associates, Atlanta.

"Don't touch" over and over again until he's in the habit of looking at you before he touches something that might be dangerous. Your watchful eyes and your disciplinary skills are the best prevention for baby-related accidents. *Remember that babies develop rapidly and may suddenly do things you may have never seen them do before, such as roll themselves over.* It only takes a few seconds for disaster to strike, so monitor, monitor, monitor your baby's whereabouts. His safety is your first responsibility as a parent.

A Safety Exercise: "See" for Yourself. . .

It would be impossible to list every possible unsafe situation that your baby could get into in your home. And even if we did, you would never be able to ward against them all and keep your sanity. The key phrase is anticipating your baby's moves and *closely supervising your baby while allowing him to explore.* One of the best exercises we've found to determine what you should move, cover, or remove from your house *before you have the baby* is to get down on your hands and knees and crawl around your entire house and yard, if you have one, looking at things from a baby's vantage point. This takes about

---

HOW'D SHE DO THAT?

It is crucial for a parent to know what their baby is capable of in order to keep the baby safe. This list should give you a *general* idea of what your baby can do and when she may start doing it. More details on baby's development are in Chapter 19, "Your Baby's First Year: Month-by-Month."

By 2 Weeks	Baby can squirm and possibly roll over.
By 3 Months	Baby can roll and grab things.
By 6 Months	Baby can crawl, pull herself up, and pull things down.
By 10 Months	Baby can stand, climb, and maybe walk.

---

a half hour and is a great help in identifying the places and things in your house that would be dangerous to a baby. You will be surprised to find that many ordinary household things that an adult would take for granted could potentially harm or even kill your child. When you are down low you will notice the following ordinary things that are hidden baby accidents waiting to happen in and around your home:

Kitchen/Dining Room

◆ Tablecloths that hang over the sides of your table
◆ Household cleaners, laundry detergent, and other toxic items in under-sink cabinets
◆ Garbage pails
◆ Pots on the stove with their handles turned outward
◆ Spattering frying pans
◆ Hot liquids, hot objects, or bowls of hot foods sitting near the edge of the dining room table
◆ Electrical appliances with cords hanging down from the table or counter
◆ Telephone cords that lead into open phone jacks
◆ An open oven door
◆ An open refrigerator door
◆ Liquor cabinets or rolling bars

Living Room/Bedroom

◆ Common houseplants are very often poisonous.
◆ Sharp-edged furniture
◆ Open dresser drawers that can be used to pull the whole thing down
◆ Chipping paint causes many of our babies to get lead poisoning.
◆ Heavy glass objects on coffee tables
◆ Tiny everyday objects that fall on the floor or rug without notice
◆ Shaky or unstable pieces of furniture
◆ Sewing baskets
◆ Desk items such as scissors, letter openers, pens, and markers
◆ Uncovered radiators, space heaters, or fans
◆ Glass or glass-topped tables
◆ Throw rugs without nonskid backing
◆ Jewelry boxes
◆ Hard candy or nuts left out in candy dishes
◆ Newspapers, books, and magazines can be toxic if chewed on.
◆ Drawers with loops for handles will invite inquisitive toddlers.

A NOTE ABOUT GUNS

Do not keep guns in your home! The American Red Cross estimates that *every day* at least one child is killed by a gun in the United States. Make sure your baby is safe from even the possibility of being shot in your home or in the home of your child-care provider!

Bathroom

◆ Baby in a bathtub unattended for one second
◆ Water that's hotter than 125°F
◆ Medicine that's not in childproof containers
◆ An open bathroom door
◆ A toilet with the seat flipped up
◆ Toxic items in below-the-sink cabinets
◆ Razors
◆ Perfumes and cosmetics
◆ Blow dryers or curling irons left plugged in or on
◆ Clothes or other items left soaking in the tub or in a basin

Outdoors

- ◆ Staircases without baby guardrails
- ◆ Painted banisters (that babies can chew on)
- ◆ Bushes and plants
- ◆ Driveways
- ◆ Open garage doors
- ◆ Open car doors
- ◆ Electric and nonelectric tools left out, or open toolboxes
- ◆ Direct midday sunlight

HISTORICALLY SPEAKING . . .

 Often granny midwives in the South would attend to sisters who were so poor that they had no place for the baby to sleep. The ingenious midwives would pad empty shoe boxes or crates, decorate them by hand, and present them to the grateful mothers as their baby's first "crib." *What We Can Learn:* Expensive cribs and designer furniture do not necessarily make a happy baby. Your sweet newborn doesn't yet know right from left, Gucci from garage sale. Resist the temptation to run up your credit-card bill by buying pricey baby furnishings and designer clothes in the name of "the baby needs this." Give your baby a clean, warm, dry place to sleep and lavish her with loving looks and attention—that's what she desires most.

Choosing a Childbirth Class

Most of the common childbirth classes are based on the philosophy that fear of birth and birthing pains can be reduced by education and the use of various relaxation techniques. Classes are given at hospitals and in private offices. They are usually begun in the seventh month and run about 8 weeks, or, in some cases, a more comprehensive class that starts earlier in your pregnancy and continues into the postpartum period is offered. You and your labor coach will learn what to expect during labor and delivery as you do simulations of the birth process in your classes. This is a great opportunity to bond with your mate and to develop confidence in your ability to meet the challenge of labor—together. The three most popular childbirth management methods are: *Lamaze*, which focuses on short breaths to manage pain; *Bradley*, which emphasizes healthy eating, muscle preparation, and slow, deep breathing to manage pain; and *Read*, which focuses on reducing fear and tension. In each method, the father or coach plays an active role in labor. As you explore, ask about class size (6 or fewer couples is best), class format, and specific emphases. Whenever possible, talk to other mothers who took the entire class and ask them about their birth experience. The big question: Were they really able to use the techniques during labor? Did they help?

Your Baby's Space

Sleeping

Your baby can sleep in your bedroom during the first few weeks of life, but after that it's best for you to give her a place of her own where all the equipment for her various baby routines is handy. Many women who breast-feed enjoy having the baby in their beds with them. Though this is controversial here in the West, other cultures have been practicing it for centuries. A mother's warm body and breathing rhythm are very soothing to a newborn baby unfamiliar with the ways of the cold world. However, there is a danger to this comfy position because either Dad or Mom can accidentally roll over on the baby if she is in the middle, and if she is on the end, she can easily roll off or be pushed off the edge of the bed. (Yes, it *does* happen.) We urge you to resist making this a habit.

Although setting up the crib or bassinet is an event parents take pride in doing when they are pregnant, the baby can do just fine sleeping in a soft, wicker laundry basket, a carry crib, or even in a drawer lined with tight-fitting padding for up to six months. A portable "sleeping kit" is a great help when you're trying to get things done in the house or the backyard and tend to the baby, too— this way you never have to be more than a few steps away from her.

Decorating

Who says a nursery should be painted pink with yellow duckies on it? Not our African ancestors! Rich oranges, golds, reds, browns, greens, and black are often used in the beautiful cloths of Africa. For centuries members of the West African Ewe tribe would commission

Consider using a traditional African Kente cloth pattern for your baby's layette instead of the usual pink or blue. Studies show that contrasting colors and interesting patterns such as these can stimulate a baby's senses without overwhelming. To find vendors that make and sell African-inspired baby furnishings, see "Decorating," below.

a special Kente cloth to mark the birth of a child. Kente cloth in general has always been reserved for special occasions, such as baby-naming ceremonies or outdoorings. Today, everything from layettes to wall hangings to baby towels is available in Kente cloth and Kente-cloth prints—a perfect way to introduce your baby to the natural beauty of her African heritage. Numerous black-owned companies offer many creative items in African patterns. You will have to search a little harder to locate them as they tend to be small or home-based businesses whose products aren't in major department stores. For more information on black-owned companies that sell culturally correct baby and infant items, contact the Black Expo USA, which specializes in presenting the wares of black-owned businesses at annual shows all around the country, at (212) 234–3400.

The Black Book, a directory of black-owned businesses, can also direct you to vendors in your area. Call (718) 638-9675 to order your city's *Black Book*.

HISTORICALLY SPEAKING . . .

 One South African ritual for pregnant women to prepare for their baby's arrival is to hang beautifully colored beads and carvings around the birth room, which is usually in the home, so that the baby looks upon things of beauty at its first sight. Earlier generations often made a special soft cloth from tree bark, which is then stained with pretty swirling patterns and used to wrap the baby in when it's born. What special touches will you surround your baby with? *What We Can Learn:* The baby's sensory world was of value to our ancestors, and attention was paid to what they saw, felt, smelled, and heard at birth and during infancy. Our ancestors felt that these were determining factors in the course of the babies' lives—and they may have a point. Determine what, if any, ethnic images you would like your baby to grow up seeing, enjoying, and ultimately identifying with. It's never too early to start.

Your Appearance

Hardly anybody buys maternity clothes anymore," says Sandra Martin, *Essence* magazine's always-in-the-know fashion stylist, "The days of buying expensive, fussy stuff are gone. Women are comfortable in their husband's shirts, tailored vests and jackets, leggings, tops, and dresses a size or two larger." Martin recalls a creative co-worker who took two elastic-waist floral print skirts, added straps to one to make a top, and wore the other as a long skirt. "It looked great!" That may not be your style but you can be pregnant *and* fine by following a few simple guidelines:

◆ Draw attention up and down. Focus on interesting necklines, flattering jewelry, and the right makeup and hairdo to bring the emphasis upward. Buy good-quality, low-heeled, slip-on shoes

Grace Huang.

and matching or patterned hose. The shoes will make your feet feel good (which is very important when you're carrying a heavy front load) and will focus the attention downward.

◆ Play up your best facial feature (like your voluptuous lips, almond-shaped eyes, or dimpled cheeks) and make it the focal point when you make up. Doing this can cut down on time, too. Be sure to find a light makeup or powder that matches your skin color and helps you enhance your healthy pregnancy glow.

◆ Invest in a sharp hat or beret in neutral or jewel-toned colors to throw on on those bad-hair days. Hat brims should be modest so as not to create another wide silhouette.

◆ Small shoulder pads that attach to your bra strap will give almost any pregnant woman a slimmer look. This works well under sweaters or tops worn with good-quality stirrup pants—a pregnant woman's favorite casual outfit.

◆ African garb looks wonderful, and works as both a beautiful camouflage and a cultural statement. The rich, bold patterns minimize your abdomen and matching head wraps focus the eye upward. Add some funky earrings and go, girl!

◆ Buy pantyhose in a larger size so they aren't binding on your abdomen. Choose knee-high hose with extra-wide bands so blood can circulate more freely in your legs.

◆ Pants with drawstring waists, vests, loose-fitting jackets, and jumpers have been a savior for many pregnant sisters.

◆ For special occasions, use a brooch, scarf, or drop earrings against a black outfit—always chic. Or, for really big deal events, call Mom's Night Out and *rent* a sexy, made-for-pregnancy evening gown, from their catalogue, 212-744-MOMS [6667].

◆ For everyday, check out the Pregnancy Survival Kit, which includes a slim-cut cotton skirt, dress, leggings, and pullover top in basic colors, all designed to coordinate and give you a city-smart look while accommodating your growing body ($150, by Bellybasics, available at major department stores).

CHAPTER 7

You (and Your Baby) Are What You Eat

Your body has been beautifully crafted to nurture, carry, and deliver a baby, but what you eat—and don't eat—during pregnancy can work against even an expertly designed system. The infant mortality rate for black babies (18.8 per 1,000 live births) in America is double that of white babies (9.3 per 1,000 live births) and almost 4 times as high as that of babies in Japan (5 per 1,000 live births), which has the lowest infant death rates in the world. Experts attribute our high infant-death rates to a combination of factors: environmental stresses, racism, poor living conditions, and lack of education about prenatal care, which includes information on a nutritious diet. Though there has been a federal initiative to reduce the number of fetal deaths among African Americans to 11 per 1,000 live births by the year 2000, experts say that not much improvement has been made to date.

Though it is true that the most informed women tend to have the best pregnancy outcomes, nutritionists say that when it comes down to who actually improves their diets, class and education don't make much difference. "You'd be surprised how many well-educated sisters are misinformed about nutrition," says Mable Everett, MPH, a registered dietician and nutritionist at Charles Drew University in Los Angeles who works with pregnant women of all socioeconomic classes. "The nutritional information many women get from a sound bite on the news or from one segment of a TV talk show isn't enough. They only focus on the most fashionable nutrition topic of the day." Sheral Cade, a clinical dietician at Parkland County Hospital in Dallas, agrees: "Most educated, well-read mothers are more *aware* of better nutritional practices, but that awareness doesn't always affect what they *do*."

As a people, we have no more good excuses for not eating healthy, particularly when we're pregnant. Gone are the days when we had to rely on the "comfort foods" high in fat, sugar, and cholesterol that have become a trademark of the black community. Our ingenious foremothers and -fathers made feasts out of the fatty "throwaways" given us by our enslavers, and thus emerged chitlins, ham hocks, pork rinds, and other black favorites. We now know that this "comfy" diet of high fat and cholesterol has led to a disproportionate number of black women and men who suffer from obesity and diet-related illnesses such as heart disease, hypertension, diabetes, and many forms of cancer.

Of course, all manner of advertising tells us to eat healthy, low-fat, light, and lean. And the black press has made great efforts to steer us in the direction of good eating. *Essence* magazine, for instance, has made concerted efforts over the years to skim the fat and salt from the recipes in its popular food section and offer more healthful ways to cook the meals many of us like. The success of new magazines such as *Heart & Soul: The African-American Guide to Healthy Living* also suggests that we are becoming more serious about improving our diets. But old habits die hard. And when you're pregnant and often feeling queasy and uncomfortable, you may lack the motivation to eat the x number of calcium servings and y number of fresh vegetables that you know you should. One problem for mothers-to-be in low-income communities is that they struggle to find fresh foods at affordable prices close to home, notes nutritionist Cade. Middle-income sisters, who can access and afford the proper foods, often buy too many empty-calorie foods and too few nutritious ones, making their struggle to eat properly equally challenging.

Take this opportunity to put your poor eating habits to rest—permanently. It will take a positive attitude, a little preplanning, and perseverance, but the rewards are great—giving birth to a baby with excellent health and getting back into shape again after the birth.

We've Always Known How to Eat Right

Our African brothers and sisters have always eaten a more balanced diet than we do here in America. Although they are quickly adopting more of our Western ways of eating, like fast food, there is a lot we can learn from looking at a typical African diet (see "Historically Speaking . . ."). For instance, in less urbanized parts of West Africa, nutritious diets and physical activity—mostly walking—characterize the lifestyle of most men and women. Since much of the food for the day's meals can be bought at outdoor produce markets daily (ironically, many of the women who sell in the markets are said to be quite large), the fish, meat, and vegetables are at their peak of freshness when they are cooked and served—no preservatives needed. Meals are usually built around the vegetable or starch rather than the meat, which, by contrast, is usually a staple of the typical American meal. Meat is often not as readily available as it is here in the West, so it is more of a special treat.

INFANT MORTALITY: HOW WE RATE

In the United States, high infant mortality rates are mostly caused by poor eating habits during pregnancy and lack of adequate prenatal care. In less-developed parts of Africa and the Caribbean, though, pregnant sisters have it much tougher than we do here in the West. There, health services are scant, and living conditions too-often barely tolerable, and hunger a way of life, even for pregnant women. We should make the most of the foods and services that are readily available to us here in the U.S.

Country	Info on Country	Death per 1,000 Births
Jamaica	Won independence from Britain in 1962	43
South Africa	Held first multiracial elections in 1994	53
Haiti	Once the world's richest colony	86
Ghana	One of the first independent African nations	109
United States	**General population**	**9.3**
	African-Americans	**18.8**
Japan	Lowest infant mortality rate in the world	5

Statistics and information from *Material World*, by Peter Menzel, 1994; *Handbook of the Nations*, Time, Inc.; and the Jamaican and Ghanian consulates.

A typical snack for an African consists of a piece of fruit instead of a bag of nacho chips, and desserts are reserved for special occasions. Their good eating habits provide a wonderful guide for eating well during pregnancy: Buy fresh foods whenever possible to maintain nutrient value, center meals around vegetables, make your favorite fruits your favorite snacks, and view desserts that are not low in fat and high in calcium, like ice-milk or sherbet, as occasional treats. With this in mind, let's examine the nutrients pregnant women require and how you can get them by making some adjustments to your diet.

HISTORICALLY SPEAKING . . .

An Average West African Menu

Breakfast: Bread and tea or a bowl of coco, a cornmeal-based porridge
Lunch: Stew with vegetables, and possibly meat, over rice. Though the stew is made with a good bit of oil, vegetables such as tomatoes or okra, spinach, or garden eggs (a fleshy, squashlike vegetable) provide the dish's main attraction, usually seasoned with onions, pepper, and ginger.
Dinner: Plantain, yam, sweet potato, palm-nut, or ground-nut soup (similar to peanut soup), and either meat, chicken, or fish. Light soup, a brothlike, tomato-based soup, is also popular.
Snacks: Fruits such as mangoes, oranges, and pineapples.
Dessert: None; reserved mostly for special occasions.
What We Can Learn: If we truly want to discover our heritage, the more balanced diet of our African brothers and sisters is a ritual to adopt! Their diet is consistent, it lacks preservatives and additives, and is naturally low in sugar and fat—a healthy eating prescription for pregnancy and for life.

Nutrients You Need

A 1991 study conducted by the Food and Drug Administration indicates that adult American women have insufficient amounts of calcium, magnesium, iron, and zinc in their diets. Most pregnant women in a series of studies conducted by the U.S. Department of Agriculture weren't eating nearly enough green, leafy vegetables, nor were they getting enough vitamin B_6 or folic acid. Deficiencies in these and other essential vitamins and minerals when you're pregnant continue to help increase the number of premature and late deliveries, low-birth-weight babies, neural tube defects (such as spina bifida and anencephaly; see "Get Your Folic Acid," this chapter, for more detail), and other birth defects. Since black women of all classes are generally in poorer health than white women, we must heed this information even more strongly than the general population. "Sisters are still eating a diet that's too high in fat and lacking in calcium and green vegetables," says nutritionist Gardenia Irish. "These poor eating habits get passed on and become family traditions."

You've heard it before—now it's especially important that you get sufficient amounts of fruits and green and orange vegetables. You'll reduce
your risk of cancer, too. Courtesy American Cancer Society.

What's Happening Each Trimester and How to Eat

First Trimester

Many women do not discover that they are pregnant until well into their first trimester and thus haven't been careful about what they ate. If this is you, you should launch a high-nutrient catch-up campaign immediately! The first three months (actually 13.3 weeks) of your pregnancy is a particularly important time to make sure you get sufficient nutrients into your body—and into the baby. The baby lives off of what you eat, and very few nutrients can be stored up in your body for the baby to use later. During the first trimester, your baby's vital organs, including the brain, are beginning to form. By the fourteenth week your baby will be completely formed. That explains why eating well during the first trimester is crucial. Your baby will not need any more calories during this trimester than you normally consume, but you should gain between 2 and 5 pounds over these first three months. Focus on getting *all* the necessary servings from the major food groups *every day at every meal*. Select the "Good" and "Better" foods on the Pregnancy Food Chart—those with higher calorie counts—if you are below your proper weight gain for this trimester. Eat healthy snacks—avoid the junk. A specially formulated prenatal vitamin supplement may be a good choice now to help you make up for any diet slips. Check with your doctor or midwife before choosing vitamin supplements; she may be able to prescribe one for you that is likely to be superior to one bought over the counter.

Second and Third Trimesters

The American College of Obstetrics and Gynecology suggest that 1 to 1½ pounds per week is an *average* amount of weight to gain during your fourth through eighth months, though it's fine to gain slightly less or slightly more in any given week. In the first trimester you may not have eaten any more than you ate prepregnancy, but during your second and third trimesters your baby will require about 300 more calories than you would normally eat. Three hundred nutrition-packed calories—not fats and sweets! Your baby's intricate brain functions are developing at a fast rate during the third trimester and her lungs are reaching maturity. Your baby will double in size in this period alone. Don't fool yourself into thinking that you can load up on high-fat, high-sugar foods to meet your extra calorie requirements. You may gain the suggested amount of weight this way, but one reason why your baby can still be born prematurely or with a low birth weight is because she didn't get the *nutrients* she needed to grow at a steady pace.

How Much Weight Should *You* Gain?

The table below is widely used by health professionals to help women determine the proper amount of weight to gain during pregnancy. A height of 5 feet and weight of 100 pounds is used as a base. Simply add 5 pounds for every inch you stand over 5 feet, in order to determine your Ideal Body Weight (IBW). Example: If you are 5'6" your ideal body weight is 130: 5 x 6 = 30; 100 + 30 = 130. Once you have determined your IBW, check it against your actual weight. Use the Prepregnancy Weight-for-Height column to see how much over or under your IBW you are. Then use the right side of the table to find your recommended total weight gain during pregnancy.

Recommended Total Weight Gain Ranges for Pregnant Women

Prepregnancy Weight for Height	Recommended Total Gain (in pounds) for Pregnancy
Underweight (less than 90% of Ideal Body Weight)	28–40
Normal (90% to 120% of IBW)	25–35
Overweight (120% to 135% of IBW)	15–25
Obese (135% of IBW)	15 or more

"I was put on complete bed rest after my sixth month. I was so bored I just ate and ate and ate until I had gained 93 pounds. I looked like a beached whale! I kept telling my husband, "Oh, honey, there's just more to love, more to love."

Pregnancy Weight Gain

The prevailing idea that you are eating for two during your pregnancy may make you feel like you have the official go-ahead to eat huge amounts of whatever you like for the next nine months. Not so. It's not how *much* you eat, but *what* you eat that makes the difference. The American College of Obstetrics and Gynecology recommends that average-height (5′5″ to 5′6″) medium-build women gain 25 to 30 pounds during their entire pregnancy. Pregnant teenagers, whose own bodies are still developing, should gain 30 to 40 pounds. A study done by the Institute of Medicine showed that African-American and Hispanic women tend to gain less weight than white women, and have smaller babies even when they gain the same amount of weight. What makes the difference? The quality of the diet! You can easily gain the proper amount of weight during your pregnancy and still not be providing your baby with the nutrients she needs to be born healthy and at full weight. While it is true that both women who have gained as few as 16 pounds and those who have gained as much as 50 pounds have had normal deliveries and normal-weight babies, in most cases it is a larger sister who gains fewer pounds during pregnancy and a thin sister who gains more than the average amount of pounds. The larger woman has more nutrient stores that the baby can live off of in addition to the calories and nutrients that she is feeding her baby. The thin woman needs to gain more than the average amount of weight because she doesn't have these stores.

Even obese or extremely overweight women should not gain less than 15 to 20 pounds during pregnancy. You will end up forcing the baby to live off of your own "reserves," the nutrient stores that are keeping *your* body healthy and energized. You will find yourself feeling overtired and sluggish. More seriously, you are running a high risk of delivering a low-birth-weight baby who may have birth defects, behavioral problems, a lower IQ, and other learning disabilities that may plague your child for life.

Conversely, underweight or very thin sisters should not gain more than 40 pounds during pregnancy. Too much weight will put stress on your system and force your body to work harder to sustain the pregnancy and all *your* bodily functions, too. You may be increasing your risk of developing pregnancy hypertension and gestational diabetes, and if a cesarean section is necessary, the extra fat often complicates the surgery. Not to mention that you are giving yourself the foreboding task of having to lose all those extra pounds postpartum. If this is you, factor a moderate exercise program into your pregnancy, with your doctor or midwife's approval. Women carrying multiple fetuses will typically gain weight more rapidly than other pregnant women, particularly in the first trimester, and should aim for a 30-to-40-pound gain overall. Steady weight gain during the second and third trimesters is crucial for all women—thick or thin—to have healthy babies.

On the next few pages you will find a Pregnancy Food Chart that will show you the 5 categories of foods we eat as well as recommended daily servings of each during pregnancy. The vitamins and minerals each category of food offers you and your baby are also noted at the top of each column. This is only a guideline; it is not meant to cause you stress. Take your pick of the foods listed and add other nutritious foods that you already enjoy. We only hope to inform you with this chart, not enslave you to a rigid diet plan. The chart provides suggestions for food servings according to fat and calorie content (labeled Good, Better, and Best) so you can get the nutrition you need without the unwanted fat. Use the chart to help you create a general eating plan that's right for you, and that is one you can follow throughout your pregnancy—and your life—without feeling deprived. Our hope is that if you spend a few weeks tracking what you eat now and make adjustments where they are needed, eating a diet that's high in nutrition will become part of your and your family's lifestyle. Experts say you can add years to your life by eating right and can also shield yourself from the host of diseases that plague us disproportionately. Eat well, gain "productive weight," and give your baby the best possible start in life.

YOUR "BABY WEIGHT"

Here's a breakdown of the 25 to 30 pounds an average adult female gains during pregnancy.

Baby	7½ pounds
Placenta	1½ pounds
Amniotic fluid	1¾ pounds
Uterine enlargement	2 pounds
Maternal breast tissue	2 pounds
Maternal blood volume	2¾ pounds
Fluids in maternal tissue	3 pounds
Maternal fat	7 pounds (essential for breast-feeding)
Total Average Weight	27½-pound weight gain

Become best friends with the fresh fruit and vegetable aisle in your super-market. If you see anything dark, green, and leafy, take it home for dinner!
© Anthony Mills, Allford/Trotman Associates, Atlanta.

Special Diets

Vegetarians

Growing in popularity among African Americans, this diet style runs the gamut from those who eat everything except red meat to those who eat only plant foods (they're called strict vegetarians or vegans). Millions more folks say they are cutting down on meat in their diets, though they would not label themselves vegetarians. Black Muslims, for instance, eliminate pork and products that contain animal shortening from their diets, due to their religious beliefs.

A vegetarian diet can be quite healthy for pregnancy, as it puts all the focus on the vegetables and fruits that the typical American and African-American diet is lacking. A serving of fish or poultry provides you with more protein and less fat than red meat. The main issue with pregnant vegetarians is getting enough protein, calcium, iron, and magnesium. The next three pages show some ways to supplement your diet if you're a pregnant vegetarian.

Best Diet Choices for You and Your Baby

Milk & Dairy Products	Meat & Meat Alternatives	Vegetables & Fruits	Breads & Cereals	Oils & Sweets
Major source of: protein, calcium, riboflavin, vitamins B_{12} and D	Major source of: protein, iron, thiamin, vitamins B_6 and B_{12}, folic acid, copper, and zinc	Major source of: vitamins A and C, folic acid, copper, potassium, and beta-carotene	Major source of: thiamin, niacin, iron, and zinc	Major source of: sugar, fat, and empty calories!
Suggestions **Best:** 1 cup of nonfat milk, buttermilk, 1% or 2% lowfat milk, plain yogurt, nonfat yogurt, fat-free pudding or 2 slices of mozzarella cheese, low-fat cream cheese (or other cheese that has less than 10 grams of fat per serving)	*Suggestions* **Best:** 3 oz., broiled, of fish, chicken, liver, turkey, ham, lean veal, beef, lamb, pork (Note: 3 oz. is about 1/2 a regular chicken breast, 1 hamburger patty, 1 pork chop.) or 1 cup of dried beans, lentils, pinto beans, chick peas, soy beans, or 2 eggs	*Suggestions* **Best:** 1 cup, raw, of cabbage, dark green salad; 1/2 cup of berries, broccoli, cantaloupe, carrots, green beans or peas, split peas, turnip, collard greens, spinach, zucchini; 2 apricots, plums; or 1 medium peach, tomato, or	*Suggestions* **Best:** 1 slice of whole-grain or enriched bread, corn tortilla, taco shell; 1/2 cup of oatmeal, grits, whole-grain rice, (such as wild rice), 5 crackers; or 1/2 hamburger bun, hot dog bun, English muffin, 1/4-inch whole-wheat	*Suggestions* **Best:** 1 tablespoon of coffee creamer, all-fruit spread, honey, sugar, olive oil, canola oil; 2 tablespoons of jelly, cream sauce, gravy, sour cream, low-cal salad dressing **Better:** 1 tablespoon of margarine,

Milk & Dairy Products

Better: 1 cup of whole milk, chocolate milk, low-fat flavored yogurt; or 2 slices of hard cheese (such as cheddar)

Good: 1 cup of milk shake, pudding, custard, hot chocolate

Need: 3–4 servings

Teens: same

Meat & Meat Alternatives

Better: 1 cup of baked beans, chili, refried beans; or 3 oz. of fried chicken, fried fish, steak, rib roast, hamburger, pork or lamb chop; or 2 tablespoons peanut butter

Good: 2 spare ribs, 2 frankfurters, 3 sausage links, 3* slices bologna, 1 can sardines (drained), 1/2 cup nuts

Need: 3–4 servings

Teens: 6 servings

Vegetables & Fruits

(*Best Suggestions cont.*) orange, 1/2 grapefruit; 1/2 cup of fruit or vegetable juice, tomato sauce

Better: 1 medium apple, banana, pear, potato; or 1/2 cup of pineapple, fruit cocktail (in syrup), peas, corn, sweet potato; or 1 cup canned vegetable soup; or 3/4 cup cow peas, kidney beans

Good: 1 1/2 oz. dried fruit; 1/2 small avocado;

Breads & Cereals

(*Best Suggestions cont.*) pancake; 2 tablespoons wheat germ*

Better: 1/2 cup of white rice; or 1 cup of pasta; or 1 biscuit, roll, waffle, pancake, flour tortilla, pita; or 1 cup dry, unsweetened cereal (wheat, corn, rice, oats, barley); or 1/2 bagel; or 1 piece whole-grain corn bread

Good: 1 muffin; 1 cup sweetened cereal; 1/2 cup granola

Oils & Sweets

(*Better Suggestions cont.*) butter, mayonnaise, vegetable oil; or 2 tablespoons of regular salad dressing; or 1-oz. candy bar (about half a bar); or chips (about 10 regular-sized chips); or 2 cookies; or 1 granola bar; or 1/2 cup of sherbet, gelatin; or 12-oz. soft drink (1 can)

Good: 1 tablespoon of vegetable oil or corn oil; 1/4 cup of maple syrup, non-dairy whipped

Needed for:
Growth of your uterus and breasts; increased blood volume; formation of strong bones and teeth; brain, heart, muscle, and nervous system development; growth of placenta

Needed for:
Digestion and appetite, red blood cell and tissue formation; carrying of oxygen to the placenta; brain development; maintenance of the nervous system; growth of placenta

1 medium french fries
1 pickle

Need: 5 or more vegetable servings— 2 should be dark green, leafy; 3 or more servings of fruit—2 should have vitamin C

Teens: 7 servings

Needed for:
Healthy skin and eyes; maintenance of immune system; formation of blood and blood vessels and connective tissue between bones, teeth, tendons, skin, and cartilage

topping; or 1 doughnut; sweet roll, piece of cake, slice of pie, 3 medium cookies

Suggested maximum 3 per day

Need: 7 or more servings—4 should be whole grain choices

Teens: 9 servings

Needed for:
Red blood cell formation; digestion and appetite; growth of bones and tissue; formation of nerve and digestive system

*These foods are high in fat and are likely to contain nitrites, a chemical additive that can be harmful to your baby; eat sparingly.

"Loose" vegetarians, who eat little meat and lots of fish, and fish-only eaters have the easiest time providing their growing fetuses with the nutrients they need since fish is a wonderful source of protein. If this is you, you will not have a problem providing your baby with the necessary nutrient. Strict vegetarians can get their protein and calcium from soy milks and other soy products such as tofu. Though connosieurs of "soy chicken" or "soy fish" may think they're getting whopping amounts of nutrition, note that they contain lower amounts of protein and calcium than you might think, and can also be high in sugar and calories. Check the labels to be sure that a serving will give you a good chunk of the 1,200 to 1,400 milligrams of calcium or the 70 to 100 grams of protein you need each day. Your prenatal vitamin supplement should help make up for the vitamins and minerals you may not get enough of on a strict vegetarian diet, particularly iron; check the label to make sure it does. For those who eat dairy products but no meat (ovo-lacto vegetarians), healthy portions—even double—of low-calorie cheese, milk, and yogurt and eggs daily will provide mother and baby with the extra protein needed during pregnancy.

"I have irritable bowel syndrome and am lactose intolerant. How can I get the calcium and fiber I need during my pregnancy without drinking whole milk or eating those 'bulking' foods that give me gas?"

Lactose Intolerants

According to the National Digestive Diseases Information Clearinghouse (NDDIC), 75 percent of black Americans have trouble digesting milk and milk products. Several lactose-free milk products and digestive aids (tablets that help to break down the lactose in milk into a digestible form) are effective and widely available. If you won't drink milk at all, you will have to eat much bigger servings of other calcium-rich foods in order to get the recommended 3 servings each day. You can get just as much calcium from a cup of chick peas, collard greens, salmon or sardines, or two cups of broccoli, kale, or turnip greens as you can from a cup of milk, except that you have to eat a lot of food to get it. Also, vitamin D and vitamin B_2 (riboflavin) are important for the formation of baby's teeth and strong bones as well as the development of muscles and the nervous system. These vitamins are mainly derived from milk products and are hard to find elsewhere. You should add an egg yolk, an extra 1-cup serving of dark green, leafy vegetables, avocado, or asparagus to your diet *daily* to make up for the loss of these nutrients.

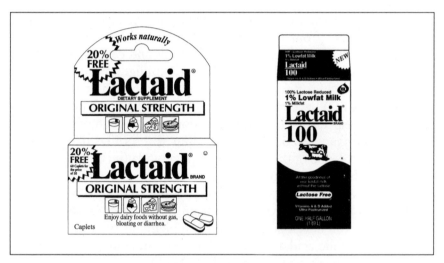

If you experience gas pain or bloating after you drink milk or eat dairy products, you may be lactose intolerant. If so, Lactaid products can help you get the calcium you need during pregnancy without suffering. Lactaid milk has a pleasant, slightly sweet taste, is easy to digest, and can be used for cooking and baking. It contains lactase, the natural enzyme that helps the body break down and digest lactose, the milk sugar found in dairy products. Lactaid milk is available in lactose-free and lactose-reduced varieties. To help digestion of dairy foods and beverages, Lactaid is also available in caplets and drops.

Wheat Allergy Sufferers

Eating wheat is an easy way to get the B vitamins, but if you are wheat sensitive it probably causes you to sneeze, hiccup, or feel congested. You can get the nutrients found in wheat—the B vitamins and other trace minerals—by eating brown rice, whole-rye bread, bulgur, foods made with whole-grain cornmeal, barley flour, oats, chick peas, kidney beans, and lentils. Note that soy products may also cause a negative reaction in wheat allergy sufferers. For more information on food allergies, contact the NDDIC at (301) 654-3810.

All women who have allergies or digestive ailments are advised to take a prenatal vitamin supplement as their caretaker directs to make sure they get the recommended doses of the vitamins and minerals they need during pregnancy. Never exceed the recommended daily allowance (RDA) because some vitamins are toxic in high doses.

GET YOUR FOLIC ACID

Derived from the word *foliage* (which means "plants"), folic acid comes mainly from dark green, leafy vegetables and also, in much smaller amounts, from some breads and cereals. A pregnant woman needs to have only about 1 milligram of folic acid per day to reduce the risk of her baby developing a neural tube defect (NTD), a congenital birth malformation. Still many women—especially black women—don't get enough of it. Each year, approximately 3,000 babies suffer with NTDs like anencephaly (absence of the brain) and spina bifida (incomplete closure of the spinal column). Medical experts recommend that women get as much folic acid from natural sources as possible. This will help protect your baby from NTDs and can also protect you from developing anemia. Supplements of .4 to .8 milligrams of folic acid are usually only recommended to women who have already had a baby with an NTD.

INGREDIENTS: STONE GROUND ENRICHED YELLOW CORN MEAL [CORN MEAL, NIACIN, IRON, THIAMINE MONONITRATE (VITAMIN B₁), RIBOFLAVIN (VITAMIN B₂)], ENRICHED UNBLEACHED FLOUR (WHEAT FLOUR, NIACIN, IRON, THIAMINE MONONITRATE, RIBOFLAVIN), SUGAR, VEGETABLE SHORTENING (CONTAINS PARTIALLY HYDROGENATED SOYBEAN AND/OR COTTONSEED OIL), LEAVENING (BAKING SODA, SODIUM ALUMINUM PHOSPHATE, MONOCALCIUM PHOSPHATE), SALT.

Ingredients: Enriched unbleached flour (flour, niacin, reduced iron, thiamin mononitrate, riboflavin), degerminated yellow corn meal, sugar, partially hydrogenated vegetable shortening (soybean oil), dextrose, leavening (sodium bicarbonate, sodium aluminum phosphate, monocalcium phosphate), salt.

Pay more attention to ingredient lists on the back of food packages like these two cornbread mixes to see how much nutrition you're really getting. Advertising can be deceptive. Remember that ingredients are always listed from most to least.

Foods and Additives to Skip for Good Health

Artificial Sweeteners

Which foods have it? Diet sodas and some "lite" or "fat-free" products; check labels

Why skip? Saccharin is known to cross the placenta and take a comparatively long time for the fetus to eliminate from its system. Also, researchers found an increase in cancer among the offspring of pregnant laboratory animals who were given saccharin. Sweet'n Low contains saccharin and should not be taken during pregnancy. Moderate use of aspartame, another sweetener used in the products Equal and NutraSweet, is generally considered safe. However, the effects of aspartame may also vary depending upon each individual's sensitivity to the product. Since not enough research has been done, the safest route seems to be eliminating artificial sweeteners from your diet and trying some of the many foods now available that are sweetened with fruit or fruit juices.

Sodium Nitrite

Which foods have it? Bacon; sausage; ham; pepperoni; deli meats such as salami, pastrami, and corned beef; frankfurters; cured pork; and smoked fish.

Why skip? Nitrites are added to foods to prevent the growth of the bacteria that produces botulinum toxin, a deadly biological poison. However, the nitrites themselves can be converted into carcinogens in our stomachs and can cause cancer. Since most of these foods contain too much fat anyway, why not just skip them altogether.

Chemical Additives

Which foods have it? Processed foods.

Why skip? Sadly, processed foods make up much of what we eat today. Most of these foods contain some kind of additive—a little chemical "something" to make a product thicker, tastier, easier to cook, longer lasting, or better looking. Some additives are relatively safe, while others have not been tested thoroughly enough to be sure. Some have caused sickness in laboratory animals or have various minor effects on people who are sensitive to them. Although it's unlikely that you can eliminate every possible additive, preservative, or artificial flavoring from your diet, you can minimize the amount of processed foods you eat. When you grocery shop, take note of products that boast "no fat"; they may contain loads of additives, salt, or sugar to compensate for the lack of nutritious ingredients and the lack of taste. *Note:* Chemical pesticides and fungicides are often found on produce such as peppers, apples, and tomatoes. Wash and peel fruits and vegetables thoroughly before eating.

NEWS FLASH: SALT IS NOT TABOO DURING PREGNANCY

As a black woman, you may never have thought you would hear this advice, but as long as you don't suffer from high blood pressure, you can salt your food to taste without worrying about negative effects on your baby during pregnancy. The amount of salt in your blood gets diluted as your body fluids increase, often leaving you with too little salt in your system. Salt helps your baby's cardiac system function. (But don't overdo.)

Foods Cooked with MSG (Monosodium Glutamate)

Which foods have it? Chinese and other Oriental foods, processed foods.

Why skip? This vegetable protein is what makes Chinese food and many packaged convenience foods taste so good. All that's tasty is not good for you, though. MSG is very high in salt and can cause you to retain water. Worse, it is known to cause burning sensations in the chest, back, neck, and face; throbbing headaches; stomach cramps; and hyperactivity. The effects of MSG on the fetus are currently unknown, although experts believe it may have the potential to cause brain damage in infants if ingested in large doses. If you're ordering Chinese food, ask them to hold the MSG.

Raw Fish, Meat, and Other Foods

Why skip? Raw fish such as sushi, and even lightly steamed seafood, can contain parasites that cause hepatitis B. The parasites infiltrate the fish through polluted waters, and even freshwater fish may be contaminated with pesticides. The infections that can arise from eating affected seafood can be worse than those that come from eating spoiled seafood and can cause severe intestinal disorders, among other diseases. Also avoid eating raw and undercooked meat, particularly steak tartar, and raw eggs (found in some health-food shakes). Raw and half-cooked meat can contain harmful bacteria, including the one that causes toxoplasmosis, a disease that can harm the fetus because it is not able to fight off infections as well as an adult. (See Chapter 4, "Your Habits and Your Lifestyle: Being Careful," for more on toxoplasmosis.)

Poorly Refrigerated or Undercooked Foods

Why skip? Poorly refrigerated and undercooked foods simply become breeding grounds for bacteria, which thrive in warm, moist environments. Bacteria causes food poisonings such as salmonella, which lives largely in uncooked meats. Salmonella can be transferred to other foods and into your system via the utensils or plates that were used to prepare the meat before it was cooked. Be sure to wash hands, utensils, and other kitchen items that were used in the food preparation stage before using them during cooking or serving. Refrigerate leftover meat promptly. If you barbecue at home, eat your meat well done during your pregnancy. If you are using the oven, a meat thermometer inserted into the center of fully cooked meat should read 140°F and the meat should not be pink. *Note:* A good rule of thumb is that hot foods should be eaten hot and cold foods eaten cold; foods should not be "warm" for too long.

Stale Nuts and Grains

Why skip? Alfatoxin, a cancer-causing mold, often develops on nuts and some grains that are sold outside, at such places as outdoor fruit and produce stands where the products are exposed.

Making Eating Right Easier

Tips on how to "sneak" more nutrition into your everyday diet:

◆ Sprinkle wheat germ (the heart of the wheat grain) on everything—cereal, salad, yogurt, pasta; you can even use it in breading for chicken, fish, or pork chops or mix it into muffin and cookie mixes. One serving of wheat germ contains a huge amount of protein and concentrated nutrients that we don't usually get in many other foods. Vegetarians should include sesame seeds, sunflower seeds, and nuts or nut butters in their meals and snacks to help get the protein that otherwise would be missed.

◆ Buy fresh or fresh-frozen vegetables and steam them instead of boiling. Not only will you save their precious nutrients from being washed out in the water, but you'll substantially improve the fresh taste and bright color of your veggies, too.

◆ Make your snacking count by including a piece of fresh fruit, a serving of low-fat cottage cheese, lowfat yogurt, whole-grain crackers, or a can of vegetable juice with whatever you are craving.

◆ Drink, drink, drink—you and your baby need lots of fluid. Add some nonfat dry milk powder to your lowfat or skim milk and get a double dose of calcium in one shot.

◆ Pack your sandwiches with dark green, leafy lettuce and tomato slices. This way you get your "salad" even when you don't feel like eating a real one. Some dark, handsome leafies to try include escarole, chickory, and romaine lettuce. The typically used iceberg lettuce contains virtually no nutrients. Another way to get your greens is to put broccoli or some other vegetable on your pizzas. Also, serve side salads in individual plates along with your family's dinner—you're all less likely to pass on it if it's served individually.

◆ Be choosy when you eat out. The entrées on the menu that are broiled, grilled, baked, poached, and steamed are the only ones for you while you're pregnant. Pick through the bread basket and choose the whole-wheat roll or bran muffin over white rolls. White bread has only 20 to 30 percent of of the amount of important B vitamins you would get in whole-grain breads, and many rolls, muffins, and buns are loaded with sugar. Also, remember to go very easy on the butter and ask for sauces and dressings on the side. How about a hearty pea, bean, or vegetable soup to go with that whole-wheat roll you chose? Soups like these, not the thick, creamy, high-calorie ones, make nutritious delicious meals with a moderate amount of calories. The best desserts: fresh fruit with a spoonful of whipped topping.

◆ Eat a potato with your meals as often as you can, always with the skin on. Potatoes are versatile vegetables, delicious steamed, boiled, and sautéed in a light sauce or baked and mashed. They contain fiber, protein, calcium, iron, thiamine, riboflavin, niacin, and loads of vitamin C, much of which is lost if you peel off their skins.

HISTORICALLY SPEAKING . . .

 In parts of West Africa even today, when a woman becomes pregnant a Yoruba medicine man is immediately summoned by her husband to attend to her throughout her maternity. He prepares a special diet for the mother to follow, which he varies from month to month as the pregnancy progresses. Often, the diet calls for some type of freshwater fish, rich in protein. They believe that the woman must eat her prescribed meal the very last thing at night before retiring and first thing in the morning upon rising—even before she speaks a word to anyone. East Africans believe that eating anything hot or drinking hot water while you're pregnant can inadvertently scald the fetus. In the Sudan, a special porridge made from millet (a grass cultivated for its highly nutritious grain) is served to women in their third trimester as they await the birth. *What We Can Learn:* Clearly, a balanced diet is highly valued by our older cultures, with the emphasis placed on eating fresh foods and foods high in nutrients. Rather than adopting superstitious customs, we can learn that our African ancestors placed a high value on nurturing and protecting their babies even while they were in the womb. To Africans, children symbolize hope, prosperity, the perpetuation of life, and the continuance of the tribe or family line. Thus, sisters are conscious that what they put in their mouths is going to nourish their little warrior, too. Do we value our children enough to think before we eat throughout our pregnancies?

"My husband, who's white, used to have to drive into South Central L.A. in the middle of the night to buy the soul food I was craving while I was pregnant. All the way there he would say, 'Baby, you know I love you, don't you?'"

Cravings and Aversions

When you're pregnant, there are a hundred things just waiting to throw you off your diet and exercise plan. Cravings, food and smell aversions, heartburn, nausea, constipation, tiredness, edema (swelling of the feet and hands), and emotional seesaws are some of the most common saboteurs. Understanding why these discomforts are occurring may at least ease your mind, if not your stomach.

Cravings are thought to be caused by the rise in hormone levels that occurs during pregnancy. This rise, which also occurs during the latter part of your menstrual cycle, causes your body to lose sugar stores, producing hunger pangs for specific foods and causing aversions to others. The women we surveyed craved everything from Neopolitan ice cream to artichokes during their pregnancies, and yes, a few sisters *did* say they craved collard greens and watermelon! Your senses of smell and taste will also be heightened during pregnancy. Sisters said they had strong attachments to certain smells like auto fuel and onions, and strong aversions to things like the smell of greens cooking or of certain aerosol sprays. Many women felt they were craving the foods that contained nutrients that were deficient in their diets, as if the baby were sending requests to feed it what it wasn't getting through their normal diets. This theory is commonly expressed by pregnant women and may even be a plausible one, according to some nutritionists, though no scientific studies bear it out. One hitch in this theory would be the fact that our bodies also crave foods that clearly *aren't* good for us, so what message is the baby sending when we are longing for a package of double chocolate Ring-Dings?

Don't wait for messages from the baby to prompt you to eat well. And don't let cravings and aversions throw you off your good eating plan. Fool your taste buds by eating something similar to but healthier than what you're craving. A craving for chocolate could be placated by carob cookies or a piece of chocolate cake made with low-fat milk and egg whites. A passion for high-fat nacho chips might be alleviated by thinly slicing potatoes (with skins), baking them on a cookie sheet, and sprinkling them with cheese. Similarly, an aversion to salad may be transformed by stuffing the dark green leafies, tomatoes, and other veggies in a whole-wheat pita pocket and adding a sliced, broiled chicken breast. Doing something to take your mind off the object of your craving or aversion may also help. If all else fails, ask your husband for a big, soothing hug. That might provide enough of a pleasant distraction and may shift your craving to some other pursuit—even one that burns calories!

◇◆◇◆◇◆◇◆◇◆◇◆◇◆◇◆◇◆◇◆

"I remember being nine months pregnant in Toys "R" Us on Christmas Eve with my husband, searching for something to get our older kids at the last minute. A woman shopping across the aisle from us had just let go of some serious gas! I tell you I had to run into another aisle and crouch down between the stuffed animals for five minutes just to keep from throwing up!"

◇◆◇◆◇◆◇◆◇◆◇◆◇◆◇◆◇◆◇◆

"I had migraine headaches, severe nausea, and every other sickness you could imagine throughout my pregnancy. I was sure I was going to have a deformed child because of how poorly I was eating. I just couldn't keep anything down. Even my own normal body odor made me nauseous!"

◇◆◇◆◇◆◇◆◇◆◇◆◇◆◇◆◇◆◇◆

"I don't even know what morning sickness feels like. I never had a moment of nausea during my pregnancy. Some say it's because I had boys instead of girls."

◇◆◇◆◇◆◇◆◇◆◇◆◇◆◇◆◇◆◇◆

Pregnancy ("Morning") Sickness

Believe it or not, morning sickness is actually a good sign that your pregnancy is going well. It also arises from the hormonal changes taking place early in your pregnancy. While some sisters reported that they had only minor "upsets" that went away by their second trimester, others suffered with morning sickness all day or for most of the nine months. Some women use up all their vacation days from work because of pregnancy-related nausea and vomiting. A survey done by *Shape* magazine's *Guide to a Fit Pregnancy* showed that about 10 percent of respondents lost more than 15 days of work because of pregnancy sickness. Other women have to be hospitalized, and still others spend a fortune trying to cure it on their own. Pregnancy sickness is a topic that everybody and their mothers (*especially* their mothers) have an opinion on or a cure for. Though no remedy is guaranteed to cure morning sickness (or all-day sickness, for some women), here is some basic advice that will help and some remedies that mothers said helped them.

◆ *Spread it around.* Eat small meals and snack often throughout the day instead of eating three big meals. This way your stomach won't have to cry out with emptiness, eliminating one major cause of morning sickness.

◆ *Skip it.* Simply avoid having to prepare the food items that make your stomach turn—invite your spouse or a family member to cook the meal for you.

◆ *Drink it away.* Cool or frozen drinks, seltzer, ginger ale, fruit ices, fruit juices, and broths may all calm your queasiness and will replace the fluids you may be losing by frequent vomiting. See "Mix It Up!" at the end of this chapter for a great shake idea.

◆ *Treat it ginger-ly.* Generations of midwives and childbearing sisters are sold on the restorative benefits of ginger—take it raw (suck on a thin slice) or in tea, ale, or cookies (if you must). Ginger is known for helping to relieve intestinal gas and stomach gripes and has a natural antinauseant effect. Lemon and raspberry leaf teas are also commonly used to calm a nauseous stomach. See "Honest Herbs" later in this chapter for more.

◆ *Munch and crunch.* Plain or whole-wheat crackers, unsalted pretzels, rice cakes, or other fairly bland carbohydrates often help morning sickness. Keep them right by your bed so you

Roni Ramos Photography, Inc.

can eat them *in* bed as soon as you wake up. Jumping up out of bed with nothing in your stomach will only feed your feeling of nausea.

◆ *Join the band.* Millions of pregnant women have reportedly found comfort wearing seasickness (acupressure) bands on their wrists. They have no known negative side effects and cost about $10 a pair at local drugstores.

◆ *Take a hike.* Relax, go for a slow walk on your lunch hour, or take a regular nap. Women who are stressed out during their pregnancies tend to be the ones who complain most about morning sickness.

◆ *"B" good to yourself.* Some studies show a decrease in bouts of pregnancy sickness in women who got adequate amounts of vitamin B, particularly B_6, and folic acid (also a B vitamin) in their diets. Check the nutrition labels of the food you are eating to make sure you get the recommended daily allowance (RDA) *for pregnancy* of B_1 (thiamin), B_2 (riboflavin) and B_6 and B_{12}. Get enough folic acid by eating dark green, leafy vegetables daily.

◆ *Get professional help.* About half of all pregnant women experience morning sickness. For many women, the nausea ends with the first trimester. For others, particularly those who have a history of this condition during pregnancy and those carrying multiple fetuses, it continues for the entire 9 months. If your sickness is unbearable, your caretaker may suggest an antacid or give you a prescription drug. If the sickness is so severe that you are not gaining enough weight, you may need to be hospitalized. Nutrients will be fed to you intravenously in the hospital and you will be given an antivomiting medication.

HISTORICALLY SPEAKING . . .

 According to *Folks Do Get Born*, a wonderful chronicle of the life and times of granny midwives in the South, typical teas "prescribed" to pregnant women included black haw-root tea to guard against miscarriage and wild cherry-bark tea to ease "body trouble," among others. *What We Can Learn:* Prescription medicine and even over-the-counter preparations were prohibitively priced and virtually unavailable to most southern black families in the early 1900s. Midwives were desperate to provide salves for their pregnant womenfolk. Herbs were a readily available, inexpensive, and effective treatment for whatever ailed you. Today we are rediscovering the value of herbal remedies but the industry remains underdeveloped. This is mostly because large pharmaceutical companies see little in the way of profit potential (plants can't be patented, so no one company can "own" the right to their use). Though the temptation to try an herbal remedy recommended to you by a family member may be great, be smart. Many herbs are much more powerful than they look. We know so little about their long-term effects, especially on an unborn child, that they're too risky to try. For now, stick to herbs that have been widely approved for safe use. Note that doctors caution against drinking senna and goldenseal teas, which are popular among blacks, during pregnancy.

Honest Herbs

Herbs and herbal teas were used by our granny midwives in the olden days for everything from thrush to body aches—and often they worked. But herbs can be powerful medicine in certain quantities, and dangerous in the hands of a novice. The effects of herbs on pregnant women have also not been studied by the medical community, thus the industry remains highly unregulated. Some herbs that seem safe can trigger allergic reactions, and others can be toxic. For these reasons, we recommend that you *use caution in choosing which herbal teas to drink during pregnancy.* Tea made from cinnamon, mint leaves, ginger root, and orange or lemon rind are safe to drink and can help ease pregnancy sickness. Raspberry leaf tea has been used for generations as a preventative for nausea and to strengthen and relax uterine muscles, making contractions easier to bear. No ill effects have been documented to date.

Mix It Up!

Experiment by mixing some of the following ingredients in your blender, according to your taste, and you're in for a treat that's loaded with nutrients and may ease your quease.

> *¹/₂ cup low-fat milk*
> *¹/₂ cup plain or vanilla low-fat yogurt*
> *¹/₄ cup concentrated or ¹/₂ cup fresh-squeezed orange juice*
> *¹/₂ banana*
> *1 cup of frozen berries, ¹/₂ cup fresh berries*
> *¹/₂ cup mango or papaya chunks*
> *¹/₈ cup wheat germ*
> *¹/₂ teaspoon vanilla*
> *¹/₄ teaspoon grated ginger root or nutmeg*
> *¹/₂ teaspoon honey or sugar*
> *juice of one lemon or lime*
> *ice cubes*

A final note: What works during pregnancy will work postpartum. A high-nutrient diet will always serve you and your family well. (For more see Chapter 16, "Postpartum Recovery.")

CHAPTER 8

Filling Your Inner Tanks:
Spiritual, Emotional, and Mental

During pregnancy, with its wildly fluctuating hormones and strange new sensations and cravings, many women feel like their bodies were invaded by a Martian from outer space! Nausea, heartburn, and your ever-enlarging abdomen can sometimes make you feel lousy. Feelings of anxiety about childbirth and impending motherhood can also conspire to overwhelm you. Arming yourself to combat these feelings during your pregnancy means attending to your three most important "tanks"—spiritual, emotional, and mental—on a daily basis. In this chapter, we will discuss each of these tanks and offer suggestions on how you can keep them filled during your pregnancy and beyond. But first, let's briefly examine public enemy number one: stress.

BY THE WAY ...

Did you know that your baby's heartbeat quickens when you are stressed out?

Stress: A Familiar Foe

The National Black Women's Health Project has estimated that 50 percent of black women are undergoing some sort of emotional distress. When you factor pregnancy into this foreboding statistic, it spells even more trouble. Studies conclude that women who are stressed out experience more morning sickness during pregnancy, more pain during childbirth, and produce more preterm babies than women who are mentally and physically relaxed. Dr. Grantly Dick-Read, an English obstetrician who helped introduce the idea of natural childbirth in the 1930s, was one of the first to point out that there was a relationship between stress and the level of pain a woman experiences in childbirth. His opinion was that the pain could be greatly lessened if mothers-to-be were taught to relax using deep breathing techniques and if they were shown how to keep fit and limber during pregnancy. Sounds like common sense, right? So why aren't more sisters practicing it?

Pascal Sacleux, Allford/Trotman Associates, Atlanta.

Since it's often the behaviors following a "stress attack" that lead to trouble for you and your baby, your aim should be to identify areas that cause you stress and learn how to dismantle their effects. For example, allowing moments of sadness or disappointment to escalate into despair can easily coax you back into old habits that can harm your pregnancy. That habit may be overdosing on junk food or, worse, smoking, drinking, or doing drugs. These indulgences may offer you a temporary respite for the stress, but they can be at the expense of your baby's healthy growth. Let's go on to discuss ways to manage your "tanks" so your feelings don't send you spiraling.

Your Spiritual Tank

"Come unto Me all ye that labor and I will give you rest."

In our opinion, grounding yourself spiritually is the most important thing you can do for yourself and your baby. Physical exercise is important, but experts agree that spiritual exercise is essential. More and more couples have told us of the good fruit they are reaping in their marriages and family lives as a result of having developed a personal relationship with God: They each have more to pour out because their spiritual tanks are being filled daily.

Being "spiritual" is no new thing to black folk. Many of our African brothers and sisters were and are quite fervent in their dedication to religious mythology, ancestral spirits, and animism (a belief that spirits inhabit objects and animals). But though many folks say they've found God in a crystal, in a statue, or in the sun, ultimately we are looking for a counselor, someone who can relate to us, somewhere to go to get embraced, replenished, and loved. "In the Spirit," the monthly column written by *Essence* editor-in-chief Susan Taylor, is one of the most popular features in the magazine because sisters are hungry for spiritual guidance. As a people, we have always come back to the Creator to seek comfort and direction, especially during difficult times. We were the first to praise God when things went well—and to accept it as God's will if they didn't.

Granny midwives in the South made it their business to pray together regularly before they went about their job "catchin' babies," often under the most horrendous of conditions. In some cultures, the expected place for a father-to-be *to be* during childbirth is on his knees in a nearby place, praying for his wife and the safe delivery of his child. (Not a bad idea, men.) What better time to get spiritually connected than when you're about to bring a life into the world? Reverend Handy Nereus Brown, a prominent African-American author and speaker in the early 1900s, gives wise instruction to sister-mothers-in-waiting. He shared the following advice about the awesome responsibility of a mother-to-be in his book, *The Parents Guide*, which was published around 1904:

> During the state of formation the mother is more responsible for what goes into the child's life than the father and should be educated as to the result of her thoughts and life upon the character of her child. Samuel [who became a faithful judge, prophet, and

priest] was conceived in prayer, formed in devotion and born in the thought of promotion. He was asked of God, trained for God, and given to God. Every mother should fix her mind on the calling of her child before conception, during formation, and deliver him to God in parturition [childbirth].

A number of fascinating studies support Reverend Brown's idea: that your developing baby can sense whether or not you are joyful and at peace about the pregnancy *and* that this "knowing" has an effect on your child's personality and predispositions.

There is a depth of joy about your pregnancy, impending birth, and motherhood that only comes when you have a deep sense of personal security, a sense that "no matter what I have to go through, I am equipped and empowered to handle it." We believe that security comes from having a good understanding of who you are so you can revel in how expertly God has created your body for just such a time as this. "Whatever spiritual life you have, make it central," says Dr. Brenda Wade, family psychologist and author. "Your center cannot be your husband or your baby, if it is, you're going to be miserable."

Here are some ways to nurture your spirit:

◆ Commit yourself to having regular "quiet time" for at least 15 minutes a day. During this time you can stay quiet and hear what God may want to tell you, you can talk to God about the struggles and triumphs in your pregnancy, you can read from the Bible, listen to a gospel tape, or do all of the above! The important thing is that you make the time to "meet" with God regularly. The Bible is full of verses that provide love, comfort, and insight to every situation. As we pray, the words often begin to "speak" to our specific situations and give us that "you can do it" spirit—something you will need a lot as your pregnancy progresses.

◆ Receive the depth of God's love for you into your being. Affirm that you are loved by God, verbally, out loud, so you can know it in your soul. Let it change and renew you. In the book of Jeremiah, God restored the people by reminding them of His love: "I have loved you with an everlasting love, I have drawn you with loving-kindness. I will build you up again. . . ." (Chapter 31). Allow His presence to build you up again each morning, freeing you to be who He made you to be—gifted, treasured, unique, important, and intended for greatness.

◆ Use a devotional handbook to help you along. Devotionals provide structure to your quiet time and can also help you keep
regular appointments with God. Some to try: Susan Taylor's *In
the Spirit*; *Mother's Devotional* by Mimi Varberg; *Bible Readings
for Mothers* by Mildred Tengbom; or check out *Chosen Vessels:
Women of Color Keys to Change* by Rebecca Florence Osaigbovo
for a look at our spiritual history and our God-ordained destiny
as black women. For nonreligious meditation try: *Black Pearls*
and *Black Pearls for Parents* (an accompanying journal is also
available) by Eric Copage and *Girlfriend to Girlfriend: Everyday
Wisdom and Affirmations from the Sister Circle* by Julia Boyd.

◆ Read or listen to inspirational teachings by men and women
whom you admire. We all get renewed as we hear others sharing their struggles and triumphs as they held fast to God.
Often there's nothing like a good "testimony" from someone
about how they overcame adversity to rev up your own spirit.
Make time to spend in meaningful, *uplifting* conversation with
other sisters—especially other women with children, pregnant
sisters, and older mothers who are pressing on with God.

◆ Pray for the baby in your womb. In their helpful book, *Praying
for Your Unborn Child*, Francis and Judith Macnutt recommend
placing your hands on your belly and thanking God daily for
the baby growing inside you. Prayers don't have to be fancy to
be effective. If possible, ask your husband to join you as you
pray for the baby. It will be a wonderful bonding experience for
your marriage and the baby will learn to distinguish his strong
voice, too (after its fourth month in the womb). If you're uncomfortable making up prayers, here's a sample: "Thank you
Lord for this baby, thank you for blessing and protecting it as it
grows into the wonderful child you want it to be. Thank you
for entrusting this precious life to us. Amen." Here also are
some Bible verses related to creation that will be helpful as
you pray for your baby: Psalms 139 verses 11–14 and 15–18;
Isaiah 49:15–16; Isaiah 42:2–4; Psalm 121; Luke 1:36–44;
John 16:21–22.

◆ Begin to formulate your personal mission statement. Promoted
by author Stephen Covey in his best-seller *Seven Habits of
Highly Effective People*, a personal mission statement should
answer the following questions: What was I born to do? What
are my deepest-held values, the ones I am eager to pass on to
my child? Imagine, if you can, your child grown up and eulo-

gizing you at your funeral. What would you want her to say about you as a parent, as a person? All of the couples we interviewed said that expecting their new arrival caused them to take a serious look at themselves, their lifestyles, and their values—this exercise is a great way to start.

HISTORICALLY SPEAKING . . .

 One Ugandan saying goes like this: "Pay attention to the pregnant woman! There is no one as important as she." *What We Can Learn:* Take this wise advice to heart and treat yourself accordingly. Regard your growing body with awe and wonder and do whatever it takes to guard that new human being forming inside you.

Your Emotional Tank

Flowers sent "just because." A pleasant call from an old friend. Praise from your boss. A shopping trip where everything you put on looks great *and* is 50 percent off. An unexpected hug and kiss from your honey (or, better yet, a warm-oil massage). These are some of the things that pregnant women say fill their emotional tanks.

Having a shouting match with your mate. Feeling unappreciated and unattractive. Feeling alone in your pregnancy. Working like a dog and still feeling like you're behind. Having no time for yourself. These are some of the things that pregnant women say drain their emotional tanks.

During pregnancy, your emotions can run amok. Some women experience mood swings and irritability, similar to PMS, which are considered normal during pregnancy; others suffer mild to deep depression. Circumstances and relationships, especially with your mate, greatly affect your emotional state when you're pregnant. Notice how most of the situations described above involve others' reactions or lack of attention to your feelings. As black women, our emotional condition is too often dependent on what others are or aren't doing *to* us. Studies indicate that when you are pregnant, this emotional vulnerability can worsen morning sickness, cause over- or under-eating, and, left unchecked, can even cause premature labor. Although we cannot totally control our circumstances or the behavior of others around us, we can develop our own sense of personal security—the key to emotional health. "It's not what happens to us, but our response to what happens to us that hurts us," says Covey.

Here are some ways to help stabilize your emotions, based on *Seven Habits of Highly Effective People*:

◆ Seek meaningful, cooperative relationships with others. When you are secure within yourself, you have the energy to strive for compromise with and a deeper understanding of the people in your life. When you aren't wrapped up in "making your point," you can be an active listener.

◆ Ask yourself: Am I listening to others, or merely hearing? Practice becoming an active, empathic listener, listening with the intent to understand instead of respond. You will be surprised as you find out what people have really been saying!

◆ Seek gratification from helping others in meaningful ways that you find personally fulfilling. Think about the people in our history whom most of us admire: Jesus Christ, Martin Luther King, Sojourner Truth, Frederick Douglass, Madame C. J. Walker, Malcolm X, Fannie Lou Hamer, Gandhi, Mother Teresa, Harriet Tubman. They are known because of their tremendous contributions to humanity, contributions they made with great passion and dedication. Many of them gave their lives for the greater good.

HISTORICALLY SPEAKING . . .

 As we all know from conversations with older women in our families, there are many superstitions in African and Caribbean cultures surrounding the precautions pregnant women should take to protect themselves and their babies from harm and evil spirits. Women in Jamaica believe that a mother should not even *look* at anything that will upset her during pregnancy, as they believe it will also upset the baby. Pregnant women are also discouraged from being involved in any "cheap talk" or potential quarrels. Some expectant Nigerian tribeswomen go so far as to cover their bellies with their hands if they see something frightening, as if to cover the eyes of the baby. What We Can

Learn: Although we reject superstition, there are scientific links between a mother's emotions and those of her unborn child. For example, studies have shown that as a pregnant woman becomes frightened, upset, or anxious, hormones like adrenaline are released into her blood-stream and the fetus becomes irritated. Several mothers who had to face family crises and other stressful situations during their pregnancies recalled that they felt contraction-like pains through-out the stressful time. And we know for sure that stress plays a role in prolonging labor. Focus on building destressing rituals into your life now. They will serve you well as the years go by.

Your Mental Tank

Mental renewal—freeing your mind from the humdrum and exploring new thoughts, reading, writing, planning, and organizing—these are all ways to keep your mind stimulated when you're "waiting for the baby." Every piece of information you take in during pregnancy doesn't have to be about pregnancy or childbirth. Take a break from the how-tos and the what-to-expects now and then and read a book about the civil rights movement, cyberspace, economic development, or youth in Asia. Write your own thoughts and opinions down on paper. Who knows? You may discover that there's a book, poem, magazine article, or movie script waiting to be written *by you*! (It worked for successful sister-author Terry McMillan and many others.)

Here are some mental stimulators for you to consider:

◆ Read more inspiring books. Here are some of our favorites: *I Know Why the Caged Bird Sings* by Maya Angelou, *The Soul of Politics* by Jim Wallis, *Beyond Charity* by Dr. John Perkins, *Brothers and Sisters* by Bebe Moore Campbell, *My American Journey* by General Colin Powell, *Gifted Hands* by Dr. Ben Carson, *My First White Friend* by Patricia Raybon, and *The House on Mango Steet* by Sandra Cisneros.
◆ Engage in meaningful conversations in which you express your feelings clearly and concisely (of course, listening emphati-cally, too).
◆ Make a list of your ultimate life goals and aspirations. Visualize

yourself doing the things you wrote down. Break them down into smaller, do-able pieces and get inspired to begin your exciting journey!

◆ Write some really good letters.
◆ Keep a journal. It will help exercise your mind as you step out of yourself to write about yourself.
◆ Challenge yourself (and your mate) to pare down to one hour of TV a day or less—spend some of that newfound time talking and dreaming out loud together. Also, the routine of restricting TV watching will help your child become more expressive and less media-hypnotized.

CHAPTER 9

Your Physical Tank

Few of our mothers were busy thinking about how they could sneak in a cross-country race during their sixth month of pregnancy. While most of us have no intention of keeping up a world-class athlete's fitness routine during pregnancy, many sisters have discovered the tremendous benefits of regular exercise and want to continue to keep their figures in check while they are pregnant. Many medical and fitness experts agree that moderate exercise can be quite beneficial for pregnant women, particularly those who had an active prepregnancy lifestyle.

The benefits of being physically fit during your pregnancy are numerous—after all, as one medical expert put it, childbirth is an athletic event. Exercise will help tone the muscles in your legs, abdominals, and pelvic area, which will aid tremendously when you're pushing the baby out. Your improved cardiovascular strength will help you manage those potentially long hours of labor with less strain and less huffing and puffing. Studies conducted by James Clapp, M.D., director of research in the obstetrics and gynecology department of the MetroHealth Medical Center in Cleveland, Ohio, indicated that women who exercised regularly during pregnancy were able to cut their labor time by one-third and generally had easier labors, reducing the need for interventions such as epidurals, episiotomies, and pain-killers. Plus, being fit when you're pregnant, just like being fit while you're not pregnant, is emotionally satisfying and boosts your self-esteem, confidence, and personal strength—tremendous preparatory steps for one of the most physically challenging events of your life. "In addition to the physical benefits, exercise is a major stress reliever," says certified aerobic instructor Alicia Villarosa, who is also a CSW. "A structured exercise routine, or even dancing to your favorite tape or CD, can cause the endorphins to kick in, lifting your spirits and giving you that 'exercise high.'"

According to the experts, the best candidates for exercise during pregnancy are women who were already doing moderate exercise regularly before they became pregnant. Moderate means you exercised aerobically *at least* three times per week, for 20 minutes or more each session. This makes sense because a regular exerciser probably knows her body's limits better than someone who is just beginning.

If you can get used to this squatting position and practice it as often as possible during pregnancy, you will give your inner thighs and pelvic muscles a great stretch—perfect childbirth prep.

Most regular exercisers can work with their pregnancy caretaker to determine whether they can continue exercising through pregnancy with a few modifications to ensure safety (see "Guidelines for Exercise during Pregnancy," later in this chapter).

Both the American College of Obstetrics and Gynecology (ACOG), which polices the childbirth industry, and the March of Dimes, which focuses on the prevention of birth defects, recently gave the green light to pregnant women who want to do more challenging levels of exercise *if they are fit for it.* (The ACOG's recommendations until 1994 cautioned against exercise routines that raise a pregnant woman's pulse rate above 140 beats a minute, as would a 20-minute ride on a stationary bicycle at a moderate speed.) If you are just starting a regular exercise program start slowly and increase the exercise slowly as you become more comfortable with the routine. If you are a smoker (even if you quit when you got pregnant) you have decreased lung capacity and should choose a less strenuous exercise routine to compensate for the additional stress to your cardiovascular system. Obese, sedentary, and overweight sisters should do the same. Women with high blood pressure or asthma should consult their practitioners to ensure safety while exercising. All women, fit and less fit, are advised to let their doctor or midwife know what type of exercise routine they are doing or are planning to do and to adhere to his or her advice.

If you were not a regular exerciser, or even if you were sedentary before you became pregnant, you can begin an exercise program during maternity. However, experts advise that you follow a simple routine. Consider brisk walking outdoors or on a treadmill at low resistance, climbing a stair machine (if your knees can handle it), taking a low-impact aerobics class, or stationary cycling a few times a week for 12 to 20 minutes each session. You should not embark on a more strenuous exercise program during your pregnancy if you were sedentary. Use the questions in the box on the next page to help determine whether your prepregnancy activity level is high, moderate, or low, so you can choose a regimen that best suits your level of fitness.

HOW FIT ARE YOU?

Circle one answer for each statement.

1. Before I became pregnant, I did an aerobic workout (for 20 minutes or more):
   once every so often (20 points)
   once or twice a week (10 points)
   three times per week (5 points)
   four to five times per week or more (2 points)

2. In my daily routine, I:
   work at my desk or computer terminal (20 points)
   go up and down stairs frequently and walk much of the time (10 points)
   walk to work often/walk briskly during lunch hour (2 points)

3. Of the following activities, I have recently participated in:
   tennis singles; lap swimming; basketball; soccer; racquet sports; roller or ice-skating; fast-paced, aerobic walking; aerobic gym workout (2 points)
   tennis doubles, volleyball, biking, softball, brisk walking, golf (without cart), bowling, leisurely walking (10 points)
   none of the above (20 points)

If you chose the higher scores on 2 or all 3 questions, you should start exercising very slowly, with your doctor or midwife's guidance. If you scored low on 2 or all 3 of the questions, you are well conditioned and prepared to continue exercising through your pregnancy. If you scored in between, choose a moderate exercise routine.

Your Body Image

The way you view your pregnant body has a lot to do with whether you will spend your pregnancy frustrated and dissatisfied or whether you will enjoy the miracle of the child growing inside your body. And how we feel about ourselves and our bodies during pregnancy is far more important than what society says. Women in most African and West Indian countries revel in the beauty of their growing bellies and breasts during pregnancy. Their fertility symbolizes the continuity of life. They bathe, oil, massage, and pamper their bodies in preparation for the great event. Research from the University of Texas at Austin showed that rural women in the last stages of pregnancy had a better outlook on their bodies than their "citified" counterparts. So, city women, listen up! "This is not a time to be worried about every curve," reminds Villarosa. "Your body's going to house another human being. It's a miracle." You have the most awesome job anyone can hold—glory in it. You are beautiful! During pregnancy, when you see your

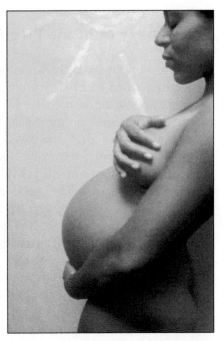

Pascal Sacleux, Allford/Trotman Associates, Atlanta.

skin "glowing," as many women do, due to the fact that more blood is flowing under your skin, enjoy all the compliments you'll probably receive—they're true. As your abdomen swells, think about how more space is being made for the baby to grow healthily. The bigger you get, the closer you come to the big day. When you see your breasts growing or leaking colostrum, think, My body can provide food for another human being (among other fun things you could say about having bigger breasts!). If you stay grounded spiritually, stay well informed about your body changes, get regular exercise, and eat well, you are sure to feel happier about your changing shape. Of course, your mate has a part to play too. His job is to keep your spirits up and love you in ways that you love to be loved, to tell you you're beautiful, and to reassure you that you are more than equipped for the task ahead. (If he didn't know this was his job, let him know!)

Being Overweight and Pregnant

If you were overweight when you got pregnant you are not alone: About one-third of black women between the ages of 25 and 34—prime childbearing years—are overweight, and 50 percent of all sisters of any age are tipping the scales. Although health officials often use weight tables that are based on the builds of white men and women to determine what our "ideal" weights should be, if you were topping those charts by 20 pounds or more *before* you got pregnant you are overweight. The good news is: Overweight women give birth to healthy babies every day. You should know, however, that there is a link between excess weight and cesarean section because the fat can hinder your uterine muscles from pushing the baby out successfully. You are also at risk for acquiring gestational diabetes. Your heart must work overtime to sustain you and the baby during your pregnancy and delivery. Overweight sisters are often discouraged to find out how difficult it is to take off that much excess weight after the birth—many never do. We encourage you to take this opportunity to decide on a healthy exercise and eating plan now that will benefit you for the rest of your life and reduce your susceptibility to numerous diseases and ailments. Follow the guidelines for exercise in this chapter and read Chapter 7, "You (and Your Baby) Are What You Eat," for nutritional help.

◇ ◇ ◇ ◇ ◇ ◇ ◇ ◇ ◇ ◇ ◇ ◇ ◇ ◇ ◇ ◇ ◇

"I was put on 24-hour bed rest during my pregnancy. I am five feet five and when I finally gave birth I was a whopping 207 pounds. Almost half of that weight was gained during the bed rest!"

◇ ◇ ◇ ◇ ◇ ◇ ◇ ◇ ◇ ◇ ◇ ◇ ◇ ◇ ◇ ◇ ◇

Bed-Rest Pregnancies

When your doctor or midwife has ordered you to stay strapped to the bed for some or all of your pregnancy, your primary concern is to nurture the growing baby that's inside you fighting for a healthy life. If you haven't already, you'll soon learn how to make lists, write notes, shop by phone, and even use a laptop computer from your bed. But even though you're bedridden, there are still leg and arm exercises that you can do (if you're well enough) to help keep your limbs supple. In fact, it may be more important now than ever to get in some form of stretching and light exercise to keep your muscles from wasting away during your wait. Here are some exercises you may be able to do from bed:

Foot circles: Moving only your ankles, point your toes and make circles with your feet, one at a time, raising them a few inches off the bed (or as much as you can lift them without straining). This will help improve your circulation and keep your ankle joints and Achilles tendons flexible.

Wrist and arm circles: With your arms outstretched in front of you, do the same circling motion with your wrists as in the foot circle stretch. If you are propped up in bed, neck and shoulder circles will help relieve tension and improve your posture, too.

Bed walk: Sit up as straight as you can with your hands palms-down on the bed on either side of you for support, without lifting your legs off the bed, bend and straighten your knees alternately, as if you're walking on air; when you bend your knee, flex your toes.

Bust Supporter: Sit up in bed, bend your elbows, and cross your arms; grasping your upper arms with each hand; squeeze your arms a bit while pressing your hands against your arms and you'll feel the flex in your chest muscles. This will give a little support to your breasts as they grow heavier, taking some of the strain off your neck and back. Palms can also be placed together with elbows out to the sides. Press your palms together and hold 2 to 3 seconds, then release and repeat.

Kegel exercises to strengthen your important pelvic muscles can be done anywhere, anytime, in almost any circumstance. Sadly, many pregnant women who attend their aerobics classes faithfully have saggy pelvic floor muscles because they didn't do their Kegel exercises. See page 199 for explanation of how to do these.

Guidelines for Exercise During Pregnancy

Exercise authorities agree on these basic rules for physical exercise during pregnancy:

◆ Determine your fitness level and choose the exercise routine that's right for your lifestyle. (Go through the questions in "How Fit Are You?" for starters.)

◆ Remember that the credo for exercise during pregnancy is "no pressure." You are not "going for the burn" here. This may be the first time in your life you are *not* required to push yourself too far or be highly competitive. (After your fifth month you'll hardly want to anyway.)

◆ Choose an exercise routine or sport that you enjoy doing and don't be afraid to vary your workout: one day an aerobic tape, next time a walk. If you like the exercise, you'll do more of it.

◆ Stick to the intensity level that your body says is enough for you. "Your body is in charge," reminds fitness instructor Alicia Villarosa, who has trained women in both prenatal and postpartum fitness. "If your body says, 'Hey, I can't jog but I *can* walk,' then you walk."

◆ Be as consistent as possible. Do your exercise as many times per week as you can. We recommend a 20-to-30-minute cardiovascular workout at least three times per week for maximum results. The ACOG recommends that regular exercising is preferable to intermittent activity—for example, exercising five times per week the first week (when you're excited and raring to go) and then only once a week for the rest of the pregnancy. Sometimes exercising with a partner will help keep you from backing out on the days when you're feeling unmotivated. A partner can also let you know if you look overtired or overheated while you're exercising.

◆ Always warm up before exercising and cool down afterward, allowing at least 10 minutes for each. This simply means doing a slower, lighter version of the activity you're about to do or the one you just did. Warm-up and cool-down exercises get your muscles loosened up for the next time you exercise. Good warm-up, cool-down stretches include neck rolls, shoulder circles, trunk twists, and leg and arm stretches. All of the workout videos listed later in this chapter have good warm-up and cool-down portions. Don't fast-forward past them!

◆ Eat some extra calories on the days that you exercise, to compensate for those you're burning, especially if you're slim. (This is in addition to the 300 extra calories you should already be eating each day just because you're pregnant.)

◆ Stay cool by drinking a glass of water before the workout and sipping another one throughout, as needed. "Water brings your core body temperature down, a very important factor for pregnant exercisers," says Villarosa. "Omitting the water is not an option when you're pregnant—drinking it is a must!" If you can, open a window to get more air circulating in the room where you're exercising.

◆ Dress in comfortable, thin layers to do your workout. An all-in-one maternity leotard made of a cotton/lycra blend, with a cotton T-shirt, cotton socks with nylon, and some good cross-training or running shoes is an ideal outfit for working out, but sweatpants and a T-shirt will also do fine. "Leotards made of Supplex or Coolmax are great because they have what are called 'wicking properties,' which disperse the heat your body is generating and keep you cooler," says Villarosa. "It works kind of the same way a disposable diaper does, keeping wetness away from the baby's skin." Cross-training or running shoes will work better for you than aerobic sneakers because they have a wider heel base that will help your growing, swelling feet. The waffle-shaped tread of these shoes will also provide more support when you exercise.

◆ Consider wearing a belly band, which is like a large piece of thick elastic, to support your belly and lower back and reduce the strain on your spine. "It's like a bra for your belly," explains Villarosa. Belly bands can be worn under your clothes whenever you feel you need the extra support. Price range: $52 with a one-piece maternity leotard, from Japanese Weekend Inc., 1-800-808-0555 for catalog and store listings; also from Prenatal Cradle, Inc., $35 to $45, 1-800-383-3068.

◆ Be extra careful when you exercise. Remember that you are carrying more weight than usual, which puts more pressure on your legs, joints, and back. Your pelvic joints, in particular, are becoming softer and looser so the baby's head will be able to pass through. This natural loosening of this and other joints may leave you more prone to injury.

◆ The ACOG recommends that you get your caregiver's approval to exercise if you had a low activity lifestyle prepregnancy or if you have any of the following risk factors: pregnancy-induced hypertension; preterm membrane ruptures; previous or current preterm labor; a surgically closed or incompetent cervix; persistent second- or third-trimester bleeding or retarded intra-uterine growth; cardiac, vascular, or pulmonary disease; chronic hypertension; or an overactive thyroid. If you know that you have had previous difficulties while exercising, talk it out with your caregiver.

Expect to Feel . . .

◆ Off-balance if you engage in a sport that requires balance, such as tennis. Your center of gravity is shifting so it may sometimes feel like your belly is arriving two seconds later than your body! "You may not have yet adapted to the changes in your body, like when you drive a fast car all your life, then suddenly you're driving a slow car trying to make it go at the same speed as the fast car," cautions Villarosa. Be aware that too much jarring will put you at risk for maternal complications, including miscarriage.

◆ Easily tired during your workout. Don't be surprised at how easily you may feel hot and sweaty. It takes less exercise to make you tired now than it did before you were pregnant because you are carrying more weight and because your baby uses up more of your oxygen.

◆ The need to urinate frequently. This is due to all the water we hope you're drinking and because your growing baby is squeezing your organs and pressing down on your bladder.

◆ Hungry during the workout. Eat a small meal an hour before you exercise and remember to drink water before you start and throughout your workout. It will help quell that hungry feeling while you work out.

◆ Small uterine contractions during or after aerobic exercise. This is normal and should subside as you change positions or walk around. If they persist and get stronger, call your caregiver.

◆ Minor swelling (edema) in your feet after your workout. This is caused by the accumulation of fluids in your tissues and should only cause you mild discomfort. Avoid wearing elastic-topped socks and elevate your legs after you're done exercising. Excessive swelling of the feet, hands, and face, however, may be a sign of complication, especially if it lasts more than a day; in this case, call your caregiver immediately.

Note: If you are dizzy, gasping for breath, nauseated, cramping, feeling faint, feeling like you may be spotting (light, vaginal bleeding), experiencing a racing heartbeat or any pain, especially in your pubic area—at any point during your exercise—stop! Get advice from your doctor or midwife about how you should modify your routine or whether you should continue exercising.

Best Exercises for Pregnancy

Stretches and Strengtheners

Kegel Exercises. Whatever you do, don't skip these! Named after Dr. Arnold Kegel of the University of California at Los Angeles, who recognized the importance of the pelvic muscles in childbirthing, "Kegels" are considered by many to be the most important of all prenatal exercises. Kegel exercises strengthen the muscles in the vaginal and perenial area—all-important muscles for a manageable childbirth. They are best done lying flat on your back with your knees bent and feet shoulder-width apart. Put a pillow under your head and shoulders for support and comfort. Contract the muscles around your vagina and anus (similar to what you would do if you had to go to the bathroom really badly but were holding it in). Squeeze as long as you can, then release. Aim to do 25 Kegels a day, holding them for 10 seconds each squeeze. Kegels can also be done in public any time you think of it since the tiny, internal movement is hard to detect. Try doing some when you're sitting in your car at a stop light or at your desk and while standing in line at the post office or waiting for the bus.

Pelvic Rock. This exercise helps prevent and soothe backache during both pregnancy and labor. It will also help you relax your lower back and the symphysis pubis, the place just above your vulva that holds the sides of your pelvis together, which will ease the baby's exit. Lie on your back in the same pose as for Kegels and exhale as you press the small of your back toward the floor; inhale as you relax your spine. Aim for 10 repetitions, back and forth, "rocking" your pelvis. After your fourth month, stand against a wall to do the same exercise, gently pressing the small of your back toward the wall.

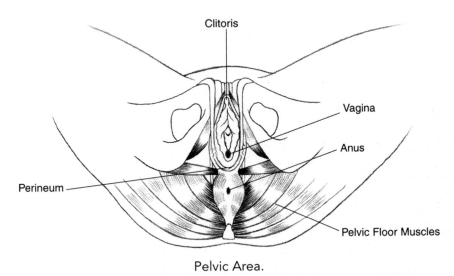

Pelvic Area.

The Cat Stretch. This will strengthen your legs and relieve lower back tension. Get on your hands and knees, with your arms directly below your shoulders and your parted knees directly under your hips. Inhale and gently bring your head and buttocks up trying not to arch your back. Exhale, lower your head, and round up your spine. Alternate the two positions, inhaling and exhaling. Repeat 5 to 10 times.

Inner Thigh Stretch/Squat. (See page 190 for illustration.) This will stretch your inner thighs, loosen up the knee and hip joints, open your groin area, and tone your leg muscles. The earlier you get comfortable with this position the better; you may need to maintain it for a long period of time during labor. Standing on your toes, crouch down until you are squatting, still balancing on your toes. Keeping you back straight, gently pry your legs open at the knees with your hands. Return to a standing position, then lower your heels. Repeat 5 times per day. Another variation of this exercise: Sit on the floor and place the soles of your feet together; lean forward and gently press the knees apart with your elbows. Repeat 5 times each day. Try sitting with your ankles crossed (the way children sit in kindergarten) as often as you can.

Aerobic Exercise

Walking. Brisk walking was one thing almost all the women we surveyed said they did for exercise during pregnancy. But Villarosa cautions against thinking that a stroll to the mailbox every day is enough to keep you toned. "If you want to stay fit walking, you have to walk purposefully and for real," reminds Villarosa. She recommends that beginners start with 5-to-10-minute walks two times per week, increasing the pace as you walk. Regular exercisers can start at 20 minutes or more four to five times per week. "Remember, you are not window-shopping or browsing—you have to haul your butt!" Take a walking class at a local fitness center such as the YWCA or call the Black Women's Health Project at 1-800-ASK-BWHP for information on walking clubs near you—you might even consider starting one with a few other pregnant sisters. Hints: You'll feel less self-conscious about pumping your arms if you get a partner to do it with you. Invest in a good, comfortable pair of walking or running shoes; your feet will thank you. A good-quality support bra or sports bra with a crisscross back will help keep your growing breasts from bouncing and can reduce sagging. If you prefer indoor exercise, try walking on a treadmill twice a week for 12 minutes at 2 to 3 miles per hour, slowly working up to 3 times a week for 25 minutes at 4 miles per hour. Don't worry if you have to stop sooner, slow down the pace, or reduce the incline of your treadmill—your body knows best.

"Swimming was the only thing that soothed my pregnancy sickness. I would actually cry when I had to get out of the pool! "

Aerobic Water Exercises. Besides walking for fitness, the women we surveyed rated exercising in a pool their favorite pregnancy workout. "You're more bouyant when you're pregnant so you'll enjoy a great feeling of weightlessness when in the water," says Villarosa. "Plus, the water naturally keeps your body temperature down while you work out, an important concern when you're pregnant." Non-swimmers will appreciate the fact that most aerobic water exercise routines don't involve actual swimming. The workout movements are basically the same as in a regular aerobic workout, only in water. A good water-fitness routine can include any of the following: walking or running the length or perimeter of the pool; doing leg lifts, front and side kicks, and flutter kicks with a board or holding on to the side of the pool. All of these great exercises offer you aerobic benefits with little or no direct impact on your body. For maximum benefit, do your water routine at least three times per week for a total of 45 minutes per session (including 10-minute warm-up and 10-minute cool-down, which is standard in most classes). Call your local YWCA to find out if one is being taught near you. Please, no diving. And, fear not, water cannot enter the womb through your vagina. If you are a bit nervous in the water, Villarosa suggests you use arm-buoys to help keep you afloat. Goggles, a bathing cap, or ear plugs also make some women more comfortable. Speedo and other brands make nonfrilly, sleek-looking maternity bathing suits for about $48 to $69.

Stationary Cycling. While cycling outdoors could be hazardous during pregnancy because you might easily lose your balance and fall, stationary cycling offers the same fitness benefits minus the risk. Stationary biking is great for pregnancy exercise because you can actually sit, and even read, while you get a good cardiovascular workout and strengthen your thigh and calf muscles. If you or your mate owns a bicycle, you may be able to purchase an inexpensive device that transforms it into a stationary bike. Check major sporting-goods stores.

Praise in the House with gospel singer Fred Hammond (Integrity Music, Inc., Mobile, Alabama) has great cuts to dance and exercise to while you enjoy the dynamic praise music that was birthed in the African-American church.

Freestyle Dancing. If you're the type that just wants to put on a funky tape and dance for fitness, do! (Just don't try too many Little Richard or Janet Jackson moves, though.) If possible, choose tapes that have continuous danceable music on at least one side so your level of activity remains fairly consistent. If possible, incorporate toning movements into your dance, such as lifting your legs and lifting your arms over your head. Aim to dance for 20 to 30 minutes for optimum benefit.

Mild-to-moderate exercise performed at least three times per week is recommended by the American College of Obstetrics and Gynecology as acceptable during pregnancy.

Massages

Gentle touches are always comforting and relaxing, and are doubly so when you're pregnant. A back or body massage (even one done by a mate or nonprofessional) can feel wonderful when your muscles are aching. The effort must be sincere and selfless. Massage is a great way for you and your husband to draw closer during this special time. Olive oil, sesame oil, castor oil, corn oil, butter, and good old Vaseline are used by midwives and husbands all over the world to help soothe a mother-to-be's stressed-out muscles. A good massage is simple to perform: It consists of repeated, rhythmic motions done with sensitivity and care. Here are some suggestions for massaging different parts of the body:

Feet, Calves: Have your partner sit up, making sure her back is well supported. Sit at her feet and place one foot on your knee. Grasp her foot, pressing firmly into the sole of the foot with your thumbs. Make circling movements with your thumbs, working up from her heel to her calves and thighs, if she's receptive.

Head, Brow, Scalp: Lie down or sit down with your partner propped against your chest. With your hands on either side of her forehead, begin to make gentle circular movements with your fingertips. Then, using all your fingers, begin to gently knead her scalp from the top of her head to the nape of her neck.

Back, Shoulders, Buttocks, and Thighs: With your partner lying on her back, firmly press on her lower back with the oiled heels of your hands, making circular movements on *either side* of her spine (never directly on the vertebrae). Move slowly up and down her back several times, massaging the top of her shoulders with your thumbs. Make your way down again, and massage her buttocks and thighs, gently kneading them with your fingers.

HISTORICALLY SPEAKING . . .

 Midwives in Jamaica, West Indies, are likely to offer a massage to a pregnant woman, using special fragrant oils to help keep her skin supple as it stretches with the baby's growth. African women of the Zulu tribe offered breathing exercises to the pregnant women in their midst, believing that it helps "strengthen" the child inside them and prepared them for birth. One Haitian tradition is that women who discover themselves pregnant will ask older women to bring them special herbs to be used in their bathwater for three consecutive days, in hopes that it would ward off any evil spirits that would harm the baby. *What We Can Learn:* It's no news to us that oil is a wonderful lubricant. We've used it in our hair and on our skin for centuries to keep them soft and glowing. Midwife Onnie Lee Logan boasts proudly in her book *Motherwit* that she only had one woman tear (in her perineal area) during childbirth in all her decades of practice. How'd she do it? When she saw that a woman wasn't dilating, she says she would "greaze mother with a li'l oil or white Vaseline. . . . It eases em and it just stretches the skin out." She'd follow that with a hot towel. "And they dilate so good . . . without needin' any lacerations." Breathing exercises can be very calming and relaxing when you're pregnant, especially if you're feeling a stress attack coming on. And an herb bath may be just the ticket after a long workday. Bring in some candles, too, for atmosphere. We strongly discourage rituals that involve the occult, whether they are part of our heritage or not. Instead of dabbling in voodoo, why not take advantage of the luxurious solitude to meditate on the miraculous construction of your body and to thank God for your many blessings?

Avoiding Exercise Hazards

While you are pregnant, it's a good idea to avoid exercises or sports that require:

◆ Short stops and starts or lateral (side-to-side) moves. You will open yourself up to muscle pulls (the last thing you need to risk now).

◆ Short bursts of high-energy output such as jogging slowly for a ¼ mile then sprinting 50 yards. This type of "peak and valley" exercising makes it hard for you to breathe freely and thus be able to deliver oxygen to the baby. It can also easily cause your body temperature—and the baby's—to rise too fast, and you both may get overheated.

◆ Lying on your back after the first trimester. Your enlarging uterus can constrict the flow of blood from your heart to the fetus.

◆ Lying on your belly.

Other sports and sports-related situations to stay away from include:

◆ Contact sports where you're likely to get shoved (like basketball), banged (like soccer or possibly bowling), hit (like baseball or volleyball) or where you may easily get off balance and fall (like roller-blading, ice-skating, skiing, or horseback riding).

◆ Muddy, icy, or slick surfaces that might cause you to slip.

◆ Whirlpools, saunas, hot tubs, steam rooms, very humid gyms or exercise rooms, basically anywhere that invites excess heat and dehydration.

Workout Videos Suited for Expectant Mothers

Some of these videos feature black women, some don't, though they may have other special features we thought you would appreciate in a pregnancy workout. As with all workouts during pregnancy, talk to your caregiver before you begin.

Buns of Steel 8: Pregnancy Workout. The tape many women love to hate when they're *not* pregnant is available for those who want to keep those curvaceous hips toned while with child. For the serious (highly active, highly conditioned) exerciser. About $10, available at most video chains nationwide.

Tyla's Mom Jam features fitness professional Tyla Reich, actress

Sheryl Lee Ralph, and other pregnant women in a low-impact aerobics workout, plus various abdominal workouts suited for each trimester. A free plastic exercise band comes enclosed with the tape and $1 of the purchase price goes to the Pediatric AIDS Foundation. $24.95, 1-800-760-MOMS.

Jane Fonda's Low Impact Aerobic Workout. Another oldie but goodie. May be harder to find, as it was produced in 1986. Includes two black women exercisers and incorporates dances like the cha-cha and the Charleston, which adds some fun to the 35-minute aerobic routine. Great for those who have been sedentary or are over-weight, newcomers to exercise, and women who dislike "jump-ing around." About $20.

Aerobics with Soul—Serengeti. For those who prefer African rhythms and more natural (yet challenging) movements, this is a wonderful video. Though there is no pregnant instructor on this tape, the smooth, low-impact movements are fine for pregnancy and post-partum fitness. You'll enjoy "moving like the animals" that inhabit Tanzania, Africa, where certified instructor Maria Nhambu Bergh was born. Bergh created the video because she was bored with the aerobics class she took after her son's birth. It's particularly nice to see beau-tiful, multihued sisters leading the exercises, as well as a variety of body types. Also available on audio tape for freestyle dancing. $24.95 for videotape, $13.95 for audio tape, 1-800-423-9685.

Kathy Smith's Pregnancy Workout. An oldie but a goodie, say preg-nancy fitness experts. The tape has been on the market since 1989 and is still a top seller. Includes low-impact segments. About $20, available at most video chains nationwide.

Integrity Music Fitness Praise Workout. Worship as you work out with this fitness routine set to "contemporary-style" praise music, featuring one pregnant exerciser. The workout alternates step aerobics with strength and weight training, so you will need a step and some hand weights to get the full benefit of the exercises. An aerobics-only video, *Fitness Praise Aerobics* includes a pregnant exerciser for you to follow. Both are $19.95, 1-800-533-6912.

Safety Note: In general, non-pregnancy videos can be used safely during pregnancy as long as you listen carefully to your body, don't move too fast, keep cool, drink water, and keep a close monitor on your pulse (heart rate). Says Villarosa, "Heat, hydration,

and heart rate are the Three H's to keep an eye on when doing aerobics during pregnancy."

MOTHER TO MOTHER
by Gail Boggs Larson

One sister's humorous story of triumph over postpartum bulge.

When I had my first baby I wanted to hurry up and show so I ate a lot. By the second baby, your stomach remembers so you don't have to help it. After 30 weeks of pregnancy my nurse-midwife told me I was dilated. So, at 30 weeks, I was ordered to hit the bed. I could only get up if it was an emergency. My spouse—a man who couldn't cook an egg before—had to learn to cook for three. And he did. (He's really into learning everything thoroughly.) He would carry me to the

*kitchen to show me the food and ask me if it was cooked yet. I felt so
bad. I had bed sores, head sores, everything, and they said if I didn't
want to see my baby in the preemie ward, I'd better lay my ass down.
Since we live near where the L.A. riots took place, we could see and
smell the smoke from our window. I asked my husband jokingly,
"Honey, how would we ever get outta here? I can't get out of the bed!"*

*At 36 weeks I was finally allowed to get up. My midwife said,
"OK, let's let it out, baby." I delivered my second beautiful daughter
that same day.*

*I was horrified when I looked in the mirror. The scale said 207. I'm
only 5'5"! I was wearing a 40F bra! I normally weighed about 125—
and I thought that was heavy. Well, 125 was no walk in the park anymore, honey. I basically went on to become a human sofa for my
children. My sexuality left for a while. Some heavy women feel sexy, but
I didn't. I started to cry. I used to look at really fat people and say,
"What's wrong with them? Just give me that body and I could work
that." Suddenly I became an advocate for the discriminated.*

*I'm an actress, so I went back to work—or tried to. I usually get the
crazy-cute-sexy-girl roles. Suddenly I was only playing roles that were
described as "the heavy, depressed friend." I was up for a big part one
week, and it was down to me and another woman, and she got it. I cried.*

*I decided to go to Jenny Craig at 176 pounds on December first (I
like to start things at the beginning of the month). By June first I had
gotten down to 132 but I went back up to 152 to go up for a part that
included a bed scene with Gregory Hines. (Wouldn't you?) I didn't get
it. Now I'm back down to 132, and those 12 extra pounds are sitting
there singing, "We love you, Gail. We ain't ne-va leav-in'."*

*I looked at myself in the mirror again at Thanksgiving and I
started crying. I began to see how I was eating. I cried to my husband, "Look how I'm eating. I'm going to stay this way forever." My
husband is so calm and supportive. He could have said, "Baby, your
ass is biiig," but instead he said things like, "Well, do you want to be
fat?" and "What do you want to do about it?" I said I needed help.
He said he would help me in any way he could.*

*My mother and sister were both heavy and both recently lost it all
at Jenny Craig. I hated them. But I was happy for them at the same
time. My sister took one look at me and said, "Go to Jenny, girrl." I
called. I asked for Jenny. The girl on the phone laughed and said,
"I'm Gina, but I can still help you." She did. And I stuck to it. I felt
like I was buying a new Saturn (the whole staff in the showroom of
the car dealership cheers for you when you make your purchase—*

really). They took pictures of me and told me I was the best client of all time. I needed that. As long as you have supportive people around, you can lose the weight. If someone told me I couldn't do it, I would have figured out a way to do it anyway.

I was drinking so much water I almost had to wear Depends. I needed a bedpan in the car just for me! But all that weight stayed off and its been off for 2 years. I now walk 4 times per week, 3 miles each time, and I promise myself I won't eat after 6, except for right before my period, when anything goes. When I'm really motivated to lose I don't eat after 3 o'clock. I drink lukewarm water and tea all the time. It's great for the bowels. I eat foods with high water content, like broccoli. I eat everything bright, tender to the touch, or raw. My husband gives me a whipped-up, high-fiber fruit drink every morning (since he's now the cook of the house). I take my drink and the newspaper in the bathroom with me and forget it—I'm ready to go!

CHAPTER 10

What's in a Name?

A good name is rather to be chosen than great riches.
—Proverbs 22

In the Bible, when God reminded ninety-nine-year-old Abraham of his commission to become the father of many nations, He said, "No longer will you be called Abram; your name will be Abraham," which means "father of many." He was given a new name to suit his new goal, his new purpose in life. Sarai, Abraham's wife, was also given a new name, Sarah, which means "God's princess." Many other biblical characters were renamed to better suit the mission they were to fulfill later in life. The story of Abraham tells us that it took many years before he actually *became* the father of many nations. (After all, he didn't even have his first son until he was nearly one hundred!) His new name reflected God's belief in his *potential* for greatness.

As we become more in touch with our rich heritage as descendants of Africa, many black parents are discovering that our African sisters and brothers are also very serious about naming their children. Historically, children were highly valued in African families and were seen as symbols of the continuity of life. In many African countries, a naming ceremony, or "outdooring," is held shortly after a baby's birth. It is the African equivalent of a christening. At this ceremony, the family celebrates the precious gift God has given them and it is often at this time that the baby's name is formally bestowed. These are major family events complete with food, special dress, and an after-party that can last all night and through the next day. Members of African communities expect that a child will grow into a man or woman of good character if they are given a name that has meaning and significance. Parents also may be given new names to signify their new role.

"Names don't have to be African to be Afrocentric. Even names like Shaquisha, which are often made up, have a certain kind of uniqueness. Though we may look down on them saying, 'What kinda name is that for a child?' Well, the answer is, it's definitely not European!"

"Ever since high school I was doodling the name Joy on my notebooks; I always liked that name. When my daughter was born I wanted her name to have the same initials in her father's name, Joel Nathaniel, so I threw all of the sounds together and named her Joy Nayelle."

What Influences Our Name Giving?

There is no such thing as the typical "black name" just like there is no "typical black" anything. Contrary to popular belief, we know that we are not a homogenous group of people. Both African-American and Caribbean black families are influenced by many different social, religious, and cultural traditions that shape their naming decisions. Of course, not every black parent is comfortable with, or even interested in, giving his or her baby an African name. Parents may feel more personal connection to their home state or island than to an African heritage they've only read about in books or watched on TV. Some parents simply give their children names they have always liked, others choose the names of biblical figures, celebrities, or relatives; some select a name from another culture with which they closely associate, and still others choose to create a totally new and unique name for their child. For example, since American-born blacks are influenced by both their African heritage and their identification with mainstream America, many of these parents choose names that will help their children "fit in" but that will also be unique and lyrical, with an "African sound." Out of these desires was born the era of "remade" names—Anglo names that were cleverly given a "black spin" by parents who added or changed some of the letters or attached an ending. The name Michelle is remade into Nishell, Wanda becomes Wandah, and Ray becomes Rayvawn. Another way black parents remade Anglo names was by adding a syllable like "La," "De," or "Sha," which some feel adds a softer sound to certain names. The name Donna became LaDonna, Anna becomes DeAnna and Rhonda is remade into Sharhonda.

"I brought home a book of traditional African baby names to show my wife, who is West Indian. She took one look and said, 'I am not going to name my child Chimichanga!'"
—*Name withheld, New York*

Black Caribbean parents are influenced by British, French, Spanish, and Dutch cultures, since most of the Caribbean islands were settled and ruled by people from these countries. Caribbean-American parents tend to be less interested in African names partly because they have a stronger sense of their own identity. There is less of a longing for affiliation with a majority-black Africa since they never held minority status on their islands to begin with. Many of the battles they fought were more about classism and the ever-present "light skin versus dark skin" issues than about black versus white. Most Caribbean-born parents adopted the traditions of their "parent" countries and thus tend to give their children names that were well thought of in those countries. "My brothers were named Rupert Kenneth and Osbert Cipriani," says Gladys Parris, a native of Grenada, an island in the West Indies once under British rule. "Names of members of the English royal family, such as Elizabeth, Victoria, Mary, Edward, and Charles were also very popular and were considered prestigious names to give your children."

"When I experienced the pain of labor and an unexpected cesarean section, we decided to give our daughter all of our favorite names at once because I said, 'This may be it for me!' Her name is Baldwin (after writer James Baldwin) Callie (after my husband's great-great-grandmother Caledonia, who bought her freedom with fourteen pieces of gold) Clara (after my mother)."

Similarly, other black parents name their children after famous or prominent people whom they admire, both black and white. Many name their children after famous black authors, actors and actresses, ministers, singers, athletes, and politicians. Some parents have used a famous person's last name to create a unique first or middle name for their child.

Black families reared close to the church often choose biblical or religious names for their children. Black Christians today give their children first and middle names in honor of famous biblical characters like John (after John the Baptist), Rachel (the fiercely loyal wife of Jacob), David (after King David), or Mary, after the child-mother of Jesus. A Muslim tradition is to name children after one of the many attributes of Allah, such as Ar-Rasheed, which means "the Watchful" or Ash-Shaheed, which means "the Witness." Though devout Muslims consider it rude to use a person's name without a prefix (such as "Ar" or "Ash"), these are usually dropped by many black Muslims today who might simply name their son Shaheed or their daughter Rasheeda.

African Names

As more of us venture to Africa and discover our innate connection to the Motherland, more and more black couples are choosing to name their babies traditional African names. The more educated you become about Africa—whether through a visit, by spending time with African friends, or by reading books and magazine articles on the continent, the more inclined you will be to want your child to share in that connectedness. "My husband and I strongly identified with the struggle of liberation in South Africa and we had close friends who were African. We were also part of the civil rights movement here in America," says mystery writer Valerie Wilson-Wesley. "When our daughters were born, we wanted to connect them with more than their American experience. Names like Tiffany and Anna didn't mean anything to us. So we named them Nandi, after the mother of African warrior king Shaka Zulu, and Thembi, a Zulu name which means 'beautiful hope.' Most of our friends named their kids African or Islamic names, too."

African names are usually genderless and typically reflect one of the following: the family's religion or status in the community, the mysteries of nature, a specific hope or virtue, a life circumstance, a particular place, the order of birth, or the day of the week on which the child was born. Special names are given to the first-, second-, and thirdborn, to boys born between two girls, the last child born, and a baby that was born ill.

The African-American parents we talked to said they would consider naming their child an African first name and many liked the idea of giving their child a special African middle name. Parents expressed that they feared saddling their children with hard-to-pronounce, hard-to-spell names that teachers, co-workers, and friends will repeatedly say and spell incorrectly—not to mention discriminate against. Ironically, most African names are spelled phonetically and are in fact easier to pronounce than some European names because they are written almost exactly the way they are spoken. The reality is if you live in America, your children are likely to experience both discrimination and peer pressure in some form whether their name is Bradley or Babatunde (a Nigerian name that means "in the image of grandfather"), so why not be bold and give them a name that's significant and meaningful?

"When our daughters Nandi and Thembi were younger they sometimes created other European names in order to fit in. Teachers could never spell them right—Nancy for Nandi, and so on. But by high school and now in college, they have both thanked us for giving them African names. Now, they will probably give their children African names too."

According to the parents we talked to who gave their children African names, most of the children went through brief periods of resentment about their unusual names, but as older teenagers and young adults, they came to appreciate their parents' bold choice. One of the keys to helping your children through this period is to reinforce to them why you chose the name you gave them and reassure them of its significance and its meaning. If you named them an African or historical name, or if you named them after a famous person, planning trips to museums, libraries, galleries, and other places of information where they can learn about African culture will be a great help. Biblical names can be explained through the Bible itself as well as through countless Bible story books on the market—so you can also teach your child biblical principles along the way. Often, children need to "see" in order to internalize what you're saying, especially since images of thriving, successful black cultures are rarely depicted in mainstream American media. "When my daughter Nandi finally saw the epic *Shaka Zulu*, about the great African warrior king, and discovered that Shaka's beautiful, strong mother was named Nandi, it suddenly hit her. 'I'm named after Nandi the African queen mother!' " recalls Wesley. "Now, when she says her name she says it loudly and with pride."

Here's a healthy sampling of some African names we liked best from each region of Africa, along with their basic meanings and place of origin. Most of the names are taken from *Multicultural Baby Names* by M. J. Abadie, (Longmeadow Press, Connecticut, $4.95) and *What to Name Your African-American Baby* by Benjamin Faulkner (St. Martin's Press, New York, $4.50). Names are unisex, except where indicated.

Swahili

(A Bantu language spoken in East Africa; considered by some to be the language of liberation)

Name	Meaning
Adhana	Call to prayer
Amini	Worthy of trust
Amiri	Commander
Akida	Leader, chief
Baraka	Blessing
Cheka	One who laughs
Chuma	Iron (strong as)
Dafina	Precious
Ema	Good

Name	Meaning
Imara	(One with) stamina and endurance
Jahina	Bold, courageous
Kabaila	Respect(ed)
Kimeta	Radiant
Kita	Firm in the face of danger
Maisha	Life
Manzili	Sent by God
Nailah	Destined to succeed
Nia	Goal-oriented
Tamba	Dancer

Zulu

(A Bantu language spoken in southeast Africa)

Name	Meaning
Amandla	Vigor(ous)
Ameni	Amen
Anelisa	Satisfied
Enza	Producer, Creator
Inkani	Self-will(ed)
Isandla	Careful
Khala	Sings like a bird
Khanya	(One who) shines
Nika	Provide(r)
Quinisa	Sustain(er), provider
Shela	Passion(ate)

Other Names from Southern Africa

Female Name	Meaning
Chuma	Riches
Magano	She is a gift
Sekayi	Happy with laughter
Sipo	A gift
Zenzele	She does it herself

Male Name	Meaning
Mahuli	Victorious
Molefi	Keeper of traditions
Ndoro	Emblem of kingship
Simba	Strength of a lion
Sipho	A gift

Other Names from Eastern Africa

Female Name	Meaning
Aisha	Life bringer
Dalila	Gentle
Eshe	Life
Kalifa	Holy child
Layla	Born at night
Najuma	Abounding in joy
Rhamah	My sweetness
Salma	Safe
Tabia	Talented
Zakiya	Intelligent

Male Name	Meaning
Ahmed	Praiseworthy
Bakari	Of noble promise
Hamadi	Praised
Hasani	Handsome
Jelani	Mighty
Khalfani	Destined to rule
Nadif	Born between seasons
Shomari	Forceful

Yoruba

(A Kwa language of the Niger-Congo family; spoken in parts of West Africa)

Name	Meaning
Afinna	Sculptor
Akewi	Poet
Akowe	Writer
Angeli	Angel
Dara	Elegant, fine
Eleda	Creator
Emi	Spirit
Itara	Zeal(ous)
Iyanu	Surprise (was a)
Laiya	Bold, brave, daring
Nifaiya	Winning, winner
Nitara	Eager
Ola	Dignity, dignified

Name	Meaning
Omnira	Liberator
Orin	Song, (singer)
Sora	Careful
Tanna	Blossom
Yanilenu	Extraordinary
Yara	Smart

Other Names from Western Africa

Female Name	Meaning
Azisa	Precious beauty
Camara	Teacher
Dayo	Joy arrives
Ekechi	God's creation
Elon	God loves me
Halina	Gentle
Jamila	Beautiful
Kelinde	Secondborn of twins
Malene	Tower
Neema	Born in prosperity
Oji	Giftbearer
Rasida	Righteous

Male Name	Meaning
Abiola	Born at the new year
Adama	Majestic
Damani	Thoughtful
Ekeama	Nature is splendid
Keita	Worshiper
Konata	Man of high station
Kwesi	Conquering strength
Mawali	There is a God
Sekou	Fighter

Hausa

(An Afro-Asiatic language spoken in northern Nigeria and southern Niger)

Name	Meaning
Asali	Origin, ancestry
Cimma	Accomplish(ed)

Name	Meaning
Darika	Brotherhood
Gwani	Expert
Kai	(Will) amount to . . .
Karimi	Charitable person
Koya	Study, learn
Kuzari	Stamina
Murjani	Coral
Nadiri	Rare, one of a kind
Nasara	Success, victory
Nema	Seek
Rai	Life
Salla	Prayer
Sarakai	Nobility
Shiru	Quiet
Suna	Fame, glory, honor
Zuma	Honey

Other Names from Northern Africa

Female Name	Meaning
Amira	Queen
Fatia	One who conquers
Karimah	Generous
Lateefah	Gentle, pleasant
Mawiya	The essence of life
Nadia	Time of promise
Nathifa	Clean, pure
Qimmah	The highest point
Shaba	Morning has come
Tahirah	Pure
Thuraia	Star of my life
Yaminah	Right, proper

Male Name	Meaning
Akil	Intelligent, uses reason
Amal	Hopes
Hashim	Crusher of evil
Jamal	Beauty
Khalid	Eternal
Malek	Owner
Naeem	Benevolent

Name	Meaning
Omar	Trustworthy
Osaze	He whom God likes
Saeed	Happy
Thair	Honest, clean
Zaid	Increase, growth

HISTORICALLY SPEAKING ...

 As Americans of African descent, our identity has changed with each struggle and each achievement. We have called ourselves black, negro, colored, Negro (resurrected during our migration to the North), and Afro-American. Today, the name African American, proposed by Jesse Jackson, is meant to give us kinship with a historical land base instead of a color. Which "label" do you use? What will you encourage your children to call themselves?

African Ceremonies

Whatever you name your baby, one of the ways you can make name-giving a special occasion is by hosting an African-style celebration where you can publicly declare your baby's name and its meaning (if any) and formally introduce your child to the world. African-inspired naming ceremonies and other rituals of baby dedication are enjoying a revival in many black families. There are two major African ceremonies that surround the birth of a baby. One is a naming ceremony in which the baby's name is bestowed and the other, a west African ritual, is called an "outdooring," in which the baby is first introduced to extended family members and friends. Both ceremonies are concerned with uniting the baby with her ancestral roots.

Naming Ceremony

An African naming ceremony is where the baby's name is officially bestowed. Traditionally, it is a small, intimate gathering of close family and friends held shortly after the baby's birth, often when she is 10 days old or younger. The Yoruba people name a boy on his ninth day of life, a girl on her seventh, and twins on their eighth. Before the ceremony is held a baby is simply called "newborn child" or Ikoko Omon. In the Baganda tribe of Africa, which holds naming ceremonies when babies are older, the paternal grandfather will recite the names of the ancestors of the clan at the ceremony and when the child laughs it is given the last mentioned name. This polygamous tribe also does naming ceremonies for several children at once. Each child's mother is to bring a piece of her umbilical cord, saved from birth. The clan chief drops the cord into a bucket of liquid. If it floats, the child is legitimate and accepted, if it sinks, the child is considered illegitimate and is disowned.

Many African-American parents hold naming ceremonies as late as 5 months after the birth, and some hold the ceremony in honor of the baby's first birthday. Since the child will already have been given a first name by this time, parents will probably bestow an African middle name on the child during the ceremony. Both men and women are invited to the event and come bearing gifts for the baby. Men's gifts are given to the baby's father, women's gifts to the mother. The elder of the family holds the baby up and then whispers its name, which may have been chosen well before its birth, into the baby's ear. This ritual is supposed to release the baby from the spirit world. Sometimes water is sprinkled in the air. This may serve the same purpose as the pouring of libations (the first drink) to the ancestors, which is done in a typical "outdooring" ceremony (see below). The elder then announces the name to those gathered and explains its meaning and significance. In some traditions, the baby's mouth is touched with water, salt, pepper, honey, oil, and koala nut symbolic of purity, power, good character, happiness, prosperity, and good fortune, respectively. A party ensues with food and dancing, as guests express their good wishes to the new parents and the baby.

Outdooring

This is an event that takes place about eight days after the birth. At this point, the baby has already been named, so the ceremony is to introduce it to its family and friends and is similar to a christening. It is also the first time the mother will have been seen "outdoors" since the birth. According to the Ghanian tradition, many members of the extended family gather and the elders (mostly the men) make speeches and tell endearing stories about the family. This may include a discussion of the name the baby was given, especially if it was named after a relative or ancestor. The baby is brought gifts by extended family members, similar to those brought to an American-style baby shower. Bright-colored dress is a requisite for attendees and sometimes the baby is clothed all in white. In some traditions, the baby's parents are considered guests of honor at the ceremony and play a passive role, allowing the elders and others to run the program and tend to the guests. In other cases, the parents share the responsibility of hosting, with the elders conducting the ceremonial aspects of the evening. The parents are usually dressed in Kente cloth reserved for special occasions (the idea is that you wear your best dress). This is a joyous and momentous day for all involved and the baby receives its official blessing and welcome into the family by the elders After that, it's party time! Libations are first poured to the ground (or into a houseplant if you're indoors) as a toast to our African ancestors. Then a spread of traditional African fare is served and the family continues to enjoy hearty fellowship, often ending with singing and dancing into the night.

These wonderful beginnings are easily replicated by black parents everywhere. Do some or all of the rituals, whatever makes you feel most comfortable. Have a big family celebration in a rented hall, or a small, intimate gathering of close family and friends in your living room. If the worship of ancestral spirits clashes with your religious beliefs (as it would for me), you may want to omit the libations from your ceremony. Instead, invite your minister or church pastor to say a blessing over the baby and create a different way to honor those who went before us. Why not do a family tree and read aloud the accomplishments and characteristics of your forefathers? Add your family's unique lore to the ceremony and celebrate the miracle of your baby's birth by starting your own tradition, African-style!

MOTHER TO MOTHER
by Monique Greenwood

**One mother's story of how she created
her own African-inspired family tradition.**

When my daughter was born, my husband and I were split as to whether to have her christened. I wanted to but my husband did not. We decided to have an African naming ceremony for her instead—even though she was already a year old. We read books on African names to get the how-tos, which weren't many, and forged ahead. We asked the couple we chose to be her "godparents" to host the ceremony in their home. Then we made sure we invited the eldest person in our family, which was my grandmother. Our baby was already a year old, so we weren't able to stick to the tradition of hosting the ceremony when the baby is 8 days old. Nor was it a small affair—we had 75 guests! My husband and I wore beautiful, specially made African garments, as did our baby daughter. We served light refreshments and finger foods first (we didn't do the African fare) and then I asked the guests to gather around so we could perform the ceremony. I announced the "godparents," a couple we chose to help guide our daughter, who made a short speech and then my grandmother, who is 87, performed the ritual of bestowing the baby's name. I asked her to do this just before the ceremony was set to start so she couldn't get nervous and back out. (You know how some older folk can be about African "roots" stuff.) Grandma held up the baby, whispered the name into her ear, which, according to African lore, breaks her from the world of the unborn into the world of the living. Then she announced her name to all the guests—Glynn Nailah. Glynn is derived from my husband's name, which is Glenn, and Nailah is Swahili for "destined to succeed." We chose the name Glynn because after my difficult pregnancy, which required me to have 7 hospital stays, I was not confident we would ever try this again, so I figured my husband better get his "Jr." now! We chose Nailah because she too endured much during the pregnancy, and even though she was born 5 weeks early she was perfect and proved that she had already lived up to the meaning of her African name. Today, at 4, she is very self-determined, not intimidated by anything—Nailah, indeed. People at the naming ceremony cried, they thought it was so beautiful. After the name was announced, we poured libations into a wooden cup and poured it into a plant—symbolizing a toast to our ancestors. With a little creativity we made a palm-size book of Xeroxed photos of Glynn's development during her first year of life and gave them out to our guests as favors. They were a hit and we've continued to make and give out a keepsake book for her birthday each year.

GLYNN NAILAH

"One Year of Pure Joy"

A keepsake baby book like the one made by Glynn Nailah's parents is a wonderful favor for friends and relatives to take home from a naming ceremony. (Cover shown left; inside page below.)

That face . . .

That adorable face. It has appeared in *Children's Business* magazine, *Baby Business*, and *The Washington Post* for a Hecht Company ad. Here's the photo Washingtonians saw in *The Post*.

Inspired to have an African naming ceremony or an outdooring for your baby? Jollof rice, an authentic West African dish, is easy to prepare and is often served at special occasions. It can be a side dish or, prepared with meat, makes a hearty main course.

JOLLOF RICE: A ONE-POT MEAL

Recipe as told by a Ghanian American

⅓ cup oil
1 large onion, chopped small
⅓ of a 16-oz. can of crushed tomato
½ 6 oz. can tomato paste
1 tablespoon fresh ginger, finely chopped
Fresh hot pepper or red pepper, chopped or crushed, to taste
Salt, to taste
1 lb. cooked beef or chicken, cubed
2 cups cut green beans, fresh, frozen, or canned (optional)
3 cups uncooked white rice
5 cups water

In medium or large sauce pot, heat oil; add chopped onion and cook until lightly browned; add crushed tomato, tomato paste, ginger, and pepper. Cook for 2 minutes, stirring. Add ½ cup water and salt to taste. Heat mixture over medium heat for 10 minutes, until thick. Add meat and vegetables, simmer at low to medium heat for 5 minutes, stirring occasionally. Add remaining water and rice, stir. Bring pot to a boil, stir, and reduce heat to low. Cover pot, cook 1 hour until rice is cooked and soft. Makes 5 to 6 servings.

HISTORICALLY SPEAKING ...

 One southern midwife recalls a humorous tale about a man named William who wanted a namesake so badly that he called his first five daughters Willie Sue, Willie Mae, Willie Kate, Willie Jane, and even Willie Bertha! When he finally had a son his wife was tired of calling the name "Willie!" and, oddly, decided to call him Bishop instead. Another story from the rural South tells of parents naming their babies after favorite foods like Strawberry Smith and China Rice. And you *know* the parents of Precious Character, Annie Cute, and Fed Wright (actual names!) had a definite message they wanted delivered through their children's names. *What We Can Learn:* Though made-up names are fun and certainly different, it's important to know that a name has the power to enhance or deflate your child's budding personality every time it's used. Give your baby a name that reflects the inner character you hope to build in her.

BY THE WAY ...

One story told in the book *What's in a Name?* (Tyndale House Publishers, Wheaton, Illinois) tells of a young boy who overheard his uncle speaking to his father. "I don't know why you named that boy Clayton," the uncle said. "Clay is dirt. That's what that name means—dirt. He'll never amount to anything." The father replied, "Well, you could be right about that." Young Clayton never forgot that conversation and grew into manhood with a very low sense of self-worth. Names are as unique and as important as your child. Knowing the meanings of the names you choose for your children will prove a valuable and esteem-building experience for both you and your child. Give names to your children that will inspire them to live up to their potential.

CHAPTER 11

Single Sisters

Single mothers are not a statistic. Neither are they a homogenous group of women who all have the same life circumstances. Contrary to society's stigma, they are not to be categorized as poor, uneducated, "loose" women. In fact, they are our co-workers, supervisors, fellow church members, entrepreneurs, actresses, neighbors, and best friends. Some are divorcées, some widows, some are teenagers, some rape victims, some had "accidents," and some have consciously chosen to bear a child alone. Their lifestyles have very little in common except that they are all women who have (or will have) a child without a marriage partner. And they are heading more than half of all African-American families in the United States.

For many single sister-mothers-to-be, the credo seems to be, "I don't need him. I am perfectly capable of doing this myself."

With pride and determination thousands of single sisters each year decide to have babies without the support of the baby's father. For a lot of these women, the credo seems to be, "I don't need a man. I

Diane Allford, Allford/Trotman Associates, Atlanta.

am perfectly capable of doing this myself." And many are indeed strong, capable sisters. But pregnancy, childbirth, and child-rearing were not designed to be solo events. And women say that it's usually after going to that first childbirth class without a coach or staying up all night with a colicky baby that the feelings of anger, loneliness, and even regret begin to surface. When we interviewed new single mothers from varying backgrounds, the key theme was that they were under some serious stress. The main issues single sister-moms struggle with are: lack of support with everyday scheduling; financial hardship; lack of emotional support; fatigue; feelings of anger, abandonment, and depression. "In my practice I find a very high degree of depression among single mothers," says Dr. Brenda Wade, a California-based family psychologist and author of *Love Lessons.* "Depression manifests itself as hyperirritablity. Very often when I see a sister on the street yelling and snatching her kid I say, 'There's a depressed woman.' " But depression doesn't have to be a requisite state of being for single mothers any more than it does for married mothers. Replenishing yourself spiritually and emotionally each day and gathering the support of family and close friends are the keys to combatting depression and enjoying your pregnancy and childbirth experience. This includes having a daily quiet time where you speak to and listen to God and where you get empowered by learning about his undying love and support of you—no matter what. "It is critical that you maintain your inner life," says Dr. Wade, who is also a single parent. "When we don't, our children pay the price." (See Chapter 8, "Filling Your Inner Tanks," for more.)

The second step to having a healthy and enjoyable pregnancy is building a support team of people who will encourage you through the rough times as well as be there to laugh with you in times of joy. Every mother, married or single, needs others to "hold her arms up" when her energy is low and her spirits downcast. As a single mom, you will face additional challenges that will test even your last few nerves. You must be able to ask for help from others when you need it. We believe it is the duty of all people in a community—particularly couples without children and single folks—to gather around single families and offer them support, love, and time, in the tradition of the African village.

The other chapters in this book will provide sound information that will help you during pregnancy, childbirth, and your baby's first year. Being well informed and clearly understanding your options will give you the confidence you need to make wise decisions about what's right for you. Read each chapter carefully and take advantage of the research and interviewing we did on the issues that are important to women during maternity. Develop your own opinions based on the information you glean. Below is some advice that we believe will speak to some specific concerns expressed by single sisters.

Pregnancy

Though you may feel alone during those long days of pregnancy, know that married pregnant women whose spouses work nights and weekends say they often feel lonely too. Marriage does *not* cure loneliness. However, the more you isolate yourself from others, the more vulnerable to depression you will be. Consider strongly the possibility of living near or moving in with a close friend or relative who you can rely on for physical and emotional support during your pregnancy. Don't try to go it alone. You are not Superwoman. Ask a close friend or relative to be your childbirth coach and attend the classes with you. Your friend should be willing to attend *all* of the classes and be "on call" the week before and after your due date in order to be with you during labor. (Note: Only 5 percent of babies are actually born *on* their due date.) Share your birth plan with your coach so he or she can be your mouthpiece during labor, making your desires known to the medical staff (see below, "Labor and Childbirth"). Other important areas where your friend can be your "accountability partner" throughout pregnancy include helping you maintain a nutritionally balanced diet; seeing that you do your pelvic exercises and take brisk walks daily (if your friend will walk with you that would be even better); accompanying you to doctor or midwife appointments; taking a keen interest in any tests that are recommended to you and helping you talk through any concerns your caretaker may express about your pregnancy; getting the baby's space organized and well stocked so necessary items are easy to reach; preparing freezable meals (such as casseroles) to be eaten during the weeks after the baby's birth.

Labor and Childbirth

Ideally, the same person whom you asked to be your coach for childbirth classes should be the one who will serve as your birth assistant. During the stages of labor your assistant may need to support you physically, for long periods of time. It will be a great help to you if your assistant was well versed in the various positions that can ease labor pains. (See illustrations in Chapter 14, "All about Labor and Delivery.") Another big job for your assistant is to help ensure that you experience childbirth in a way that's most comfortable for *you*. Your assistant should not be the timid type! For instance, if you've decided that walking around during your second stage of labor will be better for you than lying down (which it is), you should not end up on a hospital bed hooked up to a fetal monitor against your wishes. The more your assistant knows, the more confident he or she will be in mediating on your behalf. Your friend can also arrange for the care of other children while you are giving birth, if applicable.

"It was the first night back home from the hospital with my baby. I had an emergency cesarean section and I had no idea how painful the recovery would be. I remember literally crawling on my hands and knees from my bed to the baby's crib in the middle of the night to care for him. I had a lot of friends and relatives who offered to help. I just hadn't called them."

After the Birth

In several European countries, a midwife makes daily visits to a new mother's home during the first week to ten days after the birth. Many sister midwives here in the United States will also make routine home visits to help new mothers ease into the routine of life with baby. But for the majority of pregnant women, who still choose hospital birth, once you leave the premises, you're pretty much on your own.

As a single woman, having a companion will be a tremendous help during those first weeks after the baby's born. Though you may feel fine, you will find yourself getting tired very easily. Having someone to talk to, to tend to you and the baby, to warm up meals and do light housekeeping will seem like an angel has fallen from the sky into your home! Consider choosing a retired person or a friend who has a flexible enough work schedule so they can really come when you need them. Otherwise, someone who can come over for a few hours after work will do just fine, since that's about the time when your energy will be running out. Right after the birth, your friend can assist you by phoning relatives or recording an informative message about the baby's arrival on your answering machine (if you have one) to protect your recovery time once you return home. She can also help you and baby get discharged from the hospital and transport you home—remember the car seat for the baby; it's the law! When you're up and about, your friend can help you take care of the baby while you run errands. It's best to save up several errands that can be accomplished in one outing. Just not having to fold and unfold a baby stroller or buckle and unbuckle a car seat each time you need to make a ten-minute run into a store will be a blessing. You also avoid agitating your baby with the constant movement.

"I'm so sick of hearing co-workers say, 'Oh, it must be sooo hard being a single parent.' "

Your Work Life

Pregnant women and single mothers often have a hard time in the workplace. At a time when almost everyone works overtime regularly, co-workers and supervisors can view a woman's need to leave at five or frequent sick calls as compromising her job. Start out on the right foot by having an honest conversation with your boss, and work out an arrangement that's amicable to you both. In not-so-corporate settings, this usually works fine. For instance, you may agree to come in and leave work an hour later if you're experiencing morning sickness. Don't compromise your lunch hour, though. You'll need it to take a walk—or a nap—so you can be replenished for the rest of the day. Such arrangements are usually easier to negotiate in more laid-back work settings, but, on the other hand, larger companies may be more familiar with the needs of pregnant workers. Know that it will be a difficult balance to have an emotionally healthy baby and steadily advance your career. Children require a tremendous investment of time and energy—and they're worth every bit of it. If you have the education and the experience in your field, you might want to explore the pros and cons of starting a home business or working flex-time. We know of several single sisters who have been incredibly creative in inventing workable schedules so they can spend time with their babies, pay the bills, and achieve their long-term career and financial goals. Of course, such ventures must be thoroughly researched and require at least a year of careful planning before you take the plunge. Some sisters found new job opportunities in their field with more relaxed work environments, others switched careers altogether. Whatever you choose to do, it will take time. And your support network should be able to pinch-hit for you while you're in the process.

"When I told the man I was dating that I was pregnant and that I decided to have the baby, he said, 'I didn't give you permission to use my seed.' I still haven't found words that could really express how I felt in that moment. But I thank God for moving me onward to a most beautiful time in my life."

Your Baby's Father

It can also be stressful dealing with your baby's father. Be honest with him about your feelings of abandonment, anger, or frustration, but it's crucial that you express yourself without screaming and yelling; you will waste your valuable time and, worse, you won't get heard. Though you may not feel inclined to become a student of the opposite sex right now, it will help you in the long run. Lesson number one: Men respond best to communication that's straight-forward and concise. For example, say "I feel overwhelmed with the baby and I'd like you to spend at least two hours a week caring for him so I can have a break" instead of, "You don't give a damn about your child; you don't even come to see him! Last time you said you forgot, but what you were probably doing was . . ." Accomplishing this requires a good deal of inner security on your part. You *must* be operating from a place of peace in order to have a calm conversation with a man you may even hate. Do it for the sake of your child and your own personal growth. As you see yourself handling a tough situation in a rational way, you will be empowered. At best, the father will respond more positively; at worst, you conducted yourself with dignity and grace—characteristics of the handsome African woman you are.

If your baby's father is abusive toward you or the baby, get out of the relationship, and quickly. As a pregnant woman or a new mother, you have no business being with people who are hurting you. The emotional and physical toll it will take on you can jeopardize your health and your baby's life. Many single mothers have transitioned from pregnant woman to parent more successfully on their own than single women who tried to do it while living with an abusive, insensitive, and immature man. Enlist the support of your pastor, family members, or good friends to help you act on your decisions.

Just because a father is un-wed doesn't mean he's un-caring. If you have a good relationship with your baby's father—bravo! Build on that good foundation during your pregnancy and encourage him to bond with the baby immediately after birth. Studies show that if a father is actively involved with the pregnancy and the baby's birth, he is much more likely to stay involved with his child down the road. (Turn to Chapter 12, "Becoming Daddy," for more information on how you can encourage a relationship between father and baby.) Most important is that you don't drive a wedge between your baby and her father by having a negative attitude. You will have to learn to set your personal feelings about him aside as much as possible, for the sake of the father-child relationship.

"My ex-husband and I didn't have an entirely amicable separation, but I tried hard to separate my feelings for him from my actions toward my son, Jeremiah," says Lori Hicks, whose son was an infant when she and her husband separated. "I make a point of not speaking ill of him to my son. I tell him his father loves him, but is having a difficult time. We pray for him, but I make it clear that we aren't going to get back together and that his father may get remarried." Hicks notes that she also has "accountability relationships" with several friends whom she has given permission to tell her when she is making mistakes in parenting her son. "Sometimes, when I get home from work, he misbehaves just as a way of telling me, 'I miss you, Mom.' I used to punish the bad behavior without dealing with the real issue until a friend who I trust pointed it out."

"I applaud single mothers," says Donte Compton, a teen father who now has taken up his role as dad to his two young daughters, thanks to the National Institute for Responsible Fatherhood and Family Development. "When you have little people you have to be responsible for constantly, you're under a lot of stress. You want to be a good role model. You want to make sure everything is right. You want to provide. It's a job and a half."

Your Living Environment

If you are able to move "back home" with your family, and choose to do so, it should be a well-thought-out plan that's discussed openly and honestly with your parent or relative *before* you move. The chances are that if you had a rocky relationship with the folks before you became pregnant, it will only worsen when you bring a baby home with you. However, you can help reverse this by creating clear terms of agreement before you move in. We strongly recommend writing the terms down on paper—and give everyone a copy. Also, if you have an end to the arrangement in sight and show a concerted effort to stick to it, your folks are more likely to respect and help you.

Your "contract" could be written in statements such as: "We will make every effort not to speak negatively about the baby's father, for my child's sake." "You promise not to overrule my child-rearing decisions, and I will respect and consider your suggestions." "I will not leave the baby with you for more than 24 hours unless it is an emergency or an agreed-upon instance." "I promise to find a permanent living arrangement within one year." You will also want to discuss any in-home visitations by the father, if applicable, as well as any other house rules your relatives may want enforced. On your end, make sure you let them know that you will need regular times of solitude so you can relax, meditate, or just take a nap. Overall, your attitude while negotiating this deal should be one of gratitude, your tone respectful. Remember, unless you are a teenager, it is not your mother's responsibility to house you or help you raise your baby.

If you opt against living with a parent or relative, one viable solution is to share an apartment with another single mother. This way you will have another woman, hopefully a friend, who understands exactly what you're going through—because she's living it too. The benefits of this type of living situation are enormous. You can baby-sit for each other, learn parenting skills from each other, and enjoy the cost savings of shared rent, grocery bills, utility bills, and more. You may even be able to share and swap baby clothes. If you don't want to live *with* another sister, you might like to live nearby. One mother alternates baby-sitting with her sisters, who are also single mothers. They plan sleep-overs and teach the older children how to help with the babies. (However, be sure not to put the care of an infant on the shoulders of a child or young teenager—mothering your baby full time is a job only you should do.) With any of these living arrangements, you'll have the companionship that may help keep you from getting depressed and overwhelmed by the responsibility of a new baby.

"It really helps to know that you're not alone," reminds Dr. Wade. "You need to know that there's always a place to talk and receive support. It's harder for us as black women to find groups and form groups, yet it's essential." Roommate-ing may be part of the answer to this dilemma. As with any such arrangement, it will work best if you meet together first and outline on paper what each of you is expecting, even down to a chore schedule. This minor inconvenience will be a tremendous help in avoiding the petty arguments that can slowly destroy what could have been a good situation.

The worst choice you can make as a pregnant woman or new mother is isolation. Magazine articles often highlight the "strong, single mother who did it all herself," but closer inspection will show you that most didn't. Usually, there was a parent, a grandmother, a sibling, or a good friend who helped them through the fire. Whether you believe this or not, as humans, we were created to be *inter*dependent, not *in*dependent, to need others in order to be whole. When you isolate yourself from the support you need, you are putting yourself and your baby in danger. What will happen if you get depressed and are about to snap? Who is nearby to baby-sit when you need a break for an evening? What will happen to your baby if you get sick? Forming close relationships may be difficult, and even scary, but it's worth the effort. Great places to meet potential roommates are in your workplace, at your place of worship, at the playground, or at the gym, if you are a member of one. Initiating new relationships will be easier if you do it in a familiar environment among people you can trust.

◇ ◇ ◇ ◇ ◇ ◇ ◇ ◇ ◇ ◇ ◇ ◇ ◇ ◇ ◇ ◇ ◇ ◇ ◇

"The people I thought would help me the most, helped me the least. Those who I'd thought would stay on the sidelines jumped in with both feet."

◇ ◇ ◇ ◇ ◇ ◇ ◇ ◇ ◇ ◇ ◇ ◇ ◇ ◇ ◇ ◇ ◇ ◇ ◇

Your Finances

Financial hardship is another issue that often does a double whammy on a single parent. She must work in order to support herself and her child, but her expenses often exceed her income, putting her in a spiral of debt. Baby-sitters, diapers, and transportation costs are some of the major expenses that eat up big chunks of a single mother's income. So what about saving for the future? Unfortunately, even many single moms with decent-paying jobs just aren't doing it. "No one ever showed me how," admitted one sister. "The *idea* of saving was conveyed to me as a child, but the specifics of how that actually gets done were not."

Sadly, most of the single mothers we interviewed admitted that their financial futures looked bleak. "After I buy the things we need to live, that's the end of my money," says one mother who works for a New York City newspaper. "Most single mothers I know live paycheck to paycheck. I don't even have a bank account."

One way that some working mothers broke out of this dangerous cycle was by joining their company's payroll deduction plan, which automatically deducts a set amount of money from their paychecks and whisks it into an out-of-reach savings account. Some companies will even match a portion of your savings dollar-for-dollar. That's a rate of 100 percent interest! "Many people like this method because it's 'out of sight, out of mind.' They say, 'If I don't see it, it's not there to spend,' " says New York–based personal financial adviser Tara Flax. She recommends payroll savings plans as excellent vehicles for single mothers to build their nest eggs. When it comes to saving, it's important to know two things: that the right time to start saving is *always* now, and that small amounts become big amounts over time. "People often tell me they'll start saving next year, but it's much easier to start saving a small amount now and just let it accumulate," says Flax. She encourages single mothers to picture how the future would look if they didn't save, or if an emergency came up with their child and there was no money there. "I think this creates a sense of urgency in people," says Flax. For instance, many black parents, single and married, have a goal of sending their children to college. Most think that financial aid and loans will cover their child's college tuition, but the reality is that there will probably still be a gap of several thousand dollars even after the financial assistance (if it even exists 18 years from now). What then? Planning and saving are the only ways to be prepared.

There is no new strategy for how to save money; it requires a little knowledge, and a lot of discipline and faith. Here's a simple plan to help you get started: Begin by filling out an income and expenses sheet so you can see how much you're spending on what each month. Then take a piece of paper and write down your financial goals, large and small. For example, "I'd like to buy a home in ten years," "I want to send my child to piano lessons," or "I'd like to take a vacation next year." Think through the details of each goal carefully and give yourself a realistic amount of time in which to achieve them. Seek help from a financial planner or counselor, or from a friend who is saving consistently, and pull from one category to the other in order to make your goals do-able—even if it will take several years. If you're in deep debt, seek help from a debt-consolidation service in your area; they'll help you reduce bill payments to a manageable level. Commit to "paying yourself" regularly in the form of a deposit to a savings plan. It can be as little as $20 per month to start. Have your helper hold you accountable for making your deposit each payday if your company doesn't have a payroll deduction plan. This simply means she asks you each time whether you made the deposit and asks to see your bank statement at the end of each month. "Living on a budget and making sacrifices to save for something long term may seem like a drag, but it's incredibly liberating to have a handle on my finances and know that I'm on track," says one sister who recently got out of debt and saved enough to make her first IRA (Individual Retirement Account) contribution. It *can* be done! (Turn to Chapter 6, "Getting Your 'House' in Order," pages 115–17, for a sample budget sheet and more strategies on budgeting with a baby.) Two books that can teach you how to maximize your money: *The Black Woman's Guide to Financial Independence* by Cheryl Broussard, and *The Complete Financial Guide for Single Parents* by Larry Burkett. Also, if you're entrepreneurial minded, check out *Sister CEO's: A Black Woman's Guide to Starting a Business*, also by Cheryl Broussard.

MOTHER TO MOTHER
by Joy Rankin

A single sister-mom tells her triumphant story.

My story isn't tragic or heroic. It's not humiliating or embarrassing. And by no means is it a romance or fantasy. Actually, my story is no different from that of most sistas out there who have looked for companionship and love in all the wrong places.

What started as an emergency visit to the hospital (for what

I thought was a pain in my kidneys) ended in my coming home pregnant, unwed, and over thirty. The hardest part was telling my parents. They didn't even know my lover. When I think about it, I never really knew him either.

During my two-week hospital stay, I had lots of time to think about my life and how this would impact it. Initially, when I was told of the pregnancy, I immediately reacted, "There's no way I'm having this baby, it's not a part of my life's schedule." After what seemed like days of daydreaming, I was rolled downstairs for a sonogram. There in the waiting area were other women (and girls) in the same predicament. My mind began to wonder about how different each of our situations was. Beside me was a girl of maybe 16 who was ecstatic about the possibility of her boyfriend getting her a beeper (now that she was going to have his child). Across from me was another sista who was at least 8 months pregnant, about 19 years old, and handcuffed to her prison guard. I thought about how differently the cards would lay for our babies once they arrived. It was probably that very moment I decided a baby could be a part of my world. If these women with obviously challenging situations could brave the storm, I had to seriously consider this baby and my own fate. What did I have to lose? I'd traveled the world, had a master's degree under my belt, had never been pregnant, and, most importantly, I had an enormous, supportive family and numerous friends who were ready to play their part.

I never considered my lover's feelings when making my decision. He was years younger than me and we didn't have the kind of history that would take us down the "shacking-up or marriage" avenue. To be quite honest, my decision was totally based on what I could do for the baby without him. (Somehow I knew there was a 98 percent chance I would be going it alone!) But he had rights too. I had to at least tell him what I decided. When I did, I was shocked. His first and most impactful response was, "I didn't give you permission to use my seed." I still haven't found words that could really express how I felt in that very moment. But I thank God for moving me onward to a most beautiful time in my life. One full of baby, a new outlook on life, and the village He provided to help raise my child.

As this new life took over my mental, emotional, spiritual, and physical self, I felt incredibly beautiful and sexy. I actually liked what was happening to me.

So now it was time to go coach shopping. No, not for everybody's favorite leather bag, but another kind of skin, a sista! A close friend of mine had just lost her boyfriend and was having a really hard time dealing with his death and I knew just how to save her. I offered her life by helping my baby get his first look at the world. We needed her and she clearly needed us. Little did I know it wouldn't be a match made in heaven.

Right away I knew I'd be the kind of mother-to-be that would immerse herself in the experience of growing a baby. I went to Lamaze classes, talked to breast-feeding experts, and read children's books to my unborn baby daily (What can I say? I'm a librarian). Well, the Lamaze basically went like this: Once I convinced my girl-friend to move on from her boyfriend's death, she joined me weekly at the doctor's office for birthing classes. Looking back, I don't think I took immediate notice that we were the only black women in the class as Coach and Mommy. I didn't care; negative vibes just couldn't invade my private, peaceful spot. Even when my girlfriend made a comment about our appearing gay, I managed to keep her feelings where they belonged.

With everybody now in place, the only thing we seemed to be waiting for was the baby. I had all the procedures and rules down— in my mind, but not in my heart. After what I thought was a final checkup, the doctor sent me home, told me to call my friends, get my bags, and return that night to have the baby. All wasn't going as planned! I was going to have a cesarean section.

Both my grandmothers and my coach were called and told to meet at the hospital for the delivery. What we thought would be a successful natural birth turned out to be a serious C-section. And after several hours of intense anxiety, screams at my coach, and major sedation, I gave birth to a healthy and beautiful man-child!

I never thought about the dynamics of coming home and never really being home alone again. Our first night home (and all the nights to follow) we were totally by ourselves. Sure, everybody offered their services and stayed as late as they could, but no one ever volunteered to stay for the 2, 3, 4, and 5 A.M. wake-up calls. My people were there for the asking; I just didn't ask. I would never do that again.

Life with my son has been amazing. Not just for me, but for all around him. After the initial shock of announcing my pregnancy, I think my family and friends saw single motherhood in a whole new light; after all, I had the right attitude. That doesn't mean I wasn't in for some surprises. The people I thought would help me the most helped me the least. Those who I'd thought would stay on the sidelines jumped in with both feet. I learned not to count people in or out.

Knowing I can't be my son's father isn't hurtful anymore. After all, he's surrounded with positive male role models—from his grandfathers to his uncles and my male buddies. My son's world is also rich with strong, dynamic women. Most importantly, women who are going to allow him to become a man—a strong, dynamic Black Man.

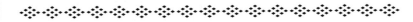

"My friends said it was easy to have a baby, that I could still party and stuff. That's basically why I got pregnant. But I found out it was all lies."

Teen Sister Mothers

Getting pregnant when you're a teenager is difficult, but it is not the end of the world. Some teen sisters wake up to the harsh realities quickly as their pregnancies mature, and begin to meet the challenges of motherhood head-on. Too many teens however, still think that pregnancy and childbirth will be easy ("Peaches and cream," to quote one young sister we interviewed), and that they can resume their prepregnancy lifestyles soon after the birth. The reality that the carefree part of their lives is essentially over forever hits many teen sisters hard.

Often teen mothers will have a strong need to mourn the loss of their freedom and their childhood. This need to grieve may show itself as sadness, anger, and irritability for "no reason," or in the new mother competing with her baby for attention and affection. Many girls thought that having a baby would solidify their relationships with the baby's fathers, which it usually doesn't. Some dreamed of birthing a cute, cuddly bundle of joy and instead got a premature, fussy baby who cries all night, and their expectations were dashed. Regardless of the mother's age, she may forget she's not dealing with a reasoning person but rather an innocent yet demanding baby. Several teens told us that they had babies because they wanted "someone to love them," or because they needed "to have something no one can take away from them." What makes teen pregnancy all the more difficult is that young sisters are still working out their own self-images, figuring out their own goals and dreams, while they have the looming responsibility of a baby that insists they be adults—now. This pressure, along with the unfamiliarity with adult ways, makes teen pregnancy and parenthood even harder.

"I remember being surprised when my doctor told me that two bags of potato chips and a box of mini-doughnuts wasn't good enough to nourish a baby," says one teen mom. Other young women struggle with chronic illnesses during their pregnancies. "I had to gain eighty pounds during my pregnancy to make up for the bulimia that I had before I became pregnant," recalls another mom, who says her diet was mostly "pickles, pizza, and hot fries." Another sister worried that her baby would inherit the diabetes that afflicts her grandmother, mother, and little sister. And everyone expressed fears that they wouldn't finish school and that their relationships with the fathers wouldn't "work out" after they had the babies. One sister told me that the great hope among single teen moms in her neighborhood was that the fathers of their *second* child would marry them.

Despite the odds, for many of our teens pregnancy ends up being the experience that grows and deepens them beyond measure. "I've matured since I had my son," said one 16-year-old. "I was all about partying before, now I'm trying to stay home for him." Another teen told us, "My son gives me a lot of courage and motivation. I'm striving to do things that I wouldn't be doing if I didn't have him. I think I'd be just sitting around."

Thankfully, more parents and grandparents are refusing to allow teen parents to "just sit around," and insist that they participate more fully in the care of their babies, even when they live at home. The days of "Mom will take care of the baby" are coming to an end. Parents and relatives are easing into the more supportive role they were meant to play. "When my son sneezed, I'd think he had a major cold," says one mom. "Once he overslept and I just knew he had a severe sleeping disorder. I would have admitted him into the hospital if it wasn't for my mother, who explained what was going on."

As far as young fathers are concerned, there seems to be a slight increase in their level of involvement with their infants. Community organizations like the Cleveland-based National Institute for Responsible Fatherhood and Family Development (NIRF) are a great help in this crucial effort. The organization seeks out teen fathers and schools them about the importance of being a presence in their baby's life. An incredible 74 percent of young fathers in the program become nurturing, involved dads, legally claiming paternity, and some even obtain custody of their infants. But many sisters still long for the closeness and everyday (and every *night*) commitment from their baby's father that's only found in marriage. "Financially he's good to us, but I need him to be there to take care of his baby," laments one teen mom. "If I need something, I just want him to get it. I don't want to have to explain why I need it. If you care about your baby, you'll be there to see what it needs; you won't even have to ask anyone."

Obviously, teen pregnancy and single motherhood is a challenge on many fronts. It is important to allow yourself to feel the emotions that are welling up inside. Only if you get down and dirty with yourself and root out the real cause of your pain will you ever be able to be a whole parent to a child. It can help to write down your "raw" feelings and look back at them later. This may be step one in your healing process. Remember to keep things in perspective and learn to accept the things you cannot change—and to change the things you can. March on, sisters. The village is here to help you—you may just have to search it out. Know that you are phenomenal women, fearfully and wonderfully made!

CHAPTER 12

Becoming Daddy

*The true measure of a man is not where he sits in times of comfort
and convenience, but where he stands in times of challenge.*
—Dr. Martin Luther King, Jr.

The fathers I encounter in my practice in Harlem give me cause
for both rejoicing and sorrow. I am inspired when I see them
struggling and juggling to fulfill their roles as parents, partners, and role models. One new father routinely brings his baby
daughter in to see me for checkups. Often he comes alone, but when
the baby's mother accompanies him, he barely lets her get a word or
a question in edgewise—this brother wouldn't even let his wife
undress the baby for the exam! He's so excited. He wants to do it
all—he wants to be Superdad.

I am encouraged when I see what I call the "too-young fathers,"
most of whom are not married to the mothers, show up at the hospital to see their babies for the first time. I always hope against hope
that when they hold that precious life they helped to create in their
arms, they will realize how important their presence as a father—a
daddy—will be in their child's life. More often than not, though, I
am saddened to hear that that one hospital visit was the most meaningful interaction they ever had with their child.

But then there are the many black fathers who shine. Not because
they had wonderful fathers as role models growing up (most didn't), or
because they are uniquely gifted, or because they are "whipped," but
because they are, simply, committed. These brothers are committed
to loving and caring for their families. They are willing to fight the
awkwardness and venture into a baby's world. They take risks, learn

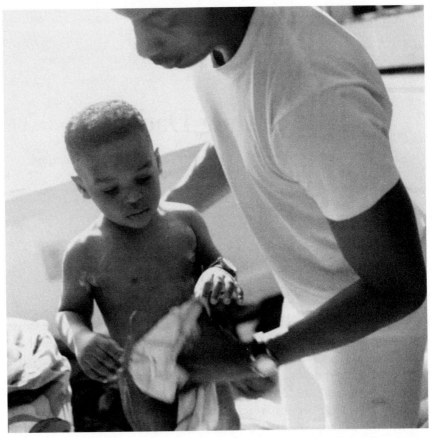

Albert Trotman, Allford/Trotman Associates, Atlanta.

from their wives, make mistakes, and try again. They are sold on the task of husbanding and fathering, and they want to do it well—from the start.

In spite of the pressures of being black men in America, brothers are becoming good fathers, and good husbands, too. How do they do it? Well, we thought that would best be answered by the brothers themselves. On the next few pages, you'll find the actual conversations we had with twelve black fathers across the country in all walks of life, each with children under 5 years old, as they candidly share their fears, struggles, and triumphs about "becoming daddy."

A Fathers' Roundtable

"I wondered what in the world I was going to offer a child. I had bouts of fear and anxiety. I couldn't believe my wife was actually pregnant."

Q: What went through your mind when you found out you were going to be a father?

Martin, 35, single, father of 1: I had flashes of everything, of what kind of parents we'd make, who this person would be, of my relationships with my mother and father, of what I had to do. I knew I wanted to be Superdad, Bill Cosby. I watched lots of family sitcoms growing up—*The Brady Bunch, The Partridge Family.* Unfortunately, they solved all their problems in half an hour. I found out that real life hardly ever imitates the fantasy world of TV.

David, 30s, married, father of 1: I wondered what in the world I was going to offer a child. I had bouts of fear and anxiety. I couldn't believe my wife was actually pregnant.

John, 29, married, father of 2: I had thoughts of the old cliché—*Father Knows Best.* I wanted to go out to work and be able to come home with peace and serenity in my heart and enjoy being with my family. But I've discovered that there are many outside forces that work against this, especially for young black families."

"We started talking to our child in the womb. We played music for her and read to her."

"We admired the way some of our friends were raising their kids, so we surrounded ourselves with those friends."

Q: How did you prepare yourself for becoming a new parent?

Carl, 32, married, father of 1: My wife and I have been married for six years so we had a lot of time to think about becoming parents. We read all kinds of parenting books—Dr. Spock, everything. We learned that there are stages that every child goes through and it really helped to read about them *first* so we knew what to look for. Also, the people we came in contact with when we moved to Los Angeles all had kids, so I heard stories, but talk can be superficial.

Steve, 39, married, father of 1: We started talking to our child in the womb. We played music for her and read to her. We got to know her before she was even born. I read every book that was written. But nothing can quite prepare you.

Salif, 43, married father of 3: It wasn't easy. I was a taxi driver and owned a restaurant when my wife was pregnant with our daughter. She would come and cook at the restaurant after doing her day job because we couldn't afford to hire anyone to work at night. We didn't have much time to prepare. We went to the hospital straight from the restaurant.

David: My wife and I gathered all these books and read them. Some of our friends really did things with their kids that we liked, we admired the way they raised them, so we surrounded ourselves with those friends.

Rick, 32, married, father of 2: My wife read all the books and we went through Lamaze classes together. We turned to our parents and friends a lot, but basically I didn't find anything very difficult. I'm very comfortable with babies.

"My father was absent, and I still remember the pain of not having him around. You start to remember things like your father promising to get you a new Easter outfit and you wait and wait and he never shows."

Q: Talk about your experiences with your own fathers. Discuss how they affect the way you feel about fatherhood.

Ray, 32, married, father of 2: My father wasn't there. My mother laid down the law. My wife's parents also separated when she was young, and she and her father still don't get along. These factors make it very important for me to be a visible force in my family. Our society had given us [black men] a raw deal and we need to counteract it with positive images. This starts at home.

Preston, 47, second marriage, father of 2: My father was absent, and I still remember the pain of not having him around. You start to remember things like your father promising to get you a new Easter outfit and you wait and wait and he never shows. I was told he was a merchant seaman. It turns out he was in jail, he later told me. I was raised in an extended family. Nowadays, kids are raising kids without the solid foundation of a support group. The role of the man in the family is very important, especially for boy children. Kids need to be motivated by both sexes.

Carl: My father showed me how important it was to have stability in a relationship. He was always there and he always paid the bills. Men in the church also helped shape my images of fatherhood. As an adult, my relationship with my father hasn't been very close. We talk and see each other a couple of times a year.

Steve: My father had to work two jobs, so I never really got to see him. That was a real concern for me with my own child. But he was a provider, an incredible man. We never wanted for anything—but time with him. When I think about a good father, I think of him being there, being very affectionate. I think this is very important, especially for black fathers. The best example of being a father is the Lord. His unconditional love. My wife and I are devout Christians and we want to raise our children with the principles of the Bible and the word of God. And in doing that you don't have to compromise your heritage.

Rick: Consciously, my father has no influence in my life. My role model and hero was my mother. She went to my games *and* worked two jobs. She is white, but is more black than my dad, who was always trying to "keep up with the Joneses." My first role models were my Little League baseball coaches. They were blue-collar workers yet they found time to give back to the community. I think this is an important quality that I will teach my children.

Anthony, 40, father of 3 from 2 marriages: I lost both my parents at a young age, so my sense of a role model for fatherhood didn't exist. Since I was raised by my godmother, I had to develop my own images of fatherhood through trial and error. After I divorced, remarried, and had another son, I've had to redefine my role as a father. I learned that each of my children needs different things from me. For instance, I have a great deal of concern about how my older son (from previous marriage) will treat women when he grows older. For my daughter, I have to demonstrate caring, and challenge the existing stereotypes about men. I have to show her that men can be loving. For my youngest son, I just have to be there.

Cornell, 28, married, father of 1: My father gave me good values, but I lived with relatives most of the time. It was a terrible experience. So my major influence for fatherhood came from the Bible. I know that God is my father and he is all understanding.

◇ ◇ ◇ ◇ ◇ ◇ ◇ ◇ ◇ ◇ ◇ ◇ ◇ ◇ ◇ ◇

"My grandfather was the perfect role model for fatherhood. He was married for more than fifty years! By example, he showed me how a man is supposed to love a woman."

◇ ◇ ◇ ◇ ◇ ◇ ◇ ◇ ◇ ◇ ◇ ◇ ◇ ◇ ◇ ◇

Salif: My father spoiled me so much, I had problems when he passed away. I began to miss school and my mother couldn't do much for me. I wasn't listening. Having a father in the house is very important. You have to take responsibility for your kids as a father. You can't just have them and leave them.

David: Even though my parents were divorced, my father and my stepdad were still good influences. My grandfather was the perfect role model for fatherhood. He was married more than fifty years, and by his example he really showed me how a man loves a woman. I really had to look at myself and get my life together. I realize that everything I do affects my daughter.

John: I don't know my father. I didn't grow up with him. I don't have any animosity now, but I'd still like to talk to him and ask him why he didn't take care of his responsibility. I have to do what I can so I won't follow down the same path as he did.

"After seeing my wife through pregnancy, I am simply amazed at how much a woman can endure. My wife became a queen in my eyes."

Q: *Were you actively involved in your wife's labor and childbirth? Tell us about it.*

Anthony: Giving birth was a team effort. We attended childbirth classes together, but at first my wife didn't think I would have enthusiasm for another birthing process since she knew I had done it before [with my first wife]. I told her that this time would be the first time with her, so that made it very special. She even bought me a T-shirt that said COACH on it. But I forgot to wear it to the hospital.

Carl: Yes, I was in the delivery room with my wife for 32 hours! Friends had told me what to expect so I felt prepared.

Martin: I was in the delivery room when my daughter was born. When she came out, it was such a miracle to me. Her face was my face, just all mushed up. So I nicknamed her Mush.

Cornell: My wife acquired gestational diabetes and there was a pretty large presence of danger. We were very prayerful about it.

David: I canceled everything in order to be at the birth. But I did book this one job that was scheduled for two weeks after the due date. Her due date came and went and the job came up. It seems like my wife went into labor the minute I got to the airport. I really regret missing it.

◇ ◇ ◇ ◇ ◇ ◇ ◇ ◇ ◇ ◇ ◇ ◇ ◇ ◇ ◇ ◇ ◇

"I wanted everything to be perfect—I sprayed the room with Lysol, I wanted to sterilize everything! It was like bringing home china. I felt like an idiot. It took me four months to get used to the experience."

◇ ◇ ◇ ◇ ◇ ◇ ◇ ◇ ◇ ◇ ◇ ◇ ◇ ◇ ◇ ◇ ◇

"When my wife admitted that she didn't know what she was doing either, that made me feel a whole lot better!"

◇ ◇ ◇ ◇ ◇ ◇ ◇ ◇ ◇ ◇ ◇ ◇ ◇ ◇ ◇ ◇ ◇

Q: *What were the first few weeks of being a dad like for you?*

David: Bringing home our baby was like bringing home china. I didn't know what to do and my wife seemed to fall into it so naturally. I felt like an idiot. I never slept. It seemed like I was always stumbling.

Steve: When I brought home my daughter it was like, "Here's the real world." We went through Lamaze, the birth, but this [coming home] is when it hit: Now there's this person who will be with us for the rest of our lives. That's reality.

Ray: For the most part I kind of felt in tune. It was a first for both of us. The second time we realized that babies are a lot more durable than we thought.

Rick: I have younger brothers and five godchildren, so dealing with babies wasn't anything new for me. I've been baby-sitting since I was three. My wife and I took turns getting up in the middle of the night and all those sorts of things. Holding and feeding the baby was no problem for me; I'm used to handling them.

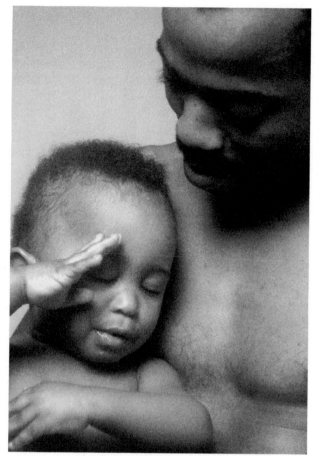

Diane Allford, Allford/Trotman Associates, Atlanta.

"Most of our men didn't spend time with their fathers talking about their feelings or struggles or hopes—they didn't hear about his life from him. So they don't see spending time this way as an important component of fathering."
—Dr. Brenda Wade, African-American family psychologist

Q: *What changes have you had to make to facilitate your role as a new parent?*

Cornell: Time has become our biggest consideration. I guess we didn't realize the amount of time a newborn would require. I try to structure my schedule so I can ease up my wife's time and she can have time for herself.

Steve: My schedule has me traveling a lot. But I want to make sure that I'm there for my child. Right now, Thursday is my day with my daughter. It won't make up for the time when I'm away, but it *is* a time when we'll be together. Also, children are like sponges; they soak up everything. I have to really watch myself.

Carl: Becoming a father changed my focus from career to family.

David: We both traveled a lot for work and I finally had to make a career change because I didn't want to drag my daughter all over the country. I wanted to establish a home environment for her. We moved here from a bigger city because I wanted her to feel free to run around in a backyard.

Donte, 23, single, father of 2: I was having problems with the kids' mother and I felt like she was being neglectful of our infant daughters. So I filed for legal custody and I've had them with me for four years now. When you have little people, you have to be responsible. You're constantly under stress. You want to make sure everything is all right. You want to provide, you want to be a good role model. Both my daughters are in day care and I drop them off on my way to work and pick them up in the evening. I'm on my own for the most part. My mother helps me out by taking the girls on weekends. I applaud single mothers; it's a job and a half.

Salif: In the beginning, my wife worked, so I had to prepare the kids in the morning, take them to the sitter, then go to work. In the evening, my wife would come home and I'd go back to work again, to my second job. It wasn't easy. Parenting is much easier in Senegal, where I'm from. There, the whole village cares for the children. Here, no one cares.

Preston: When I had my first child in college at age 25, I thought I was doing a great thing by working all the time to provide for my family. I almost missed out on my son's growing up. Now, with my younger sons, every evening we have a family lesson where we talk about how snowflakes are formed and all sorts of things like that. It's great.

"My wife knows the difference between a feed-me scream and a change-me scream. I'm still kind of guessing—I have to take a look."

Sometimes the man is trying to be a father but the mother gets in the way. Sisters have to realize how much they are hurting their children by doing this. Children must be allowed to get to know their fathers—even when they're not great guys. —B.W.

Q: What did your mate do, if anything, that helped you relate to your baby better?

David: She told me that she didn't know what she was doing either. That made me feel a lot better! But she seemed to have a natural way with the baby. She coached me on a few things, like holding, burping, and changing. I learned by watching her. I always felt like I was going to break the baby, but my wife encouraged me not to be afraid.

Anthony: Actually, since I had been through it before and she hadn't, I was able to answer questions my wife had. She's in the medical field and also did a lot of reading about pregnancy and birth. We helped each other.

"All of a sudden, here's this new little person demanding your wife's attention."

Q: How has the baby affected your marriage?

Anthony: There's a lot of communication between us and commitment to each other. I wanted to have another child and we waited a couple of years for it to happen. I knew a child would benefit from her intelligence and I wanted her to experience the fullness of womanhood. When we had our son, my wife and I became even more of a team than we were.

Steve: One adjustment that can be hard to make is the fact that all of a sudden, here's this new little person demanding your wife's attention. That takes some getting used to.

David: After you see this woman, the woman you love, with a child coming out of her, she becomes a queen in your eyes. It's another link in our relationship. It has brought my wife and I closer. A man has to make a decision now to put his family first.

Preston: New children help consolidate a marriage. I always wanted more kids but my first wife was very much a career woman. My wife enjoys a balance of career and family.

John: When my son was born, my wife and I weren't getting along. At the time, the idea of having another child didn't make sense. You have to work together from the very beginning. You can't have a lot of conflict. It's hard to raise a child when you're at odds with each other.

"We can't be as spontaneous as we once were."

Cornell: It's a new stage in our life. It's scary and exciting and we're sharing the anxiety and joy. There's a whole new level of understanding and support. When a commitment has been made by both parties, parenting only strengthens a relationship.

Carl: We can't be as spontaneous as we once were. We used to go to the Caribbean every year and we haven't since we had our son, but we expected that.

Steve: My love for my wife has matured. It's a much more secure love. We are great friends.

"I just want to teach them to live right."

"I want them to know that their real home is in Africa, so they'll know where they come from, who they are."

Q: As a father, what are some key things you plan to teach your children?

John: I want to teach my children to respect their bodies, to live healthy, to respect others, and to learn you can't always get what you want in life. I want to keep my children in church so they are kept busy with lots of good activities and their mind won't be idle. I just want to teach them to live right.

Salif: It's important for me to teach my kids through example. They know their father. They know what I do, that I work 16 hours a day. I also want them to know that their real home is in Africa, in Senegal. I sent the two youngest there for a year so they could learn the language and get to know their grandparents. This way they know where they come from, who they are.

"I would like to build a sense of responsibility and honor in her, to instill a good work ethic and to help her see the value of keeping her word."

Martin: My childhood was full of color and energy. I smiled all the time. I was simply loved. It's important that your life be good on the inside. I want that for my child.

Carl: My father was the one who introduced me to sports, so I want to get my son into it too, when he's older. I feel that sports transcend life. It teaches you how to work with people, how to be a team player, how to win and lose graciously; you learn to deal with adversity and to work hard. I also want to teach him honesty, respect for your fellow man, the ethics of work, and the concept of competition.

Ray: I don't want my daughters to grow up with the stigma of sexism, thinking they are not as important as men. I want them to be focused and have high self-esteem.

Cornell: I would like to build a sense of responsibility and honor, to instill a good work ethic, and to help her see the value of keeping her word. I also want her to keep in mind her self-esteem, the fact that her parents love her and the knowledge that God loves her.

◇ ◇ ◇ ◇ ◇ ◇ ◇ ◇ ◇ ◇ ◇ ◇ ◇ ◇ ◇ ◇ ◇ ◇

"As a pastor, I've done ninety-five funerals for young people who have been killed. My son takes a lot of time and energy, but I have to be there. When fathers aren't there kids turn to other sources for support. What I'm doing by being here is trying to save my family."

◇ ◇ ◇ ◇ ◇ ◇ ◇ ◇ ◇ ◇ ◇ ◇ ◇ ◇ ◇ ◇ ◇ ◇

Our Legacy of Strong Black Fathers

An examination of the African family shows that a father's role as protector and provider was quite revered. The father of a large family was held in high esteem by other villagers. In some parts of Africa, fathers play a vital role of support even as their mates are in labor, and are often held responsible for the outcome. Though not allowed inside the birth room, Ugandan fathers are expected to be in a nearby place praying for the safe delivery of their son or daughter. Some South African fathers make sacrifices to their gods on the baby's behalf. Kenyan fathers even take off their belts and pants in a symbolic gesture of support for their laboring wives during a difficult birth! The Bible itself urges men and fathers to be self-controlled, temperate, worthy of respect, and sound in faith, in love, and in endurance. More mature men and women are told to be examples for the younger generation in word and deed. Fathers and mothers are commanded to "train up their children in the way they should go" and it promises that if done well, "it will not depart from them."

Yet even with all this great wisdom to guide us, fatherlessness is still the biggest problem in American society, and is a virtual plague in the African-American community, some say. According to Haki R. Madhubuti, author of *Black Men: Obsolete, Single, Dangerous? The Afrikan*

American Family in Transition, fathers are the missing link in the lives of many young African Americans. In an increasingly dangerous and unpredictable world, absent fathers add tremendously to the insecurity of children. Other than the period of chattel slavery, there has never been a time when the absence of black fathers has been so prevalent. In fact, nearly two-thirds of black babies are born out of wedlock and more than half of black families are headed by women.

Not surprisingly, the problem of absentee fathers in the black community is largely a class issue. In his book, *Two Nations: Black & White, Separate, Hostile, Unequal,* Andrew Hacker notes that in depressed black neighborhoods, hardly any of the households have a male parent in residence. As a functional alternative, boys spend much of their time with groups of youths their own age, where they devise their own definition of masculinity. "It is difficult to teach males to nurture children when they have not had fathers themselves," says Charles Ballard, president of the National Institute for Responsible Fatherhood and Family Development, a Cleveland-based nonprofit organization devoted to teaching young, inner-city men how to become good fathers. His religious-based program boasts an incredible 74 percent success rate, with a few fathers like Donte, from our roundtable, even becoming primary caretakers for their children.

Thankfully, more and more "middle-class" brothers are making a conscious effort to be there for their families, physically and emotionally. But before we decide that fatherlessness is someone else's problem, we should note that even well-educated, hardworking black men in their thirties are twice as likely to be separated or divorced than their less-advantaged counterparts. This would suggest that just giving a brother a degree, a job, a house, and a car does not a good father make. For a black man, "success" often comes with more emotional stress and pressure that puts more strain on their marriages. Add a couple of babies, some new bills, and the radical change that many marriage relationships undergo when a child enters the picture, and you can see how the unraveling begins.

Sisters have their part to play in the making of an emotionally absent dad too. The fact that African-American women have dominated child nurturing and childrearing in our culture has inadvertently helped brothers feel purposeless as caregivers for their children. Often, a woman wants and needs to involve her mate more in the care and nurturance of their child, but she can sabotage her own efforts by playing the role of critic when he shows initiative. Brothers are often treated as baby "helpers" instead of as fathers with a duty to provide daily care for their children—from the start. Ironically, this happens at just the time when many men are feeling like real grown-ups and want to get with the "family-man" program—similar to the way young African men feel when they return from their initiation period and become accepted by the other warriors. Women must realize that having a child is a sink-or-swim time in many brothers' lives, one in which they can either flourish or flee, even if they're only fleeing emotionally. In order to flourish in this new role as dad, a man must have two basic things: a deep commitment to learning how to be a good husband and father—whatever the cost—and the undying support of a good woman by his side. With these two factors in mind, here is a synopsis of the "Afrikan American Father's Pledge" from Madhubuti's *Black Man: Obsolete, Single, Dangerous?* (Third World Press, Chicago) and some of the promises made by Promise Keepers, an interracial group of Christian men, including hundreds of African-American fathers. Below these are some practical ways that you and your mate can help each other become fulfilled as parents.

An Afrikan American Father's Pledge

1. I will study, listen, observe, and learn from my mistakes as a father.
2. I will openly display love and caring for my wife and children. I will hug and kiss my children often.
3. I will teach by example, introducing my family to new, developmental activities regularly.
4. I will read to or with my children as often as possible.
5. I will try to make life a positive adventure and make my children aware of their extended family.
6. I will never be intoxicated, "high," or use foul language in front of my children.
7. I will be nonviolent in my relationships with my wife and children.
8. I will maintain a home that celebrates Afrikan-American history and culture.
9. I will teach my children good values such as self-discipline and honesty, and I will encourage them toward economic independence.
10. I will provide my family with love, security, and spiritual guidance and will encourage them to exercise their responsibility to the less fortunate of this world.

Promise Keepers, a fast-growing Christian organization, emphasizes adherence to biblical values and highlights the importance of a man having a firm foundation in God in order to be the spiritual leader in the home. It also recognizes the value of external relationships. Summarized, some of their promises include:

A commitment to loving and protecting your wife and family and raising children according to biblical values.

A commitment to practice spiritual, moral, ethical, and sexual purity.

A commitment of time, talents, and resources to the church and support of the local pastor.

A commitment to reach beyond any racial barriers to demonstrate the power of biblical unity.

A commitment to pursue vital relationships with a few other men, understanding that they need brothers to help them keep their promises.

Dad's: Don't forget to check out Tony Evans's *No More Excuses: Be the Man God Made You to Be* (Crossway Books). It's good stuff!

Supporting Your Mate: What Works

Men

◆ Talk to your wife, explain to her that you aren't used to being around babies or having emotional intimacy and that you need help. That's what marriage is all about!

◆ Don't be afraid to play with your baby. Babies usually enjoy being held in a man's strong, firm arms, or against a bare chest. It makes them feel safe. And most squeal with delight if you lift them over your head—just as long as you hold them securely.

◆ Don't shrink away from the baby if she's crying or sick, especially in the middle of the night. Developing a relationship with your child means being able to soothe and comfort her in these moments, not just playing with her when she's fed and happy. Take comfort: Your wife doesn't always know what to do either; it just seems that way. Sometimes a baby *does* need her mother, especially if she's breast-feeding. Don't let this make you feel unwanted or incapable. It's just nature calling.

◆ Make changing diapers, washing diapers, and picking up baby things as much your job as your wife's—a daily habit. Don't allow "traditional" ideas about who does what to sway you from your commitment to being a fully involved partner.

◆ Accept the fact that you and your wife have lost some freedom that will not be regained until your baby grows up and leaves home.

◆ Accept the fact that your work environment may be unsupportive of your efforts to become family centered instead of work centered.

◆ Talk about your baby to as many people as can tolerate it. It will help you continue to walk what you talk.

◆ Offer to take the baby with you when you go to the store or on short trips outside (longer ones if you're able). Use a front or back carrier to help the baby bond with you during your outing.

◆ Sing, dance, tell stories, and make silly (but not scary) faces to your baby—she'll love it, and you.

◆ Read "Sex after Birth" in Chapter 16 before your wife does, and surprise her with your sensitivity!

"I wanted to encourage my husband to bond with our six-month-old daughter, so I decided to consistently make a big effort when he came home from work. We would hear his car in the driveway and I'd say, 'Jasmine, Daddy's home! Yay! Let's go meet him at the door with a big hug!' And we'd run to the door to greet him. Of course, sometimes I had to work up the enthusiasm, but it was worth it! He really felt missed and loved. And their relationship continues to improve."

Women

◆ Genuinely encourage every interaction your husband makes with the baby. Men need verbal affirmation, especially when venturing into a "woman-dominated" area—give it freely and frequently. Often, men like to play with their babies as a way of getting comfortable with them. Do not discourage this; most times mothers worry that Dad is playing "too rough" with the baby—he's not. Babies, even newborns, are much more durable than we think. As long as a newborn's head and neck are not allowed to tip back, playing is fine.

◆ Don't hover over your mate when he's feeding or changing the baby. He's already afraid that he may be doing something wrong. If you delegated the task, let it go. He does not have to do things exactly the same way you do them; let him work things out by his own experience. Learn from him.

◆ Verbally acknowledge the ways the baby responds to your mate—when she laughs if he tickles her feet, for instance. Once he's discovered "their special thing" he'll enjoy doing it again and again and will develop confidence in his new role.

◆ Regularly discuss the baby's changes with your husband; ask for his input.

◆ Regularly have a "date" together where you discuss how things are going in your relationship. One daunting statistic tells us that more than half of the men who cheat on their wives do so while she is pregnant or shortly after the baby is born. This is a time of drastic change in your marriage; it's crucial that you both keep communication lines open so you can maintain intimacy.

GOOD THOUGHTS

My Dad and Me
by Melody Marie McGill, aged 12

I love my dad very much and he loves me.
My dad takes me places and does things for me.
My dad took me to this 3-D movie. We had to wear weird glasses. Also my father bought me a Game Gear.
He might not still be with my mom but I still love them both.
He doesn't even have to take me places or buy me things.
Just me spending time with him is good enough for us.

HISTORICALLY SPEAKING . . .

 A West African father is handed his child shortly after birth. Lifting her up to the heavens, he recites the following prayer, "Welcome into our midst, may thou grow up to be a true and healthy woman/man amongst us." And all present say, "So be it!" Young Ugandan fathers are taken aside by the elders in their communities and are taught how to care for their pregnant wives. They are told pearls of wisdom like, "If your wife makes you angry while she is pregnant, go over to the neighbor's and scatter your anger there!" *What We Can Learn:* Our men have a heritage and a legacy of strong, responsible leadership in the home and of the family, too. There is also a common string in both the tribal traditions and modern programs designed to strengthen men in their roles as fathers. That cord is community and family support: an older man teaching a younger man the right way; a mother-in-law who forgoes criticism and teaches by her attitude and her actions; good friends who share their lives with you. We have learned how to network with each other in the business arena; now we need to develop deep, lasting, interdependent relationships with people that will build us up on the inside.

CHAPTER 13

Coping with Chronic Conditions and Illness During Pregnancy

E ven if you have a chronic condition or if you become ill during your pregnancy, it is likely that you can still have a normal labor and deliver a healthy baby as long as your condition is properly treated. Below is an alphabetical list of common conditions and illnesses, with emphasis on those that afflict black women disproportionately.

Asthma

Asthma, if controlled, has minimal effect on pregnancy, but on the flip side, pregnancy *can* affect asthmatics. In one-third of the cases, the asthma improves; in another third, it stays about the same; and in the last third (usually severe asthmatics), the asthma worsens, usually in the second trimester.

Before conception or in early pregnancy: Quit smoking. Avoid environmental triggers like pollen, animal hair (consider asking a friend to keep your pet), dusts, molds, tobacco smoke, household cleaning products, and perfumes. You may need allergy shots. Take your prescribed medicine before you exercise. Treat asthma attacks immediately with your prescribed medicine so your fetus is not deprived of oxygen. If medication doesn't help, go to the emergency room or call your doctor. Take drugs only as prescribed for your pregnancy. Make sure you get your immunizations to help avoid getting colds, flus, or respiratory infections.

The normal breathlessness of late pregnancy isn't dangerous, but treat any increased asthma attacks promptly. You can decrease the chances of your baby becoming an asthmatic by breast feeding exclusively for the first six months.

Diabetes

Most diabetics have normal pregnancies, but the key is keeping your blood sugar levels consistently stabilized before, during, and after your maternity. Your doctor can put you on a special program to prepare you for conception. If possible, the ideal combination of doctors you need are a diabetologist, a neonatologist (a newborns' doctor), and an obstetrician. See if your hospital-insurance carrier covers this. Your health and your pregnancy must become priority number one in your life for roughly the next year. You'll be glad to know that diabetic women in one study took such excellent care of themselves, they and their babies had fewer problems than non-diabetics.

If you have Type 1 diabetes (insulin-dependent) you already know that your pancreas is not producing enough insulin. Insulin helps transport glucose, or sugar, throughout your body to be used for energy. Most black diabetics have Type 2 diabetes—where the pancreas produces insulin but the body doesn't respond well to it. Your developing baby will make additional demands on your body for glucose, and if there isn't enough insulin available to provide it, it will obtain what it needs from other sources in your body. If this happens too often, you and your baby will be in serious danger. Coma, severe birth defects, and even death can result.

Expect to be monitored more closely than usual by your doctor, possibly once a week throughout the pregnancy. Many specialists recommend in-hospital training for diabetics before or early in pregnancy. You will be switched from oral to injected insulin when you become pregnant, to protect yourself from hypoglycemia (low blood sugar). Your medications may vary throughout pregnancy. Adding more fiber to your diet may reduce your insulin requirements, but you should follow a diabetic pregnancy program that is geared specifically for *you*. Eat regularly and exercise moderately. Get lots of rest, especially in the third trimester. Monitor your blood sugar at least four times a day. Contact your doctor immediately if your levels are above or below recommended ranges. If you have retinal or kidney problems, they may worsen during pregnancy, but return to "normal" after delivery.

For unknown reasons, stillbirths occur more to diabetic women than others—another reason to be extra cautious. If complications arise in late pregnancy, your baby may be delivered early, vaginally or through cesarean. You'll be admitted into the hospital for delivery around your thirty-seventh or thirty-eighth week, and given an amniocentesis to test the maturity of your baby's lungs. Every doctor should use an ultrasound device to locate the fetus's position immediately before inserting the needle for amniocentesis. The doctor might want to induce labor. If he or she uses Pitocin, ask to receive it intravenously rather than by injection. While it's true that many cesareans—33 to 75 percent, according to the National Institutes of Health—are unnecessary, it can be a lifesaver for the diabetic mother and her baby. After the birth, most hospitals will immediately place the baby of a diabetic pregnancy in the neonatal intensive care unit, as they tend to require more care. There, the baby will be monitored for respiratory problems that may result from excess glucose in the baby's bloodstream and for other organ abnormalities. Babies born to diabetic mothers are also often larger than other babies, which can preclude vaginal delivery.

Despite the somewhat daunting description above, many women with well-controlled diabetes have carried their babies to term safely and have had normal, vaginal deliveries—so can you, if you give yourself the best possible care.

Gestational Diabetes

A Northwestern University study found that black pregnant women are nearly twice as likely to develop gestational diabetes as whites. This refers to diabetes that is developed during pregnancy and generally ceases after delivery—though it can return later. In gestational diabetes, the hormones secreted by the placenta during pregnancy interfere with a woman's glucose levels, throwing them off balance and causing the disease. The effect on the baby is that it may grow too big for vaginal delivery, and could develop hypoglycemia after birth. Such children may later develop diabetes, obesity, or abnormal intellectual growth. More than half the women who develop gestational diabetes develop permanent diabetes later on. If you are 25 or over and pregnant, and have any history of diabetes in your family, ask for a glucose tolerance test. Gestational diabetes can be controlled through diet and/or insulin. The use of exercise to treat or prevent hyperglycemia in pregnancies complicated by gestational diabetes or insulin-dependent diabetes is currently being investigated.

Epilepsy

With expert medical care, preferably before conception, epileptics have a 90 percent chance of having a healthy baby. You'll need constant supervision and possibly frequent adjustment of medication. Epileptics are prone to excessive nausea and vomiting, but are not any more likely to experience miscarriage, preeclampsia, or premature birth than the average woman. The slight increase of birth defects in epileptic mothers may be due to certain anticonvulsant drugs, but some of the defects appear related to the epilepsy itself. Ask your doctor if you can be weaned from medications before conception, or if you can use a less risky drug. Frequent seizures may be more dangerous to your fetus than the drugs that control them.

The greatest risk of abnormalities is in the first trimester, medication shouldn't affect the fetus much after that. Ask for ultrasound or alpha-fetoprotein tests to check the fetus. If you've taken valproic acid (Depakene), check for neural-tube defects such as spina bifida. Epileptic women often develop folate-deficiency anemia. Your doctor may prescribe folic acid, vitamin D, or vitamin K.

Most women find that pregnancy doesn't negatively affect their epilepsy. If it does, due to vomited medication, ask about taking a time-released anticonvulsant at bedtime.

Breast-feeding is generally safe, since epileptic medications pass to milk in low doses. But if your baby is unusually sleepy after you've taken your drug and breast-fed, tell your doctor.

Fibroids

Though uterine fibroids affect 20 to 50 percent of all women, some medical research contends that black women show more susceptibility to them than other women, though no one yet knows why. Fibroid tumors are the most common cause of an enlarged uterus, next to pregnancy. The tumors, which are balls of muscular and connective tissue, tend to show up in us in our thirties and forties, our prime child-bearing years and earlier than they commonly appear in white women.

Fibroids often grow in the muscle wall of the uterus or on the surface of the uterus. Less often, they develop in the interior uterine cavity or in the cervical area of the uterus. The formation of fibroid tumors is related to the production of the hormone estrogen, which increases in pregnant women and in women on birth-control pills. Fibroids may be present for many years without producing any bothersome symptoms. A woman may have one large tumor or several smaller ones. Symptoms of a fibroid tumor depend on its type and location, and can include a mucus-like vaginal discharge, irregular periods or periods with heavy bleeding and cramping, severe lower abdominal pain, back pain, incontinence, and painful urination. Fibroids can be tricky to diagnose as they grow in different ways and sometimes resemble ovarian cysts. Some women can feel them when they press around their lower abdomens, but they can be officially diagnosed through a pelvic exam or ultrasound.

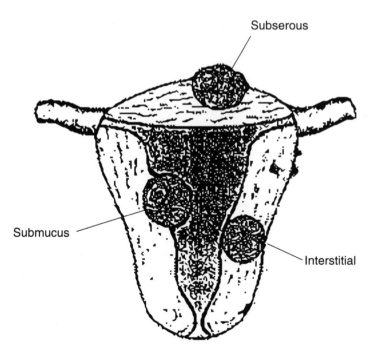

Fibroid Tumors.

Contrary to popular belief, fibroids do not cause infertility, though they may complicate pregnancy. Like the baby growing in your womb, fibroids need blood to live, and compete aggressively for it, thus reducing the blood supply available to the fetus. Miscarriage is also a higher risk for a pregnant woman with fibroid tumors, however, many women have full-term pregnancies despite their presence. Treatment for fibroids is usually recommended when the tumor is larger (about the size of a 12-to-14-week pregnancy), as it is likely to cause some complication eventually. Otherwise, doctors often prescribe watchful waiting. Holistic treatments that may be effective include eliminating dairy products from your diet and reducing stress. Myomectomy is a surgery that, in most cases, removes the fibroids and leaves the uterus intact, though with a weakened uterine wall. This procedure is recommended mostly to women with large tumors who want to have children immediately; there is about a 50 percent chance of successfully getting pregnant afterward. In some cases the fibroids are deeply embedded in the wall and cause the uterus to bleed profusely and result in scarring after a myomectomy. Pregnancy can cause an already-existing fibroid tumor to enlarge due to the increase in the production of estrogen, which can be quite painful. However, myomectomy during pregnancy is discouraged as there is a high risk of miscarriage. For a complete report on fibroids contact the National Women's Health Network's Information Clearinghouse at (202) 628-7814.

Heart Disease

Nowadays heart disease shouldn't bar anyone from pregnancy except those who have a very limited normal life. Many heart-diseased women have easy pregnancies and deliveries; some even experience improved heart conditions. You'll be closely supervised, and must rest to avoid extra strain. Take at least two naps a day and sleep 12 hours at night. Call your doctor if you get a chest infection, a temperature, or swelling of the hands, face, or feet; and rest in bed.

More black women than whites are obese and more black women have diabetes—both contributing factors to heart trouble. Thus, black women are more than twice as likely as white women to have hypertension and/or heart disease. The bias toward the white male in medical research has largely ignored the effects of diseases on women, both black and white. Only recently has the frightening severity of heart disease in black females been universally recognized. Coronary Artery Disease (CAD), is a type of heart disease that can be diagnosed by your cardiologist, who can also offer an opinion as to whether or not your heart can handle a pregnancy. If your condition is mild or moderate, you'll likely carry safely to term under close medical supervision. Your cardiologist will ask you to follow strict instructions, such as avoiding physical and emotional stress, possibly staying in bed, taking your medication faithfully, not gaining excess weight, eating a low-fat diet, moderating sodium intake, taking iron supplements, wearing support pantyhose, and quitting smoking. Near the end of the pregnancy you'll probably have more ultrasound scans and nonstress tests. If there are no heart or lung complications, your delivery should be as normal as any woman's, though forceps might need to be used to help expel the baby. If your disease is severe, and you are not yet pregnant, ask your doctor about corrective heart surgery in order to enable a safer pregnancy.

Hypertension (High blood pressure)

Pregnancy can raise one's blood pressure. Black women are more than twice as likely as white women to develop hypertension, especially if it runs in your family. Your pregnancy will be considered high risk, so you'll see your doctor or doctors more often and must follow their advice faithfully. If your blood pressure remains under control, with good care you and your baby should do well though you may have to go to the hospital earlier than most. Recent studies show that even hypertensive women with kidney impairment can usually have successful pregnancies. Anxiety and stress can raise your readings, so learn relaxation techniques. Rest often, and curtail physical activity to ease strain on your heart. If you have high blood pressure and are not yet pregnant, consult your doctor before conception.

You may be asked to monitor your blood pressure daily with a home kit. Eat a balanced diet; you may be advised to limit sodium. Drink more water—up to a gallon a day—to flush out excess body fluid. Take rest breaks, morning and afternoon, with your feet up. If your job involves high stress, seriously consider leaving work until your baby arrives. Get help—paid or volunteer—if you have other children. Raised blood pressure in late pregnancy can be a sign of preeclampsia. If this is the case, your blood-pressure medication may be changed and low-dose aspirin may be prescribed. Be alert to signs of pregnancy complications such as bleeding, dizziness, or high fever, and if you experience any of these contact your physician immediately. You will probably visit your doctor more often and receive more tests than a woman with a low-risk pregnancy would. Pregnancy is especially risky if your blood pressure remains very high and/or you have serious side effects such as retinal hemorrhages, severely impaired kidney function, or an enlarged heart.

Blacks may be more susceptible to high blood pressure than whites because of a salt sensitivity inherited from our ancestors. The theory is that many blacks on the slave ships died because of diarrhea and salt losses, which led to dehydration. Those who survived were likely to have bodies that retained more salt and water. The gene for salt retention that helped us then is hurting us now, especially when combined with the high-fat, high-salt diets of many black Americans, plus high stress levels. Blacks in Africa don't suffer the same high rates of hypertension as American blacks do.

For now, you can't control what genes you inherited, but you can control your diet and exercise habits, and take steps to manage stress, especially during your pregnancy.

Hepatitis

Hepatitis is a viral inflammation of the liver that causes nausea, fever, abdominal pain, weakness, loss of appetite, and, often, jaundice. It appears most commonly in two forms (though there are four): Type A is most common and is usually mild; it is unlikely to harm the baby. Type B is transmitted through kissing, blood transfusion, or sexual contact, and can be harmful to your baby. You may have been tested for hepatitis B during your prenatal exams and should be receiving periodic blood tests to monitor the disease if you have tested positive. Eating well and resting are recommended treatments. Eighty percent of babies become infected during delivery if the mother is infected, and thus become carriers. Bathing and vaccinating the baby immediately after birth and continuing periodic vaccinations until she is six months old can often prevent her from becoming a carrier.

Lupus or Systematic Lupus Erythematosus (SLE)

Lupus is an autoimmune disease that primarily affects women aged 15 to 64, and more black women than white, although it is not common. Pregnancy doesn't seem to affect the long-term course of lupus. Some women find that their lupus improves during pregnancy; for others, it worsens. Flare-ups seem to increase after delivery. It's unlikely that any woman will pass lupus on to her baby. It seems that women who conceive when their lupus is quiet will do best. SLE women who have severe kidney impairment or lupus anticoagulent in their blood have the poorest prognosis. Ideally, kidney function should be stable at least 6 months before conception.

Low daily doses of both aspirin and the steroid prednisone may reduce overall risk. Some steroids don't cross the placenta, and some do but may serve to quicken the baby's lung maturity. Your pregnancy will be more complicated than most, with more frequent tests and possibly more physical limitations. Work closely with your obstetrician or maternal-fetal subspecialist, and with the doctor who treats your lupus.

Multiple Sclerosis (MS)

Multiple sclerosis and pregnancy seem to have little effect on each other. Nevertheless, early and regular prenatal care, with regular visits to your neurologist, are a must. You may be prescribed iron to prevent anemia, or stool softeners to prevent constipation. If you've had urinary tract infections, you may be given antibiotics. MS probably won't affect your delivery. Most women with MS find that their condition stabilizes with pregnancy. In later months, with weight gain, any problems you had with walking may worsen. If you need steroids, prednisone may be safe in low doses, but have your doctor check any MS medication for safety of use during pregnancy. Risk of relapse increases for 6 months after delivery, but doesn't seem to affect the overall lifetime relapse rate. Take iron supplements as prescribed, minimize stress, get adequate rest, avoid infection, and avoid raising your body temperature as with hot baths or exercise. Discuss with your doctor when you can go back to work. Breast-feeding is possible, even with occasional steroid intake. If you need large doses, you can pump your milk and discard it until the drug is gone from your milk. Bottle-feeding may be an appropriate way to supplement breast-feeding in this case.

Most MS mothers can stay active for twenty-five years or more after diagnosis and can raise their children without much difficulty. But if MS interferes with your functioning when your child is young, look for tips on baby care for parents with physical challenges (see "Physical Disabilities" on pages 273–74).

Obesity

Most overweight mothers have healthy pregnancies and deliveries. Ovulation is often erratic in obese women, so accurately dating a pregnancy is tougher. It's more difficult for doctors to determine the height of the fundus, the size of the uterus, or the fetal size and position through manual means. Being overweight raises the risks of hypertension and diabetes, which in turn can complicate pregnancy (in the form of preeclampsia and gestational diabetes). A large mother can produce a big baby, even if she doesn't overeat during pregnancy. If a cesarean is necessary, a fatty abdomen can complicate both the surgery and recovery from it.

You will probably undergo more tests than the average woman, with early ultrasound and at least one glucose tolerance test or screening for gestational diabetes. Quit smoking, and reduce other pregnancy risks. Obese women can gain less weight during pregnancy than other women without harming their fetuses. Your diet must contain at least 1,800 calories and be packed with vitamins, minerals, and protein. Exercise, following your doctor's guidelines. For future pregnancies, try to get close to your ideal weight before conception.

A woman is considered obese if she's 20 percent over her ideal weight, and very obese if she's 50 percent over. Obesity is a big problem for us, as well as for the larger society. From ages 18 to 65, black women are heavier than black men, white men, or white women. A third of black women ages 25 to 34 are overweight. (One-quarter of the overall American population is overweight.) About one-third of African Americans are obese. In black women, poverty seems to create conditions that lend to obesity. Being fat predisposes us to diseases such as hypertension, heart disease, and diabetes. Medication, proper eating habits, and exercise can help control these diseases and stabilize the weight.

Some physicians believe that the risks of obesity are greatly exaggerated. A study in South Africa showed that a group of 210 poor rural black women had very few weight-related health problems in spite of an obesity rate of nearly 20 percent. Of course, these women were active and enjoyed a mostly vegetarian diet of corn, brown bread, fruits, vegetables, beans, and occasional dairy items and meat. Interestingly, other studies have shown that Westernization and urbanization in Africa, including the adoption of the high-fat Western diet, sends obesity rates and disease rates soaring. For a healthy eating plan during pregnancy see Chapter 7, "You (and Your Baby) Are What You Eat."

Physical Disabilities

Good news: There's no evidence of increase in fetal abnormality among mothers with spinal-cord injuries, nor among those with physical disabilities not related to hereditary or systemic disease. Delivery will be more difficult for you, but not for your baby, and vaginal delivery is possible in most cases. Women with spinal cord injuries are more susceptible during pregnancy to kidney and bladder problems, palpitations, sweating, anemia, and muscle spasms. Your contractions may be painless, so you'll have to learn other signs of labor. It's important, though, to find an obstetrician or a maternal-fetal subspecialist who's experienced in dealing with disabled women. Or find a supportive doctor who's willing to learn "on the job." Later, get a referral for a pediatrician or family doctor supportive of the physically challenged parent.

Your special measures during pregnancy and parenting will depend on your particular physical limitations. In any case, restrict your weight gain to the recommended 25 to 35 pounds. Eat well, and keep up your strength and mobility through physical therapy. Plan your route to the hospital well in advance, and prepare the hospital staff for your special needs. Remember, you may be alone when your time comes. Leave early for the hospital to avoid traffic delays. Make sure your obstetrical unit is wheelchair friendly.

Modify your home for your special child-care needs. Your husband will need to be a more-than-equal parenting partner. Some ideas to make life easier: Get in-home assistance, paid or unpaid; tailor the changing table to accommodate your wheelchair, purchase a crib with a drop side; use a baby carrier (leaving your hands free for your wheelchair); consider using a diaper service. For your emotional tank: Join a support group for disabled parents so you won't feel alone in your situation.

Sickle-Cell Anemia

With today's major medical advances, a woman with sickle-cell disease can have a safe pregnancy and a healthy baby—even with complications like heart or kidney disease. Pregnancy adds stress to the body and increases the chance of a sickle-cell crisis; the risks of miscarriage and early delivery are increased with this disease. Preeclampsia is more common in sickle-cell women, but whether it's because of the disease or being more prone to hypertension is unclear.

Find an obstetrician who's familiar with sickle-cell and who works closely with a maternal-fetal subspecialist, internist, or hematologist. You should have frequent prenatal checkups: every two or three weeks up to the thirty-second week, and once a week after that. Vitamin and iron supplements may be prescribed. You may need blood transfusions. You're as likely to have a vaginal delivery as anyone else, and you may receive antibiotics afterward to prevent infection. If both parents have the sickle-cell gene, your baby could inherit a serious form of the disease. Your husband should be tested; if he has the gene, you may want to see a genetic counselor. For a referral call your March of Dimes.

Sickle-cell anemia strikes 1 out of 12 African Americans. It can also be found in Caribbeans, Southeast Asians, East Indians, Latin Americans, and Mediterraneans, though less frequently. Having sickle-shaped, rather than round, red blood cells may have helped our African ancestors survive malaria. These odd-shaped cells can pile, stick together, and clog blood vessels, reducing circulation. The disease can lead to death. About 8 percent of blacks carry the sickle-cell trait. It's not contagious and cannot be passed through a blood transfusion. When both parents have the trait, their baby has a 1 in 4 chance of getting the full disease. The baby also has a 1 in 4 chance of having normal blood cells, and a 2 in 4 chance of carrying the trait, which has no symptons.

All newborns should be tested. In many states, hospitals have mandatory screening, and newborns are tested within a few days. Signs of sickle-cell disease in children include leg ulcers; hands and feet that swell and turn red, hot, and painful; slow growth; frequent colds and sore throats; jaundice—yellowish tinge in the whites of the eyes; painful joints, especially in the hips and shoulders; and sickle-cell crisis, which is severe chest, abdominal, arm, and leg pain. If your child has the disease, he or she will need medication and constant monitoring. A new treatment using butyrate—a fatty acid—has proven promising in clinical trials.

MOTHER TO MOTHER
by Monique Greenwood

A determined sister shares her story of going through pregnancy with fibroid tumors.

I had a fibroid tumor the size of a lemon for two years before my husband and I decided to get pregnant. We decided to go ahead anyway and after three months of trying we were pregnant. By the end of my first trimester I had lots of bleeding and excruciating pain in my abdomen. Because of the fetus growing in my womb, the fibroids—there were now two—were deprived of their blood supply, which they feed off of. It became so bad that I had to be hospitalized and was given painkillers.

At four months, I was already having contractions. I was given more drugs to stop the contractions. Still, they continued. By this time one of the fibroids was the size of a melon. I was huge! My doctor ordered that I have complete bed rest for the rest of the pregnancy. My company sent over a fax machine and a computer so I could work from bed. At home, I was hooked up to a fetal monitor 24/7. The monitor was hooked up to my telephone line and the doctors would "call in" and check the baby's condition every few hours. (Isn't technology great?) I was taught how to give myself medication intravenously at home to help control the contractions. After a while, though, the medication no longer worked. I needed a stronger drug that could only be administered and monitored at the hospital, because it was toxic in certain doses. The doctors said the medicine wasn't harming the baby. I spent so much time in that hospital that I developed quite a rapport with the hospital staff. Everyone knew me (or knew of me) and seemed genuinely concerned about me and the baby. I must say that I was treated wonderfully. One nurse even helped me to do exercises from bed. When I wasn't in the hospital, a nurse would come to my home to give me steroid shots to help the baby's lungs develop faster in case of a pre-

mature delivery. I still had seven weeks till my due date when they did an amniocentesis and determined the baby's lungs were in fact developed enough for her to be born. That day the doctor took me off the medicine, and our daughter, Glynn Nailah, was born, five and a half weeks premature but at eight pounds, three ounces! We stayed in the hospital for five days because they thought she may have kidney problems. Then, finally, we brought her home.

The pregnancy was an emotionally difficult time for me and my husband. We weren't prepared for everything that happened. My doctors had never had a patient like me before. My husband got a pager so he could always be available to me. He would make breakfast for us every morning, pack me lunch in a cooler and Thermos, and leave it by the bed before he left for work because I couldn't get up. Neighbors would check in on me during the day.

Do we want more children? you ask. The answer is yes. But I admit, I'm afraid. The fibroids are still there, though they don't bother me. I still have to wear a size 14, and the tumors make me look like I'm always four months pregnant. Many doctors have advised me not to have a myomectomy (an operation in which the tumors are removed) because of the risk of scarring that would leave me with a 50/50 chance of conceiving. And 50/50 doesn't mean it will be the same again.

PART TWO

LABOR TO POSTPARTUM

CHAPTER 14

All About Labor and Delivery

The long-awaited moment has come—or will come soon. Are you ready? In this chapter you will learn about, and see illustrations of, the stages of labor, pain management techniques, vaginal birth, cesarean section, episiotomy, and epidural. You will also learn about technologies and medications available during childbirth and a myriad of other important details surrounding the birth experience. The more you know about what happens when you leave your home to give birth, the more confident you will feel when your time comes.

What to Prepare

Before you rush off to the hospital or birth center—if you're leaving your house at all to give birth—be sure to go through this list of items first. We suggest you gather and pack as many of the necessary items as you can by your eighth month, just to be safe.

What to Bring to the Hospital or Birthing Center

Your doctor or nurse midwife should provide you with a list of things to bring to the hospital or birthing center. They include the following items:

In the Car

◆ Car seat for baby, properly adjusted beforehand. (It is a law in most states and at most hospitals that babies can't leave by automobile unless they are in a car seat; the hospital staff will check for this); remember extra blankets to pad the car seat so the baby will lie securely.
◆ Plastic sheet or trash bag for you to sit on in case your water breaks (or insert a disposable baby diaper in your underwear to catch any fluid)
◆ Pan or bag, in case you feel nauseous

For Mother

◆ A watch with a second hand for timing contractions
◆ Light snack or juices for energy in labor (yes, it's okay)
◆ Toiletries such as soap, toothpaste, toothbrush, deodorant, and hair creme
◆ Sanitary napkins (though usually provided by a hospital)
◆ Hairbrush, comb, and hair accessories
◆ Glasses and/or contact lenses
◆ Nightgown (one that's easily opened for breast-feeding if you are planning to)
◆ Robe and slippers, for walking the hallway
◆ Socks for labor
◆ At least two changes of underwear (or more, depending on how long you plan to stay)
◆ Change of clothes to come home in

For Baby

◆ Undershirt
◆ Socks or soft booties
◆ Sleeper or outfit for the trip home
◆ Receiving blanket
◆ Soft cap
◆ Bunting outfit, preferably one that covers feet (for cold weather)
◆ Diapers

Miscellaneous

◆ Insurance forms
◆ Hospital preadmission forms, if necessary
◆ Copy of your birth plan

◆ Two or more extra pillows for labor
◆ Tape player and cassettes of soft music (don't forget its adapter or batteries)
◆ Camera or videocamera
◆ Address book or phone list of people to call after the birth
◆ Spare cash or change to make phone calls with or buy snacks at the hospital
◆ Good book or baby name book (if you haven't yet decided)

GOOD THOUGHTS

Gospel singer Larnelle Harris is one of many artists who provide great music to labor to. Here are comforting lyrics from his song "It's Only Thunder" (*Gospel Greats*, Benson Music Group):

Child it's only thunder
There's no need to be afraid
For as quickly as it started
The storm's gonna pass away
So if you're seeking peace of mind
Come on and sit here by my side
And you'll appreciate the wonders
'Cause child, it's only thunder.

What to Prepare for a Home Birth

Your midwife will probably instruct you to purchase a birth kit, which includes all of the items for a home birth, or you may be asked to gather the items yourself. They can include any or all of the following:

◆ Plastic sheeting to cover the bed and floor
◆ Towels
◆ Gauze pads
◆ Cord clamp
◆ Tape measure
◆ Bedpan
◆ Vaginal lubricant
◆ Antiseptic fluid and unperfumed soap

- ◆ Kettle
- ◆ Sanitary napkins
- ◆ Nursing pads
- ◆ Soft baby cap

What You Should Know before Giving Birth

Modern medicine, advanced technology, and research have done much to help ensure that more babies are delivered safely in complicated deliveries. However, technology can also be abused or used unnecessarily, too often causing a chain reaction of complications that might have been nonexistent if nature had been left to work on its own. For instance, once a woman is hooked up to an electronic fetal monitor, studies show that she is much more likely to have a cesarean section. Why? Because any indication of fetal distress detected by the EFM may alarm your physician, who might bypass attempting several possible natural solutions and go straight to a C-section, "just to be safe."

The more information you are given about each piece of technology and each procedure, the better equipped you are to help make wise decisions about your and your baby's care with your doctor.

Technology, Surgery, and Drugs Used in Labor and Delivery

Electronic Fetal Monitoring

There are two kinds of electronic fetal monitoring (EFM): external and internal. Both kinds of monitoring are used to measure the baby's heart rate in response to its movement and your contractions. In external EFM, two large belts are placed around the mother's abdomen to hold two small sensors in place. One is an ultrasound device that detects the baby's heartbeat, the other measures uterine contractions. Internal fetal monitoring is more accurate than external monitoring, and can only be done after the mother's water has broken or the membranes (amniotic sac) are artificially ruptured by the doctor or midwife. In this case, an electrode attached to a long wire is passed through the mother's cervix and is attached to the baby's scalp to record the baby's heartbeat while a soft tube called a catheter is also threaded through the cervix into the uterus to record contractions. Both types of monitoring are connected to a machine that continually charts a readout of the results on a piece of paper.

EFM became standard procedure in most hospitals during the 1980s, but in recent years its use has been called into question. There are many controversial issues surrounding the use of EFM. On the positive side, EFM can be helpful if you are at risk for complications during pregnancy (if you have diabetes, high blood pressure) because it provides the doctor with a visual analysis of the baby's condition over a period of time, helping him or her assess whether the baby is under stress or not receiving enough oxygen. On the other hand, critics of EFM, including most midwives, cite several reasons for its misuse. First, several recent studies have found that EFM is no more efficient than using a Doptone (hand-held ultrasound instrument to record the heartbeat) or fetoscope (a stethoscope placed on the abdomen) periodically through the labor and recording the results. Secondly, since EFM use became widespread in the United States, cesarean rates have doubled (even tripled in some areas). This is in part caused by differing interpretations of the meaning of changes on the graph readouts—is the baby in trouble (for instance, if meconium is present in the amniotic fluid) or is it simply an unusual pattern that may be altered by a change of the mother's body position? When in doubt, your doctor may prefer to play it safe and opt for a cesarean.

There are other drawbacks to the use of EFM. When external monitoring is used in labor it prevents the mother from moving around—an essential part of helping labor progress. Being "tied up" this way will increase the likelihood of a stalled labor or a labor that drags, and makes changing positions to help ease birthing pains more difficult. Also, EFM use has brought an increase in forceps deliveries, as doctors attempt to bring the baby out more quickly, and an increase in maternal and fetal infections caused by bacteria entering through the tubing and wire involved in internal monitoring.

Speak with your doctor or midwife about his or her use of EFM during delivery *before* you go into labor. You may want to request monitoring with a fetoscope, Doptone, or telemetry. Telemetry is a fairly new option that monitors your baby's vital signs through electrodes attached to the baby's head and is strapped to your thigh. This will allow you to roam freely without being tied to the bedside machine. Drawbacks include the possibility that the baby may develop a rash and may feel pain while it is hooked up. Ask whether your hospital has one of these devices and if so, get your practitioner's opinion on its safety. This is an important issue, as some hospitals have a requirement that women be hooked to an EFM from the time they arrive and every 15 minutes thereafter.

Fetal Scalp Sample

This is a quick test that takes a blood sample from your baby's head to determine her ph level, which can tell whether or not she is getting enough oxygen. It is not routine and is often done after an EFM indicates an abnormality. Another EFM should be done to confirm any findings obtained from the scalp sample.

Induction of Labor and Pitocin

Induction of labor (artificially starting labor) may be performed for a variety of reasons. In some cases labor may be induced if the gestation is at, near, or past term and either mother or child is considered to be at risk if the pregnancy continues much longer. Induction may be done if the mother has an illness such as high blood pressure, diabetes, or a worsening case of preeclampsia. Occasionally, induction may simply be performed by breaking the mother's membranes, and if the cervix is not "ripe" or ready to dilate (see illustrations, page 300), hormonal prostaglandin gel may be applied to it. However, more often than not, the drug Pitocin will be used to stimulate regular contractions. Pitocin is an artificial form of the natural hormone oxytocin that your body produces during labor. Pitocin is administered intravenously with an IV inserted in the mother's arm or the back of her hand. The amount of Pitocin is gradually administered until regular, strong contractions occur. Because the uterus receives this hormonal boost in an unnatural way, Pitocin contractions are usually more painful and closer together than regular contractions. Women who receive Pitocin often require pain medication or an epidural to help them handle the pain.

In theory, Pitocin should only be used out of necessity in critical situations when your placenta is determined to be functioning at a decreased level and is thus having a negative impact on the fetus. However, nowadays it is commonly used to jump-start a stalled labor or speed up irregular contractions. Some doctors routinely induce labor if the pregnancy continues two weeks past the due date, mostly because there is a higher incidence of fetal death associated with pregnancies that are longer than 42 weeks. Often the placenta begins to function less efficiently at this point, which can put the baby in danger. (See "When Baby Is Overripe" later in this chapter.) While Pitocin can be useful in pregnancy, it can also lead to complications. Because contractions are stronger with Pitocin and because they are regulated artificially rather than by nature, you will require continual electronic fetal monitoring. Strong, Pitocin-induced contractions may also limit the amount of oxygen the baby receives, resulting in fetal distress. (Fetal distress detected by EFM is more common in Pitocin-induced labors.) Once the doctor determines fetal distress, she may opt to do a cesarean section.

It's important to remember once again that no two labors are alike, and that nature doesn't always work according to the time lines and progression of labor that are described in textbooks and in birth classes. Prepare yourself for the possibility of a long labor (particularly if this is your first child) both mentally and physically, so you won't be tempted to jump at the opportunity of taking anything that's offered to you for relief. This is where a midwife's experience may be useful. Midwives are not licensed to administer drugs, and instead focus their skills on using natural alternatives to Pitocin, such as nipple stimulation (studies and time-tested experience have both found that your body produces effective amounts of oxytocin when stimulated) or movement during labor to produce oxytocin, and are willing to wait out a manageable but long labor with relaxation techniques.

If induction is recommended for you in advance, make sure you discuss the reasons and need for it thoroughly with your caretaker. If it isn't a necessity, inquire about other options. In some cases Pitocin can help a dragging birth and a quickly tiring mother get over the last hurdle to delivery after other alternatives have been tried and failed. If Pitocin is recommended while you're in labor, you may not be in a position to ask questions, but preparing yourself ahead of time and understanding the process can help you work more effectively with your birth attendants.

Episiotomies: The Long and Short of It

An episiotomy is a surgical cut made in the perineum as the baby's head begins to "crown" or become visible from the outside to enlarge the vaginal opening before birth. It cuts thorough soft tissue, muscles, and nerves. A local anesthetic is injected into the perineum shortly beforehand to keep the mother from feeling any pain. The

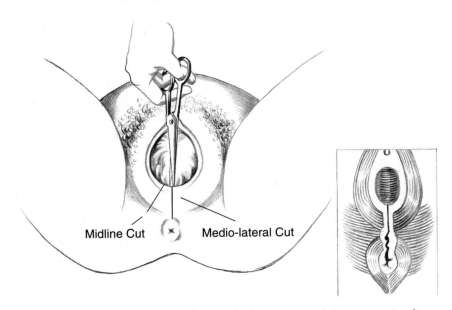

Midline Cut   Medio-lateral Cut

Episiotomy—something we hope to help you avoid. Episiotomies have become almost standard procedure in hospital births in the United States, used in 80 to 90 percent of first births and roughly 30 to 50 percent of subsequent deliveries. Many women suffer painful aftereffects for months. Shown, midline cut and medio-lateral cut; inset, a midline episiotomy that has torn into the rectum.

cut is repaired with stitches shortly after the baby has been delivered—though the aftereffects can last a long time, especially if the cut or the stitching was done haphazardly.

Much controversy surrounds this little snip. In the past, when women were drugged and immobile on their backs during labor, physicians used to perform episiotomies to widen the vaginal opening for the forceps they used to pull babies out. Also, with women on their backs and their feet raised in stirrups, tearing was much more common because of the uneven pressure the baby's head placed on the lower part of the perineum. Throughout Europe, particularly in countries such as the Netherlands and Sweden where midwifery is common, the incidence of episiotomies and tearing are significantly lower. Women are allowed to give birth at their own pace; the hurry to get the baby out quickly is less of an issue.

Of course, episiotomy is a good option if there is a serious problem—such as if the baby is losing oxygen or is in an odd position and cannot be turned manually. Episiotomies can shorten the pushing stage of labor by anywhere from 5 to 20 minutes, though rushing the birthing process has no advantage for the health of the baby except in emergency situations. Proponents of episiotomies also claim that a neat cut heals more quickly than a jagged tear of one's own. While this is true for extreme natural tears, it's often difficult to tell in the middle of labor whether a woman will have a large tear or small "first-degree" surface tear that heals much more quickly than an episiotomy incision, which severs more layers of muscle. And many women don't tear at all.

The most obvious and common drawback to an episiotomy is the soreness and pain you may feel afterward. Most women who have episiotomies are unable to have sex without great discomfort for many weeks and even months after they give birth. Other risks associated with episiotomies include abscess or infection, and the possibility of a hematoma, a collection of blood under the suture site caused by hemorrhage that may be extremely painful for weeks. While roughly 15 percent of women experience some degree of urinary incontinence after birth, time usually mends this problem (postpartum Kegel exercises can help) and research has not found that episiotomies decrease incontinence.

Some practitioners prefer not to perform episiotomies unless they think it absolutely necessary during the delivery. They will prepare you in advance not to need one by having you do Kegel exercises, perineal massage, and apply hot compresses, or encourage you to try vertical birthing positions during labor. Finally, most obstetricians in the United States perform episiotomies on a majority of their patients having their first child and on almost a third of those who have had one or more already. What's worse is that some physicians routinely do midline episiotomy cuts, which extend from the vagina all the way through to the anus. If you're delivering with an obstetrician, speak with him or her in advance about a preference not to have an episiotomy performed unless absolutely necessary.

A great preventative measure is to practice Kegel exercises and perineal massage (see Chapter 9, "Your Physical Tank") on your own and practice your relaxation techniques for birth. Ask your practitioner to tell you how stretchy your perenium looks and feels a month or so before your due date, while you can still do something about it. Also ask to be shown alternative vertical birthing positions that can reduce the pressure of the baby's head on the perenium. If you are familiar with the positions, you can assume them easily and without much prompting.

"I felt completely different after my second baby was delivered without an episiotomy. I was up and about, feeling good, in two days. It really tripped me up the first time. This time I knew I didn't want it and I knew what to do to avoid it."

Forceps and Vacuum Delivery

In about 10 percent of all births, forceps or vacuum delivery are used. Though today's forceps are hardly the horrid, patched-together spoons employed centuries ago, there is controversy surrounding the use of forceps in delivery. Many mothers are given drugs and anesthetics to "help" them during labor to the point that they are unable to *do* the labor, thus creating the need for more "help" from forceps.

Forceps are tongs (like salad servers) that are inserted into your vagina one side at a time, after which the baby's head is slowly and gently pulled out. Your cervix must be fully dilated before forceps can be used and the baby's head must have descended into the pelvis and stalled there. If your practitioner determines that you need a forceps delivery, you will be given an injection of anesthesia into your perenium to deaden the pain and your legs will be placed in stirrups. An episiotomy will be performed and then the forceps will be inserted. The forceps are removed once the baby's head is delivered.

Vacuum extraction, more popular in Europe than it is in the U.S., is used in lieu of forceps when there is a stalled second stage of labor. Your cervix does not have to be fully dilated for vacuum extraction to be performed. It takes about 10 to 20 minutes and consists of a small cup being placed on the baby's scalp through the vagina. When the vacuum is turned on, the cup is suctioned to the baby's scalp and the baby is carefully pulled out while the mother pushes. There may be some swelling on the baby's head where the cup was, but it should disappear within a few days of delivery.

Managing Labor Pain: "You *Will* Toil in Labor"

Understanding Pain

Some women who have short, efficient births, particularly if they had a mild early labor, may consider their childbirth a breeze compared to what they had been expecting. But women who had long, drawn-out labors with significant contractions throughout (particularly those with back labor or a very large baby) may feel like they have just been hit by a car. Regardless of the experience, labor hurts and it's wise to expect pain. But realize that your experience with labor can depend just as much on your attitude toward pain and your efforts to relax, cope with it, and work through it, as on the physical circumstances.

Pain *does* have a purpose. Pain is your body's way of telling you to respond to the stimulus and do something about it—namely, relax. Fear, on the other hand, can obstruct labor by causing you to tense your muscles, including your uterine muscles as they contract.

"I found that if I made a deep oooob sound through my contractions, it helped me cope with the pain and made my labor more productive. Don't let anyone tell you not to make noise, as long as you're making productive noise."

"My husband had the song 'No Woman, No Cry' playing in the background throughout my labor!"

Dealing with Pain Naturally

There are several ways you can practice relaxation and pain management during labor. The first part of this process is knowing yourself and what kind of stimulus you do (and don't) respond to. Do you like to be touched and massaged, or do you prefer to have your own personal space? Do you relax to music, a warm bath or shower, or both? The same relaxation techniques you use normally can be useful in labor. However, when birth day actually arrives, be willing to try as many different techniques as possible, because labor has its own set of techniques for relaxation as well (such as changing labor or birthing positions), and one may work well at one stage of labor, while another works better during the next. While it helps to try to practice them beforehand, you may not know whether they work for you until you're actually in labor. Here are some proven techniques that have worked to alleviate pain for many women in labor:

◆ Take a warm bath or shower to ease pains.

◆ Use breathing techniques to prevent you from clenching your body during the tough spots.

◆ Use different forms of touch. Try deep kneading, massage on your shoulders, back, hands, legs, or feet, or try light rubbing, caresses or fingertip touches on limbs, the sides of your brow, etc. Practice forms of touch with your partner beforehand to see which are most appealing to you. Having your partner support you with affectionate touch that conveys love and support can also work wonders, such as a gentle kiss on the forehead, holding your hand, smoothing your hair, or wiping your brow. Partners: Remember that your lovingly intended touch may not be the right action at the right time. Don't get upset if your wife suddenly says, "Stop it!" or "No. Not there!" Sometimes the wrong kind of touch can cause a woman to lose her concentration or hinder her from relaxing. In the midst of hard labor a woman may become irritable in her efforts to focus, especially when she's having trouble dealing with the pain. Your job is to help her stay focused in whatever way she needs you to.

◆ Pray between contractions. Recite the Twenty-third Psalm and think about being beside those "green pastures" and "still waters"! Getting recentered can bring powerful feelings of peace and assurance and can take your focus off the pain and back to the fact that you *can* do it.

◆ Use distraction techniques such as a focal point, or visual imagery (imagine yourself scaling a mountain and reaching the top, or holding the baby in your arms). Some mothers bring photos of smiling babies to focus on during labor.

◆ Bring whatever music relaxes you at home to the labor room. While the voices of doctors, midwives, nurses, friends, or family members may be whirling around you, the background sound of soothing, familiar rhythms can cut through the voices and reach you when other methods seem difficult or too exhausting.

◆ Change positions during birth if you have the desire or if one seems to cause you added discomfort.

At some point in labor, usually in the strongest, final contractions before you begin pushing out the baby, even your relaxation techniques won't seem to do the job of helping you through the pain. It's at this point that all of your mental preparation and the birth philosophy you've developed play a part. If you place high value on the experience of labor—the task, struggling to overcome the pain, leading to the final reward of seeing your baby—you are likely to muster up the needed strength to make it over the hurdle. If the process is not as important to you, particularly if pain and exhaustion are causing you so much stress that you are unable to relax, then it may be best to ask for some form of intervention. Neither decision is wrong at this point, and you shouldn't feel guilty for choosing one path over another. The ultimate goal is the healthy and successful delivery of your baby.

HISTORICALLY SPEAKING . . .

 Expectant mothers in Uganda fear that they will become the talk of the village if they let themselves scream during childbirth, so they try to bear the pain in silence. In contrast, women giving birth in the Sudan believe that there's no point in trying to be courageous and quiet, lest you make yourself susceptible to the "evil eye." Some Southern midwives contended that married women made more noise during birth than single women, the latter of whom they say didn't feel the need to "put on a show" for anyone. *What We Can Learn:* How will you be in childbirth? Will you let it all out or will you attempt to be in control until the very end? Interestingly, research indicates that much of the screaming during childbirth is more connected to the fear of the unknown than to actual pain experienced. Women who have had thorough prenatal care and are aware of what will happen during the various stages of labor are said to be less fearful and frantic when the time comes, and thus tend to have easier birthing experiences. Though we live in one of the most technologically advanced countries in the world, we can certainly learn

much from the simple relaxation techniques used in other lands—why not find one you think would work for you and give it a try? All you have to lose is some pain!

Narcotic Pain Relievers

Barring a medical need, the choice to use analgesic pain relief will be left up to you. The best approach is to have a balanced view of childbirth medication. You shouldn't feel like a martyr if you don't take it or a failure if you do. Ideally, in most labors it's best for both the mother and the baby not to use narcotic pain relief, as no medication is considered without some risks or side effects. For example, the most common forms of narcotic pain relief, Demerol and Fentanyl, as well as the narcotics Nubain, Stadol, and Numorphan, can all cause sedation and drowsiness in the mother, a decrease in the strength and frequency of contractions (which can slow or stall the labor), and can cause respiratory depression and feeding difficulties in the newborn directly after birth, depending on when or how the drug was administered. These symptoms typically leave within a few hours after birth. Some women dislike how they felt fuzzy or stifled after taking the analgesic, and how it made them feel out of touch with the rhythm of their labor.

Others experience few or no side effects and enjoy the freedom from sharp pain that medication provides (narcotic analgesics take the "edge" off the pain, but don't eliminate it entirely). In some cases, when a woman becomes frustrated by the pain and becomes overwhelmed, a dose of analgesic can give her the brief respite that allows her to gather herself together and work through the end of the labor.

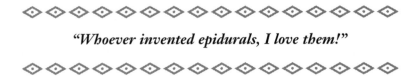

"Whoever invented epidurals, I love them!"

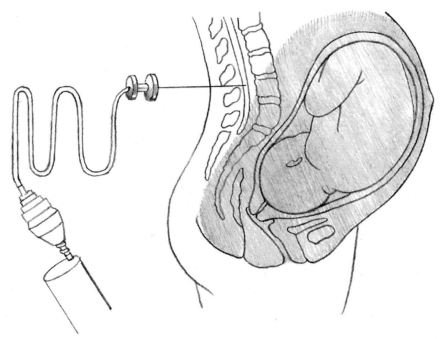

An *epidural* will anesthetize your abdominal area (see shaded area). Once it is administered most women can no longer feel their contractions and will be dependent on their coach or caregiver to tell them when to push; this makes you more likely to have an episiotomy.

Epidural Anesthesia

An epidural block is used to help relieve the pain of labor. With the woman either sitting up or lying on her left side, a local anesthetic will be administered to the lower back, then a numbing medication is injected into the spinal cord. The needle is connected to a thin tube through which the drug can be regulated and readministered throughout the labor (and delivery, if needed). It usually takes 15 minutes or less, depending on the type of drug used, until the woman is completely numb in the lower half of her body. Blood pressure is usually monitored frequently while the epidural is in place, and a urinary catheter, a slender tube that will help draw urine from the bladder, is inserted because the anesthesia numbs the feeling to urinate. Continuous electronic fetal monitoring is also necessary during an epidural because it may cause the baby to have a slowed heartbeat.

In some cases an epidural may be necessary, such as if a cesarean section must be performed, if Pitocin-induced contractions are too difficult for a woman to handle, or if a woman is struggling through exhaustion and tension that are interfering with her labor. In other cases an epidural may be elective, meaning that it is simply a pain-relief option available for women if they want it. Most women who have epidurals suffer few if any complications, and many are thrilled at its ability to eliminate most of the pain from labor. Women who are fighting the limits of exhaustion and fear during childbirth may be able to gain control of themselves and relax after the epidural is administered, which in some cases can help move a stalled labor.

However, there are drawbacks and risks associated with epidurals. An epidural can cause labor to slow or stall, since women are less likely to feel their contractions or the urge to push, and women must lie stationary while it's administered rather than moving around or standing up. Women who receive epidurals are also twice as likely to have forceps deliveries or vacuum extraction, since diminished contractions can slow the baby's progress and keep it from rotating naturally through the birth canal. In a small amount of cases the covering of the spinal cord, called the dura, is punctured accidentally (known as a "spinal tap"), causing a severe headache that can last several hours or a few days. If the needle punctures a vein, it can cause dizziness or seizures. Finally, an epidural can deprive you of the feeling of accomplishment and control, making you more of a passive than an active participant in your baby's birth. Because there are risks and drawbacks involved with epidurals (as with most interventions), it's important for you to weigh these drawbacks and benefits ahead of time so that when you are experiencing the pain of labor, you can make the best, informed decision for you and your baby. Pudendal blocks are another form of anesthetic that numbs the nerves in the lower part of the pelvis only. This reduces the pain produced by the pressure of the baby on the pelvis, but not much else.

Cesareans

A cesarean section (or C-section, as it's commonly known) is an incision made in the mother's lower abdomen and uterus as an alternative way to deliver the baby when a vaginal delivery is considered risky or impossible. Cesarean sections were once mostly done with vertical outer incisions, as in our illustration. The horizontal or lateral cut (also known as the "bikini cut") is the method preferred by women today because it's located lower in the uterus (below the bikini or panty line) and because it is extremely unlikely to rupture

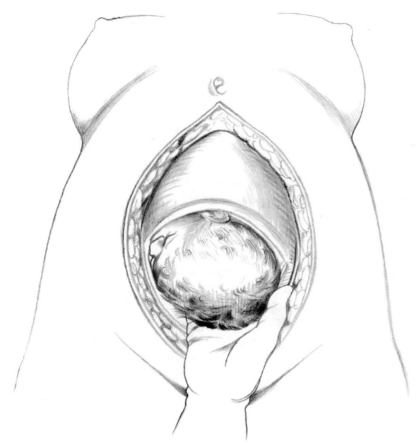

In a *Cesarean section* two incisions are made, one on the flesh and tissue (vertical cut shown), and another on the uterus (transverse cut). You may request a transverse or bikini cut, where the outer incision is made just above the pubic hairline. However, what is actually done when the time comes will be at the discretion of your physician. The baby is then lifted out headfirst as shown.

in future pregnancies. This may not be the preferred choice of your doctor, though, as it is more awkward to lift the baby out when this type of incision is made. Again, discuss your preferences with your practitioner, so you will both be "on the same page" should the need arise for a cesarean.

An epidural or spinal anesthesia, which numbs the mother from the waist down yet allows her to be awake during the delivery, is usually administered before the surgery. In some emergency situations such as with bleeding or fetal distress, a general anesthesia is given, which puts the woman completely asleep (note that in this situation the husband or birth partner is usually asked to leave the surgery room until after the delivery).

Five percent of all births in the United States were cesareans in the 1960's. Today 25 to 30 percent of all babies born are delivered by cesarean section (the rate varies slightly depending on the area you live in). Yet the increase in cesarean rate over the last thirty-five years has not improved the infant mortality (death) rate, and other industrialized countries with lower infant mortality rates boast lower C-section rates. Then why are so many cesareans being done in the United States? This question has stirred controversy in the medical community and has resulted in extensive research and debate. Generally, the medical establishment in the United States has determined in the last several years that unnecessary cesareans are being performed. These surgeries are usually the result of the birth practices in this country and the high rate of interventions used in labor.

For example, one of the greatest reasons cited for a cesarean is a term known as *failure to progress,* or *uterine dystocia.* Failure to progress is determined when the cervix has not dilated enough after 16 to 24 hours of labor, depending on the assessment of the individual physician. A good reason to perform a cesarean at this point would be after a fetal monitor picks up a steady pattern of fetal distress, which should be confirmed by a second opinion (but often is not) or a fetal scalp sample that indicates decreased oxygen in the baby's blood. But labor does not follow a timetable, and some women's labors may normally and naturally stop, stall, or gradually work themselves up over a few days. Although this route is more tiresome than a comparatively quick labor, there is no scientific evidence that a long labor in itself is harmful to the baby or decreases the amount of oxygen the baby receives. If a mother has already been admitted to a hospital when the labor stalls, electronic fetal monitoring can aid her by indicating that although labor is progressing slowly, both mother and baby are doing fine and there is no need for intervention (such as inducement or a cesarean).

Women who have repeat cesarean births account for almost a third of cesareans performed, although research now finds that 70 to 90 percent of women who have a cesarean can go on to deliver their next child vaginally (see "Vaginal Birth After Cesarean" later in this chapter). Doctors admit that fear of lawsuits plays a role. High rates of C-sections are often found in areas where malpractice lawsuits are common, as well as in metropolitan areas with "diverse" populations.

Fetal distress is another common reason for cesareans, although irregularities in the readings can be ambiguous and do not always prove that something is wrong (see "Fetal Distress" later in this chapter). Since a cesarean section is considered to be a safe and efficient procedure, a doctor may decide not to take a chance and perform the operation, which in some cases may be wise. Others may forgo the opportunity of receiving a second opinion or trying alternate tests to confirm the distress.

There are ways you can reduce the likelihood of having a cesarean. Start by choosing your caregivers carefully; consider a midwife or select a doctor who encourages natural births. Labor at home as long as you can, in order to decrease the chance of receiving any interventions designed to "hurry you up." Second, research has proven that keeping in a vertical position during labor, particularly if you are walking and moving about, can shorten labor, increase the efficiency of your uterus, and can aid dilation and effacement. Factors that can keep you from being upright or from moving around can be having a routine IV, continuous electronic fetal monitoring, or having an elective epidural. Use pain relief medication and interventions such as epidurals wisely, only after natural relaxation methods have failed. Avoid continuous EFM, or request that periodic fetoscope monitoring be performed instead.

Even though it's wise to enter labor prepared to do all you can to have a safe vaginal delivery, in birth you should always be prepared for the unexpected. Roughly 6 to 10 percent of all deliveries do require a cesarean. Reasons for *necessary* cesareans include:

◆ An extremely difficult birth position for the baby, such as a transverse (horizontal or crossways) breech, footling breech (one foot first), or frank breech (buttocks first), particularly if the baby weighs 9 pounds or more
◆ Severe illness in the mother that can endanger her health if the pregnancy continues much longer, such as maternal diabetes or an uncontrollable case of eclampsia
◆ An active case of herpes in the mother at the time of delivery that could infect the baby during its passage through the birth canal
◆ A prolapsed umbilical cord that could potentially cut off the baby's oxygen supply
◆ Placenta previa or placenta abruptio, which can cause severe bleeding and endanger both mother and child (see Chapter 15, "What-ifs During Pregnancy and Childbirth")

◆ Cephalopelvic disproportion, the rare case when the baby's head is too large to fit through the mother's pelvis. (This is often too difficult to determine until the mother is in labor or right up to labor.)

If you find out in advance that you may need a cesarean, there are some questions you can ask your doctor. Make sure the procedure is explained thoroughly to you. Will you be using general or spinal anesthetic? Will your husband or partner be allowed to stay with you during the surgery? If the reason for the cesarean is because the baby is breech, can a manual turn (called external cephalic version) be attempted first? Afterward, will the baby be allowed to room in with you overnight? Your husband or partner may be allowed to stay overnight as well to give you a hand with the baby when it needs to nurse. How many days will you need to spend recovering in the hospital before you can return home? Be sure to discuss these questions in advance.

Vaginal Birth After Cesarean (VBAC)

In the past, once a woman had a cesarean she was expected to have one with every subsequent pregnancy. This was because the type of incision used, a vertical cut made in the upper part of the uterus, was more likely to rupture under the strain of labor contractions. Nowadays, most women are given a horizontal "low-transverse" incision or "bikini cut" on the lower, thinner part of their uterus that heals with a stronger scar and is highly unlikely to rupture. The American College of Obstetricians and Gynecologists now recommends that vaginal deliveries after cesareans become the norm for most women, even those who have had two cesareans. Not only does a vaginal birth pose less risk and offer a shorter recovery time than a cesarean, but the mother is allowed to have the satisfaction of and participation in a vaginal delivery.

Research shows that roughly three-fourths of women with previous cesareans who give birth with experienced VBAC birth attendants have successful vaginal deliveries. If you are considering a VBAC, be sure to look for a doctor or midwife who is supportive of your desire for a vaginal delivery, and does not label you as a "high-risk" patient (the same holds true for the hospital you plan to give birth in). To find an experienced and supportive VBAC doctor, speak with friends, childbirth educators, or cesarean or VBAC support groups. Find out about the hospital's attitude toward VBAC patients. Will you be required to have continuous electronic fetal monitoring (not a good sign) and will you be allowed to use a labor-delivery-recovery room? As a VBAC patient, you can even consider the option of giving birth in a birthing center as long as an obstetrician is assigned for backup support and the midwives have experience with successful VBAC deliveries. Don't be afraid to ask either doctor or midwife their VBAC success rate (a good figure is 70 percent or better).

As a VBAC candidate your own confidence and attitude can play a large part in the success of your delivery. Do as much research on birthing as possible, understand all stages of the birthing process, practice relaxation techniques, and know what your birthing options are. Information and a willingness to explore different options that can enhance and ease your labor (such as water birth or using different birthing positions) can help you conquer any fears that may arise in the delivery.

Labor and Delivery

Understanding What's Going on in Prelabor and Labor

As your delivery day approaches it's important for you to understand what happens during labor, as well as the vocabulary of labor that your doctor or midwife will be using. Before the baby can move into the birth canal, your cervix, the neck of your uterus, which the baby must descend through, may begin to *efface* (thin out) and *dilate* (open). This can begin happening a few weeks or few days before you give birth or may not begin until the day. Dilation is measured in centimeters, and effacement is measured in percentages. When you are fully effaced (100 percent effacement) and your cervix dilates to its maximum width of 10 centimeters (wide enough for the baby's head to fit through), you're finished with the first stage of labor and are ready to start pushing out the baby.

Before this happens, though, there are a few other changes you may notice in your body. As your cervix begins to thin out and open, you may lost your *mucus plug*, the clear, jellylike mass of mucus lightly tinged with blood that seals off the opening of the uterus while you are pregnant. The mucus is usually light pink or tinged with brownish red. This can occur a week or two before labor, but more often it happens only a day or hours before labor actually begins. You may also notice when the baby descends into your pelvic cavity, also called *lightening* or *dropping*. This can happen from four to two weeks before delivery if this is your first full pregnancy, but is more likely to happen during labor if you've had children previously (although there are always exceptions). Generally, if you've dropped you'll notice that your abdomen is now lower and thrust forward, and there is less pressure against your diaphragm and ribs. However, the baby now rests more heavily on your bladder, causing you to take more trips to the bathroom throughout the day. Your bag of waters, really amniotic fluid, may or may not break anywhere from six hours to right before the onset of labor.

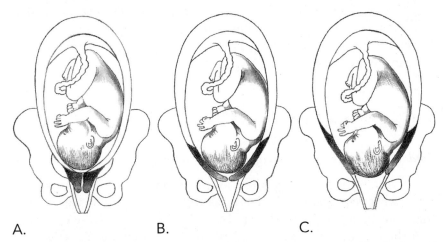

A.   B.   C.

Cervical Effacement and Dilation. Your cervix is normally thick and strong (A), but as you have contractions it begins to thin out allowing the baby to drop down (B). This thinning is known as effacement, which then progresses to full dilation (C), which means your cervix has opened and you are ready to push.

How far the baby has moved into your pelvis is measured in *stations* of descent. As your baby's head (the most common presenting part to move first through the cervix) rests near the top of your frontal pelvic rim, the baby is considered at −4 station. At this particular station the baby is considered *floating*, meaning that although it's resting low it can easily reposition itself and "float" back up again. Eventually, the baby progresses farther down the pelvis from −3, −2, −1 stations until it reaches "0" station, also called *engagement*, when the widest part of the baby's head has entered the pelvic inlet, and your birth attendant (you are now well into labor) can feel that the head is level with the tips of your pelvic bones, called "spines." From here your baby will continue to descend through +1, +2, and +3 station, until it reaches +4, when it is visible from the outside.

Prelabor and Labor vs. False Labor

Even before labor begins your body can send you a variety of signals to let you know it's preparing for labor, otherwise known as prelabor. However, these symptoms may be more noticeable in some women and less noticeable in others, while some women may simply ignore them or pass them off as something else. Also, depending on each individual pregnancy, the prelabor signs may start weeks or only hours before real labor begins. However, being aware of these changes in your body can help prepare you for the unexpected.

Prelabor Signs

◆ Dropping
◆ Loss of your mucus plug or "bloody show" noticeable; the mucus plug is a jellylike mucus that may either be clear or tinged with blood (be sure to call your doctor immediately if you find yourself bleeding bright red); this can also occur during labor
◆ An increase in Braxton Hicks contractions, which may be stronger and more frequent
◆ Diarrhea or loose bowel movements
◆ A sudden loss in weight (up to 3 pounds of fluid) or no weight gain
◆ Increased or thickened vaginal discharge
◆ A sudden burst of energy or "nesting" instinct, a desire to clean and prepare for the baby

Real Labor Signs

◆ *Contractions*
　◆ Are typically felt radiating from the lower back to the front; may feel like menstrual cramps, deep internal pelvic pressure, or rhythmic low backache
　◆ Gradually show a pattern of regular intervals that increase in intensity, duration, and frequency (longer, stronger)
　◆ Are intensified when you walk or move around, and don't stop when you lie down or change positions
◆ *Breaking of Your Bag of Waters*
　◆ May be either a steady trickle or a gush of amniotic fluid
　◆ Fluid may be clear, straw-colored, pinkish peach, or green
　◆ Contractions may increase or intensify now that your water

has broken (*Note:* about 10 percent of women have their membranes rupture before they actually begin labor. For these women, labor contractions usually begin within 12 hours. If this happens to you, be sure to notify your doctor or midwife. Take note of the time your membranes ruptured, the color of the fluid, the amount, and the odor.)

False Labor

◆ *Contractions*
  ◆ Tightening is only felt in the front, not accompanied by cramps or internal pressure
  ◆ Are irregular, may stop and start, and don't show a general pattern of increasing intensity and duration
  ◆ Tend to disappear if you change positions, walk around, rest, or take a warm bath or shower
◆ *Mistaken Bloody Show*
  ◆ Dark brown or reddish brown clots in discharge or spotting may be caused by an internal exam or sexual intercourse

Note: Stay Hydrated! While it's important to keep drinking fluids throughout your pregnancy, this becomes crucial toward the end of your pregnancy, particularly if you live in a hot area or are giving birth in the summer. In the eighth and ninth months when you are already likely to feel an increase in Braxton Hicks contractions, dehydration can trigger even stronger and more frequent contractions that can easily be mistaken for labor. Dehydration is not good for you or the baby, and can increase your risk of urinary tract infections. You should be drinking 3 quarts to 1 gallon of fluid a day (approximately eight 8-ounce glasses), and more if you are exercising or staying outside in hot weather.

Preterm Labor and Premature Rupture of the Membranes

Labor is generally considered preterm or premature if it occurs before the end of the thirty-sixth week of pregnancy (although some doctors consider 36 weeks and up full term). Preterm labor may be more likely to occur if you have fibroids or other malformations in your uterus, high blood pressure, a chronic illness, experience bleeding in the second trimester of your pregnancy, are carrying more than one fetus, or have had several induced abortions (see Chapter 13, "Coping with Chronic Conditions and Illness During Pregnancy"). Sometimes there seems to be no known reason or link as to why a woman goes into labor ahead of time.

Signs of preterm labor can be strong menstrual-like cramps, lower back pain, pressure in the pelvic floor, and bloody show (see "Real Labor Signs," pagse 301–302). An obvious sign that preterm labor is about to occur is premature rupture of your membranes (PROM). About half of all preterm pregnancies will begin labor 24 hours after the membranes rupture. If a woman doesn't go into labor after 24 hours there is a risk of infection or prolapse (slipping down) of the umbilical cord. However, if your doctor determines that the baby is too young to be born, you may be hospitalized and efforts will be made to keep the pregnancy going. (When the amniotic fluid begins leaking it doesn't immediately run dry; your body and the baby continually replenish it, although it may continue to leak.)

If you show any signs of preterm labor or premature breaking of your membranes, call your doctor or midwife immediately.

When Baby Is "Overripe"

It's the day after your due date, nothing's happening, and your doctor just told you that nothing's changed since last week. Is this baby ever coming out? Before you begin to worry, remember that a due date is actually called an *estimated* date of delivery (EDD), and that the medical establishment considers a normal, full-term pregnancy anywhere from 37 to 42 weeks gestation. Only about 5 percent of all babies are actually born on their EDD. If your pregnancy does go past 42 weeks, there are a few things you must consider before choosing your options. There are several reasons for your caretakers to be concerned about a postterm pregnancy. Babies who continue in the womb past 42 weeks are at higher risk for an abnormal heart rate and the possibility of meconium aspiration, when the baby excretes greenish waste from its bowels into the amniotic fluid and then inhales it into its windpipe. There is also a concern that the increased size of a postterm baby (a condition called macrosomia) may cause a difficult delivery or a labor that doesn't progress. Finally, there is also a risk that the placenta will begin to lose its ability to function well, and that the amniotic fluid may decrease, causing the umbilical cord to get pinched.

Despite these concerns, on the positive side, know that most babies (more than 90 percent) born between 42 and 44 weeks do not face these risks and are unaffected by their lengthened stay in the womb. Part of the reason for this is inaccurate estimation of the due date. After delivery, a majority of babies thought to be postterm are actually well within term. For whatever reason, others simply stay in the womb a few extra days without harm.

Faced with this information, you and your doctor or midwife can choose a course of action (or inaction, as the case may be) when your baby seems to be overdue. You can choose simply to wait it out and be patient, with no monitoring, or you can be examined each week with a series of tests to ensure the baby's well-being. This usually involves having nonstress tests done with an electric fetal monitor, using ultrasound twice a week to measure the level of amniotic fluid, and having you perform a fetal kick count each day (see pages 39–41). If all seems to be well, you will probably be just fine to wait it out until baby is ready to be born. Another option is for your doctor to induce labor artificially by breaking your bag of waters and then inducing you with Pitocin. Although it's convenient, unless the baby is clearly at risk or showing signs of distress, this is probably not a wise option.

When to Call Your Doctor or Midwife

The best way to answer this question is to ask your doctor or midwife in advance. However, there are a few points that will help you avoid spending several hours of a slow early labor pacing the hospital halls, or making a mad dash through traffic at the last minute (you may have heard of someone whose baby was born on the freeway for this very reason).

If this is your first child and your labor seems to start slowly and mildly, it's probably in your best interests to labor at home as long as possible. *Arriving at the hospital too early and spending hours in the labor room can not only get tedious and uncomfortable, but can put you at risk for unnecessary intervention* such as getting an IV or electronic fetal monitoring in early labor, which can keep you strapped down, causing a slow labor to stall or drag. However, if this is your second or third child and your previous labors went quickly it's probably best to call your doctor or midwife as soon as you feel the first series of regular contractions, even if it's early labor. If it's still early in the day your doctor or midwife may want to be notified if you've begun labor, but if it's the middle of the night general guidelines for when to call your doctor and head to the hospital are:

- ◆ If your water breaks (particularly if it's stained green or brown)
- ◆ If your contractions are coming roughly five minutes apart or less for an hour

◆ Regardless of their distance apart or length, if the contractions are strong and painful, severe enough to stop you in your tracks and require all your attention and concentration. (In some rare cases women progress through labor and delivery with contractions that never get closer than five minutes or more apart.)

Call your doctor or midwife immediately:

◆ If you are bleeding or notice any bright red spotting
◆ If you feel any sudden, severe pain in your uterus that is unlike any contraction
◆ If you continually feel faint

Finally, when in doubt, call your practitioner regardless of the time of day or night. If it turns out to be a false alarm you won't be the first

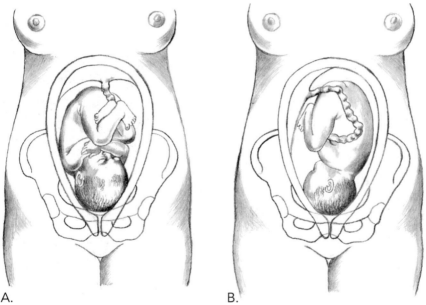

A.   B.

(A) *Posterior position* of baby: If your baby is in the posterior position, you are likely to experience painful backache during labor. This is because the larger part of the baby's head is presenting itself first, with the back part of the head resting on your spine. Your labor will probably be longer and more erratic than usual. (B) *Well-flexed position:* Most babies lie in this position—his arms and legs are bent and his head is curled onto his chest. His head lies near your pelvis. You may be able to determine the position of your baby roughly by feeling the contours of your abdomen with your palm.

woman to mistake the signs of labor, and at the very worst, you may get sent home from the hospital or doctor's office. At the very best, your unease and intuition may help you arrive at the hospital in the nick of time, possibly rescuing you or your baby from a critical situation.

Coping with Back Labor

What Is It?

When the baby is facing a posterior position during labor, this means that the back of the baby's head, rather than its face, is facing your spine, and you are said to be in "back labor." During each contraction the hard back of the baby's head is ramming into your spine.

If you are in *back labor,* your partner should massage your back using the heel of his hands or even his fists to apply counterpressure.

Thus, lying on your back can be very painful. The posterior position of the baby can usually be detected both internally and externally by the caregiver once labor has begun and the membranes have ruptured. More often it's noticed immediately by the mother if almost all of the pain of each contraction is felt in her back. This poses no risk to either mother or child, but it does mean a very uncomfortable labor. Rocking on your hands and knees and kneeling down with your butt in the air and your arms and head on a pillow will help take pressure off your lower back. Warm compresses, a hot water bottle, or a warm shower directed to your back will also help to ease the pain.

The Trouble with Lying Down

Although movies and television continually portray women giving birth flat on their backs, maybe slightly propped up at best, it's time for us to understand the disadvantages of this position and realize that there are better alternatives. Back-birthing became popular in the early 1900s when doctors (instead of midwives) began managing births. Having a woman lie on her back made it more convenient for them to reach the baby, and to use forceps and surgical interventions when necessary. This soon became standard practice and the trend continues even today. The main problem with giving birth on your back is that you are working against gravity. With the weight of the baby and the uterus lying on your back, not only can you increase the feeling of backache with contractions, but you compress the large blood vessels that run along the back of your spine, which in turn can decrease the amount of blood and oxygen the baby receives. Finally, this position is comparable to pushing the baby out uphill, and may put added strain on your perineum, increasing the chance of tearing or needing an episiotomy.

Some good alternatives to laboring on your back include squatting, either assisted by furniture or your partner, and sitting up in a birth bed, propped with pillows so you are semi-upright with your knees bent and drawn close to your body (see illustration).

Sitting up during active labor will use gravity to help pull the baby down and out better than lying down.

Stages of Labor

First Stage of Labor

There are three stages of labor. During the first stage, your contractions work to open your uterus. This is the longest stage of labor, and is divided into three different parts or phases: latent, active, and hard labor (also known as transition). In some women, these phases seem to overlap or blend together. In others, they are clear and distinct. Remember that while there are general guidelines as to what a "typical" labor should be like, each woman's experience can vary. Most first-time mothers will have a longer labor, particularly in the first stage, than women who have had children before. However, even some women with first pregnancies may hurry through this stage or even sleep through the first two phases. Contractions may seem so mild or irregular they may continue at their usual pace throughout the day, hardly realizing how far they are progressing. On the other hand, most women will feel their contractions getting increasingly stronger throughout the first stage. Remember, labor can stop and restart, or can stall for hours with contractions coming roughly the same distance apart. Throughout your labor you must be alert to an *overall pattern* of increasing frequency and duration, particularly if contractions become stronger and more uncomfortable or painful.

First Phase: Early Labor (Approximately 0 to 2–3 centimeters dilated)

What's Happening in Your Body: Contractions are generally slow and dull at this point. Women describe these contractions as pelvic pressure, heaviness or tightening in the pubic bone, backache, or like menstrual cramps. Contractions may be anywhere from 5 to 30 minutes apart, and last 30 to 45 seconds (contractions are usually farthest apart in the beginning of this phase, and become progressively closer throughout the rest of your labor). During this phase the baby may drop into the pelvis. Other symptoms of this phase, particularly if it occurs over several hours of distinct labor, may include bloody show, nausea, and/or diarrhea (your body's natural way of emptying your bowels before birth).

How Long It May Last: This phase of labor may occur over a few weeks of mild contractions or may happen in a few hours of unmistakable labor.

Your Reactions, What You and Your Partner Can Do: In the beginning of labor, the latent phase, the contractions may feel so fuzzy that some women can hardly tell when they are starting or stopping. If this phase occurs over a few weeks or even a few days, you may not even realize it is taking place. If your contractions are distinct and seem to be coming 6 to 7 minutes apart or less, time them. It's at this time that you should call your doctor or midwife and let them know what you are feeling.

When you first realize you are actually in labor you may feel both excited and anxious. Most women are able to carry on a conversation during or between contractions, depending on their severity. Use this time to finish packing, do light housecleaning, or take a bath or shower if it helps you relax. Eat light snacks or meals, drink plenty of fluids, and try emptying your bladder at least once every hour. If it's early in the day and you feel up to it, try to stay on your feet or take a walk—this can help encourage your labor to keep progressing. If it's late at night or you are tired, try relaxing and getting some sleep to rest up for a potentially long night or long day ahead. During this time your birth partner should be nearby and can help pack, clean house, play a game with you, or give you a massage—constantly providing physical and emotional support.

HISTORICALLY SPEAKING . . .

 When "that time" approaches, an African woman's attendant might massage her vagina with butter or oil to make the delivery easier. Southern midwives followed in our African sisters' footsteps and used all types of oils and even petroleum jelly to help a woman in labor. Zulu women were way ahead of Mr. Lamaze, and have been practicing breathing techniques during labor for centuries. These women sometimes count the stars through the hole in the roof of their huts as a distraction and may use one star as a focal point during hard labor. *What We Can Learn:* Freedom. That's a key component to a successful labor. Do everything to make sure that you are able to try positions, breathing or grunting techniques, have music, pray out loud, or do whatever helps you have an effective labor.

Second Phase: Active Labor (4 to 7 centimeters dilated)

What's Happening in Your Body: Your body begins the process of reaching 100 percent effacement and dilating your cervix. As your contractions become stronger, longer, and more frequent, you may feel one or more of the following symptoms: increasing backache, heavy pelvic pressure, the breaking of your bag of waters.

How Long It May Last: This phase on average lasts 2 to 4 hours, although many women can experience wide variations.

Your Reactions, What You and Your Partner Can Do: Most women can't continue hanging around the house at this point, and find themselves unable to talk during contractions, focusing inward instead.

Some women become irritable, ignoring their external surroundings. During contractions you can experiment with different positions to help ease your pain, such as kneeling, squatting, leaning against your partner, or rocking on your hands and knees. During this phase you should contact your doctor or midwife and go to the hospital or birthing center.

A WORD TO THE WISE

A good time to arrive at the hospital is when you are about four to five centimeters dilated. If you go too soon, they may send you home or, worse, they may admit you and your labor may then stall for hours. If this occurs, there is likely to be pressure from the hospital staff to induce your labor.

Third Phase: Transition (8 to 10 centimeters dilated)

What's Happening in Your Body: This is typically the shortest but most difficult part of labor. Your cervix is dilated completely by the end of this stage and the baby descends into the birth canal. Your legs may tremble and you may feel waves of nausea and a desire to vomit. The contractions come quickly and hard—2 to 3 minutes apart—and may be 60 to 90 seconds long, with very sharp peaks. During this phase the sharp peaks last through most of the contraction. To many women, these contractions feel continuous because of their severity and the inability to rest or relax in between them. Your doctor or midwife should examine you internally at regular intervals to check your progression. If your caretaker is someone you've never seen before, introduce yourself and ask them to do the same and to explain what they're about to do. Your partner should not have to leave the room during the exam. After the exam, ask how dilated you are each time; this information can really help you psychologically.

At the end of this phase of labor, you may feel an overwhelming desire to push (although some women do not), but wait until your doctor or midwife confirms that you are fully dilated. Otherwise, you'll be pushing the baby against a half-closed cervix, which could case edema (swelling) of the cervix, making delivery even harder.

How Long It May Last: 15 minutes to one hour.

Your Reactions, What You and Your Partner Can Do: This is the time when you will have to work the hardest to stay relaxed. Many women feel frustrated or frightened at the pain, and are tempted to panic or ask for pain-relief medication. It's important to remember, though, that transition passes quickly (rarely lasting longer than an hour—sometimes lasting only through 15 or 20 contractions). Pain-killers or epidurals are especially not advisable at this time because by the time they are administered and begin to take effect you will be ready or almost ready to push. At this point they can dull your senses and deaden your ability to participate fully in pushing.

Throughout this phase remember to use every resource to help yourself relax. Keep doing shallow breathing, play soothing music, or stand in a warm shower. Stay off your back, either by sitting propped up, or squatting or standing supported by your partner. Use visual imagery—imagine "releasing" or "letting go"—to keep your pelvic muscles relaxed. *During this phase it is important that your partner be prepared to do any of the following:* take care of checking you into the hospital or birth center, wipe your brow with a damp washcloth, offer you ice chips or sips of juice, encourage you through the contractions, write down the length and intervals of your contractions, remind you to relax your pelvic floor (to help avoid an episiotomy) and to keep your body loose, massage your back, hold your hand, offer a distraction (conversation about other things, jokes, photos of healthy babies, card games, etc.), go with you to the bathroom, be a "gatekeeper" for you (making you aware of any drugs or procedures being done to you), be ready to hold you up if the contractions become overwhelming. It's okay to make noise in labor, but screaming uncontrollably may be more of a sign of fear than pain and can make you tense up even more. Turn counterproductive noise into productive noise: Try grunting or moaning when you push.

◇ ◇ ◇ ◇ ◇ ◇ ◇ ◇ ◇ ◇ ◇ ◇ ◇ ◇ ◇ ◇ ◇

"I knew I was really loved when I saw my best friend and coach pouring olive oil on my vagina during my childbirth. Now that's a friend for life!"

◇ ◇ ◇ ◇ ◇ ◇ ◇ ◇ ◇ ◇ ◇ ◇ ◇ ◇ ◇ ◇ ◇

EAT, DRINK, AND DELIVER

Eating lightly and drinking fluids are fine during the late stages of labor, unless you are expected to need surgery. It will be much better and more comfortable for you to drink fruit juice (the sugar will give you extra energy) from a cup while you are walking around than to have an intravenous drip stuck into your arm feeding you fluids and confining you to the bed. Don't be afraid to assert yourself. Be sure to empty your bladder as much as possible to give your uterus adequate room to function.

Second Stage of Labor

The second stage of labor involves pushing your baby out. You may be surprised to know that some women experience a brief period of sleep or a lull in contractions at the start of this stage that can last 10 to 20 minutes. It's almost as if your body is congratulating you, saying, "You've gone through the hardest part. Now rest before we finally push this baby out." Whether or not you experienced a period of rest, many women, particularly those who are unmedicated, feel a renewed burst of energy as they begin to push. You may feel the ability to "push the pain away" through your contractions. Up until now you've been a passive participant in labor, simply trying to ride out the contractions. Suddenly you have the ability to *do something about it*, and applying this counterpressure force to the pain can feel exhilarating.

What's Happening in Your Body: Now that your cervix is fully dilated, your baby begins to descend through the birth canal as you work to push it out. Contractions at this time are generally less intense and farther apart. As the baby's head distends your perineum or "crowns" (the baby's head is visible to those who are watching), you may feel a stretching or burning feeling. However, this feeling quickly leaves because the pressure of the baby's head against your nerves soon numbs the skin. Once the head has fully crowned, one more contraction or so may nudge the head out. Amazingly, the baby knows to turn its head toward your right or left thigh at just the right time to help navigate its shoulders under your pubic bone. Your next contractions may do all the work for you to push the shoulders out one at a time. The baby's slippery, wet body quickly slides out. If you desire, you may reach down and help "catch" the

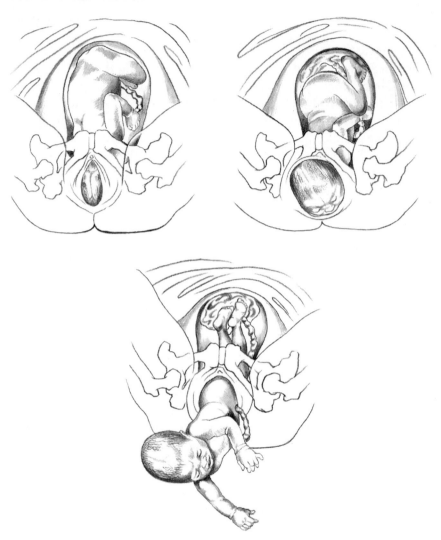

The baby is born.

baby when it's coming out. The doctor or midwife will of course help the baby up to you if you aren't able to do this. Holding her on your abdomen keeps her warm and she is comforted by the sound of your voice and feel of your heartbeat, something Zulu women feel is essential to help the baby begin to know her mother. While you are bonding with your baby for the first time, the doctor or midwife will clamp the umbilical cord that has connected you both throughout pregnancy once it stops pulsating. Your baby is born!

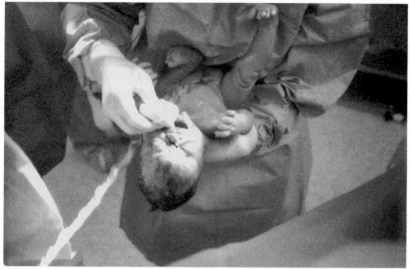

A.

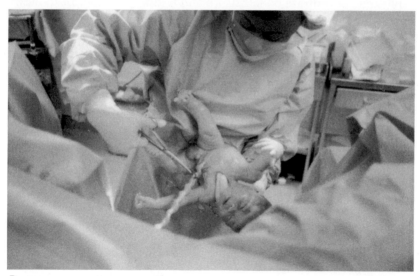

B.

(A) When your baby is delivered her nose and mouth will be suctioned to remove any mucus. (B) Then the umbilical cord will be cut as the placenta loosens itself and prepares to be expelled. Allford/Trotman Associates.

How Long It May Last: The second stage lasts an average of 1 to 1½ hours for first-time mothers (although this can also vary widely) and much shorter (sometimes only 10 or 15 minutes) for those who have already had children.

Your Reactions, What You and Your Partner Can Do: As you begin to push remember that pushing does not necessarily have to be a long, strained effort where you are using every ounce of strength, holding your breath, and bursting blood vessels. Not only is this exhausting, but it delivers less oxygen to the baby and puts you at greater risk of tearing your perineum. Pushing directed by your doctor or midwife may be necessary if you don't feel the urge yourself, but in most cases pushing is best done on instinct. *Wait until you have an overwhelming urge to push,* and then bear down with as much pressure as you comfortably can for 5 or 6 seconds, then exhale and take a deep breath before starting again. Continue these short, frequent pushes (3 to 4 per contraction) through each contraction, and then rest until the desire to push wells up again.

During this time, particularly as the baby's head begins to crown, it's important for you to keep the muscles on your pelvic floor relaxed to avoid tearing or an episiotomy. Don't tense up, but instead breathe deeply and concentrate on letting go and letting out. Your birth partner can remind you to stay relaxed (he can repeat over and over, "Relax your pelvic floor"), encourage you to breathe through your pushes, and offer massage or hold your hand (not clenched). Your birth attendants can also perform perineal massage at this time. As soon as the baby's head fully crowns stop pushing and let the contractions do their work. Your labor attendant will let you know if you don't feel the stretching and burning sensation or can let you see it for yourself with a mirror. You might like to reach down and touch the top of the baby's head at this time, a thrilling reassurance that your baby is about to arrive.

HISTORICALLY SPEAKING . . .

 African and African-American folklore is filled with stories that surround the third stage of labor, delivery of the afterbirth or placenta. Some Jamaican women and Southern midwives alike thought that blowing in a blue bottle would help a woman expel the afterbirth. Many believe that *the yindlu ya nwana* ("the house or hut of the child") has a spiritual significance; others believe that it is the baby's twin and that the child's future is linked with wherever it is placed. Some East African parents make sure that the placenta is buried wherever they hope their child will go when she grows up. *What*

We Can Learn: Before you go grabbing the placenta out of the doctor's hands and making plans to bury it on the nearest college campus, remember that these were superstitions (which are based on fear) and rooted in a belief in the occult. Cultural rituals are great as long as they are in line with your own belief system.

Third Stage of Labor: Delivering the Baby's "Hut"

The third stage of labor contractions deliver the placenta or afterbirth from your uterus. Your practitioner will pull gently on the cut umbilical cord until your placenta is expelled. It is an amazing organ that looks like a piece of liver. Don't be afraid to look at it. All of the placenta must be delivered intact or else serious infection or hemorrhage can ensue. Your uterus contracts and tightens around the blood vessels when the placenta is expelled, so there should only be slight bleeding, if any. Afterwards, if an episiotomy was needed or any tearing occurred, your doctor will stitch your perineum.

What's Happening in Your Body: Although they slow down and become relatively painless, your contractions continue every few minutes. There may be a gush or trickle of blood as the placenta separates from the uterine wall. In the excitement of seeing your new baby, you may be oblivious to this happening. You legs or entire body may shiver or shake due to the loss of heat produced by the departure of the baby and the placenta from your body; this is quite normal.

How Long It May Take: This final stage can last a few minutes to a half hour.

Your Reactions, What You and Your Partner Can Do: Your reactions can vary greatly, yet they are all normal and healthy. To varying degrees most women are relieved that the whole process is over, and feel pride and joy at the new life they hold. Some are bewildered by the unfamiliarity of this bloody, greasy stranger in their arms. After the initial excitement of the delivery some women are exhausted and simply feel ready for food and sleep. Others remain too excited to take a nap and hate to think of the baby being separated from them.

While the placenta is being delivered you can try to nurse your baby. Nursing stimulates release of the hormone oxytocin, which in turn stimulates contractions that help shrink the uterus (this is why women, particularly after second or third pregnancies, feel painful, crampy contractions during the first few days when they nurse their babies). Depending on the plan you discussed with your labor attendant, your partner can spend time holding or bonding with the baby, or help give the baby its first bath. This is also a good time to roll the tape for keepsake videos or pictures of the new "first" family.

HISTORICALLY SPEAKING ...

 Forget about Daddy cutting the umbilical cord; some tribal Kenyan women actually chew it off themselves after the baby's birth! Southern women had a tradition of throwing the cord straight into the middle of a fireplace on the seventh day after birth. If it touched the floor or the back of the fireplace, they said the baby would have a chronic backache. Others say the cord should always be cut long: "Long cord, long life." Baganda women of Africa carefully wash the cord and preserve it for use at the child's naming ceremony. A funny European folk tale contends that a baby's penis can grow as long—or as short—as his umbilical cord is cut! *What We Can Learn:* Women in earlier days were incredibly resourceful—who needed instruments like scissors back then? You are just as resourceful as those women were; the first step is believing that you are. The cutting of your baby's umbilical cord is symbolic in the sense that the lifeline that connected the two of you during pregnancy is now severed, though the bond between mother and child will last a lifetime.

What Happens Next

- ◆ The baby is weighed and his body length and head circumference are measured (weight may drop 10 percent in the next day, but that is normal).
- ◆ Shots or medication may be given to the baby (such as eyedrops, vitamin K shot, blood sample taken, and possibly hepatitis B shot).
- ◆ An Apgar test score is given to the baby immediately after birth and is based on five areas of sensitivity. Black babies will be checked for the color of their mucous membranes of the mouth, the color of their lips, palms, hands, and soles of the feet; the

whites of their eyes will also be checked. An Apgar score of 7 or more is good.

About the Apgar

The Apgar score is a way of quickly assessing how well your baby made the transition from being a fetus to being a self-sufficient individual. The purpose of the test is to observe the general condition of your newborn so that any immediate problems can be identified and treated. Five areas are assessed, which include overall appearance and color, pulse rate, reflexes, muscle tone, and respiration. The Apgar test is given 2 to 4 times to your baby: at 1 minute after birth, and then at 2 and 5 minutes after birth. Some doctors will also give a 10-minute Apgar score.

A score between 7 and 10 indicates that the baby is in good to excellent condition. A score of 6 is fair, and a score of 5 or less is poor and may indicate a need for lifesaving efforts. The 5-minute Apgar score most closely correlates to how well the baby will do in the newborn period.

Apgar Table

SIGN	POINTS		
	0	1	2
Appearance (color)	Pale or blue	Body pink, extremities blue	Pink (even in black babies)
Pulse (heartbeat)	Not detectible	Below 100	Over 100
Grimace (reflexes)	No response to stimulation	Grimace	Lusty cry
Activity (muscle tone)	flaccid (no or weak activity)	Some movement of extremities	A lot of activity
Respiration (breathing)	None	Slow, irregular	Good (crying)

Our sincere hope is that you have an uncomplicated, satisfying birth experience, as millions of women before you have had. However, if difficulties arise, we want you to be as prepared as possible. The next chapter will help you to understand some of the complications that can arise during pregnancy and in childbirth such as unusual bleeding, uterine, placental, and umbilical cord abnormalities, cesarean sections, slow labor, and miscarriage. Chapter 16, "Postpartum Recovery," addresses how to care for your body and your emotions during the postpartum period.

CHAPTER 15

What-ifs During Pregnancy and Childbirth

What-ifs are not something most mothers-to-be are anxious to talk—or read—about. But we want you to be educated about the things that can occur in pregnancy and child-birth so you will be that much more prepared should any of them happen to you. Don't read these descriptions with a spirit of fear but rather with a desire to arm yourself with knowledge.

In Pregnancy

Bleeding

During Early and Mid Pregnancy: Light bleeding before 28 weeks does not necessarily indicate a serious problem. It may be a sign of hormonal changes or may signal that the egg is attaching itself to the uterine wall. Brownish discharge, heavy bleeding, or any bleeding that is accompanied by abdominal pain can signal miscarriage or ectopic pregnancy. If you experience bleeding and your pregnancy is intact, you will probably be advised to restrict your activities until at least the fourteenth week. Abstain from sex and strenuous exercise until fetal movements have been felt for the twentieth week for a first baby and the eighteenth week for a subsequent baby. If the bleeding continues and abdominal pain appears or worsens, this usually means the uterus is contracting to expel the fetus.

During the Third Trimester: The two main causes of bleeding now are: *abruptio placentae*, a very rare condition where part of the placenta comes away from the uterine wall; and *placenta previa*, a condition where the placenta is located over or very near the mouth of the uterus, instead of being attatched to the upper uterus. See "Placental Problems," this chapter, for more detail.

Blood Clots

Women who are overweight, anemic, or have varicose veins are a bit more susceptible to venous thrombosis, a blood clot that forms in a vein, usually in the thigh or calf. Your leg or legs will feel tender to the touch. If the thrombosis is deep, you will have pain and swelling in your legs and may also have fever. Left untreated, this can be life-threatening as the clot rises into the lung area and causes bloody coughs and chest pain. Notify your caregiver immediately if you experience these symptoms. Depending on the severity of the clot, your doctor may prescribe elevation of the feet, special compression stockings, topical treatments, and anticoagulant drugs. Medicinal treatment will probably be continued for a few weeks after you deliver.

Chicken Pox

Only if you are one of the few adults today who didn't have chicken pox as a child, and thereby becoming immune for life, do you need to be concerned about this itchy irritation. If you have never had chicken pox, you can get a varicella immunization shot before you conceive, though it is still unclear whether this will protect the baby from contracting it. Chicken pox is most dangerous for your fetus if you contract it during the first six months of your pregnancy, when some of the baby's most vital organs are forming. In rare cases, chicken pox can manifest itself in fetal deformities and growth retardation. The last days before delivery is the second worst time to contract chicken pox, since any infection you get at this point is more likely to be passed on to the baby and you will not have the time to develop and pass on the protective antibodies to help the baby fight it off. The baby's brand-new immune system may not be able to cope well. Alert your caregiver immediately if you are exposed to people with the pox during your pregnancy, especially at those crucial stages. Take comfort in the fact that the Centers for Disease Control says that most healthy full-term babies who develop the pox after the first few days of life should not suffer any more severe complications than an older child.

Chorioamnionitis

An infection of the amniotic fluid and fetal membranes, this disease may be a major cause of premature labor. The difficulty in diagnosis is that in some cases no symptoms show, and no simple test can confirm it. Treatments can also vary widely, though this situation is improving with medical advances. Often, the first sign is a rapid heartbeat in the mother, then a fever over 100.4°F and, often, uterine tenderness. The amniotic fluid may smell bad if the membranes have ruptured; if they're intact, the vaginal discharge from the cervix may have an odor. Lab tests will show increased cell count, and the fetus may score low on a biophysical profile. If the pregnancy is near term and the membranes ruptured, and/or the fetus or mother is in trouble, the baby will be delivered. Otherwise, large doses of antibiotics will be given and the mother and baby will be monitored until the fetus is more mature or the mother's or baby's condition declines.

QUICK HELP FOR COLD/FLU/FEVER

Get to bed as soon as you can, drink lots of fresh citrus juices, force yourself to eat, and gargle with salt water if you have a sore throat. Take cool showers if you have a fever. Call your doctor if your cold lasts more than one week or if your fever is more than 102°F for two or more days. Don't take aspirin; your doctor can prescribe a pregnancy-safe medication if needed.

Cytomegalovirus (CMV)

Cytomegalovirus is part of the herpes family. It often has no symptoms and can only be diagnosed by a blood test. Some 20 to 60 percent of preschoolers carry this virus and can excrete it through saliva, urine, or feces for months or even years. Fortunately, around 80 percent of American adults have antibodies for CMV in their blood. The chances of your contracting CMV with adverse results to your fetus are small. The virus isn't very contagious, and most adults got CMV in childhood and it isn't likely to be reactivated now. About 1 percent of babies are born with the virus, and few of these show the ill effects of in utero CMV such as jaundice, high-tone deafness, and eye problems. Developing CMV for the first time while pregnant poses the most serious risk to your baby.

CMV can come and go without your knowledge. If you're not sure you've had it before, your doctor may advise you to take a leave of absence from any job associated with many small children, such as nursery school worker, at least for the first 24 weeks of pregnancy. Other doctors recommend wearing gloves on the job, washing carefully after changing diapers (which you should do anyway), and not kissing the toddlers or eating their leftovers. It's unlikely you'll catch CMV from your own toddlers at home. Symptoms to watch for: fever, fatigue, swollen lymph glands, sore throat. See your doctor whether these symptoms mean CMV or not.

CMV is the most common cause of babies born with viral infections though most have no signs at birth. Complications can develop later, such as mental and neuromuscular defects and vision and hearing problems. Some signs include abnormalities in the blood, brain, and various organs. Some symptoms resolve themselves; others threaten health or life. CMV causes about 3,000 children to become handicapped in the United States each year. The baby excretes the virus from its nose and mouth and in its urine.

Most women already have antibodies against CMV so you should not let fear keep you from breastfeeding. Experts say that the benefits of breast-feeding outweigh the possibility of transmitting CMV through the milk.

Down's Syndrome

Down's syndrome occurs when an extra chromosome appears before or immediately after fertilization, giving the fetus 47 chromosomes per cell instead of the normal 46. Either the mother's egg was damaged in the embryo stage, or, in about 20 percent of cases, the father's sperm was damaged. In 4 percent of cases, one chromosome broke and attached to another within an egg or sperm, or environmental factors may have caused the defect to the child itself in utero.

Down's syndrome and other chromosomal abnormalities are relatively rare, but are more common in older women because their eggs are older and have had more time to be exposed to drugs, X rays, infections, and so on. Possibly, 25 to 30 percent of Down's cases involve a defect in the father's sperm for the same reasons—age and exposure. Some studies suggest that there may be an increased risk if the father is over age 50 or 55. The risk of having a Down's syndrome baby increases with age from 1 in 10,000 at age 20 to 1 in 100 for a mother who's 40. The typical age that's used as a "cutoff" age—35—is arbitrary and is only a way for doctors to test as many fetuses as possible for Down's syndrome without exposing more mothers and babies than necessary to the risks of some types of prenatal diagnosis. Although children of parents over 40 are at particular risk, 80 percent of Down's children are born to women *under* age 35, simply because this age group bears the most children.

For a woman under 35, the alpha-fetoprotein test is recommended first. If it is normal, it may preclude the need for an amniocentesis. *Understand that despite these tests, Down's syndrome, when detected, cannot be treated or prevented.*

More males than females have Down's syndrome. Get input from a genetic counselor, pediatrician, maternal-fetal subspecialist, or other professional especially if your partner has a family history of a disease or condition such as hemophilia or Down's syndrome. A chromosome count can be done by scraping the inside of your mouth and doing an examination of the swipe under a microscope.

Down's babies are characterized by mental retardation, a flat face, and slanting eyes. Though this may be a daunting prospect for a new parent, know that Down's children are often exceptionally loving and lovable and, with the right care, can learn to take care of themselves and even read and write. Their retardation ranges from very mild to severe. Down's children can have heart and intestinal defects, ear infections (causing speech and hearing problems), respiratory conditions, leukemia, premature aging (after age 35), and symptoms of dementia. Their life expectancy is around 55 years.

Ectopic Pregnancy

An ectopic pregnancy occurs when the ovum fails to reach the cavity of the uterus, but is trapped in the fallopian tube and grows there. This type of pregnancy cannot come to term. If it is not stopped, the tube will eventually burst which can result in maternal death. Surgical treatment is mandatory to remove the fetus, and the whole tube if the damage is extensive. Your fertility will be reduced after an ectopic pregnancy.

Symptoms: pain in lower abdomen, usually one side (where the ovum is trapped); vaginal bleeding; and fainting, accompanied by a positive pregnancy test. Call your doctor. Ectopic pregnancies have increased, possibly due to the use of IUDs (the coil inflames the tube and the egg cannot travel to the uterus), and the rise in sexually transmitted diseases that go untreated.

Group B Strep

There are no symptoms for this infection so you should be automatically tested for it during your prenatal exam in about your seventh month. Your caregiver will take a vaginal sample, called a culture, for this purpose. Antibiotic treatment, administered when you are in labor, will protect you and your baby if you test positive.

Incompetent Cervix

Normally, the cervix is closed so the fetus remains in the uterus and doesn't fall into the vagina. With an incompetent cervix, the end of the cervical canal is open. The cause is unknown; the condition is very rare, unless the cervix has been damaged. A previous difficult or rapid delivery of a large baby may have injured the cervix or an unskilled abortion or other surgery may have damaged the muscle fibers that hold the cervical opening closed. An incompetent cervix usually remains hidden until the first miscarriage. The cervical canal starts opening the fourteenth week, and by the twentieth has dilated to about 1 inch—large enough for the bag of waters to bulge into and eventually break. A sudden loss of water is followed by a miscarriage with little pain.

Before or during the next pregnancy, a special stitch can be inserted around the cervix to tighten it. The cervix is usually stitched around the fourteenth week, under a general anesthetic. At term, the stitch is removed without anesthetic, and labor follows shortly, induced or naturally, though some women may wait a week or more. This treatment has a high success rate and most pregnancies proceed normally.

Intrauterine Growth Retardation (IUGR)

Several factors can contribute to delivering a low-birth-weight baby, whether it's premature or to term. Maternal illness, maternal lifestyle, placental inadequacy, and other factors may slow down fetal growth. This is called IUGR. If IUGR is diagnosed under prenatal care, steps are taken to reverse it. IUGR is more common in first pregnancies, in fifth and subsequent pregnancies, and somewhat more common in women under 17 and over 34. In most cases there are no outward symptoms. Carrying small is not a sign of a small baby any more than carrying large or much weight gain signifies a large baby. Your doctor may measure your abdomen with a tape measure, then suspect your uterus or fetus is small for date, or small for gestational age. An ultrasound examination will confirm or rule out IUGR.

Prevention of IUGR before conception: gain weight if you're underweight; space your pregnancies at least six months apart; get a rubella shot; check for a malformed uterus or other problems with reproductive or urinary organs; avoid toxic substances or environs. During pregnancy, of course, get the best possible treatment and nutrition, get adequate rest, and control or eliminate bad habits (smoking, drinking, etc.).

Miscarriage

Also called spontaneous abortion, miscarriage is when the fetus is expelled by the uterus before the twenty-eighth week. (After the twenty-eighth week it's called a stillbirth.) Medically speaking, "abortion" and "miscarriage" are synonymous; in popular speech, "abortion" is induced, and "miscarriage" is spontaneous. One in 10 pregnancies may end in miscarriage and they are most common in the first trimester. One-third of all first pregnancies abort. Many women spontaneously abort before they even know they are pregnant and barely notice the occurrence. An early miscarriage may suggest that the womb needed a "trial run" before carrying a pregnancy to term, or it may indicate the presence of a sperm or ovum defect that would have produced an abnormal fetus.

Causes of miscarriages include incompetent cervix (see previous page); incompatible blood type—your body develops antibodies against your partner's blood type, causing fetal death; hormonal deficiency—the uterine lining cannot support and nourish the fetus; misshapen uterus or uterine fibroid tumors; malfunctioning or maldevelopment of the placenta; diabetes.

Early miscarriages occur during the first trimester; late miscarries, between the end of the first trimester and the twenty-eighth week. In early miscarriage, clots or grayish matter may be passed as the miscarriage actually begins. Another sign is vaginal bleeding, heavy or light, with or without abdominal pain, perhaps with passage of mucus and a slight backache or discomfort in the lower abdomen. Any bleeding during the first 28 weeks of pregnancy is considered a threatened miscarriage until proven otherwise. Describe the bleeding to your doctor precisely: when it started, color of blood, light or heavy, intermittent or persistent, spotting or flowing, odorous or not. Report also accompanying symptoms such as nausea, vomiting, cramps, pain, fever, weakness, and so on. Spotting or staining without any other symptoms is not considered an emergency; if this happened in the middle of the night, you can wait till morning to call the doctor. With any other kinds of bleeding, call the doctor immediately, or go to the emergency room. Light or spotty bleeding in the second or third trimester usually isn't serious, but again, notify your doctor. If you are bleeding heavily, lie flat and keep your room cool. Don't take any medicines or alcohol. If you pass clots or membranes, or the fetus and placenta, collect them in a clean container for the doctor to examine.

If the fetus is shown alive through the ultrasound or Doppler device, and the cervix hasn't dilated, chances are good the threatened miscarriage will not occur. Female hormones, once routinely given for early bleeding, are rarely used today for fear they'll harm the fetus if it lives and may not be very effective. In rare cases progesterone will be given to women with a history of miscarriages and low hormone production. Late miscarriage is usually related to the mother's health, the condition of her cervix or uterus, exposure to certain drugs or toxins, or placental problems. An incompetent cervix may be stitched closed and may prevent a threatened miscarriage.

If miscarriage is incomplete, you'll need surgery to remove the remaining tissue, to prevent further hemorrhage and pelvic infection. Bleeding after miscarriage signifies that not everything has been expelled. High temperature and abdominal pain following miscarriage indicate infection.

Miscarriage, especially during the second trimester, deeply affects the woman, not just because of the loss of the baby, but because of sudden withdrawal of pregnancy hormones. You may be afraid for your fertility, or your ability to carry to term, or of carrying an abnormal baby in the future. It's normal to feel anger and grief, but avoid feeling guilty or blaming yourself. You will probably want to be alone, but fight it. Isolation will only deepen your feeling of loss. Of course, you and your husband may try for another pregnancy when you are both ready. Doctors recommend that you wait three to six months before trying to conceive again. In the meantime, to help guard against future miscarriages, pay strict attention to controlling any chronic disease such as diabetes or hypertension, preventing and treating infections, or surgically correcting the uterus.

Multiple Fetuses

Here's a fact you may not know: Twins are more common among blacks than whites. Two out of every 100 births are twins, up from 1 in 100 a generation ago, because of fertility drugs, in vitro fertilization, and the fact that more women over 35 are giving birth. Modern technology makes twin births less of a surprise, and the woman and doctor better equipped to care for a multiple pregnancy. Multiple births (three or more) are increasing at a faster rate than twin births.

Identical twins come from a single egg and share the placenta. Fraternal twins come from two fertilized eggs. Your doctor will be alerted to possible twins if there are twins in your family, or if your uterus is growing unusually large. The electronic fetal stethoscope can hear two heartbeats. Two heads can be felt, as well as multiple arms and legs. Ultrasound will confirm multiple fetuses, and twins can be diagnosed for certain by the eighth week.

Your prenatal care should emphasize avoiding anemia, checking blood pressure frequently, and getting extra rest to prevent low blood pressure, which can cause premature labor. One unfortunate result of carrying twins is that you might have more nausea than usual during the first three months of your pregnancy. Multiple pregnancy puts extra pressure on your joints, ligaments, and digestive organs. Your uterus may seriously crowd your digestive organs, so eat little and often. Don't gain too much weight, and watch your posture. Your larger uterus may cause shortness of breath, hemorrhoids, varicose veins, and abdominal pain. Alert your doctor if you experience any of these discomforts. You may have to give birth in the hospital because of the risk to the second baby if it's not born immediately after the first. Because you are carrying twins you may be automatically considered in the high-risk-pregnancy category.

If you are small-boned, your uterine expansion will be noticed earlier than on a larger-framed woman. Because a single fetus's heartbeat can be heard in several locations, hearing two or more heartbeats in the uterus confirms multiples only if the heart rates are different. No factors increase a woman's chances of having identical twins. For fraternal twins, factors include nonidentical twins in the mother's family, advanced age (women over 35 more frequently release more than one egg), use of fertility drugs, and in vitro fertilization.

Hypertension, anemia, and abruptio placentae are some complications more common in multiple pregnancies. Your doctor might prescribe early maternity leave, help with housework, and bed rest, depending on how your pregnancy is going. You may be prescribed a vitamin-mineral supplement.

Not surprisingly, multiple fetuses are more prone to poor fetal growth than single fetuses, especially in the third trimester. If one or more fetuses are growing poorly, intensive surveillance, usually in the hospital, is needed. The babies will be delivered when the lungs of the largest fetus are mature, or when it becomes risky for the smallest fetus to remain in the uterus. Fortunately, such circumstances are infrequent.

If both twins are cephalic—head down in the womb—delivery should be no problem. If one is breech (head up), the cephalic will usually be born first and open up a wide enough canal for the second baby to be delivered easily. If both babies are breech, or one is transverse (lying across the womb), or the babies are large, a cesarean may be safest.

HISTORICALLY SPEAKING . . .

 In many African cultures, the parents of twins are usually thought of as dangerous and powerful individuals. They are feared by others in their village, and all who have come in contact with them since the birth must be purified. Twins were considered abnormal or evil, and thus were often not allowed to live. One theory is that two babies born at once to a village where food is scarce would put an undue burden on the parents. In other parts of Africa, twins are considered to be gifts from the spirits, and their parents are believed to be able to see the future and bring good crops to the village. *What We Can Learn:* Twins are a delight and a challenge—they will certainly keep you hopping 24/7! Your biggest challenge if you are carrying twins is to take care of yourself so you do not deliver prematurely. Multiples are 10 times more likely to arrive before 32 weeks and weigh less than 3.3 pounds. Some things that parents of twins must think through: possibly buying a minivan; making adjustments to the home; how to pay for schooling; whether to separate them when they go to school; and giving them extra help with speech development.

Placental Problems

With the prevalence of fibroid tumors and cesarean deliveries, scarring of the uterine wall is becoming more common. It is this scarring that increases the risk of a woman having placental problems during pregnancy. There are three kinds of placental problems. In *placenta previa*, which occurs most frequently, the placenta adheres to the lower part of the uterus and is lying between the baby and the cervix. The danger is that the placenta, the baby's food and oxygen source, may "deliver" before the baby. Vaginal bleeding is one sign of possible placenta previa, but an ultrasound can make a sure diagnosis. In about half of all cases a cesarean section is performed to ensure a safe delivery. In *abruptio placentae* the placenta detaches from the uterus before the baby is born. This is often found in women who smoke or have hypertension. The symptoms include light to heavy bleeding, cramping, and abdominal aches. Ultrasounds are less conclusive in detecting placenta abruptia than placenta previa. With close supervision by your caregiver, most cases turn out fine. Be aware that you will probably be asked to restrict your activities and possibly be ordered to bed rest for the remainder of the pregnancy, depending on the severity of the placental separation. A cesarean section may be advised. In *placenta accreta* the placenta adheres to the uterine wall and will not deliver itself after childbirth. It must be surgically removed.

Preeclamptic Toxemia/Preeclampsia (PET)

Preeclampsia, or pregnancy-induced hypertension, occurs most often in first pregnancies and creeps up slowly throughout the pregnancy. It causes an abnormal elevation of the blood pressure, water retention, and protein in the urine. Black women are particularly prone to high blood pressure, so cutting down on salt and fatty foods, exercising moderately, and, once again, learning how to manage stress is crucial. Rarely occurring before the twentieth week of pregnancy, PET has no known cause, but has been associated with poor nutrition. A little aspirin, or a lot of calcium, may reduce the risk, as will making sure you don't miss any of your scheduled prenatal visits so it can be detected early.

Toxins, which damage the cells that line the blood vessels, are found in the blood of preeclamptic women. They may be produced as an immune system's reaction to the pregnancy. Signs of PET include raised blood pressure—an increase considered small ordinarily, yet abnormal during pregnancy; protein in the urine—signifying kidney damage; swelling of feet, ankles, hands, or face, often accompanied by puffiness around the eyes and neck due to excess fluid; excessive weight gain. You may have headaches, visual disturbance, mental dullness, and, in the late stages, even fits. Risk to the fetus grows with the increase in your blood pressure. PET may cause premature labor. Treatment is hospital admission, bed rest, sedation, and monitoring kidney function and blood pressure. In rare cases a cesarean may be necessary. If your blood pressure decreases and remains constant, you may return home after four or five days. Very soon after delivery, swelling goes down, and blood pressure and kidney function return to normal.

Severe preeclampsia can progress quickly into serious eclampsia, with convulsion and sometimes coma. Untreated, it can cause permanent damage to the mother's nervous system, blood vessels, or kidneys, and can cause growth retardation and oxygen deprivation for the baby. Preeclampsia can start during labor and delivery or even after birth, so mothers with sudden blood pressure elevations are carefully monitored for blood pressure, urine, reflexes, and blood chemistry.

A preeclamptic woman generally will not be allowed to go past her due date (40 weeks), since the postterm uterine environment will deteriorate more rapidly than normal. With severe preeclampsia, many doctors will induce labor preterm (at least 28 weeks); such deliveries should happen in a major medical center or hospital that is well equipped to handle any difficulties. Other doctors prefer prescribing bed rest, medication, and close monitoring, so the fetus may develop more.

Urinary Tract Infection

Common in pregnant women. Treatable by taking an antibiotic prescribed by your doctor (one appropriate for pregnant women), drinking lots of water, keeping your vaginal and perineal area very clean, fully emptying your bladder when you urinate, and getting proper rest. The most common form of UTI is cystitis; when treated it is not known to cause harm to the baby. If it goes untreated, however, and escalates to a kidney infection, you are endangering your baby's health and may deliver prematurely.

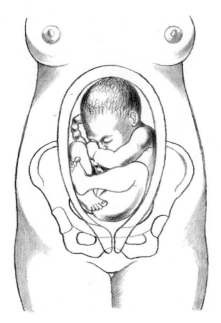

Baby in Breech Position.

In Childbirth

Breech Delivery

This occurs when the baby fails to rotate itself to the headfirst (or cephalic) position for delivery, as it does by about the eighth month in the majority of cases. It may be lying feetfirst or buttocks first in the womb.

Many schools of thought exist when it comes to discussing how to encourage a breech baby to turn. Nurse midwives and some obstetricians usually prefer to attempt to turn the baby manually by using a skill that involves putting pressure on the mother's abdomen. Unfortunately, babies turned this way have a tendency to turn back. Others say that acupuncture techniques are highly successful. In either case, an experienced professional should be the only one you allow to make such an attempt. Some women have found success using prayer and meditation as a way to encourage breech babies to turn. The mothers become calmer and more centered and thus were able to relax the nerves in their uterus, allowing the baby enough room to turn.

Nevertheless, if your baby does not turn, you can have a normal delivery, though you will probably need an episiotomy to make more room for the baby to come through. Both you and the baby will get a bit more bruised than usual, but that should diminish within a week after the birth. Be prepared to debate with your caregiver about this; many doctors will prefer to do a cesarean section to deliver a breech baby.

Cesarean Section

Often, the decision to have a cesarean section instead of a vaginal birth is made during labor. Many sisters have gone into the hospital fully expecting to give birth vaginally and ended up having a C-section. One good thing is that in less than 15 minutes, you will have your baby.

Here's what you can expect if this happens to you: A slim tube called a catheter will be inserted into your lower back to keep your bladder drained during the surgery. If there is time, a muscle relaxant may be given to you prior to the insertion of the tube to make the process more comfortable. Next you will be anesthetized from the abdomen down with an epidural, or, in emergency cases, you will be put to sleep. Your blood pressure and heartbeat will be monitored throughout the surgery through a cuff on your arm and several small suction discs on your chest. You will be fed fluids through an IV (intravenous) drip inserted into a vein in your arm. A screen will be placed at your shoulders so your bottom half remains sterile for the operation. Your view of the surgery will be blocked by this screen, however, you may request permission ahead of time to touch the baby when it is delivered. If extra oxygen is needed, an oxygen mask will be placed over your nose and mouth. Two incisions are made (see illustration in Chapter 14), one through your skin and muscles (usually a vertical one) and another through your uterus (usually horizontal). Your water bag will be broken and the baby will be lifted out headfirst. As soon as the baby's shoulders are out, the drug Pitocin will be administered to help your uterus contract and reduce the bleeding. The umbilical cord will then be clamped and the placenta removed. The rest of the operation should last about a half hour and will consist of your uterus and abdomen being stitched up (today's stitches are often clamps that look like staples). Your clamps will be removed in about five days. You will experience the same afterbirth contractions as in a vaginal birth. If you were planning to nurse, you still can, though you will prefer the lying down position to do it. See Chapter 14, "All About Labor and Delivery" for additional info on cesareans.

A NOTE ABOUT "BIKINI CUTS"

You may not always be able to have the popular horizontal "bikini cut" that leaves a smaller and less visible scar on your abdomen after a cesarean section. Especially in obese women, making a horizontal skin incision is discouraged by physicians because it doesn't provide as much room to remove the baby as a vertical cut and is a more time-consuming procedure. In emergency cesarean sections, a vertical skin incision is likely to be made because it provides more immediate access to the baby. Even a woman who has had a previous cesarean with a horizontal incision is likely to have a vertical incision the second time to avoid cutting through the scar tissue. The horizontal incision, though, is said to be stronger and less likely to rupture. Make your preference known to your doctor if at all possible.

Cord Prolapse

Occasionally, when the amniotic membranes rupture, the umbilical cord slips, or prolapses, through the cervix or even well into the vaginal canal, carried by the rush of amniotic fluid. During delivery the baby's presenting part can then compress the cord, reducing or even cutting off the baby's oxygen supply. Prolapse is most common in premature labors (because the baby's presenting part is too small to fill the pelvis) or when the foot or another part besides the head comes out first, allowing the cord to slip down. Prolapse is also more common when the membranes rupture before labor begins, rather than after.

A prolapsed cord can be felt in the vagina or can even be seen hanging. Get on your hands and knees to reduce pressure on the cord. Support a protruding cord gently with warm wet gauze pads or a clean towel. Don't press or squeeze the cord. Go immediately to the hospital. You may then be injected with a saline solution in your bladder to cushion the cord or it could be tucked in and held with a special tampon. An emergency C-section may have to be performed.

Meconium Staining

When a baby is postmature (more than two weeks overdue) or if she is undergoing some stress or discomfort, she may have a bowel movement while in the womb. The stool will pass into the amniotic fluid, which will have a greenish brown tint to it when your sac or water breaks. The danger is that the fetus may inhale the stool and fluid into her lungs, causing her to aspirate. Your caregiver may want to keep a watch on the fetus via an electronic fetal monitor during labor if meconium is found in the fluid. The baby's airway will usually be thoroughly cleaned after birth to ensure that her lungs are cleared of the meconium.

Rh Blood Incompatibility

About 80 percent of the population has Rhesus positive (Rh+) blood. Special attention is given to Rhesus negative (Rh−) mothers; if your partner is Rh+, your baby is likely to be also. If your Rh+ baby's blood cells leak past the placenta into your bloodstream, your body will react with antibodies to destroy what is called the Rh factor. This will likely happen during delivery. There's little danger to your first baby, and possibly enough antibodies won't form to endanger subsequent pregnancies. However, your doctor should test you throughout pregnancy for such antibodies. Enough of them may damage the developing baby. This happens in less than 10 percent of Rh− women.

After delivery, the mother is tested for Rh+ antibodies; if they're present, she'll be given an injection of anti-Rhesus globulin to destroy the Rh+ cells in the baby's blood, so no more antibodies will be produced. This should be done after every delivery or abortion/miscarriage, so future babies won't be endangered by Rh blood incompatibility. If not done, the future baby will be closely monitored, and given an intrauterine transfusion if necessary. A cesarean may be done before term, and the baby given a transfusion after birth to replace its damaged blood cells. The baby will be given Rh− blood so as not to trigger more antibodies. In 72 hours the antibodies will have disappeared and the baby will be naturally replenished with its own healthy Rh+ blood.

Thanks to medical advances, Rh incompatibility is less of a threat than it was a generation ago. The attacking antibodies cause fetal anemia—mild or serious, depending on the level of antibodies. In the twenty-eighth week of pregnancy, the Rh− woman without antibodies is given a dose of Rh immune globulin. Another dose is given her within 72 hours after delivery, if the baby is Rh+ (also after miscarriage, abortion, amniocentesis, or bleeding during pregnancy).

336 ♦ LABOR TO POSTPARTUM

Amniocentesis is used to determine the fetus's blood type, if the mother has a history of Rh antibodies. Use of Rh vaccines has reduced the need for transfusions in Rh incompatible pregnancies to less than 1 percent, and may wipe out the need for transfusions in the future.

Shoulder Dystocia

This is an unexpected occurrence when the baby's shoulders get stuck between your pelvic bones on its way out of the birth canal. Your caregiver will probably try to rotate the baby's shoulders gently one at a time or may put pressure on the pelvis so the baby gets "unstuck." Extensive flexing of the mother's knees sometimes helps. The baby's collarbone can be broken to facilitate the birth. The collarbone and shoulder will be wrapped and will take about eight weeks to repair. You must be careful that she doesn't sleep on the affected shoulder until the bone is repaired. Natural options should of course be attempted first, but an episiotomy (vaginal cut) may be necessary. Unfortunately, in some dystocia cases, the cut can tear into the rectum, causing weeks of painful postpartum recovery.

Slow Labor

It is not uncommon for a woman in labor to experience periods as long as 24 hours between "happenings." It may be because you are in false labor, you could be too tense or panicky, or you may have been given medication too soon. There are some things you can do to help your labor progress: (a) walking can help you relax and concentrate—the activity itself can help stimulate the labor; (b) continually emptying your bladder can help your baby descend, and mineral oil or an enema can help you move your bowels, if you are having difficulty; (c) your amniotic sac (water bag) can be broken if it hasn't ruptured on its own—usually, labor follows within 12 hours; (d) if your cervix is not dilating (opening) to make way for the baby's passage, it can be treated with a special hormone gel called prostaglandin, or oxytocin may be administered, especially if you are physically and mentally exhausted; (e) in active labor, sitting upright as much as possible or squatting uses gravity to help labor progress. Which decisions are made about what to do when your labor isn't progressing will often depend on your caregiver's philosophy. Some doctors and most CNMs will do everything possible to facilitate a vaginal delivery, as long as some progress is evident and the baby is not in danger. Many doctors will opt for a C-section after a few hours of active labor, particularly if you have a large baby and a small pelvis. Others may attempt to rotate the baby's head so it is in a better position to be delivered vaginally. Having a close, communicative relationship with your caregiver will benefit you in situations like this one when quick decisions have to be made.

Uterine Rupture

This is a tear in the uterus that usually occurs during a difficult or extended labor. Women who have had uterine surgery, and thus scarring, are most suceptible, as are women who have had many previous children (five or more). If you are in labor, your contractions will usually stop, you may feel faint, and you will feel a tearing sensation as well as severe abdominal pain. Vaginal bleeding is not necessarily a symptom. Your doctor will perform a cesarean section and proceed to repair your uterus. Only in extreme cases can the uterus not be saved.

CHAPTER 16

◇ ◇ ◇ ◇

Postpartum Recovery

Psychologists say that most women think holistically and globally. Marriage, parenthood, job, family, church, friends, recreation—all seem intertwined, one affecting the other. A man's thinking, on the other hand, is described as being more compartmentalized, like lockers in a gym, each with its own door that is opened and then closed after each use: Wife. Child. Work. Church. Extended Family. Friends. Hobbies.

That may be about to change. Now that you have this baby all to yourselves you both need to learn how to think more like the other. If you have decided to go back to work, you will need to compartmentalize your thinking a bit in order to function on the job without driving yourself crazy with worry about the baby at home. Your husband will need to think more about how his role as a career man overlaps and affects his new responsibilities as Daddy. One thing is sure: Your time is no longer your own. The baby sets the pace now, and basically, you rearrange your life accordingly. You cannot be as spontaneous as you may have been, and you will have to become more responsible than you were as a childless couple. Couples say the sooner you make peace with what is and what can no longer be, the sooner you can both begin to enjoy this challenging and immensely fulfilling new season in your lives.

Your Emotions

One of the first things you may notice is that you are on an emotional roller-coaster. Many sisters spend their whole pregnancies gearing up for the big event—childbirth—but then they don't know how to feel when it's over except relieved. You will find that you are no longer the center of attraction: The baby is, even though she wouldn't be here without your labor of love. Be prepared for this. It's important that your mate be your number-one cheerleader now to help fill that emotional void, loving you in ways he knows you want to be loved. (If he doesn't know, tell him gently, again and again.)

Close relatives and friends can also help even out the emotional ups and downs you will experience. Fortunately, most of us are quite accustomed to managing job challenges, physical challenges, relationship challenges, and other day-to-day stresses, so we have lots of practice as jugglers. However, caring for a home, the baby, the bills, your husband, and a million other details can overwhelm even the most together sisters. This baby area may be totally new to you. Maybe you didn't grow up around babies or dirty diapers or breast-feeding women, and feel ill equipped to manage this new part of your life. Ask for help. Give people, including your partner, specific tasks to perform, even if it's just "Sit with me for a minute." Mothers, grandmothers, sisters, and aunts are wonderful to have around when you bring home your baby. They can help you take care of her, prepare food, tidy up, get some *real* sleep, and offer good advice. The problem occurs when you don't see eye to eye with what Mama's telling you to do with "that baby." Be respectful and learn from them, but make sure you assert yourself and your wishes clearly: No one else is *this* baby's mama but you.

Use your creative abilities to come up with solutions to the problems that will inevitably come up with a new baby in the house. Read all you can about what your baby's thinking and feeling and how she is growing. Our fellow African and African-American brothers and sisters have been birthing and raising babies successfully for centuries with far fewer resources that we have today—you can do it, too!

Postpartum Anxiety

Depression after childbirth has been talked about so much that women have come to expect it as a natural part of the birth experience.

But feelings of sadness, of being overwhelmed, and of inadequacy are common among mothers—of newborns and of 10-year-olds. Mother-hood is a stressful experience. It is a time of immense joys, too. It is a new phase of life that takes adjustment. Though many speculate that the depression is *caused* by the drop in hormone production that occurs after birth, much like premenstrual syndrome, this has yet to be proven conclusively. Some experts conclude that the traumatic and exhilirating experience of having a baby, then being separated from it in the hospital, may induce depression, sleeplessness, and bouts of crying. Interestingly, research has shown that women who have home births shed very few after-birth tears.

A smaller amount of women experience a deeper, lingering de-pression that lasts more than two weeks and hinges on a basic in-ability to cope. A woman who is experiencing this depression may not be able to talk about her emotional state and can seem beyond comfort. She may feel resentful—even hateful—toward the baby. Her whole identity has changed overnight and she finds it too hard to deal with. A woman's home environment, her marital state, her financial state, institutional racism, and other socioeconomic factors contribute greatly to—or can even cause—the depression. This is not a condition to be ignored. This is when a woman needs the support of a mate, relatives, and friends to help make it through the day. A regular phone call just to talk—about *her*. Homemade meals. Volun-tary help with the baby or the housework. She needs these human contacts more than she needs psychotherapy, tranquilizers, a drink, or a good smoke—routes many women take. (Though there is nothing wrong with deciding to see a good therapist.) But she may not ask people she knows for help, close family and friends may be far away, and those around her may not have the courage to "get involved" on their own initiative. *Social isolation is a key cause of postpartum depression.*

Most of the solutions experts offer to ward off depression include doing things with other people and making time for yourself. Here are some more ideas: Do some form of moderate exercise regularly in the mornings with another mother; write, draw, paint, or even sew to exorcise your sad feelings; spend a few minutes alone talking to God or reading a Psalm; write out a simple outline for your day and schedule in at least a half-hour for yourself; make a priority of taking naps or just sitting down with your feet up for some time each day; read something you're interested in or listen to inspiring music each day; remind yourself that mothering is a hard job and you're doing your best.

"After I delivered, I had a hemorrhoid the size of a golf ball. Even my midwife said, 'Wow, that's a wicked one!' If I had a gun I would have shot it off my body it was so painful!"

"I was totally unprepared for how 'messy' I felt after giving birth. I was so swollen and leaky and my empty stomach felt all spongy and flabby. Those pictures of a radiant woman in a long, flowing nightgown cradling her baby are a joke. I felt like I had a basketball between my legs!"

Your Body: Recovering from Childbirth

It is quite common for women who have just given birth to experience some of the following in the days and weeks after childbirth:

◆ Slight leaking of urine when you cough or laugh due to a relaxing of the muscle around your urethra.

◆ A plump, moist, heavy-feeling vagina due to the muscles that opened up to accommodate the baby's passage and tissues that have swollen to help heal you up.

◆ A soft, flabby abdomen. Most women still look about six months pregnant for a while after giving birth.

◆ Full, heavy breasts with darker nipples than usual due to lactation; breasts may ache.

◆ A bruised feeling between your vagina and anus (called the perenium), for obvious reasons, and especially if you had an episiotomy; area may also feel numb for the first few weeks.

◆ Backache, due to the strain of pushing the baby out and/or receiving an epidural. May persist off and on indefinitely.

◆ Strong contractions or "afterpains," signaling that your uterus is shrinking back to its original size of less than 1/4 pound. You will feel these most when you are breast-feeding or when your nipples are stimulated.

◆ Pinkish vaginal discharge or bleeding, similar to a period, for about a week, and, for some, several weeks. If blood is bright red and heavy-flowing, foul-smelling, or accompanied by fever, you may be experiencing postpartum hemorrhage possibly due to the incomplete removal of the placenta. Use only sanitary napkins and call your doctor or midwife.

◆ Small blood clots from your vagina, especially after you wake up in the morning, or when you breast-feed.

◆ Constipation, gradually lessening after the first few weeks. Drink lots of liquids.

◆ Fear of having a bowel movement because of episiotomy stitches. (Not to worry—they won't pop.) Again, drink lots of liquids and eat prunes and raisins.

◆ Stinging urination can be alleviated by standing up over the toilet (the way a man does) instead of sitting on it or twisting your behind to the side of the toilet so the urine flow doesn't touch as much of the bruised tissue. If that fails, pour water on your vagina as you urinate or urinate as you shower.

◆ Hemorrhoids due to extreme pressure on the anus during childbirth. If severe, ask your practitioner for a topical treatment or a medicated suppository.

◆ Engorged (hard, painful) breasts, occurring in the first few days after your milk comes in. It is best relieved, believe it or not, by breast-feeding or expressing milk.

◆ Headaches; may persist if you had an epidural.

◆ Tiredness.

◆ Overall body aches.

If You Had Cesarean Surgery

A cesarean is considered major surgery and it may take you months to recover from it fully. You will be spared the perineal pain a woman who gave birth vaginally will experience, but you will probably feel some of the following in the days and weeks after the birth:

◆ General pain at the incision site after the anesthesia wears off. A good sign that the wound is healing is if the pain turns into burning and itching in the ensuing weeks.

◆ Difficulty urinating after the catheter (the tube that was inserted into your urethra so you could empty your bladder during the surgery) is removed. Drink lots of water, walk around, and have a bedpan nearby so you can "go" as soon as you feel the urge.

◆ Intestinal gas, common after abdominal surgery, is relieved by pulling in your abdomen and exhaling simultaneously. Grunting as you exhale helps expel the gas. If you had an emergency C-section you were probably given general anesthesia, which can cause secretions to collect in your chest. Grunting as you exhale also helps clear this up.

◆ Pain holding the baby on your lap, especially to breast-feed. Sit up in bed and place the baby on a pillow next to you with the things you need to tend to her. Lie down on your side to breast-feed the baby or use the "football hold" position. (See Chapter 18, "Caring for Your Baby," for how-to photos.)

◆ Redness, swelling, or oozing at the incision site indicates possible infection. Your doctor or midwife will prescribe antibiotics.

Pain Soothers

For Vaginal/Rectal Area
Sanitary napkin soaked with witch hazel or an antiseptic solution
A medicated pad
Oils like chamomile and lavender in your bathwater or used on a wet towel or diaper to "sop" the area
A warm sitz bath
Soft toilet paper
A crushed-ice pack
Cool water poured on your vaginal area over the toilet
Kegel exercises (if it doesn't cause pain). See Chapter 9, "Your Physical Tank," for how-tos.
Lying on your side

For Backache
A back massage

For Breasts
Hot or cold compresses

For Cesarean Recovery
Sponge bath (no baths or showers) until your stitches or clips are removed, approximately five days after the birth
Leg-bending exercises to get your circulation going and to prevent thrombosis (blood clotting in the legs); essential if you have varicose veins

Postpartum Checkup: Bring Your Concerns

Some women wonder why they have to wait six weeks to have their postpartum checkup. Most sisters want to know after the first week whether everything is going right "down there," and they want to ask questions about things they are feeling. The reason is that six weeks is considered your body's official recovery time. Your uterus should have returned to its normal size and your vaginal muscles should have regained their tone. If you had a cesarean section, your incision should be healing nicely by the sixth week. If for some reason you would like to be checked sooner, feel free to ask your practitioner if she will do so. You should not be denied. Jot down any concerns you may have and discuss them with your practitioner at your checkup.

Many nurse-midwives consider it routine to visit a woman in her home within the first two weeks of the birth. During that visit she checks both the mother and the baby and often ends up answering the mother's many questions about everything from breast-feeding to diapering to sex to how to help her three-year-old adjust to the new baby. This personal touch, which is also offered by many wonderful black and white doctors, is an essential component—especially for us. Unfortunately, most insurance carriers are not too fond of a practitioner spending more than 12 minutes with any one patient, so the pressure to get you in and out is always on. Nonetheless, personal care can mean the difference between whether a woman who's trying to breast-feed with engorged breasts in the midst of disagreeing relatives continues or gives up. The bond of caring that develops between practitioner and patient early on positively affects how a mother cares for herself and her baby down the road.

Medically, expect to be checked in the following ways:

◆ Blood pressure
◆ Weight
◆ Uterus
◆ Cervix
◆ Vagina
◆ Episiotomy wound and/or cesarean incision
◆ Breasts
◆ Anus
◆ Birth control
◆ Other concerns you may voice

Eating

Hopefully during pregnancy you added good things to your diet that might have been missing and replaced bad eating habits with better ones. Why stop now? You learned that steamed vegetables, broiled fish, and whole-wheat bread are full of good nutrients that are good for your body's functions and ward off many of the diseases that plague us. Even though you're no longer pregnant, they still do their job. Continue your good eating plan for the rest of your life!

There is no special diet a woman needs to follow after the birth of her baby, except that she should be eating nutritionally sound meals, low in fat and sugar, to stay healthy. You should get approximately 300 to 500 extra calories per day if you are nursing. If you are really anxious about taking off the weight, weigh yourself weekly. Even with the extra calories you should be slowly losing weight. If necessary, you can gradually cut down on the extra calories after the six-week postpartum period.

Mothers and medical experts have known for centuries that breast milk is an amazing substance that is able to maintain its basic composition and quantity even when a mother isn't eating well. What you eat now is less important to your breast milk than how nutritionally sound your diet was during pregnancy, when the breast milk was being made. It's still important to get the vitamins and minerals that will help you stay healthy and aid in your recovery and fortify your breast milk. Protein (animal or plant) will aid in the repair of your sensitive vaginal and perineal tissues. A sufficient amount of iron is necessary to replace the hemoglobin you lose when you bleed postpartum and later on during your periods (remember those?). Following your pregnancy diet as best you can will help ensure that you get sufficient amounts of vitamins A, B, C, and folic acid. Be sure to get between three and five servings of calcium (from cheese, milk, yogurt, collard greens, etc.) in each day. (See Chapter 7, "You (and Your Baby) Are What You Eat," for more on this.) All new mothers, particularly those who are breast-feeding and who are strict vegetarians, should continue taking their pregnancy vitamin supplement for at least the first six weeks postpartum. Afterward, you can begin taking a standard multivitamin/mineral supplement.

"Just the smell of food made me put on weight, even though I was breast-feeding. It took hard work to get it off."

◇ ◇ ◇ ◇ ◇ ◇ ◇ ◇ ◇ ◇ ◇ ◇ ◇ ◇ ◇ ◇ ◇ ◇

"When I breast-fed the weight just dropped off of me."

◇ ◇ ◇ ◇ ◇ ◇ ◇ ◇ ◇ ◇ ◇ ◇ ◇ ◇ ◇ ◇ ◇ ◇

Getting Back into Shape . . . Slowly and Steadily

Your focus for the first several months should be on nurturing your baby, not on fitting into your jeans. You did more aerobic exercise by giving birth than Jane Fonda probably does in a week! Reject the notion that you are not beautiful or the idea that you can become instantly slim again two weeks after the birth. You can get back into shape with committed, regular exercise, but your body requires at least six months, if not an entire year, in which to do so. Several important studies support the finding that women who exercise after giving birth do not lose weight or fat faster than those who didn't exercise, although their bodies probably look more toned.

Of course, you are not off the hook if you want your prepregnancy body back. If you ate properly and exercised moderately while you were pregnant, getting back into shape will not be an impossible task, though it will require concerted effort—especially around that tough-to-firm-up belly. Exercise postpartum can also help you regain your posture, strengthen your muscles (particularly if you do abdominal toners), and make your head happy. Taking time out for yourself is crucial to help replenish your mental and physical energy, especially during your baby's first year. Mothers say it's very satisfying to take a short break from the baby, do their exercises, and then reunite with her again later with their tanks refilled. Dance to some funky music that makes you slide that pelvis and move those hips, as in African dance, and you will be helping to firm up the areas that got loosened up most during pregnancy and childbirth. Consult your doctor or midwife first, and with their okay you can start exercising after your six-week postpartum recovery period. Begin with five minutes of toning exercises each day and gradually work up to an aerobic workout. (See Chapter 9, "Your Physical Tank," for exercise and exercise video suggestions.)

If you have chosen to breast-feed, you made a smart decision, not only for your baby, but for your body, too. When you ask sisters with newborn babies how they got back into shape so fast, they say, "It's the breast-feeding, girl. It's amazing." And it is. Breast-feeding mothers tend to lose baby weight faster than nonnursing mothers because the energy expended and calories burned during breast-feeding give the effect of a mini-workout. Done *frequently, consistently, and without supplementation of any kind*, breast-feeding also can suppress the return of menstruation, thus acting as a kind of contraceptive—though it shouldn't be relied upon. Generally, nursing women resume their periods later than non-nursing mothers because frequent breast-feeding helps to delay ovulation. Not getting pregnant again a few months after you give birth is certainly one way to go if you want to regain your shape!

HISTORICALLY SPEAKING . . .

 Most tribal African women, like many sisters here in the West, don't have the luxury of taking six months off from their jobs and household responsibilities to bond with their babies. And, needless to say, in the rural South during slavery few black women were able to stay in bed more than a day, and many were back in the fields the day after the birth—with the baby in tow. One southern midwife recalls that black mothers got to stay in bed longer if they had a "winter-time baby," since the fields didn't need as much attention during the colder months. *What We Can Learn:* Obviously, planned exercise was not needed in the lives of our hardworking forebears. But today, exercise time must be creatively carved out by the new mother for both her physical and mental recovery. Massages, heat treatments, cold packs, and herbal teas are some of the methods tribal women employ to soothe their aching bodies. During the postpartum period, sisters today might adopt some of these comforts, as well as resuming the activities they participated in during the early months of pregnancy, such as fitness walking, then gradually ease back into a full aerobic regimen.

Pascal Sacleux, Allford/Trotman Associates, Atlanta.

◇ ◇ ◇ ◇ ◇ ◇ ◇ ◇ ◇ ◇ ◇ ◇ ◇ ◇ ◇ ◇ ◇ ◇

"I tore a lot during my delivery and it took me nine months to get comfortable with sex again. I really thought something was wrong with me."

◇ ◇ ◇ ◇ ◇ ◇ ◇ ◇ ◇ ◇ ◇ ◇ ◇ ◇ ◇ ◇ ◇ ◇

"One night we were trying to have sex and I was still so big that my husband looked like he was mountain climbing! I said, 'Call me in a year, please.' "

◇ ◇ ◇ ◇ ◇ ◇ ◇ ◇ ◇ ◇ ◇ ◇ ◇ ◇ ◇ ◇ ◇ ◇

"We waited six weeks after the birth to have sex only *because the doctor told us to. We couldn't have waited one minute longer!"*

◇ ◇ ◇ ◇ ◇ ◇ ◇ ◇ ◇ ◇ ◇ ◇ ◇ ◇ ◇ ◇ ◇ ◇

"Six weeks!? I could have waited six months to have sex. I was so afraid of conceiving again I was praying during our love-making, 'Oh Lord, please don't let me get pregnant again.' "

◇ ◇ ◇ ◇ ◇ ◇ ◇ ◇ ◇ ◇ ◇ ◇ ◇ ◇ ◇ ◇ ◇ ◇

Sex After Birth

Sex. The final frontier. These are the voyages several postpartum sisters made back into the world of lovemaking—and each one has a different tale to tell. A few couldn't wait for sex to resume. Many said they wanted to wait longer. Others hoped he'd never ask. Still other sisters wanted intimacy but were deathly afraid of getting pregnant again. What were the common threads in all of these sisters' stories? That their childbirth experiences and new feelings of motherhood deeply affected their desire—or lack of desire—to make love again. Here are some sensual solutions that may work for you both:

◆ Lack of vaginal lubrication as a result of hormonal changes can make tissues sore during intercourse, as do the wounds of a rough delivery. *Possible Solution:* Have your husband ever-so-gently massage your entire vaginal area with a lubricant using light strokes with his fingertips; if you enjoy it, continue. If not, stop—and try again another time.

◆ Lack of desire can also be a result of hormonal changes after childbirth and may extend until your period resumes. *Possible Solution:* You will probably need a lot of tenderness, space, intimacy, and affection to feel secure about sex again—hand holding, hugging, massaging, and the whispering of sweet nothings are all part of the buildup to intercourse for us. Your husband needs to romance you, like he did when you were dating (hopefully)—after all, you're worth it.

◆ Concern about breasts—are they for feeding or fondling? Most breast-feeding women struggle with this early on. You may revel in your role as food provider for your baby and have difficulty switching back into the sexy-woman role—even if you want to. *Possible Solution:* Encourage your husband to be near as you breast-feed the baby as often as possible. Help him to feel included so he can see the beauty of your new role, and not feel resentful. The moments you share as you both watch your well-fed newborn fall asleep at the breast can be the beginning of a new level of intimacy. Why not follow with a warm oil massage that is both soothing and sensual?

◆ Leaky breasts may be annoying and embarrassing, interrupting lovemaking. *Possible Solution:* Laugh about it and continue. By now, if your mate was by your side during the many unglamorous aspects of your pregnancy and childbirth, you both should be un-embarrassable! If it's really disturbing, try not to stimulate the nipples.

◆ Interruptions by the baby may occur just as lovemaking has begun. *Possible Solution:* Learn your baby's routine and create a little space for your lovemaking that's beyond her reach, like when she's napping or after her evening (or afternoon) feed. If she was well fed, she's likely to sleep for a few hours, just long enough for a romantic interlude. Call your husband and remind him of how much you're looking forward to the evening. His mission can be to pick up dinner and some fragrant oils on the way home from work, anticipating all the way. . . .

Communicating with your partner is everything when it comes to sex after childbirth. You must be able to say, "Yes, this is good" or "No, that hurts." Tune in to each other's needs even more than you did before the baby—you've both changed and you need to rediscover each other through loving conversations and lots of understanding.

GOOD THOUGHTS

Selected verses from the lovers in the Song of Songs (in some
Bible translations it is called Solomon's Song)

Him to Her
How beautiful you are, my darling!
Oh, how beautiful!
Your eyes are doves.
Your lips are like a scarlet ribbon;
your mouth is lovely.
Your two breasts are like two fawns
that browse among the lilies,
You have stolen my heart, my sister, my bride;
you have stolen my heart with one glance of your eyes.
How delightful is your love, my sister, my bride!
All beautiful you are, my darling;
there is no flaw in you.

Her to Him
How handsome you are, my lover!
Oh, how charming!
And our bed is verdant.
Let him kiss me with the kisses of his mouth—
for your love is more delightful than wine.
Take me away with you—let us hurry!

His mouth is sweetness itself;
he is altogether lovely.
I delight to sit in his shade, and his fruit is sweet to my
    taste.
This is my lover, this is my friend.
His left arm is under my head,
and his right arm embraces me.

Part Three

Introduction to Your Baby

CHAPTER 17

◇ ◇ ◇ ◇

The Newborn:
Getting to Know Your Baby

By now you've probably discovered that your baby doesn't look exactly like the sweet-faced cherub on the Gerber box. After all, he worked just as hard as you did to be born! Most of the odd things you will notice about the baby's appearance are due to two factors: the baby lived its nine months curled up in a ball inside the small, watery environment in your womb and is showing the stress of having fought its way through a narrow birth canal. Here are some perfectly normal things you'll notice about your baby that may not look perfectly normal to you:

- ◆ An oval-shaped head that's soft at the top
- ◆ Puffy face and eyes
- ◆ Legs that may be bowed and pigeon toed
- ◆ Curled fists
- ◆ Flexed arms
- ◆ Swollen genitals
- ◆ Ears that may appear matted or pressed toward the head or the cheek
- ◆ Body looks bruised (unless you had a cesarean)
- ◆ Blotchy, wrinkled skin, which may begin to peel and crack during the first week of life

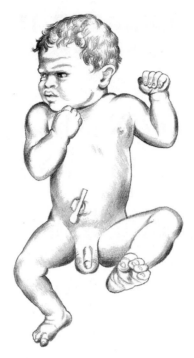

The Newborn

Your Newborn's First Checkup: What to Expect

Within minutes after birth your baby will receive his first check-up. The nurse or doctor will:

- ◆ Clear the baby's airways by suctioning his nose
- ◆ Clamp and cut the umbilical cord
- ◆ Assign an Apgar score at 1 minute and 5 minutes (see Chapter 14, "All About Labor and Delivery," page 319)
- ◆ Administer eyedrops or ointment to prevent any bacterial infection
- ◆ Observe body parts to make sure they are normal
- ◆ Record the passage or lack of passage of urine and stools
- ◆ Give a vitamin K injection to enhance the clotting ability of baby's blood
- ◆ Weigh baby
- ◆ Measure baby's length
- ◆ Measure head circumference

◆ Obtain blood from infant's heel to screen for several inherited diseases. The list of diseases screened for varies from state to state. They may include phenylketonuria (fe-nul-key-tun-oo-ree-ah) or PKU, hypothyroidism (hi-po-THIGH-roy-dism), and sickle-cell anemia

◆ Obtain blood from the umbilical cord for the Coombs test, which screens for antibodies that would indicate Rh sensitization has occurred, and to determine the baby's blood group and type.

THE AVERAGES

Average baby weight: 7½ pounds; 95 percent of newborns weigh between 5½ pounds and 10 pounds.

Average baby length: 20 inches; 95 percent of newborns measure between 18 and 22 inches.

Average head circumference: 13.8 inches; Typical range is from 12.9 inches to 14.7 inches.

During the next 24 hours, your doctor will check the following:

◆ Weight, which probably has dropped since birth
◆ Length
◆ Head circumference
◆ Heart sounds and respiration
◆ External examination of internal organs
◆ Newborn reflexes
◆ Hips
◆ Hands, feet, arms, and legs
◆ Genitals
◆ Umbilical cord stump
◆ Hepatitis B vaccine (optional at this time)

Parents are usually surprised to see their baby at delivery. You may expect to see a baby who is already washed and hungry, with eyes that are fully alert and who looks something like you. You may also expect a baby who is ready to bond and is warm and affectionate, when in fact newborn babies *require* attention, *require* bonding, *require* a whole bunch of things—but they are not very *giving*. Avoid the pain of disappointment by understanding that your newborn baby is not going to look at you lovingly, at least initially, and is not going to be capable of giving too much—except the delight it brings you to know that he's arrived safely.

Newborn babies want to feel warm and relatively tightly bundled, which helps them to feel secure. A baby that's not bundled feels like we would feel if we were in space without gravity or familiar surroundings. They are usually very sleepy and don't look around much until they start to feel hungry. Newborn babies are most awake during feeding time but will fall asleep while eating.

The baby has been in a very protected environment throughout the gestational period and probably the first pain and discomfort your baby has experienced is during the labor and delivery process. One thing that can really help you as a new parent is the realization that babies cannot distinguish the difference between pain and discomfort; everything that is uncomfortable is the worst it can be. So a hunger pain is really a desperate thing to a baby. Since your baby received continuous nourishment through the umbilical cord whenever he wanted it during his time in the womb, this is his first experience with hunger. It's very helpful to remind yourself of these things when you are getting frustrated with your baby's cries. Depending on the weight of the baby, he may feel hunger anytime between birth and the first 5 hours of life. Urine and stools will usually appear within the first 24 hours.

How Babies Look

Head

The head is the biggest part of the body that comes through the birth canal. In order to fit through it, your baby's skull bones shifted and actually overlapped during the birth process to permit easier passage. This is known as molding. You can feel ridges on your baby's head caused by the molding process. Molding is less noticeable in breech babies (where the baby's head is not the first part into the pelvis), and may not be present at all in cesarean births because the molding happens due to squeezing of the baby's head through her mother's pelvis. Don't worry; your baby won't have a conehead for too long. Within a few days or weeks, your baby's head will become round, although the longer her head was squeezed, the longer it will take to right itself. The molding process rarely has any impact on your baby's brain.

You will see that your baby's head goes from narrow in the front to relatively wide at the back. In the widest part of the head is the area that took the most pressure going through the birth canal. It is called the biparietal diameter. That area on either side of the head could have been squeezed during the birthing process, causing a superficial trauma called a cephalohematoma (seh-fuh-lo-he-ma-TOE-ma). You will see some irritation, a bit of bleeding and/or swelling between the scalp and the skull bone on either or both sides. This trauma is superficial—it is not the brain that is bleeding or swollen—and it has no impact whatsoever on your baby's brain. You will find that without any treatment the trauma will repair itself over the next two weeks.

When you touch these areas they may be sensitive, so be gentle when combing your baby's hair during the first few weeks. You may feel fluid there. Don't be alarmed—this is perfectly normal. You will also feel lines on your baby's head. These lines are where the plates of skull bones have come together. They feel just like fractures would feel. Don't worry about them; they too are natural and will go away in time.

The soft spots on the top and back of your baby's head are called *fontanels*. These diamond-shaped spaces are where the plates of the skull have not grown together yet. You can sometimes see and feel pulsing there. Be assured that tough membranes covering the fontanels are designed to protect your baby's head, so it is not as vulnerable as you would suspect. As your baby's skull bones grow together, the soft spots gradually get smaller. The soft spot at the top near the front of the head should close at 12 months; having the space open for this length of time will accommodate brain growth and growth of the head. The fontanel toward the back of the head is much smaller and closes much sooner than the other, by two months of age.

You may see a nick or bump in the baby's head approximately a millimeter long. This occurred during labor while the baby was hooked up to the fetal monitor.

Your baby's head will look quite big since it is about one fourth the size of her body, whereas our adult heads are about one-eighth the size of our bodies. On the first day of life, your baby is able to lift her head a few inches off the mattress when lying facedown. She can also turn her head 180 degrees from one side to another. This is probably a protective mechanism whereby the baby can protect her air-way. However, be careful not to put the baby on a very soft mattress because she can only lift her head up a few inches. The soft mattress may smother the baby because her head will be too low into the mattress.

Your newborn baby does not have good head control because her neck muscles are so weak and her nervous system is incomplete. So when picking up a newborn be sure to support the head with a few fingers behind the head and neck. (See "Lifting Baby," in Chapter 18, "Caring for Your Baby.")

Hair

The hair on your baby's head can be a totally different color than that of either parent. The reason is that very often there are recessive genes not seen for a very long time in either family that reveal themselves only when two parents with the same recessive genes get together. This is often seen in those of us from the Caribbean, where it is not uncommon to find people with brown complexions, blue eyes, and blond or straight hair. When this happens it is somewhat shocking to the parents. The newborn hair color, however, is not a reliable predictor of later hair color. Babies' hair falls out and is replaced by new hair by six months of age. Your baby may be born with no hair on her head, a full head of hair, or anything in between. Do not be alarmed if your baby still doesn't have much hair by five months. Hair growth is genetically programmed, as is every growth aspect of your baby, even though it can be influenced by environmental factors such as nutrition.

HISTORICALLY SPEAKING . . .

 Some African tribesmen will shave their baby's head after their naming ceremonies and bury the locks in the same place as the afterbirth or "hut of the baby" was buried. Maybe you'll want to keep a lock of newborn hair in a special baby keepsake book.

Neck

Although you may not see it, babies *do* have necks. Newborns have very short necks relative to the rest of their body but all the skin is there and is actually folded on itself. This represents a challenge to the mother in terms of cleaning the neck. Be careful to clean between the folds of the skin to prevent rashes, which can easily occur because perspiration, dirt, and food collects there. Also, since a newborn's head is too heavy for his neck, make sure you hold the neck securely until the baby is at least three months old.

Eyes

Your newborn's puffy, swollen eyes were caused by medication put in the eyes right after birth and from the trauma of delivery. The current medications are erythromycin ointment or silver nitrate. In most states in the United States it is a law that these forms of pro-phylactic eye care be used to prevent scarring of the newborn's cornea by the bacteria during her journey through the birth canal. This prevents the vision problems that were frequently seen in the United States prior to the institution of this law. However, these drops can cause swelling due to chemical irritation. The swelling usually goes down by the end of the second or third day, at which point you will start seeing your baby's eyes better.

Another cause of eye swelling in your newborn is the fact that water accounts for approximately 70 to 75 percent of your baby's weight, as compared to 60 to 65 percent of the adult weight. You will find that when you lay the baby down on one side the eye closest to the mattress will tend to be more swollen. That is why it may be a good idea to switch the side on which you lay your baby to rest periodically.

Similar to hair color, it is difficult to determine what a newborn baby's true eye color will be. The reason is that the eye color is over-shadowed by the deep blue color inside the baby's eyeball (vitreous humor), which can be seen through the thin eyeball coating of a newborn. By six months of age, the eyeball will thicken enough so that you can tell what the baby's true eye color is. Eye color, too, is hereditary. Like hair color, recessive genes may lead to your baby having a different eye color than the mother, father, and perhaps anybody in the immediate family.

Your baby may also have bloodshot eyes (scleral hemorrhage), resulting from pressure on the baby's head as it went through the birth canal. The bloodshot area may appear to be increasing in volume as it spreads and moves toward the dark-colored iris. It may even encompass the dark part of the eye, but the redness in the eye should disappear within a two-week period.

Babies are sometimes born with cataracts, for a number of rea-sons, including prematurity, heredity, prenatal infection, metabolic reasons, maternal diabetes or prediabeties, as well as chromosomal defects. Cataracts can obscure vision and can grow or shrink during the baby's lifetime. Your pediatrician will be on the lookout for this problem.

It is quite natural for babies to move one eye and not the other. Sometimes an eye may be deviated (turned inward or outward) due to early eye-muscle weakness. As the baby's eye muscles strengthen, the eyes should come into alignment by about nine months of age. If they do not, your pediatrician will refer you to an opthalmalogist.

Mouth

On the roof of most babies' mouths are two pearly white swellings about the size of a ballpoint-pen point. These two bumps on the palate are called *Epstein's pearls*. Epstein's pearls are just collected cellular material and fluid and have no purpose or negative consequence to the baby. Other cysts of similar appearance, called retention cysts, may be seen during the newborn period and will tend to dissolve within the first few months of life.

Between the floor of the mouth and the bottom of the tongue you will find a band of skin. If it is farther back, the tongue can protrude and elevate from the mouth very easily. If it goes to the tip of the tongue, it will limit the movement of the tongue. This is where the phrase "being tongue-tied" comes from. Years ago, the doctor would typically cut the band of skin. Nowadays, because this condition rarely affects eating or speaking, it is left alone. Often it will separate slightly from normal wear and tear, painlessly allowing for more range of motion of the tongue.

Once in a rare while a baby is born with teeth. These teeth have no function and will fall out without incident usually before the natural (called "deciduous") baby teeth appear. Rarely do they need to be removed. Your pediatrician will observe them and will make recommendations accordingly.

Ears

The shape of your baby's ears will usually resemble that of family members. Some babies are born with a folded ear caused by being in cramped quarters for so long. Do *not* tape the ear back; instead, when you lay your baby to sleep, make sure the ear is bent back against the head. In time, the ear will correct itself. Some ears, however, are genetically programmed to stand out!

Some babies inherit from a parent a tiny hole, that looks like a pin prick, in the upper front portion of the ear or in the curlicue part of the ear. It is of no importance when it is a very shallow hole in the skin. On very rare occasions, the hole can go fairly deep into the skin and can possibly cause problems such as infection.

Remember that your baby can hear from birth. You will notice that she will turn her head to sounds and will actually blink from loud noises.

◇ ◇ ◇ ◇ ◇ ◇ ◇ ◇ ◇ ◇ ◇ ◇ ◇ ◇ ◇ ◇ ◇

"Soon after the baby was born, everyone in my birthing room wanted to have some of the baby's vernix. They looked crazy spreading it on their faces and necks!"

◇ ◇ ◇ ◇ ◇ ◇ ◇ ◇ ◇ ◇ ◇ ◇ ◇ ◇ ◇ ◇ ◇

Skin

A newborn baby's skin is loose, wrinkled, and usually not brown, as you were expecting. The baby's body may be covered with *vernix caseosa* (kay-zee-OH-sah), which is a white, thick, cheesy substance that served as the baby's own skin lotion protecting it from the amniotic fluid and helping it pass through the birth canal. Most is washed off during your baby's first bath soon after birth. What is left looks like dry skin. That dry skin is actually the vernix adhering to the skin. On the baby's wrists and ankles where movement occurs, cracking may be seen. Though you will be tempted to slather cream on the baby (you know how we hate ashiness) these are the only places where petroleum jelly should be applied within the first two weeks.

Dark, fine, or fuzzy hair called *lanugo* may cover your newborn's body. You may find it on the baby's ears, back, cheeks, or shoulders. Lanugo is a gestational remnant that has no function. It should disappear within a few weeks, by the fourth month at the latest.

Black babies often have light skin at first, which gets darker as the babies age. A baby's true color appears in spurts during his first year, He may have a light face and darker body parts, for instance. This is normal, as the color eventually evens itself out on the entire body.

Sometimes two parents with dark skin may create a baby whose skin is, and remains, light. Recessive genes could cause your baby to have different-colored eyes or skin from anybody else you know in your family. These recessive genes come from the racial mixtures in our family histories. Every aspect of a person (height, eye, skin color, etc.) is genetically controlled by two components: one from

Francis Charteris, Allford/Trotman Associates, Atlanta.

his mother and one from his father. Usually one of these genes has more control than the other and is called the dominant gene. So a dark person can have a dominant dark gene and a nondominant light gene. Occasionally both genes act together (recessive genes) to produce an equally combined effect, which at times can be quite startling. That is how two dark skinned parents can have a light skinned baby.

Birthmarks

Birthmarks come in various shapes, sizes, colors, and textures. Some are present at birth, while others show up sometime later. Most disappear later in childhood. Following are the names of different kinds of birthmarks and their characteristics.

Mongolian spots are more common in babies of color. They look like dark green bruises of varying sizes and are usually located on the baby's bottom, but may be found all over the baby's back. They will usually disappear during early childhood but may last through adulthood.

Café au lait spots, when found in babies of color, are tan or dark brown, irregularly shaped areas of varying sizes that may become progressively darker or lighter as your child ages. When limited to three or four, these spots are of no consequence, but will last throughout your child's life.

Stork's bites are flat patches of pink to red irregularly shaped spots usually located at the nape of the neck in the newborn baby. The same kind of redness can be found on the baby's face involving the eyelids and the eyebrows. These reddened areas usually fade as time goes by and are of no serious consequence.

Strawberry marks are raised marks that range in size from very tiny to palm-sized and are caused by immature vascular materials that broke away from the circulatory system while the baby was developing in the womb. They are very common and may be apparent at birth or may show up during the first few weeks of life. Most of these marks will disappear by the child's tenth birthday or sooner. They are not harmful and should not be treated or surgically removed, as this can lead to unnecessary scarring. If scratched, they may bleed. Apply pressure to stop the blood flow.

Body

The *clavicle* (collarbone) often gets stressed during delivery. If the baby is very large (more than 9 pounds) relative to mother's pelvic size, even with great care there can be a fracture of the clavicle. The fracture is usually not deforming and heals very rapidly and with little intervention. At the end of two weeks you can see it healing nicely.

Some babies are born with *inverted* breast nipples. This condition poses no problem for the baby and may correct itself as time goes by. The only concern may be for a female who grows up and wants to breast-feed her own baby. A woman with inverted nipples will have to work with her doctor or midwife to make breast-feeding possible.

A newborn baby girl or baby boy's breasts may be swollen due to the effect of the mother's adult hormones. That is, as the fetus develops in the mother's womb, he is exposed to maternal hormones, which cross the placenta. Since both boys and girls have mammary glands, that hormonal exposure can cause swelling of the breast and even leakage of milk in the baby. Every now and then, the milk gets trapped in the breast tissue and cannot come out, so your baby's breast can become very red and inflamed, even causing fever in some babies. This problem is called *mastitis*, and is treated with warm compresses, and occasionally, antibiotics. Swelling of the breasts usually disappears in three to five days.

Down the middle of the chest near the breastbone you will find a little point of bone that sticks up. This is called the *xyphoid* (zy-foid) *process*, and is actually just the tip of the breastbone. It has no real function and gets harder as time goes on. Parents are sometimes frightened by it, although it is nothing to worry about and causes no discomfort to the baby when you touch it. The real significance of this spot is that you would need to locate it to perform cardiopulmonary resuscitation. (For more about performing CPR on infants, see "Basic Baby Emergencies," pages 471–72.)

The umbilical clamp that the doctor puts on your baby right after birth is used to prevent bleeding from the navel. The clamp will stay on until the cord is adequately dried, which usually takes about 36 hours. Alcohol should be applied to the stump during this time to keep it clean and to dry out the area faster. The umbilical stump itself will shrivel and fall off about ten days after birth. (See "Umbilical Cord," at the end of Chapter 18 for more information on umbilical cord care).

Babies tend to have wide abdomens, which often expand noticeably after eating. Initially, the baby's stomach is about the size of his or her fist. As time goes by, the stomach stretches and enlarges, so the period between feedings will become longer.

Babies have small hips relative to the size of their abdomen. Your physician will check that the baby's hips are properly in their sockets. Dislocated hips are fairly common in newborns. If the hips are not in place, your physician will work with an orthopedist to position them properly. The treatment should be completed within a few months and often there are no long-term effects.

Legs and Feet

Newborns keep their knees bent at all times. If you stretch out your baby's legs, you will find that they quickly spring back to their original position. This is because of a naturally flexed resting tone that babies retain from the cramped confines of their mother's womb. You may feel creaking in the knees when handling the baby. This creaking comes from looseness of the knee joint and should not be a concern. It will disappear as the baby ages.

The bones between the knees and ankles—called the tibia and fibula—are bowed inward in newborns. This is called *internal tibial torsion* and is seen in all babies, probably because the long bones had to take the shape of the uterus. The tibia will straighten in later infancy and childhood. Parents often confuse bowleggedness with this condition. But remember, what is commonly known as bowlegs is actually a bend in the bone between the knees and the hips (which is called the femur), not between the knees and the ankles.

The newborn's feet are very often twisted or bent upward. This, too, will correct itself in time. The baby's toes can be bent or curled under. The feet may look mottled and bluish and the baby can become easily chilled. Sometimes the foot itself is curved inward, called *metatarsus abductus*. This usually corrects itself. Only if the inward curve looks too tight and inflexible will the doctor suggest the use of special shoes or serial casts to train the foot to turn straighter. The soles of most babies' feet look flat. At this young age, one can't tell if the foot looks flat because of the baby's natural fat pad or because the baby really has flat feet. Only time will tell.

Arms and Hands

A newborn's arms are flexed. Her hands remain curled in fists, ready to take on the world. Her fingernails may be quite long and should be trimmed so she doesn't scratch herself—or you. Alternatively, you could cover her hands with mittens. Babies' hands are generally cool and slightly blue because initially, they manage their temperatures poorly.

Genitals

A newborn's genitals are usually swollen and some newborn girls have vaginal discharge—a very sticky, white, gooey material. Some mothers become obsessed with trying to remove every little bit during changing time, which can injure the baby since it is a very sensitive area. It is a natural discharge and is usually not infectious. It comes from exposure to mother's adult hormones during pregnancy. It should go away in about two weeks.

Also don't be surprised or upset to see vaginal bleeding, usually around the second week of life, which is caused by withdrawal from maternal hormones at the time of birth. This is similar to women who stop taking birth-control pills and have withdrawal bleeding several days later. Remember, your newborn has a uterus and all other female organs that will respond to hormones. The vaginal bleeding resolves itself very quickly and should not be a cause for alarm.

You and your pediatrician have to differentiate between actual bleeding and uric acid crystals. Uric acid is a breakdown product of the muscles, seen as a result of the natural trauma of delivery and dehydration. With this you would see salmon-colored paste or a crystal-type material that would be deposited on the diaper after the baby urinates. These crystals could be mistaken for blood to the untrained eye. This, too, is harmless and will pass in a couple of weeks.

Undescended testicles is a condition where one or both of the testicles have *never* been observed to be in the scrotum. Note that the testes in boys start out in the same location as the ovaries in girls. In the last trimester of gestation the testes descend into the scrotum. Sometimes there is a delay in this natural descent and your pediatrician and urologist will observe this condition for possibly one year before surgical or medical intervention. An undescended testicle does not cause pain and does not interfere with urination. It usually descends on its own. But if it hasn't descended on its own by the time your child reaches three months, new data indicates that it probably won't descend and surgery is therefore recommended. The surgery should be done by the time your child is six to twelve months old. If surgery is not done in a timely fashion there can be shrinkage of the testis (atrophy), infertility later in life, and possibly tumor formation.

Occasionally throughout the day your baby boy will have erections. This is a normal result of neurologic control of blood flow to the penis and is nothing odd.

The most common hernia found in infancy is the umbilical (navel) hernia. This is recognized as a painless bulge at the navel, which seems to get bigger when your baby cries or strains to have a bowel movement. Often parents feel guilty that they were responsible for the hernia because they let the baby cry too long. In fact the hernia is a natural space between the belly muscles that allowed the umbilical cord to pass through the baby's abdomen when she was in the womb. That space remains there and can be found well into the first five years of life before it closes naturally. It may not be apparent initially, but it's there. Don't worry. It's usually only cosmetic.

Inguinal (IN-gwuh-nul) *hernias* occur when part of the intestine slips into the groin area. Usually the intestines slide back into place, but occasionally they can become trapped and require surgical repair. If this bulge persists when your infant is not crying, or is tender to the touch, contact your pediatrician.

Circumcision

If you have a baby boy, you will need to decide if you want him circumcised. Circumcisions are usually performed while your baby is still in the hospital as long as the baby is not sick, at your request. It is a simple surgical procedure whereby the foreskin that covers the tip of the penis is cut off in order to expose the tip and the opening of the urethra (the tube leading from the bladder to the tip of the penis). Your baby will feel pain during the procedure, but you can take comfort in knowing that the procedure only takes about five minutes to complete and approximately two weeks to heal. If you make your decision after the birth, the best time to perform circumcision is when your child is about nine to twelve months old. By this point your baby's system is more mature and better able to handle anesthesia.

Although it does cause pain and stress in the infant, no long-term psychological problems have been attributed to circumcision. Your decision may be based on social or religious reasons. Ask yourself such questions as: Is the baby's father circumcised? Do I mind if my child is different from other children? If you do decide to have your baby circumcised, the physician will tell you to apply petroleum jelly to the area on the diaper that comes in contact with the baby's penis. By the end of the second week, the redness of the penis should have diminished and ultimately it will begin to look normal.

Though most babies in my practice are circumcised, the medical community has been divided in their opinion as to whether they should recommend it for their patients. In 1971 the American Academy of Pediatrics released a statement saying that "there are no valid medical indications for circumcision in the neonatal period." Since then, the AAP has twice stated that there is no absolute medical indication for routine circumcision of the newborn (in 1975 and in 1983). Now, at a time when there is a decreasing rate of circumcision in the United States, new evidence suggests that there may be a slight advantage to the procedure.

The potential benefits of having your baby circumcised are numerous. It decreases the risk of cancer in the penis, urinary tract infections, and the transmission of venereal disease to their sexual partners. Studies indicate that boys or men who become circumcised later in life do not show a decrease in the above afflictions. This suggests that circumcision during infancy may be a better choice.

Reflexes

The functional set of reflexes that your baby is born with is called the motor system and the perceptions that your baby is born with is called the sensory system. These are briefly explained in the next two sections.

Your baby was born with a number of reflex actions, which form the basis for early mental development. They include:

Sucking: Sucking begins when baby's soft palate, mouth, lips, cheek, and chin are stroked.

Gag reflex: An object in baby's throat is automatically expelled.

Tonic neck reflex: When placed on the back, baby turns head to one side, with the arm on that side extended straight out and the opposite arm flexed. (Appears anywhere between birth and two months. Disappears at about six months.)

Startle (Moro) reflex: Head drops back, back arches, arms fly out to sides, and fingers and legs extend when sudden noise or contact is made, or when the baby feels the sensation of falling. Disappears at about four to six months.

Babinski reflex: Toes spread out and foot turns in when soles of feet are stroked. Disappears between six months and two years.

Rooting reflex: Head turns in direction of stimulus when cheek is stroked, with mouth open. Disappears at about three to four months.

Walking or stepping reflex: Makes stepping movements while being held in the upright position, when one foot touches a surface. This reflex, as with other reflexes seen in the newborn period, are primitive reflexes and disappear in the first several months of life.

Palmar grasping reflex: When palm is stroked, or when an object is placed in the palm of the baby's hand, his fingers wrap tightly around object. When you place your thumb at the base of the baby's toes, the toes will curl around it. Disappears at about three or four months of age.

The Five Senses

Touch

Your newborn baby is sensitive to touch all over and is sensitive to how he is being held. A young infant can actually sense if the person holding him is anxious or angry, and will adjust his behavior accordingly. The secret is *relaxed support*. Your baby should feel secure whenever he is held. This is why some babies like men so much, as they often have bigger, stronger arms. Use your chest and abdomen to support the baby as you hold him. (See "Carrying Baby" in Chapter 18, pages 401–402.)

Smell

The sense of smell is believed to be well developed at birth, although how discriminating this sense is, of course, is difficult for researchers to measure. Babies can distinguish between their mother's breast milk and other breast milk soon after birth, however.

Hearing

Hearing is well developed at birth, although young infants have difficulty turning to the side that the sound comes from. The startle reflex in reaction to loud sounds will assure you that your baby is able to hear. Don't expect more than just a minimal response to other sounds because the baby is unable to coordinate such an effort.

Taste

It is difficult for researchers to determine just how discriminating and developed a baby's sense of taste is. It has been found, however, that babies react to sweet, sour, and salty tastes. They also have been found to differentiate among plain, slightly sweetened, and very sweet water.

Sight

Vision is not as well developed as hearing is at birth. At first, your baby's vision will be blurry, but not long after birth she will be able to see your face while you hold her in your arms and can see distinct patterns and brightly colored objects. They see most clearly at a distance of about 8 to 10 inches, which is about the distance of a baby's eyes to a mother's eyes while the mother holds the baby at her breast.

CHAPTER 18

Caring for Your Baby

This illustrated chapter offers how-to's on the following topics:

Pediatricians—Choosing One
Feeding
  The Decision to
    Breast-feed
  Breast-feeding and
    Bottle-feeding
  Introducing Solid Foods
  Weaning
Bathing
  Shampooing and Haircare
  Safety Issues
Breathing
Burping
  Spitting Up
Carrying Baby
Colic
Crying
Diapering
  Diaper Rash and Other
    Rashes

Discipline
Dressing
  Swaddling
Hair and Scalp Care
Hiccups
Immunizations
Lifting Baby
Nail Care
Pediatric Visits: What to
    Expect
  2 Weeks
  2 Months
  6 Months
  9 Months
  12 Months
Skin Care
Sleeping
Teeth
Umbilical Cord
  Umbilical Hernias

Pediatricians—Choosing One

Your hunt for a pediatrician should begin before your baby is born. While general practitioners and family physicians often accept babies and children as patients, the ideal choice for your baby is a pediatrician. In addition to four years of medical school, pediatricians also have three years of specialty training in pediatrics.

How do you find a pediatrician? The best way is through recommendations from friends and family members with children. If you don't have any friends or family members with children, or if they are not satisfied with their pediatrician, try other avenues. Ask your obstetrician or midwife for a recommendation. Call the local medical society. See if the hospital in your neighborhood has a referral service. As a last resort, open up the Yellow Pages. Of course, your insurance carrier may limit your options.

Once you have a handful of names of pediatricians who are not too far from home (you will not want to travel too far to see the doctor with a sick baby), it would be a good idea to interview them in person or over the telephone. Just because the doctor was great for your friend doesn't mean you'll think he or she is great for you. Here are some good questions to ask when interviewing:

- ◆ What are your office hours?
- ◆ What is your philosophy on child care?
- ◆ To which hospital do you admit your patients?
- ◆ What insurance do you accept?
- ◆ Where did you go to medical school?
- ◆ What additional qualifications do you have?
- ◆ What referral sources do you have in case the child needs a specialist?
- ◆ How long does it usually take to get an appointment if the child is ill?
- ◆ Do you do immunizations in the office?
- ◆ Are blood and other specimens taken at the office?
- ◆ Are you able to give assistance on behavioral issues to parents?
- ◆ Do you do behavioral assessments of the child as time goes on?
- ◆ How can you be reached outside of regular calling times?
- ◆ Ask specific questions that may concern you, perhaps regarding breast-feeding, discipline, or alternative medicine.

Be aware of the pediatrician's communication skills. Reject a doctor who talks over your head or lectures to you.

It would be surprising if the pediatrician charged you for the time it took to talk with you, but keep in mind that the time she is giving you is time away from her patients—and time is money. So be courteous and acknowledge this at the start of the interview. Then go through your concerns and questions in a concise way so the interview doesn't go to an extended period of time (about 15 to 20 minutes should suffice). Usually you can tell within a few minutes if you can easily communicate with this person and whether she's being sincere.

In the first year of life, you should take your baby to see the pediatrician at 2 weeks of age, 2 months, 6 months, 9 months, and around the time of her first birthday. These visits are your opportunity to ask any questions. Before you go to your appointment, jot down the questions and problems you wish to discuss so they are not forgotten.

It is a very good idea for both the mother and the father to accompany the baby to the pediatrician at every visit. Get away from the notion of the mother being the sole or primary caretaker for the baby. Fathers have a lot to contribute to a child's welfare, and many want to be more involved but don't know how or are intimidated (see Chapter 12, "Becoming Daddy," for how you can help your mate engage with the baby).

Feeding

The Decision to Breast-feed

Do you have a close friend who breast-feeds her baby? Does your mother think breast-feeding is for the "olden days"? Does your mate have problems with the idea of "sharing" your breasts? Did you receive a three-month supply of formula as a baby shower gift? Are you easily intimidated and embarrassed? Have you ever been sexually abused? All of the above will affect your decision about how you will feed your baby—from breast or bottle. Make the choice before, rather than after, your baby is born. Think about it, read up on it, ask friends about it, and discuss the pros and cons of each feeding method with your mate so you can make the right decision for you and your baby.

Breast-feeding offers unmatched bonding times with your baby, but it also requires patience and a supportive partner. *Many women have stopped breast-feeding after a few tries because their husbands were critical of it or embarrassed by it.* Bottle-feeding initially allows for a more predictable feeding schedule, but it requires prepreparation. Regardless of your choice, be assured that nestling your newborn in your arms as she receives her nourishment—physically and emotionally—from you and your husband will make some of your most precious memories together.

We, and the American Academy of Pediatrics (AAP), hope that you will strongly consider breast-feeding or expressing your breast milk and bottle-feeding it. The AAP recommends that mothers breast-feed their infants because breast milk is the perfect food for your baby. Your body was designed to provide life-sustaining food to your baby until she is six months old—why not take advantage of it if you can? While formulas attempt to replicate breast milk, none do a perfect job. And you will find that pediatricians, obstetricians, nurse-midwives, and even manufacturers of infant formula also agree that breast milk is best.

Here are some frequently asked questions and answers about breast-feeding that can help you make your decision:

Q: I'm a career woman and will be returning to work in two or three months. I understand that weaning the baby once she has become accustomed to the breast is difficult. Should I even consider starting to breast-feed?

A: The answer is yes! I like to think of it like this: If I was offered the chance to eat like a king for six weeks or three months, would I pass it up if I knew all I could eat after that time was Spam? No, I wouldn't. It's the same with breast-feeding. I believe two or three months of the best source of nutrition for your baby far outweighs any of the discomfort encountered in the conversion from breast to bottle. In fact, very young infants may wean more easily than babies who have nursed for nine months or more. Give the breast milk for as long as you are able. Many babies wean easily. Weaning is really a matter of time and persistence on you and your husband's part and there are some good techniques that will help ease the transition (see ahead).

Q: I have a two-year-old who has become so demanding since the baby was born that I question whether breast-feeding is right for my family.

A: Truly, this is a challenge, but not an insurmountable one. As with any human interaction, knowing the needs of the individual and what he regards as important is the beginning of successful communication. Toddlers are no different. One must pace with them and meet them where they are. You've come to know them over the past years and although they tend to be unreasonable, they have specific likes and dislikes, which can be catered to in order to carve out that half hour or so that it takes to nurse your newborn. Since being replaced by the new baby is his greatest threat, it has been suggested that the concept of sharing can be introduced by using one arm to interact with him (say, by helping him enjoy a toy) and the other to nurse the newborn. This will probably only be necessary early on as he is becoming accustomed to your interacting with the new baby. Doll play in which you act out the nursing process may be of some help.

Q: My husband was in favor of the idea of my breast-feeding our newborn, but now that I'm doing it he seems unsupportive and even jealous, though he denies it. What can I do?

A: The rhythm that mothers achieve in caring for their newborns is often so remarkable it can seem to a man that his wife and child have built their own little world together—a world in which men are not needed or wanted. Your husband may feel much less pivotal in your life than he had been prior to the baby's arrival. After all, it is a huge change in your married life! The key is communication and empathic listening. Talk with him about how he's feeling about being a new father. Invite him to sit with you as you nurse the baby (maybe during an evening feeding). Affirm him with your words. Encourage him to participate in the baby's care as often as possible and cheer his efforts along. It's likely that he just wants to make sure he's still an integral part of the picture—assure him that he is.

Breast-feeding

There are advantages to both breast-feeding and bottle-feeding, and the choice is yours to make. Happy and healthy babies have been raised on both feeding methods.

The merits of breast-feeding are:

◆ The baby bonds with you best as she enjoys the touch and smell of your skin and the warmth and security of nursing at your breast.

◆ The composition of breast milk is ideally formulated to meet the nutritional needs of a baby. No man-made formula has yet been able to match its high quality.

◆ The composition of breast milk automatically adjusts to meet a growing baby's changing needs. For instance, the breast milk of mothers who deliver premature babies tends to be higher in salt, nitrogen, protein, and sugar (lactose) to help the baby thrive faster. The composition of breast milk also varies through the feeding. For instance, more fat is found at the end of the feeding than at the beginning. It is believed that the higher fat content makes the milk more satisfying and "signals" the end of a feeding.

◆ Breast milk provides infection-fighting properties that help protect newborns against bacterial and yeast infections.

◆ Breast-fed babies get fewer allergies.

◆ It is convenient, economical, and time-saving, since you don't have to prepare bottles. Traveling with baby is made simpler since you don't have to carry formula and bottles.

◆ Breast milk is already sterile.

◆ It satisfies baby's strong sucking urge. Bottles require much less sucking and thus may force the baby into thumb-sucking to fulfill their need.

◆ You can breast-feed your baby at night while lying on your side in bed; no need to hold up a bottle.

◆ A breast-feeding mother will generally regain her figure faster because making breast milk uses up calories in the mother and breast-feeding causes the uterus to contract quickly, helping your abdomen return to its prepregnancy shape.

Things You Should Know: Technical

◆ Colostrum is what your newborn will receive during the first few nursing sessions, before your breast milk comes in. Colostrum is a watery, yellowish substance that is full of immunities and very good for your baby. Don't let anyone tell you that you are not "feeding that baby enough"! You are. Your milk will come in about two to six days after birth. Breast-fed babies don't get a lot of milk initially, but they don't require a lot of milk the first day of life. Most babies just want to sleep in that first 24-hour period.

◆ The size of your breasts has *absolutely nothing* to do with your ability to nurse. Breasts are usually larger at the time of delivery, and full-term infants tend to have small mouths. Also, the new baby has never nursed before, so clearly you will have to work with your baby to get her to latch on. I liken it to a dance in which both partners are initially awkward, but after you've got the basic steps down you are both moving together to the rhythm of the music. (Actually, playing soft music while you nurse can help both you and the baby relax.) You will have to shape the breast to fit into the baby's mouth.

◆ As the placenta is delivered there is a sharp drop in the amount of estrogen and progesterone in your body. This allows for the release of prolactin, which triggers the production of breast milk. The swelling of the blood vessels and milk-producing sacs causes discomfort in the breasts called engorgement. This may start on the second day after delivery and continue for one or two days. Some mothers have little if any pain and mothers who have nursed previously have much less pain than first-time mothers. Expressing the milk manually after applying a warm compress often helps. Some mothers find that alternating hot and cold compresses to their engorged breasts works even better. The best cure for emptying painfully full breasts, however, is nursing.

◆ After your baby suckles on your breast for a few minutes it will cause you to release hormones that cause the milk to be let down from the milk glands and ducts. This, not surprisingly, is called let-down. Don't get frustrated if it takes a few minutes before the pins-and-needles sensation of let-down occurs. As time goes by, milk flow will occur before the baby begins suckling. Many mothers will attest to the fact that their milk begins to flow spontaneously when feeding time approaches.

◆ The more your baby suckles and empties your breasts, the more milk you will make; in other words, breastmilk production is based on a supply-and-demand concept. So nature has seen to it that initially, when your infant needs less milk, you would have very little volume but high-caloric milk. As your infant's needs increase and she nurses more often to satisfy herself, you would make more milk. The key then is to allow her to feed on demand and try to avoid giving the bottle if possible in order not to interfere with the natural stimulation of your milk production. Your milk will eventually flow so bountifully that you will have to express the excess and freeze it. Breast pads, available in most maternity stores and many drugstores, will be necessary at that time.

◆ You can exclusively breast-feed your baby until she is nine months old, though many infants will become interested in solid foods at around six months of age. (See "Introducing Solid Foods," page 390, for more detail.) Breast milk satisfies a baby's thirst as well as its hunger, so no other juices or even water are needed for the first four months. My opinion is that additional water may help your baby handle any food products that may get into the breast milk.

◆ Breast-fed babies often have more frequent bowel movements than bottle-fed babies, at a rate of perhaps five or six a day. You may also find that their stools are fairly loose, granular, and curdy and have a greenish color. They are usually less foul-smelling than those of formula-fed babies.

◆ During the first week of life dehydration is a concern, especially with breast-fed babies, due to some mothers' low milk volume. In fact, most pediatricians require that newborns be seen in the office at two weeks of age to reevaluate their weight. Most babies (especially breast-fed infants) will tend to lose up to 10 percent of their birth weight during the first week of life. That weight should be regained by the end of the second week. The need for nursing mothers to eat adequately (approximately 2,500 calories per day) and drink well (approximately eight 8-ounce glasses of fluid per day) is to assure the production of adequate milk volume and calories. Dehydrated newborns will have few wet diapers, will not wake for feedings within four or five hours, as is normal, and will have weak cries and sucks.

Their eye will become sunken and the soft spot on their heads will sink in when they are held in the sitting position.

◆ Your baby may need more milk than usual when she is going through a growth spurt. These generally occur at three to four weeks, six to seven weeks, and twelve to thirteen weeks. Breast-fed infants will simply take more milk.

◆ Give your baby a vitamin D supplement, as breast milk is not rich in this vitamin. Supplements usually come in drop form and contain other vitamins such as A and C, which will also benefit breast-fed babies.

HISTORICALLY SPEAKING . . .

During slavery, black wet nurses were often called upon to breast-feed slave owners' babies so white mothers could convalesce or wouldn't have to be interrupted for feedings during the night. The Sudanese, and people of many other cultures, believe that the child inherits physical characteristics from the woman who feeds them. (Wonder how *that* idea would have gone over on the plantation?) *What We Can Learn:* The benefits of breast-feeding are innumerable—our African ancestors knew it, granny midwives knew it, and Southern white folks knew it so well they didn't mind a black woman breast-feeding their baby. We should hear this message—it is also for today. Breast milk has the right balance of protein, fat, and carbohydrates to meet baby's nutritional needs. New data suggests that breast-fed babies have higher intelligence quotients and grow up into healthier children. Even one month of breast-feeding is unquestionably better than none at all.

"People reacted to my choice to breast-feed as if it was a new and amazing thing I was doing. They told me I was 'such a good mother' willing to make 'such a sacrifice' for my child. Meanwhile, I thought it was the most natural thing in the world."

Things You Should Know: Nontechnical

◆ *As instinctive and natural as breast-feeding is, it also requires some learning.* If you didn't grow up seeing mothers nurse their babies or if you don't have close friends or family members who breast-feed, you will appreciate the breast-feeding how-tos on pages 383–86, which provide instructions and photos of how to nurse your baby. If you are willing to tough out the initial adversities, breast-feeding will be a rewarding experience for you both.

◆ *You will have to face a public that, by and large, is not sensitive to or approving of breast-feeding.* In our sexually permissive society, breasts are seen more as sexual playthings than as beautiful, life-giving instruments. Be prepared to face the funky attitudes of some store managers or park attendants if you decide to breast-feed in public places. (It is, however, a great opportunity to stand up for women's rights.)

◆ *Millions of dollars' worth of advertising will keep telling you how much easier bottle-feeding is.* And formula companies are constantly coming out with products that make bottle-feeding simpler. Ironically, these same companies are underwriting pamphlets and brochures advocating breast-feeding as the better choice. Arm yourself to stick to your decision to breast-feed and know that millions of African, African-American, and Caribbean mothers (and others) around the world are with you!

"When I gave birth to my son, the first thing my aunt said to me as I fumbled to nurse him with my 'A' cup breasts was, 'Girl, you ain't got titties enough for that!' I was so upset! But I was determined to breast-feed and I did."

Things You Should Do

◆ Gently massage your nipples during the last month of pregnancy. This is a great way to prepare your breasts for feeding, especially if you have inverted nipples. Use both your hands to stretch your areolae horizontally and vertically.

◆ Insist on getting the help you need from the hospital or birthing center staff (or a lactation counselor) in order to start out breast-feeding on the right foot (no pun intended).

If you opted for a nurse-midwife to attend the birth, she will surely provide support for you as you learn the dance of nursing.

◆ Relax, relax, relax! If you are nervous or uptight, that is what you communicate to the baby; this can definitely adversely affect your milk flow and frustrate the baby. Make sure you have at least 45 minutes set aside to feed so you don't feel rushed. Take your time and persevere; you and baby should soon settle into your own "groove."

◆ Lightly stroke your baby's cheek with your breast or fingertips. She will instinctively turn her head toward it and open her mouth.

◆ Let your baby nurse as often as she likes so you can build up an adequate milk supply. For this reason, try not to supplement your breast milk with artificial formula. *Supplementing often sabotages successful breast-feeding.*

◆ Alternate the breast you offer first at each feeding session because your baby will suck most vigorously at the first breast you offer her. Some babies favor one breast over the other. This may simply be because she feels more comfortable lying on one side rather than the other; your stronger arm may feel more comfortable than your weaker arm; or one breast may be a better provider than the other. Don't be too upset if you cannot get your baby to enjoy that other breast. Your "lop-sided" breasts should return to their prepregnancy sizes after weaning.

◆ Avoid soaping the breasts when you shower, to prevent nipple dryness. Wear a well-fitting, cotton nursing bra and use breast pads to soak up any leaking milk. Tissues will not work well as substitutes for breast pads. They will stick to you when they get wet and will be painful and annoying to remove. Massage your breasts and nipples to help prepare them for breast-feeding. If you're nipples are sore, put a few drops of olive oil on the breast pad for lubrication. This way, you are not inadvertently feeding the baby any chemical creams. Also, always leave your breasts open to the air for a while after nursing. It will be comforting not to have any material at all rubbing against them.

Getting a Good Latch

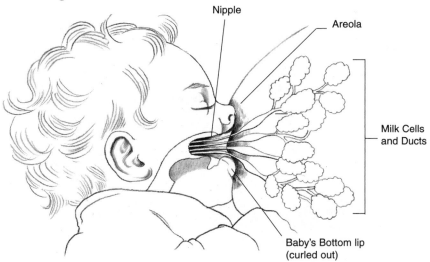

Nipple

Areola

Milk Cells and Ducts

Baby's Bottom lip (curled out)

This transparent breast shows you how a "good latch" looks from the inside and outside. The baby is considered latched on when your nipple and most of your areola is inside her mouth and her tongue is underneath your nipple. Her bottom lip curls outward and cups your areola. Remember, it is the action of her jaw, not her lips, that forces the milk ducts and milk sacs to spew out the milk.

Breast-feeding Positions

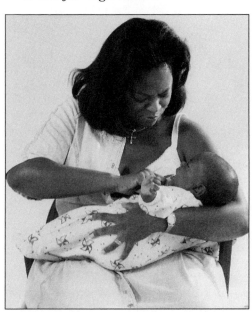

One position to breast-feed in is to sit comfortably in a chair holding your baby cradle-style with his head in the crook of your arm and your hand supporting his body. Note: If you are tense or hurried, your baby will get tense too and it will hamper the process. Try to settle down, take a few deep breaths, move to a quieter place, hum a lullaby, or whatever works—and begin again. Tickle the baby's cheek with your nipple to attract him to the breast if he seems distracted. If he still does not want to nurse, don't force him. All photos of baby care in this chapter are by Halley Ganges, New York.

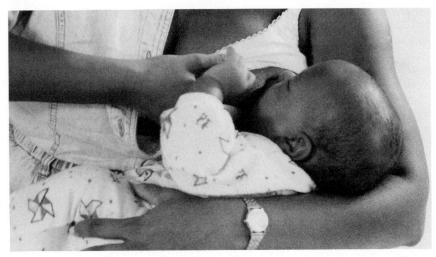

Use your other hand to hold and position the breast. Place your thumb on top of the areola and fingers beneath it to position it properly into your baby's mouth. If you have ample breasts, you will need to press the top, fatty part of your breast away from the baby's nose once he latches on to avoid hampering his breathing. If you see your baby's cheeks moving steadily, he is latched on and feeding well. When you notice this motion stopping, he is probably finished. To "disengage" your breast from the baby's mouth without pain, place your finger in the corner of his mouth and gently dislodge the breast.

Some women prefer the coziness of breast-feeding while lying down. Others find this position a blessing after a cesarean section as it takes the pressure of the baby's weight off their abdomen. To feed your baby this way, lie down on your side with pillows supporting your head, neck, and upper body. Tuck your arm under your head as shown, but do not use it to prop up your head; your arm and back will get tired halfway through the feeding. Lay the baby on her side, facing you, and draw her close to you with your other hand. Once you have positioned yourself, follow the same steps as previously outlined. You can vary this position by sitting up in bed, propped up by pillows. Cradle the baby in your arms and bring her body across your lap. Put a pillow on your lap to help bring the baby closer to your breast if necessary. Follow the same steps for positioning the breast and areola as previously outlined.

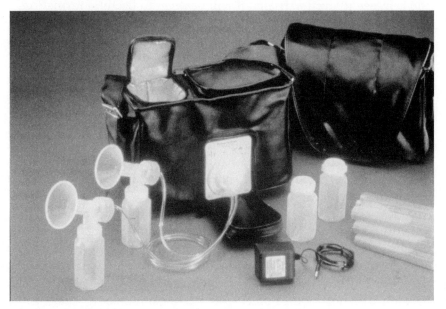

The Pump N'Style from Medela makes carrying a breast pump to work easier, $198.

Expressing Your Milk. If you are going back to work outside the home, you can express your breast milk, store it, and bottle-feed it to your baby whenever the need arises. You will most likely need a portable electric breast pump that offers strong suction (or a manual one if your flow is very good). Some popular, high-quality breast pumps are made by Medela (shown) and Egnell. Some of the more "industrial strength" models may be too costly to own, but you can probably rent one from the hospital or birthing center where you delivered for about $30 per month. Many of the infant formula companies make portable breast pumps that can operate either by battery or plug-in. Prices range from about $20 to $100. Some women with slow flows need more suction power than the lower-priced models offer. Call the La Leche League in your area to discuss your individual needs and obtain recommendations or dial Medela's 1-800-TELL-YOU line for info on where to rent or buy breast pumps in your area.

To express the milk at work, you'll need a quiet place, such as an empty office, and a refrigerator to store the milk in until you are ready to leave. Express the milk twice a day and refrigerate it; put it in the freezer when you get home, unless you plan to use it within 48 hours. You can freeze the milk for months. However, do not thaw and refreeze it, even partially; it will be open to bacteria formation.

Your Diet. You will not need to eat as carefully as you did when you were growing the baby in your womb, but you will need about 2,500 calories a day; 200 to 500 more calories than normal. Breast-milk production and breast-feeding will help burn off the extra calories. Not getting the nutrients you need can have an ill effect on the quality of your breast milk—and on you. Eating a poor, junk-food diet, for instance, can force your body to draw upon its own nutritional stores to fortify the breast milk, leaving *you* nutritionally deficient. Fatigue, irritability, and sickness may result. Since you did so well with your eating during pregnancy (right?), it would make sense that you continue to eat a well-balanced diet postpregnancy. Eat nutritious foods, especially those high in calcium, and drink plenty of liquids. Dairy foods, chocolate, and certain pungent spices in the foods you eat (used excessively) may irritate your baby. If you notice that your newborn is suddenly disinterested in breast-feeding, think back on whether food or spice you ate recently may be causing the problem and cut down on it. Express milk ahead of time if you are going on vacation, for instance, where you may have less control over what you eat. While on vacation, you can express and dump the potentially irritating breast milk and feed the baby the milk you previously expressed. For help constructing a balanced diet, turn to chapter 7, "You (and Your Baby) Are What You Eat."

Breast-feeding mothers should limit alcohol consumption to the occasional drink or glass of wine. Certain medications, including antibiotics, should be avoided by breast-feeding mothers, though some over-the-counter preparations are acceptable in proper dosages; consult your physician if you are unsure.

HISTORICALLY SPEAKING ...

 Long before the advent of formulas like Similac and Enfamil, a can of Carnation PET milk (evaporated milk) added to a can of water and 2 tablespoons of Karo corn syrup sufficed as the rudimentary formula many mothers used to feed their babies. Feeding babies this mixture has a long history in our culture because it is less expensive than formula, it is easy to prepare, and was more widely available to us than formula. The premixed formulas, once they did come along, were expensive and inaccessible to most black families, so the homemade recipes prevailed out of necessity. Mothers also believed that it tasted better than formula *(to them)*; however, it was not necessarily better-tasting—or nutritionally adequate—for their babies. *What We Can Learn:* Though a baby can be kept alive by this and other inexpensive, homespun mixtures, they are lacking in many of the essential vitamins babies need during this important stage in their growth. Please don't risk your baby's good health to save a little money. Generally, table foods like mashed vegetables, potatoes, and fruit without spice or salt or added sugar makes good baby food, but should only be fed to babies who are six months of age or older. Feeding her properly will pay off in fewer trips to the doctor and fewer nights spent sitting up with a sick baby.

Bottle-feeding

The advantages of bottle-feeding are:

◆ Fathers, sitters, and other people can easily feed the baby. The father can share equally in night feedings, giving you an extra break to sleep (though you can also express breast milk into bottles).

◆ A mother doesn't have to be concerned about how her breast milk may be affected by what she eats or drinks, her personal habits, or the medication she takes.

◆ You can feed your baby in public without fear of embarrassment.

Things You Should Know

◆ One decision you will have to make if you choose to bottle-feed your baby is whether to use a cow's-milk formula or a soybean formula (see "Milk Allergies" for information on the latter). The second decision will be whether to use a powdered, concentrated, or ready-to-pour formula (unless you are going to express your breast milk and bottle-feed it). Discuss your choice of formula with your doctor or midwife. The caloric content of each formula is made to match the content in mother's milk, usually 20 calories per ounce. A few formula makers have attempted to reengineer the protein fraction—or the curds and whey—to make their product more like breast milk. Powdered formulas are the least expensive, and ready-to-pour formulas are the most expensive. Powdered and concentrated formulas require you to mix them with tap water. We recommend that you invest in a good water filter to remove chemicals and impurities from your tap water. Boiling the water first, on the stovetop or in a microwave oven, will also kill most of the bacteria. Cool the bottle to room temperature (not hot). On the flip side, it only takes an hour for bacteria to double in number, so don't leave a cold bottle on the counter "to warm" too long. Follow the instructions on the label for specific preparation details.

◆ It is best to use a high-iron-content formula to prevent anemia, unless your pediatrician advises you otherwise. Some of the most popular formula brands are available in low-iron versions also, though all soy formulas are high in iron. Iron can cause constipation in some babies, but this is a much less serious condition than anemia.

◆ Formula-fed babies have less frequent bowel movements, usually one or two a day on average. The stools are usually yellow. If they are dark brown, your baby may be constipated. Make sure to check the expiration date on the formula and do not use cans that are dented or otherwise damaged.

◆ Do not prop up the bottle as a substitute for you holding your baby. Your baby needs to have her emotional needs as well as her hunger pangs satisfied. Not only is propping up a bottle emotionally detrimental, but it is also very risky since your baby will be more susceptible to choking and ear infections.

◆ Remove the bottle if the baby falls asleep while feeding, since leaving it in can lead to tooth decay—or worse, choking.

◆ You will need at least six bottles with graduated measurements on the outside, six nipples, a nipple brush, and a bottle brush.

Milk Allergies. Milk allergies and intolerance are very important to be aware of, especially as such a high percentage of black adults have trouble digesting milk. In infancy, a milk allergy is more common than complete intolerance. It is a reaction to the protein in the milk and often presents itself as nasal congestion, vomiting, watery stools, and bloody spit-up. A milk allergy may be suspected if your baby has persistent nasal congestion. Your pediatrician may want you to try a different milk, such as a soy formula, and see if the baby's condition improves. It has been found that 85 percent of children who are allergic to cow's milk will not be allergic to soy formulas. Nutramigen is a predigested formula that is recommended for those who are allergic to both cow's milk and soy formulas.

What About Soy Formulas? Soy formula is also generally a good choice for mothers who are breast-feeding because it's an easier transition to go from breast to supplementation with the soy than with animal's milk.

All soy formulas have a high iron content, so feeding your baby soy is consistent with the U.S. surgeon general's recommended amount of iron a baby should have daily. The disadvantage to soy formulas is that they are expensive and harder to find in some areas. The smell of babies' stools is generally a little stronger with soy formulas and the stools may be bulkier.

Prosobee is an excellent choice and contains added essential amino acids, since soybeans are deficient in essential amino acids. Prosobee had the advantage of not having any animal sugar or protein in it. When your child has a lot of diarrhea, it is good to use Prosobee, because it contains no lactose or sucrose so it is much easier to digest. Isomil is similar to Prosobee but it does contain sucrose. Babies may like it better because it has a sweeter taste.

If your baby is allergic to cow's milk, the formula of choice is Nutramigen. It is very easily digestible and babies get fewer allergies with it. However, it is expensive, foul-tasting, and foul-smelling. Fortunately, most newborn babies don't have a sophisticated sense of taste.

When Should I Feed the Baby? When you were born, the general thought was that babies' feedings should be on a strict schedule dictated by the clock. Nowadays, the prevailing view is that babies should be fed on their own time schedule, *when they need and ask for it.* It has been found that babies fed on demand, rather than being forced into a schedule, get into their own timetable more easily and may eventually require fewer feedings.

Introducing Solid Foods

Some mothers want to start giving their baby solid foods at a very early age—as young as two months—so the baby will sleep through the night. This is inappropriate because it can lead to serious problems. Do not—repeat *do not*—do this. Babies who are given food at a very young age tend to have more allergies and a higher incidence of childhood obesity. Stomach upsets and constipation or diarrhea are also common in babies who are fed solid foods too early.

When your baby is about six months old you can begin to introduce solid foods *while you continue to breast- or bottle-feed.* Don't give her an ultimatum in your desire to have her "graduate." She may signal you that she's ready for solids by acting dissatisfied after nursing or bottle-feeding. Or, she may want to be nursed or bottle-fed more than usual. Introduce one food at a time, a few teaspoonfuls at a time, until she seems to get the hang of it. To begin, place the food on the tip of a small, plastic-coated spoon and place it between her lips. Soon she will open her mouth and take an entire spoonful. Make sure the food is not spicy or salty and is well mashed or puréed. Potatoes, vegetables, and fruits make great first-time meals, as does rice or barley cereal mixed with breast milk or formula. Bananas are good, too, but once the baby tastes the sweetness, she may not want anything else.

Invest in some good bibs (some mothers suggest using a baby rain slicker) and an apron for yourself, as babies take a while to pick up dining etiquette. Hopefully, you'll be able to relax and make mealtimes fun.

Weaning

There is no rule of thumb about when is the right time to wean a baby from the breast or bottle. Mothers wean their babies anywhere from the sixth week to the sixth month, depending on their lifestyle choices. Breast milk alone for the first six months of your baby's life will provide her with superior nutrition. After six months, it's recommended that you supplement the breast milk with the introduction of solid foods. On average, babies who are going to wean themselves do so between nine and twelve months of age.

Whenever it occurs, weaning should be accomplished *gradually* over about two weeks. Not only is this gradual approach better for the baby than the "cold-turkey" method, but it will be more comfortable for you, too. As the baby nurses less often, your milk production will diminish naturally. If you stop breast-feeding suddenly, your breasts will remain full of milk, which can be painful.

A gradual weaning means expressing your breast milk into bottles a few weeks before you have to return to work or want to stop breast-feeding. Give the baby one bottle a day for one week, then two, and then three bottles, so she can get used to the different feel of the rubber nipple while you are still nursing. The last nursing sessions to give up should be the first morning feedings and the last night feedings. When switching to having to do a bottle, be certain that the milk flow of the nipple is not too fast. Breast-fed babies are used to having to do a lot of sucking. You may have to experiment with bottles with different-shaped nipples until you find one your baby accepts. If your baby is old enough to drink from a cup, and is willing to do so, then a good way to wean is straight from the breast to the cup.

For babies who were exclusively bottle-fed, keep in mind that they haven't had as much sucking time as have breast-fed babies so it is important to wean from bottle to cup more slowly, on their own timetable. Some babies naturally give up the bottle when they are ready.

By two months of age, some babies will only require one night feeding, although this varies from infant to infant. Most babies try to feed themselves between ten and fourteen months of age.

Bathing

It's natural to be afraid of bathing your baby. That initial concern is a healthy one, but remember that this is a person who has squeezed himself through a birth canal smaller than his head! Your baby has demonstrated his strength and determination by surviving the gestational period, labor, and delivery. The healthy aspect of anxiety is that parents are cautious and proceed from a posture of cautiousness to a posture of more liberalness as they see what works.

Do not submerge your baby in a bath or the sink until the umbilical cord has fallen off and the area has healed (see "Umbilical Cord" at the end of this chapter for how to care for the umbilical stump). Also, if your baby boy was circumcised, wait until his penis has fully healed until you give him a bath; sponge-bathe him until then. Don't feel obliged to give the baby more than a sponge bath two or three times a week until he is old enough to get really dirty, usually at the crawling stage.

For a sponge or tub bath, you will need:

◆ A towel with hood
◆ A washcloth
◆ A mild soap
◆ Tear-free baby shampoo
◆ Diapers
◆ Change of clothes
◆ Towel or robe to cover your clothes

Use lots of water to get the soap off your baby since any soap left on the skin and scalp could be quite irritating. Bathing too often can also lead to dry skin. Unless you live in a very humid environment, two or three baths a week should be sufficient, as long as you thoroughly clean your baby's bottom after each bowel movement and regularly wash her hands, face, and genital area.

When bathing your baby, find a way to hold her that works for you. The football position seems to work well. Make sure the room is warm and that there is no draft. If your baby gets very upset at bathing time, it may be that she senses your anxiety. It could also be that she doesn't like to be totally naked (anymore). Try covering and washing one part of her body at a time. Also try distracting your baby with singing or a soothing voice. If you are really having trouble getting her into the bath, try taking a bath with her, and perhaps even breast-feeding your baby while in the bathtub. If there is a part of the body that your baby gets particularly upset about getting cleaned—which can spoil her mood for the entire bathing process—either save that part for last or wash it at another time during the day.

Bathing before bedtime will help your baby relax for a restful sleep. Avoid baths just before or after a meal. Don't be surprised if your baby frequently urinates and has bowel movements in the tub. Do not treat your baby to a bubble bath too often because it could be irritating to his genitals and urinary tract. When you do use bubbles, be sure to rinse the genital area thoroughly with clean water. Even sitting in soapy water for too long can cause irritation, especially to a baby girl's vaginal area. Though some products are advertised to be mild for hands and lather very well, detergents such as liquid soaps

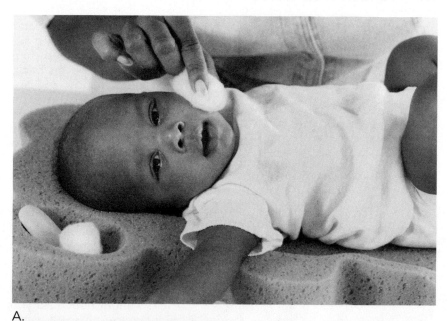

A.

B.

Newborn's Sponge Bath. (A) Place your baby on a flat surface with waterproof padding or on a sponge-bath cushion. Leave his T-shirt and diaper on for now so he won't be cold. We will start at the face and work our way down. Begin by wiping his face with a moist cotton ball, wiping each eye (use a separate cotton ball for each to avoid infection), using outward strokes. Do the same with his ears, mouth, and the rest of his face and neck folds. (B) Hold your baby in a football carry with his head over a bowl or sinkful of lukewarm water. Wet his scalp with the water, using a washcloth. Shampoo his head with a mild soap or no-tears baby shampoo and massage his scalp with your fingertips. This may only need to be done once a week. (Make sure you use your fingertips and not your fingernails.) Rinse, using the washcloth and water. Pat his head dry.

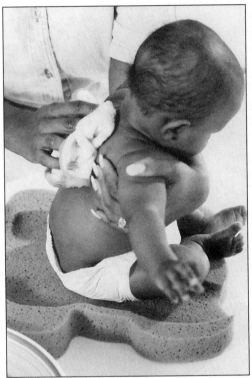

(C) Remove his shirt only and prop him in a supported sitting position, holding him firmly as you wipe his back, chest, arms, hands, and fingers, remembering to wipe in-between places and skin folds. If his umbilical cord is still healing, avoid getting water on his midsection. Clean the navel area with a cotton swab dipped in alcohol. Towel him dry and put on a clean top.

(D) Remove the baby's diaper; soap and rinse the genital area, bottom, legs, and feet, remembering nooks and crannies. Baby boys may squirt without notice, so you might drape an extra washcloth over the penis while you clean the rest of him. Diaper and dress your baby's bottom half.

C.

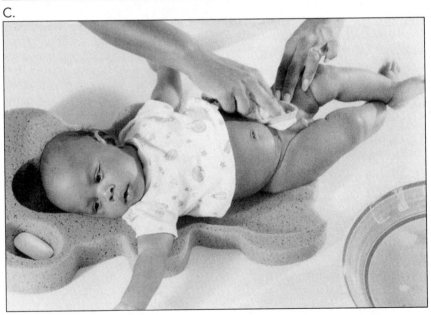

D.

should not be used to bathe your baby because they are very irritating to your baby's genitals.

Powders can be dangerous! Your baby can breathe in fine talcum powder and injure her lungs when an excessive amount of powder is used or if it is used incorrectly. The proper way to use powder is to put a small quantity on your fingertips and then rub it onto the skin. Powder should not be found on the sheets and blankets in the baby's sleeping space if you are using the right amount.

Once the circumcised penis is healed, the only care it needs is normal washing with warm, soapy water. The uncircumcised penis in an infant also does not need special care, and you will find that at this young age you cannot retract the foreskin, so do *not* try. Simple rinsing of the penis well with water is adequate to clean this area. Remember, the foreskin of the uncircumcised penis is usually very tight. Attempting to retract it will often cause painful cracking of the foreskin. Your baby boy will have frequent erections throughout the day, which, in part, serve to stretch the foreskin gradually and naturally.

HISTORICALLY SPEAKING . . .

 Calabash leaves steeped in a pool of warm water is a royal bath for Haitian newborns. Many West African babies are "rubbed down" with coconut oil immediately after birth. Tribal women in Zaire will scent their baby's bathwater by using a sweet-smelling vine from the forest, the place where they believe babies originate. The Dinka people of the Sudan feel so strongly about bathing that they call a baby's first year of birth "the bathing period." They also believe that if a child grows up to be clumsy or unpoised, it is because he was improperly bathed during this period in his infancy. Midwives of the African Baganda tribe help a newborn learn to breathe by blowing up its nose; tribal women of the Ivory Coast splash their babies with cold water. In parts of West Africa, the baby is placed facedown on the midwife's lap, her head is tilted upward, and she is immediately taught to drink from a gourd (similar to a cup). She is determined to be "full" once the midwife observes her swelling abdomen. These babies are also taught how to get accustomed to falling by being thrown up in the air two or three times right after birth, and

sometimes are held upside down by their legs, too. *What We Can Learn:* Though some of these tribal rituals may seem unusual or even downright scary (don't attempt them at home!), it's good to remember that babies are tougher than we adults think they are. Newborns *do* need firm support at the head and neck when being held, but often parents tend to be so cautious and nervous they transfer their anxiety to the baby, who begins to cry. As you start to relax and realize your baby's ever-increasing abilities, you'll soon be holding her with one hand and vacuuming the rug with the other!

Shampooing and Haircare

(See B, in newborn bathing photos.) The baby should be held in the football position with one arm (nondominant arm). The scalp should be washed with a gentle no-tears baby shampoo. Wet the baby's head, squeeze on a small amount of shampoo, and gently massage the entire scalp. With the scalp thoroughly lathered, tepid water can now be poured repeatedly over the baby's scalp with a cup to remove all of the soap. If you wish, you can massage a little baby mineral oil into the scalp. Using a very fine toothed comb, comb the baby's hair while scraping the scalp a bit, and you can remove a lot of the cradle cap that way. Don't be afraid to comb the hair and scrape the scalp. This will not be unpleasant to most babies. Cradle cap is a seborrheic dermatitis of the scalp and is quite common in young infants. The last part of the cradle cap that will be removed will be the part that's over the soft spot. The soft spot will retain it because it will actually sink a little when you try to move the comb across it. Shampooing your baby too frequently can cause a dry and flaky scalp. Once or twice a week should be sufficient.

Your newborn baby's hair will probably be fine in texture and not well-rooted in the scalp. Most babies will have a large bald area on the back of their heads that stretches from ear to ear. This is normal and occurs because the baby spends so much time laying on those parts of its head. The hair will thicken and take on its genetically programmed texture as baby's first year progresses. We recommend using a damp comb or soft baby brush to style the hair. *Loose* braids or "pigtails" are fine, but avoid using rubber bands or heavy baubles to secure them. The pulling of the bands and the weight of the baubles will cause the already fragile hair to break. Use plastic-coated bands or barrettes instead. If you are braiding the hair regularly, remember to vary the

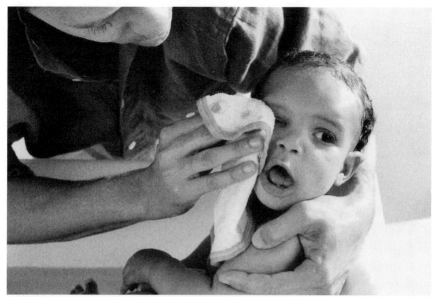

A.

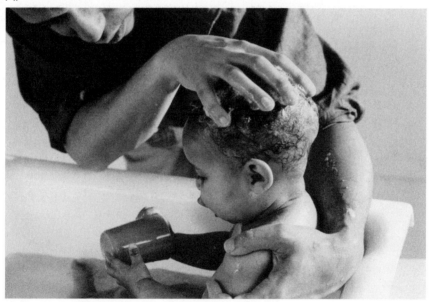

B.

Baldwin's Baby Bath (for older infants). (A) Run about 2 inches of water into a baby tub, preferably one with rubber grips on the bottom. Undress your baby and sit her in the tub, supporting her as necessary with your arm and hand. Don't let her slip! Wipe her face, starting with her eyes, and so on, remembering ears and neck folds. (B) Shampoo her head, massaging with fingertips from front to back so that soap

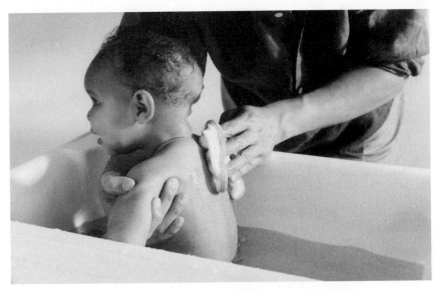

C.

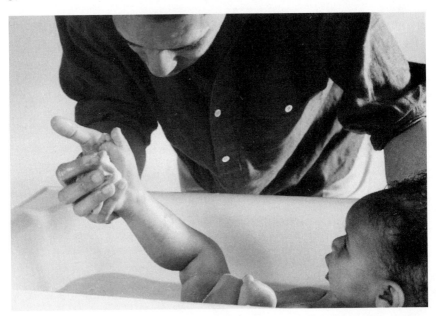

D.

drips behind the head not onto the face. Rinse the head by pouring water from a plastic cup over the baby's head from front to back, so it drains down her neck and back. You may need to tilt her head upward to facilitate this. (C) Lightly soap the baby's body, including genitals, then her back. (D) Remember to clean between the toes! Lift baby out of the tub and wrap her in a soft towel to dry.

place you part the hair every few days. *Straighteners, chemical relaxers, and hot combs are not to be used on a baby's hair!* It is much to fine to withstand these preparations. Light mineral oil may be applied, as necessary.

Safety Issues

Never leave your baby unattended in the bath for even a second. Don't even turn your back on your baby in the tub to retrieve a towel behind you. An inch of water in the tub is enough to drown your baby if she is left unattended—*a curious, crawling baby can even drown in the toilet!* Also, be sure electrical appliances are far from the tub. Never leave your hair dryer, curling iron, or other appliances plugged in while in the bathroom—whether they are on or off—because the baby can grab them. If she's in water she can be electrocuted. If you are a homeowner, turn down your water heater temperature to 120°, and test the water temperature with the inside of your wrist before putting your baby in the water. For details on how to make your home safe for baby, see chapter 6, "Getting Your 'House' in Order."

Breathing

Nasal congestion is common in most babies from time to time. Babies breathe though the nose, so if the nostrils are congested you will have one miserable baby due to the anxiety of not being able to breathe through the nose. Nasal congestion can result from the drying effect of the heat in your home. Dry air causes nostrils to become dry and swollen. A vaporizing humidifier, 20 to 30 minutes in a steamy bathroom created by running hot water in the tub, and salt-water drops for the nose are all good for alleviating congestion.

Babies have a different kind of breathing pattern than we do, and it may seem quite irregular to you. Their breathing is more periodic than that of adults. Sometimes you can't see the respiratory effort because it is so shallow. Babies also breathe very fast. It can be very frightening to see because babies pant, breathing mostly in the upper portion of their lungs. Another frightening thing babies do is hold their breath up to 10 seconds. *Don't be alarmed.* This is a part of the periodic breathing of babies. After a period of panting, it is not unusual in a newborn to have a pause in breathing, followed by more panting.

A.   B.

There are three ways to burp your baby: (A) The shoulder brooch burp, as shown; rub or pat your baby's back until he burps. (B) The sit-up-and-spit-up position, where the baby sits on one side of your lap, as shown, with one hand supporting him at the chest. Lean the baby forward a bit and use your other hand to rub or pat his back. The take-it-easy burp position (not shown), where the baby lies across your lap. With his head tilted to one side and supported by your hand, rub or pat the baby's back with your other hand.

Burping Baby

Burping your baby is an important step in the feeding process. If your baby is not properly burped, she may cry, be very fussy, and have difficulty sleeping because of air trapped in her stomach. One burp during a pause in feeding and one burp after the meal is usually sufficient. If your baby doesn't burp after a few minutes, that's okay. Drape a diaper or towel across your shoulder or knees if your baby tends to spit up. Keeping her upright for a while after a feeding may lessen her spitting up.

Spitting Up

Some babies spit up when they burp. Spitting up is caused by a gas bubble underneath the food that comes to the surface of the baby's tummy and pushes the food up and out. Some babies who spit up may lose most of their feeding. If that is the case, you may have to feed her a little more afterwards, or feed her earlier for the next time.

Carrying Baby

To restate one new father's observation, "The baby seemed to me like a set of expensive china." This may be how you feel, understandably, about handling your newborn, especially after all the older, more experienced helpers have gone. However, not to worry; your baby is tougher than she looks. With basic knowledge and a little practice you'll get the hang of it in no time.

Here are four comfortable ways to hold a baby properly. Let's call them the Cradle, the Shoulder Brooch, the Football Hold, and the Front Facer. The Cradle and the Shoulder Brooch are the two "holding positions" that people are most familiar with. The Cradle is simply

A.

B.

cradling the baby in your arms with her head and neck in the crook of your elbow supported by your forearm. The traditional way to carry the baby is in the Shoulder Brooch position (so coined by my West Indian friends) when you hold her on your shoulder with one hand supporting her upper back (neck and head if a newborn) and the other under her bottom. (A) To hold her in the Football *(left)*, lay the baby on your forearm with your hand cradling her neck and head. Make sure your arm is close to your body for added support. One leg should be on each side of your elbow. This one-handed position is great for newborns since they are small and light. Daddies, in particular, seem to love it. (B) The Front Facer *(right)* requires two hands but allows the baby to examine his new environment, which is usually a treat. His hands also get to move more freely in this position. Face the baby to the front with his back leaning on your chest. Support his chest with one hand and let his bottom sit on your forearm.

HISTORICALLY SPEAKING . . .

 African babies are with their mothers constantly until about the age of 2— usually wrapped in a cloth sarong, in a goatskin wrap, or in a *doek* or headscarf on her back. See chapter 6, "Getting Your 'House' in Order," for how to tie a sarong. A South African woman bonds with her baby as she walks down a road to fetch water, as she shops in the market, and as she goes about her work. When a mother isn't carrying the baby on her back, she swings her around and carries her on the hip, also a convenient way to breast-feed when the need arises. The mother is so in tune with her baby's body that she can feel when the baby is about to urinate or have a bowel movement and simply lets her down. *What We Can Learn:* Our African sisters don't need ten-year studies to tell them that babies who are carried frequently are more content and better behaved than babies who are not. Why not try using a sarong in a vibrant African Kente cloth pattern to carry your baby in for a few months? Or, for the less adventurous, consider the Baby Wrap, a back-carrier designed by an African woman. To order one, call (303) 757-5564. Either way, you'll probably end up with a happier, quieter baby and you may get some compliments, too.

Colic

Most people think of colic as a gastric phenomenon. They believe that something uncomfortable is happening in the baby's tummy. In fact, colic is just an umbrella term for "I don't know why the baby's crying but I'm about to go out of my mind." A colicky cry is a very intense, incessant cry and it really does frighten most people who are around the baby. The child is in a total panic and there doesn't seem to be anything that will calm her.

Colic does not have to be a gastric ailment, but it often can be. A problem-elimination approach to determine the cause of the crying is essential. Systematically go through your baby's last few days: How did I prepare her food? When did I last feed her? What did I feed her? Sometimes in the middle of the night you may have made formula and accidentally made it too concentrated, for instance: That can cause diarrhea and dehydration. Parents can also overheat and thereby denature (break down the nutrients in) the milk, making it more concentrated and harder to digest. Some babies are sensitive to certain types of food. Your baby may also have a milk allergy.

When breast-feeding mothers eat a lot of green, leafy vegetables, such as spinach and broccoli, their babies tend to have more gas and explosive stools. The same goes for mothers who drink a lot of orange juice and other citrus juices. Though both green leafies and citrus juices are good for you, you may want to restrict or exclude them for a while to see if your baby reacts positively.

Regarding allergies to milk, almost everybody who drinks milk at a very young age has some bleeding from irritation of the gut. This irritation can be anything from microscopic to actually finding blood in the stool from drinking whole-milk products. The most common cause of rectal bleeding in babies is cow-milk-protein allergy. So what mother eats and what baby eats really do have an effect on how the baby responds and what the baby's personality is like. When the mother goes on a bland diet, a colicky baby seems to improve after a day or two. If you suspect your diet is giving your baby discomfort, omit the food you think may be irritating to her and express your milk and discard it for 24 to 48 hours.

Colic usually doesn't start until two weeks of age and peaks at about six weeks of age. Take heart: By three months of age, colic usually miraculously goes away, so try weathering this period as best you can.

Crying

When you are weary of hearing your baby cry, just remember that crying is the *only* way newborns have to communicate. Babies develop "differential crying" in the first 24 to 48 hours of life. That is, they will have a minimal cry for little things and a louder cry for more important needs. Soon you will learn to distinguish what your baby is trying to tell you with each type of cry. How loud or ferocious your baby's crying may be does not always indicate the *severity* of the problem, though. This is because babies' young nervous systems do not permit them to modulate their level of crying to the severity of their pain or discomfort. So a cry for food to the baby is quite desperate. Learn to be calm when your baby cries and use the problem-elimination approach to figure out what the crying is all about. If feeding, diapering, cuddling, rocking, and everything else does not calm your baby, speak to your pediatrician. Also contact the pediatrician if the crying is accompanied by any health symptoms.

Crying is important in that it allows your baby to inhale deeply, expanding the lower portions of her lungs and allowing for better air exchange.

There is controversy as to whether picking up your baby each time she cries will spoil her. Remember, your baby has been carried for the entire gestational period. At birth she was taken from her mother's womb and made to lie on a relatively firm mattress, alone. It is natural that she would feel a need to be held continuously. To that extent, reproducing her gestational experience as closely as possible by bundling her in a warm blanket is often soothing. When your baby cries, however, other reasons for the crying should be sought.

It has been found that some babies behave particularly poorly on days just before there is an advancement in development. Well-regarded pediatrician and author T. Berry Brazelton describes three baby "types": the quiet baby, the average baby, and the active baby. In his theory he explains a slightly different approach for each baby's personality. Get to know your baby's type by observing how she reacts to things, her sleeping and eating characteristics, and her level of sociability so you can better care for her. Finally, remember that the baby will not behave this way forever, and as you learn to cue in to your baby, you will be able to comfort her more easily and quickly.

Pacifiers are useful in quieting your crying baby because of his natural desire to suck. However, realize that you are conditioning the baby to put something in her mouth whenever she needs to relieve tension or upset. Does this idea sound familiar? Think about compulsive smokers, overeaters, nail-biters. They operate on the same strategy.

The La Leche League does not recommend the use of pacifiers in breast-fed babies because of concerns about nipple confusion. In this situation, babies who are breast-fed might tend to prefer the rubber nipple over the mother's breast. Initially, this can be a real pain for breast-feeding mothers. One positive aspect of using a pacifier is that it helps the baby exercise and strengthen her oral muscles. However, pacifiers can cause your baby to have a higher roof palate and, later, buck teeth. There are currently orthodontically correct pacifiers that address this problem. Please know that once your infant becomes comfortable sucking a pacifier you may find it quite a challenge to remove it. Consider that your baby will benefit more from receiving the comfort and attention of her parent than she will from a rubber sucker.

"I was at my girlfriend's house and her baby was playing for hours in a disposable diaper that was so full it was yellow on the outside. I gingerly said, 'Shouldn't you change her?' and she replied, 'No, no, it's a disposable; they're very absorbent. When it's only urine I don't worry about it.'"

Diapering

In our parents' and grandparents' day, cloth diapers were *it*. Even when disposables came out, cloth diapers were still the preferred choice of many mothers because they allowed for better air and heat exchange than disposables, and because they are much softer. Today it seems there is a trend toward returning to cloth diapers. (Just as we return to everything else: platform shoes, bell-bottoms, and Afros!) Their ease of use has improved: They can be found in many department stores, and are offered in the same hourglass shape that disposables are (so no folding) with Velcro closures to eliminate pinning. Cloth diapers (including laundering costs) will also run you less than half the cost of disposables.

To their credit, today's disposable diapers are more absorbent and are engineered actually to "pull moisture from baby's skin," as their many TV commercials attest. Gels now used in disposable diapers also cause the urine to be pulled away from baby's skin. But there are significant drawbacks you should consider. While disposables keep the baby drier, this tends to placate parents into fewer diaper changes, leaving the door open to all types of rashes. Disposable diapers are also one of our planet's greatest pollutants, and even the biodegradable ones reportedly take close to 100 years to degrade. We urge you to consider the implications of your choice. Of course, cloth diapers are more time-consuming and not as aesthetically pleasing as disposables.

In the first week, you will have two or three wet diapers a day. After that, you will have to change between 80 and 100 diapers a week with a newborn. Frequent changing will avoid irritation and diaper rash. You should change your baby's diaper before or after every feeding and whenever there's a bowel movement. Changing a baby every time she urinates is a good idea, but don't drive yourself crazy trying to keep up. If your baby sleeps with a wet diaper, you do not have to change her, unless you are treating persistent diaper rash.

Be sure to fold the diaper below the baby's navel if it hasn't completely healed.

For a change of pace, we decided to demonstrate the diaper technique showing a mother using cloth diapers. Just follow steps A through E if you've decided to use disposables.

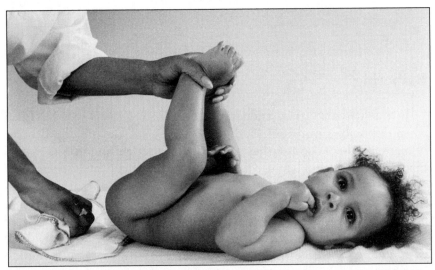

(A) With your baby on a flat surface, unfasten the dirty diaper, lift the baby's legs at the ankles, and roll the diaper toward the baby. Wipe any stool with the back end of the diaper and set diaper aside.

(B) Holding baby's ankles with one hand, lift up the baby's bottom, and wipe the baby's genitals and buttocks with a wet cotton ball, damp wash-cloth (low cost), or baby wipe (more expensive). Allow baby's bottom to air-dry for a minute. If you are treating a rash, apply the appropriate oint-ment. Hint: Give baby a toy to play with during changing time so she may be less fidgety; a pacifier may also do the trick for the moment.

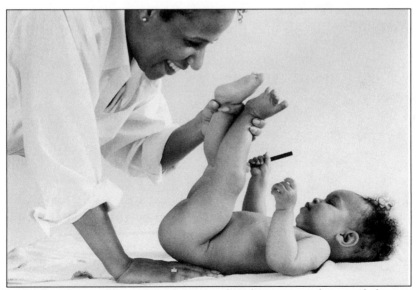

(C) Holding her ankles again, raise up her bottom and spread the new diaper down underneath her. The top edge of the diaper should be at waist height. For disposable users, the adhesive tabs should be at the back of the diaper. Position her properly on the diaper.

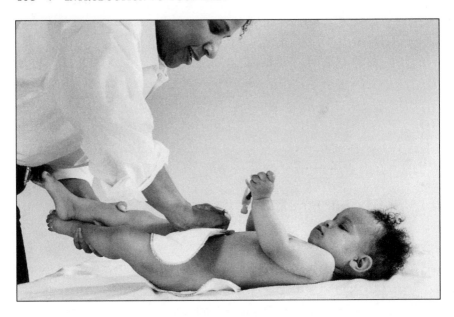

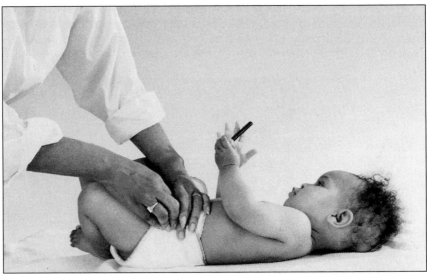

(D) and (E) Bring the front of the diaper up over the front of the baby and tape or Velcro the diaper securely on either side.

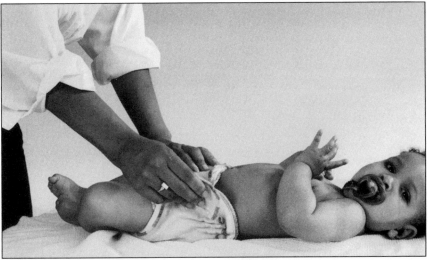

(F) Cloth diaper users will then put on baby's waterproof pants. Be sure to take the baby off the changing table!

For cloth diaperers: (G) Take the dirty diaper to the bathroom and empty it out into the toilet. Swish it around so you get most of the stool off.

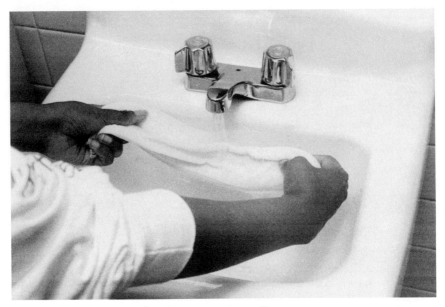

(H) Run the diaper under the tap to rinse. Squeeze out excess water.

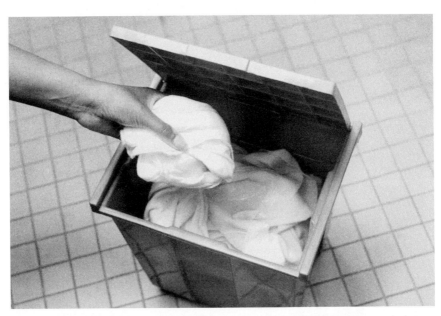

(I) Drop the diaper into a pail of water and bleach or water and detergent to soak for later laundering. If the idea of doing this repels you, consider using a diaper service. They will launder and deliver 80 clean diapers to your door each week for about $15.

Diaper Rash and Other Rashes

There are various rashes that are common in newborn babies: diaper rash, heat rash, miliarial rash (infant acne), and atopic dermatitis (a dry, scaly rash that appears on the neck and joints). Most will go away by themselves or with treatment by your pediatrician. Rashes in the diaper area are caused by the heat and moisture produced from the diaper and the urine. It starts out as chafing. Any rash that lasts long enough can turn into a yeast infection if the diaper area remains hot and dark enough.

Diaper rash is little bumps that appear for several reasons, often from an irritation, fungal, or bacterial infection or allergy. Usually it is not an emergency. Yeast is a common cause of persistent diaper rash. The most common causes of diaper rash are tightly fitting diapers, too much ammonia in your baby's urine, infection due to bacteria or yeast, an allergic reaction to food, or something in the air. In addition, diaper rash can be caused or aggravated by rubber pants, detergents, powders, perfumes, alcohol, lotions, and fabric softeners.

To prevent diaper rash, change your baby's diapers frequently and clean the diaper area carefully each time with warm water. Consider putting baking soda in the water when you are doing the baby's laundry and in the bathtub as a neutralizing agent for bacteria or fungi. Let your baby go diaperless as much as possible. Also, let the diaper area dry before putting on a new diaper.

To treat simple diaper rash, change your baby's diaper frequently, allowing the area to be exposed to the air and light. Apply A and D, Desitin, or a generic-brand zinc oxide ointment to the area. If your baby's diaper rash persists, consult your pediatrician. Cortisone creams and antifungal creams are often prescribed.

Discipline

By the tenth month, your baby is becoming more mobile. Continue to set limits with him so he will avoid dangers, as well as learn what is appropriate and inappropriate behavior. How to set these limits is a very critical issue. Reacting to inappropriate behavior with a yell, a shake, or a hit will only frighten and confuse your baby. It can easily discourage his developmental stage of exploration, which can have negative long-term consequences, according to noted researchers.

Instead of yelling or hitting, try a firm "No" when he is behaving inappropriately, then immediately show him the right way to behave in that situation and have him model it. This way your baby's impulse to explore will not be stifled, but rather channeled in an acceptable way. Soon he will learn what is acceptable behavior and what is not, without stifling his impulse to explore. Setting limits requires you to be consistent and firm. Hitting just escalates into harder hitting.

Also, instead of taking good behavior for granted, be sure to praise it often. This is important for the child's self-esteem, and to let the child know that he pleases his parents. Setting no limits gives a child a sense of insecurity because he feels that no one cares what he does. When you set boundaries you help him to find order in this "new" world and, more importantly, you begin to develop his moral character.

Dressing

The biggest mistake that parents make when it comes to dressing their baby is overdressing. While overdressing is done out of protectiveness and love, it can actually make the baby miserable. At best, it can cause the baby to be irritable, but it can also lead to prickly heat bumps, or even worse, heat stroke.

Dress the baby in as many layers as you're wearing (yes, it's true). Carry along extra clothes in case the baby seems uncomfortable, gets her clothes damp with sweat or spit-up, or the weather changes. Infants do need a little more protection than you do, but don't get carried away. If the baby's undershirt is damp, take off some clothes. The baby will tell you if she's too cold by constricting her face or by becoming blotchy in her complexion.

Don't be too concerned if your baby sneezes. Babies sneeze very easily, even at the slightest temperature change. Sneezing is a good thing in that it helps the baby to clear her nostrils of mucus.

Summer and winter hats are very important accessories in your baby's wardrobe. Hats are crucial when the weather is cold, or even cool, since 25 percent of body heat is lost through the top of the head. In the summer, choose a lightweight hat that will protect the baby's head without overheating him.

When selecting clothes for your baby, look for those that will be quick and easy to put on and take off. You want to make dressing time as simple and fun as possible. Look for wide neck openings, snaps, loose sleeves, and stretchable fabrics. Make sure zippers are held away from the baby's skin when zipping up or down. Sleepwear should not contain strings or ties, since they can strangle the baby. Buttons can also be a hazard to babies since they can bite them off and choke on them. Look for 100 percent cotton clothes, since this material breathes and is absorbent.

Some parents, especially those of Caribbean and Hispanic origin, put amulets (little charms) on the baby in the belief that this will prevent somebody from putting a hex on the baby. We encourage you to reject superstition (which is based on irrational fear) and concentrate on your baby's safety instead. A necklace may look nice hanging around the baby's neck, but she may accidentally choke herself with it. No jewelry, including earrings, is recommended for an infant.

Opinions differ on when the baby should start wearing shoes. Generally when the baby starts walking well she only needs to wear shoes outdoors. Prior to the time your baby starts to walk, shoes aren't really necessary, but if your floors are cold or may have splinters or other sharp objects, you should cover her feet with soft, leather-soled

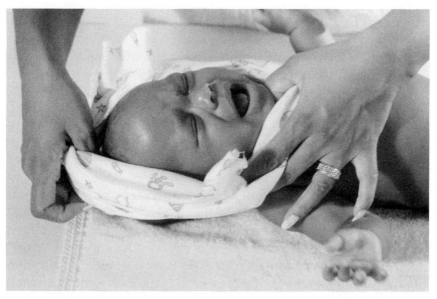

A Tip for Getting a Top over the Newborn's Head. With the baby on a flat surface, scrunch the top and stretch its neck opening as wide as you can. Get the baby's face through the opening first and then ease the shirt over the back of the head. This way, his face is "hidden" from you only for a short time. As you can see, though, he still may not like it! Once the shirt is over the head completely, reach your fingers into the sleeves and navigate the baby's arms through. (If you wait for the baby to help you with this, you'll be waiting a long time.)

moccasins, socks with rubber tracking on the bottoms, or slippers. Regular socks are often too slippery and will encourage falls.

Make sure you go to a shoe store where there are professional salespeople available to measure your baby's feet and recommend the proper size. Proper fit is essential. Your baby's foot will grow very rapidly at this age, so check for the correct size every three months. The common belief that babies need high-topped shoes for ankle support is false. These shoes actually impede the range of movement needed for the baby to walk easily.

Swaddling

Swaddling is simply wrapping a baby fairly tightly in a receiving blanket. Many newborns like being swaddled until they are three to four months old. It provides a sense of security, warmth, and the sensation of being constantly held and touched on all sides.

Hair and Scalp Care

Your baby's first hair will be very furry and will tend to fall out on its own. This process can happen very rapidly, leaving baby with periods of complete baldness. Don't worry, you may notice that the quality of the hair is changing (as it gets replaced) rather than that your baby is balding.

You will find it easier to groom your child's hair when she isn't tired or hungry. Give her a toy to play with. She may also enjoy looking in the mirror while you groom her hair.

Braiding a baby's hair in tight braids or cornrows can cause irritation of the scalp. This irritation will look like little bumps at the hair shaft where the follicle leaves the skin. Tight braiding can also lead to patches of baldness and thinning of the hair. If you part the baby's hair, change its location every few days to prevent the hair from thinning around the part. If you need to use a blow dryer, be sure to use only a low or cool setting to prevent burning your baby's scalp.

Mild cradle cap, which looks like greasy scales on the surface of the scalp, is normal. This can be treated with a massage of mineral oil or petroleum jelly, followed by a shampoo. In a severe case of cradle cap, your baby will have heavy flaking and/or brownish patches and yellow crustiness. Your pediatrician may suggest a special medicated shampoo to follow the mineral oil or petroleum jelly massage.

Babies with cradle cap should wear a hat as infrequently as possible since the condition is aggravated by a sweaty scalp. Occasionally, cradle cap will persist throughout early childhood.

Baby acne can also be found on the scalp. To learn how to treat this, see the skin care section later in this chapter.

Hiccups

Hiccups are normal, and are quite common in infancy. Their cause is unknown but a prime suspect is gas bubbles. Hiccups typically occur after crying for long periods of time and after eating. Burping the baby or giving her warm or room-temperature water can usually alleviate some of the gas, and the hiccups should stop. If you were in the midst of feeding the baby, try resuming the feeding—the hiccups will usually go away.

Without intervention, hiccups will usually stop by themselves after about 5 or 10 minutes. Babies don't seem to mind having hiccups. Incidentally, babies have been found to have hiccuping spells while in the womb.

Immunizations

During your baby's first year, it is important that she is immunized against several serious and potentially fatal diseases. An immunization contains dead organisms or weakened live microorganisms. When the immunization enters your child's body, her body builds up antibodies or resistance to the microorganism. Thus, if your child is exposed to the disease in the future, these antibodies will prevent your child from getting sick.

The healthy newborn arrives in this world already partially immunized by her mother. Breast-fed babies receive additional antibodies from the mother through her breast milk. However, *all* babies still need additional protection that can only be gained through immunizations.

Realize that when your child is exposed to other children, even though your home may be clean and your baby is healthy and eats healthy foods, the child is going to be exposed to a barrage of germs. Siblings will bring back germs to younger children who are home all day. Children don't respect each other's space; they're all over each other. And they are exposed, even more than adults are, to airborne and contact kinds of germs due to their natural tendencies to be playful and their inexperienced immune systems.

While many parents are fearful of their children being immunized, black parents may be partially apprehensive because of the involuntary experimentation conducted on our ancestors by the U.S. government. One infamous example is the Tuskegee Experiment, where black men with syphilis were withheld treatment in order for "researchers" to see what the final stages of the disease looked like. Some parents are still suspicious that vaccines are a way for the government to exterminate our children. You can be assured that the same vaccine lots are given to children regardless of race, color, or creed. Immunizations are here to save our children's lives—and are, for the most part, very successful in accomplishing this.

While a cold can make you feel miserable, eventually you get better. There are, however, other illnesses that can cause serious permanent damage to your child, and may even result in death. Measles can kill. Mumps can sterilize baby boys. Polio can paralyze. Tetanus kills. Rubella is responsible for birth defects. Immunizations are an easy way of protecting your baby from needless suffering.

Some infants do have reactions to certain vaccines, but these reactions have no long-term consequences and usually last only a day or two. The series of DTP vaccines (which prevent diptheria, tetanus, and pertussis—also known as whooping cough) can lead to such symptoms as pain, swelling, and/or redness at the injection site, fever, fussiness, and drowsiness. Symptoms usually show up about 12 to 24 hours after the injection. In extremely rare circumstances, the pertussis component of the DTP vaccine can cause brain damage. However, children who get pertussis are 10 times more vulnerable to brain damage than children who get the vaccine that prevents it.

Measles vaccine causes a fever a week later, which lasts only a few hours. Children who have a low seizure threshold can have a seizure as a result of the fever. Note that it's not the vaccine directly causing the seizure, but the fever. If your child begins showing signs of a serious reaction to any vaccine, contact your pediatrician immediately.

The scar that most of you have on your arms was from a smallpox vaccine. Because that vaccine was so successful, smallpox has been virtually wiped off the face of the earth. Therefore, there is no need to give the smallpox vaccine anymore. The hope is that the diseases we currently immunize against will soon also be wiped off the face of the earth too.

You may want to bring a favorite toy to the pediatrician and hand it to the baby right after her shot. A bottle or breast may also comfort the baby. Although you may be anxious about your baby getting shots, try to hide this anxiety from your baby and instead be available to comfort, stroke, and soothe her. You may want to discreetly hand the pediatrician the toy or a treat to give to the baby so your child associates some positive things with the pediatrician.

It is important for parents to keep precise records of their baby's immunizations. Your pediatrician will also keep a record.

Here is a list of diseases your child should be immunized against:

◆ Hepatitis B (HBV)
◆ Haemophilu influenza type b (HIB)
◆ Pertussis (whooping cough)
◆ Tuberculosis
◆ Measles
◆ Mumps
◆ Rubella (German measles)

Recommended Immunization/Test Schedule for the First Year*

Baby's Age	Immunization/Test
Birth	HBV (Hepatitis B vaccine)
1–2 months	HBV
2 months	DTP (diptheria, tetanus, pertussis)
	Polio
	HIB (Haemophilu influenza type B)
	HBV
4 months	DTP
	Polio
	HIB
6 months	DTP
	Polio
	HIB
	HBV
6–18 months	DTP
	Polio
	HIB
12 months	Tuberculosis, skin test for presence
15 months*	Measles, mumps, and rubella vaccines
	Polio
	DTP

*The immunization/test schedule may vary slightly from doctor to doctor.

After one year of age, your baby will need an additional series of shots for DTP, another dose of polio serum, and a single shot for mumps, measles, and rubella (MMR). There is also now a combination vaccine called Tetramune that immunizes against DTP and HIB in one shot.

Lifting Baby

Be aware that for a newborn baby, who felt so securely supported in amniotic fluid inside your uterus, being lifted and put down can feel like a scary roller-coaster ride. When adequate support isn't given to the head and neck, the baby will get a sensation of falling and you will see a startle reflex. Gradual and gentle movements are much better for the baby. So when lifting her, be sure to support the neck carefully with one hand and the lower back or buttocks with the other. If you pick up a baby who is lying facedown, put your hand under the chin and neck and place your other hand under the baby's bottom. Use your arms as a support. (Putting her in the cradle hold

Picking up and putting down your baby involve very similar techniques. Here, we are putting down an exhausted young man. The head, neck, and lower back are supported. Once baby's whole body is securely on the mattress, slip your hands out from under him.

after this will probably be best and easiest.) Bend your body toward the baby so she will have to spend less time in the air.

Nail Care

It is important to keep your baby's fingernails short and rounded so that she does not scratch herself too much. Furthermore, dirt can collect under long nails.

It is not advisable to clip the baby's nails because they will be left with a sharp edge. Instead of scissors, use an emery board to file down the nails and to round out any sharp edges. Emery boards are very safe and won't hurt the baby's skin like scissors probably would.

If you do use scissors, use special baby-nail scissors, which have rounded tips. Press the baby's finger pad away from the nail as you cut. It's a good idea to manicure the nails when the baby is fast asleep. If you put your finger in the baby's palm, she will instinctively wrap her fingers around your finger, making your job a little easier.

Babies' fingernails grow rapidly and are very thin and soft. Toenails grow quite slowly and often look ingrown, but this is usually nothing to worry about.

If your baby has a torn nail, put a baby Band-Aid over it until it grows long enough that you can trim and shape it.

Pediatric Visits: What to Expect

You will spend a good bit of time at your pediatrician's office as your child grows, but especially during your baby's first year. If you keep a record of your baby's developmental and behavioral milestones (which is an excellent idea), bring it along on your visit in case the doctor has any questions. Then add to this record what occurred during the doctor visit, including immunizations, weight, height, head circumference, and any other pertinent information.

One thing that your pediatrician will do at every visit is measure and plot your baby's weight, height, and head circumference. The pediatrician then uses a standard growth chart (like the ones on pages 421–24) to determine whether your child is growing proportionately (that is, if she is not too heavy or thin for her length, and if her head is not too big for the length of her body), and to determine how she compares to other babies her age in the United States.

Growth charts are derived from an assessment of thousands of boys and girls throughout the United States. The charts commonly in use today were created many years ago, so they may not be as accurate as we'd like them to be. Furthermore, they do not distinguish between babies who are bottle-fed and babies who are breast-fed, who typically experience different rates of growth in their first year.

Each growth chart is composed of seven curve lines, which have on one axis the age of the child and on the other axis the height or weight the child might be. The chart will allow the pediatrician to see how your child's growth ranks with that of other children in the United States. It is probably even more important to see if the child's weight, height, and head circumference are in proportion. Babies tend to decrease in the rate of growth after the third month of life. Remember that each baby grows at his or her own unique rate. Some children have a growth spurt and then slow down, others decrease in their growth only for a short time and then go up again, others have a continuous rise, while others' plotted growth charts may look like a staircase. Remember to look at yourself, your mate, and the physical characteristics of both of your family members' before you jump to conclusions about your baby's growth. As the old saying goes, "the apple doesn't fall far from the tree."

Here's what you can except during your baby's first year of visits to the pediatrician.

2 Weeks

At the 2-week visit your baby's doctor will:

◆ Measure and plot weight. Check to see that the baby has regained her birth weight. Babies lose about 10 percent of their birth weight during the first week of life, so at the 2-week visit your baby should weigh about as much as she did at birth.
◆ Measure and plot length.
◆ Measure and plot head circumference.
◆ Assess vision and hearing.
◆ Report on results of neonatal screening tests. If not given previously, screening tests will probably be given now.

2 Months

At the 2-month visit your baby's doctor will:

◆ Measure and plot weight.
◆ Measure and plot height.

◆ Measure and plot head circumference.
◆ Administer immunizations.
◆ Give a physical examination.
◆ Conduct a developmental assessment, including checking for head control, vision, hearing, etc.

Weight for Age–Boys

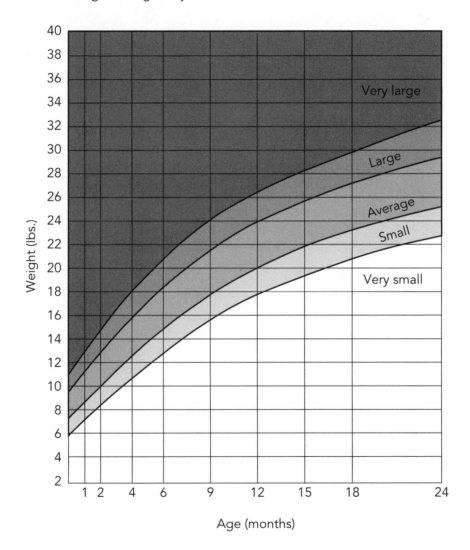

Adapted with permission from *My Health Diary*, 1992, by the U.S. Department of Health and Human Services, Health Resources and Services Administration, Washington, D.C.

Weight for Age–Girls

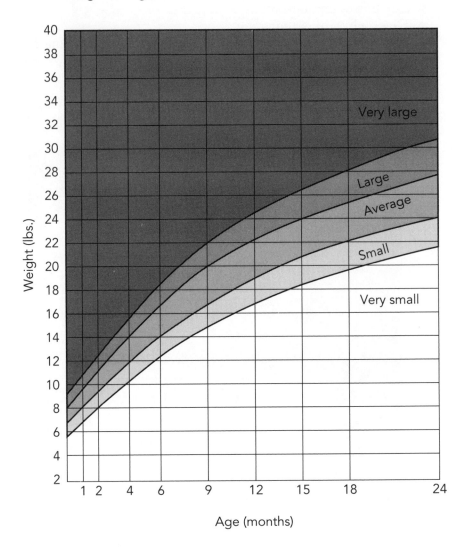

Age (months)

6 Months

At the 6-month visit your baby's doctor will:

◆ Measure and plot weight.
◆ Measure and plot height.
◆ Measure and plot head circumference.
◆ Administer immunizations.

Length for Age–Boys

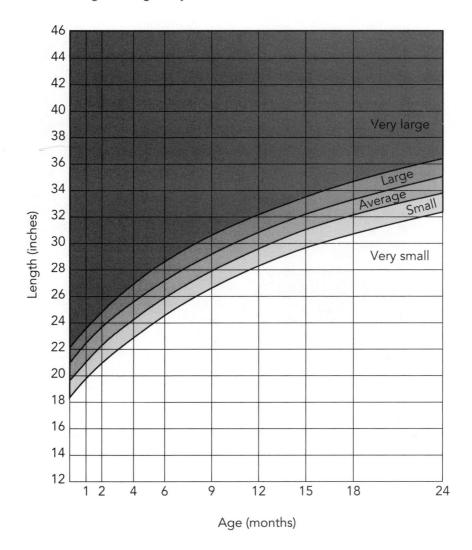

- ◆ Give a physical examination.
- ◆ Check mouth for arrival of teeth.
- ◆ Conduct a developmental assessment, looking for head control when sitting, vision, hearing, ability to reach for and grasp objects, to roll over and bear some weight on legs, social interaction, and vocalization.

Length for Age–Girls

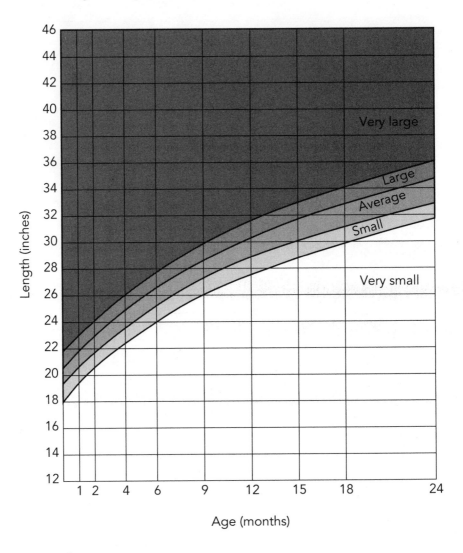

Age (months)

9 Months

At the 9-month visit your baby's doctor will:

◆ Measure and plot weight.
◆ Measure and plot height.
◆ Measure and plot head circumference.
◆ Administer immunizations.
◆ Give a physical examination.

◆ Conduct a developmental assessment, checking ability to sit independently, to pull up with or without help, to reach for and grasp objects, to rake at and pick up tiny objects, to look for a dropped or hidden object, to respond to his or her name, to recognize such words as "Mommy," "Daddy," etc., to enjoy some social games.

12 Months

At the 12-month visit your baby's doctor will:

◆ Measure and plot weight.
◆ Measure and plot length.
◆ Measure and plot head circumference.
◆ Administer immunizations.
◆ Give a physical examination.
◆ Check feet and legs when standing supported and unsupported.
◆ Conduct a developmental assessment: ability to sit independently, to pull up and to cruise or walk, to reach for and grasp objects, to pick up tiny objects with pincer grasp, to respond to his name, to feed himself, to use a cup, to cooperate in dressing, to recognize simple words, to play some social games.

Skin Care

Your newborn baby's skin may look dry and start to peel after a few days. Mothers usually think that this is dry skin, but it is actually vernix caseosa, which is the white, thick, cheesy substance that protected the fetal skin from amniotic fluid and helped your baby pass through the birth canal.

When the vernix peels off, the skin will resemble snakeskin. It takes about two weeks for the vernix to peel off. During that time, parents should *not* apply oils or lotions to the baby's skin because that will lock the vernix in place and actually prevent it from peeling off as it was meant to do. If it doesn't peel off, you'll end up with heat rash and other rashes to contend with. You should not use lotions and oils until after the second week of age. An exception to that rule is if the baby has cracking around the joints. These areas may tend to get cracks and sores, so you can put a little Vaseline there. But limit the Vaseline to those joint areas. After two weeks of age you can use lotion or oil on the baby's skin as necessary. See what works best for your baby. The thinner the lotion is, the more quickly it will get absorbed. Petroleum-based jellies last longer than lotions and creams.

Baby acne can appear on the scalp as well as on the face and shoulders. Baby acne is caused by hormones generated by babies of both sexes in the first weeks of life, making the oil gland overactive. It usually disappears by three or four months of age. Shampooing the scalp daily will help treat baby acne on the scalp.

◇ ◇ ◇ ◇ ◇ ◇ ◇ ◇ ◇ ◇ ◇ ◇ ◇ ◇ ◇ ◇ ◇

"I slept with the baby in my bed almost every night and I never rolled over on her or dropped her. My mother's instinct kept me from harming her; it was no problem."

◇ ◇ ◇ ◇ ◇ ◇ ◇ ◇ ◇ ◇ ◇ ◇ ◇ ◇ ◇ ◇ ◇

"I know a woman who propped her baby on pillows on her bed and went to take a phone call. The baby turned herself over, fell off the side of the bed facedown into the wastepaper basket, and asphyxiated."

◇ ◇ ◇ ◇ ◇ ◇ ◇ ◇ ◇ ◇ ◇ ◇ ◇ ◇ ◇ ◇ ◇

Sleeping

Babies tend to sleep a minimum of 14 hours during a 24-hour period. The *average* newborn baby sleeps 16½ hours each day in the first month of life. But this average means that some normal babies sleep 10 hours a day while others sleep as much as 23 hours. Do babies dream during all of that sleep time? Studies say they do. But what they dream about only the Lord knows.

Sleeping with their baby is the most natural thing in the world for parents to want to do. This desire comes out of an instinct for protection and bonding. However, there are safety hazards in terms of smothering the baby, crushing the baby, and dropping the baby off the bed. This problem has been an issue for parents since the beginning of time—literally. Book One of Kings tells us the story of a poor woman way back in 970 B.C. who smothered her baby accidentally. During the night this woman's son died, it says, "because she lay on him." If you know that something has the potential to harm your baby, you should take action to minimize it. After three months of age, the baby should have established a somewhat regular sleep pattern and needs to learn how to fall asleep by himself. The baby-in-our-bed habit can exacerbate separation anxiety, not to mention inhibiting your sexual relationship.

A newborn baby's body is about as pliable as pudding, so there is a lot of shifting when they sleep. Be sure that your crib bumpers or liners are securely fastened. Mothers like to use very soft pillows for their babies. Don't! Babies can barely lift their heads off a flat mattress, so imagine their faces sinking into a fluffy pillow—they will suffocate. Soft mattresses, soft quilts, and all pillows are hazardous to your baby. (See "SIDS Update" box.)

Most babies are not light sleepers and won't be awakened by typical household noises such as the television, the dishwasher, and the washing machine—in fact, these sounds might lull them into a deeper sleep. A sudden loud noise, however, will most likely wake up the baby with a fright. You may also notice that they will make sucking noises and other interesting sounds as they float into sleep—just like us. This is nothing to worry about.

Believe it or not, some babies start sleeping through the night at six weeks of age. At that point, their stomachs have stretched large enough so they can hold enough milk for six hours. Those six hours may not be the six hours that *you* want, however. Your baby may sleep from 9:00 at night until 3:00 in the morning or 11:00 at night until 5:00 in the morning. Getting by on less sleep than you used to may serve as your official induction into parenthood. Even the sleep-through-the-night babies don't really sleep through the *entire* night without waking up intermittently, especially in the first year. But hope is in sight. Your baby is likely to develop the habit of taking one or two long naps during the day as he gets older and expends more energy. This new level of activity should make it easier to put him to sleep at night, exhausted.

Whether you will go to your baby every time she cries during the night is a decision you and your mate must make. Be aware that what you do will set the stage for what the baby will begin to expect—and count on. If you have established a pattern of getting up for many months, you will have a mighty hard time breaking him of this expectation. Your best bet is to let the baby cry and fall asleep on his own for several nights; make every effort to deal with the crying without going to him—or at least without feeding him. Offer comfort by rubbing his back or patting him instead, if it upsets you too much to go cold turkey. The crying periods should become shorter and shorter each night, if you are consistent. Of course, if you hear a cry that sounds like he's in pain, you should go to him. (See "Crying," this chapter, for more on this.)

You can coax your baby into a reasonable sleep schedule by keeping her active during the day and developing a quiet "wind-down" routine that leads to sleep time at night. This way she can anticipate and know when sleep time occurs. That routine could be singing to her while you rock her, feeding her and talking softly to her in a dimly lit room, putting her in a baby swing, going for a short stroll, playing soft music as you rub her back, or any number of ideas like these. Rocking re-creates the motion your baby felt while in your uterus and will often put your baby to sleep. The routine for daytime naps should involve less fanfare than for nighttime sleep, so the baby can differentiate between the two. Early on, when there is little activity, the baby's naps should always be less than four hours. Otherwise she may sleep all day and stay up all night!

SIDS UPDATE

A recent recommendation from the American Academy of Pediatrics is not to put babies to sleep on their stomachs because this sleeping position has been identified as a risk factor for sudden infant death syndrome (SIDS), which affects Native American and black babies more than it affects whites (though the reasons may be largely socioeconomic). The theory is that if a baby sleeps facing downward on a surface that's soft and fluffy, he may asphyxiate. Laying your baby on his right side aids in digestion, especially good if he's just been fed because it takes pressure off of his stomach. Putting him on his back may cause choking.

Teeth

Signs that your baby is teething include chewing on her hands, an increase in drooling, and the need to bite on something. The age when infants start teething varies widely from baby to baby, though the typical time for the first tooth to erupt is at four to six months of age. Heredity plays a large part in this. Asking your parents when your teeth came in may help you see a pattern. The first tooth to appear is usually the lower middle incisor. The full set of primary teeth is typically all in by about two and a half years. Teeth usually push through in upper and lower pairs, with the lower pairs usually appearing before the upper pairs.

The spacing and position of primary teeth are no indication of how the permanent teeth will look, so don't start worrying about braces just yet. Girls usually start teething earlier than boys.

Not all children are distressed by teething, but many times it is a difficult period for babies. There may be swelling and inflammation of the gums, and sometimes fever. To soothe the baby and temporarily alleviate some of the pain, try rubbing the gums with ice, a Popsicle, a cool spoon, or a refrigerated, "liquid" teething ring. Don't be surprised if the discomfort your baby is experiencing upsets the daily routine that you have established. Once the teething period is over, your schedule should go back to normal.

You should start regularly cleaning your baby's gums as soon as the first teeth appear. A good way to clean baby's teeth and gums is to use a moistened, gauze-wrapped fingertip as a toothbrush. Once the baby has a full mouth of teeth, switch to a toothbrush.

When a tooth is injured, you should bring the child to a dentist.

Do not put the baby to bed with a bottle of anything other than pure water. Doing so may result in damage to the baby's teeth caused by the overgrowth of bacteria that eat the sugars in milk and juices.

Discuss the use of fluoride with your pediatrician. It can help your baby develop healthy teeth—even while they are still forming. He or she should know the fluoride concentration of the water in your community supply, and can also tell you if the formula you are using contains added fluoride.

HISTORICALLY SPEAKING ...

 Is your baby's teething making you grit your own teeth? Granny midwives, some of whom were very superstitious, had a "cure" for that: Tie the tooth of a hog—or a dog—on a string around the baby's neck to calm her down. Women of the African Baganda tribe believe that if a baby's upper teeth come in before the lower ones, it is a sign that the child will mistreat the mother in later life. *What We Can Learn:* Teething is a

mysterious thing to most parents. Babies cry for what seems like hours on end, and appear unconsoled by even the best of efforts. Surprisingly, though, teething is usually not very painful for the baby. Thus, most of the cries are not ones of real distress (as long as she has something to gnaw on), but rather they signal that the baby is tired or upset *in addition* to being perplexed about this strange, new feeling of teething. Often a long, comforting hug, rub, or lullaby will be just the solution.

Umbilical Cord

The plastic umbilical clamp that was placed on your baby to prevent bleeding from the navel will be left on until the cord has adequately dried, which usually takes about 36 hours. A medical professional will remove the clamp at the appropriate time. Remember that the cord has *no nerves at all* and touching and manipulating it causes *no* pain to your infant. Parents are often quite apprehensive about dealing with this area because it often looks infected—although it usually isn't—and might contain tinges of blood. It is imperative that you quickly overcome your fears because you must clean the area regularly and properly to avoid infection, prevent a very foul smell, and ensure that the cord falls off in a timely manner.

The umbilical stump will turn black a few days after birth and shrivel up and fall off anywhere between one and four weeks after birth, although it usually occurs about ten days after birth. At that time, you may notice what looks like a crater with pus on it. Don't be alarmed—it's just healing tissue.

Alcohol should be applied to the stump in order to keep it clean and to dry out the area. The drier the stump, the faster it will fall off. After it falls off, apply alcohol around the edges of the crater during each diaper change, using sterile cotton balls, sterile gauze pads, or alcohol pads. Do not put dressing over the area because it needs exposure to air to heal quickly. The navel should close up within three days.

Furthermore, parents should make sure that the baby's undershirt is not over the navel and that the diaper is turned down. These steps are very important to allow for drying of the navel and the umbilical stump.

Before the umbilical cord falls off, do not bathe your baby in a tub. Only sponge-bathe your baby at this time, and avoid wetting the navel when doing so.

If you are careful to clean the area with each diaper change and to fold the undershirt up and the diaper down, an infection in this area is very unlikely. Signs of an infection include significant redness, swelling, or tenderness around the base of the cord. Although redness could also be caused by the alcohol, seek medical attention at once since the umbilical cord leads deep into the body and can spread infection rapidly. Infection will most likely be treated with antibiotics. Also see your pediatrician if the navel has a puslike discharge or a very foul odor. (A slight odor is normal.)

After the umbilical cord stump has fallen off, you should continue to wipe the area around the navel with alcohol periodically for several days. Even after the cord has fallen off, it is not unusual for a tiny amount of fresh or dried blood to appear. If there is more than a tiny amount of bleeding, see your pediatrician. Once the umbilical cord has fallen off, you can submerge your baby in the tub.

Whether your baby has an "innie" or an "outie" belly button has nothing to do with the way the stump heals. It has nothing to do with the way the umbilical cord is cut, either, so don't blame your physician if your baby didn't get the type of belly button you were hoping for! Most outies flatten with time but may stay as they are if children stretch them (as many do).

HISTORICALLY SPEAKING . . .

 The practice of tying cloth or taping coins around the baby's navel gets its roots from Afro-Caribbean tradition. The thought was that if you covered up the navel you would hold in whatever was jutting out. Maybe this has something to do with the origins of the term *belly button,* named such because originally we had a hole in our bellies but now it's "buttoned" up!

Umbilical Hernias

Umbilical hernias tend to be more common in black babies than in babies of other races. An umbilical hernia is a space (between the two large bands of muscles that grow down the center of the baby's abdomen and encircle the navel) that persists even after the umbilical cord stump has fallen off. When the baby coughs or sneezes, or does anything that increases abdominal pressure, the belly tends to poke through this little hole, looking like a soft water balloon.

Parents tend to get very upset by umbilical hernias because this fairly long section of the belly can poke through the little hole; it can even be as long as a finger. Umbilical hernias are painless to the child, though. To avoid this poking out, parents from various cultures put coins in the hole or various types of tape or belly bands (a piece of cloth with ties) around the infant. However, these homemade remedies don't work and can actually cause problems. Belly bands go around the entire abdomen, and since babies use their abdomen to breathe, the band becomes like a girdle and restricts breathing. Parents have the whole weight of their culture encouraging them to do these things, but we encourage you to resist the pressure from relatives and friends to do something that is potentially harmful to your baby.

It is best to use no kind of treatment at all and to allow the hernia to close naturally. By the age of four or five years, the umbilical hernia usually closes on its own. Therefore, physicians usually do not repair the hernia surgically unless it hasn't closed by the time the child is five years of age. If the baby's umbilical hernia is so large that the pediatrician feels it's not going to close, or if there is a strong family history of hernias not closing, the physician may intervene earlier. Surgery to repair an umbilical hernia is simple and safe, although it is always best to avoid surgery if possible.

An "outie" belly button, by the way, is not a hernia. A hernia will expand when the baby cries while a normal outie will not.

CHAPTER 19

Your Baby's First Year: Month-by-Month

The first year of life is a period of rapid change in your baby's physical appearance, as well as in her social and intellectual development. It is also a period of major adjustment for the parents and siblings.

Before you read this section, we would like to emphasize two things. First, understand that each child develops skills and abilities at his or her own unique pace. Although the *sequence* of development is fairly universal, the *month* when each developmental milestone is reached differs from infant to infant. *Please don't be alarmed if your baby hasn't reached a developmental milestone during the month suggested in this book.* These are just to be used as general guidelines. Babies who were "late" speaking their first real word have just as much chance of becoming literary giants and television news commentators as the baby whose mother told everyone she's been saying "Mama" since the day they brought her home from the hospital. Resist the urge to compare your child with other children and reject promptings to speed up your baby's development to suit other people's—or your own—expectations. Be confident that your child has been fearfully and wonderfully made by God. Avoid making comparisons from one child to another, especially in front of the child, as this can hurt her self-esteem.

If you are truly concerned that your baby is not developing properly, certainly discuss this with your pediatrician. Keep a notebook record of your baby's milestones. This will be useful in discussions with your pediatrician, and when your child is older she may enjoy learning about her development. There are many things to look at before you, or your pediatrician, reach the conclusion that your baby isn't developing well. These include alertness, appearance, general disposition, eating habits, proportion of height and weight increases, and reaching basic developmental goals for her age range. If your baby is *consistently far behind* in these areas over a period of months, it may suggest a physical or developmental problem that should be further investigated by your pediatrician.

As parents, your job is to facilitate your child reaching her fullest potential. This will be hard to accomplish unless you keep committing yourselves to seeing things from the baby's point of view. By doing this, you will be much more in tune with your baby's growth and accompanying frustrations, and you will lay the foundation for a relationship that is based on understanding rather than the emotion of the moment.

The stimuli we recommend in this chapter will help facilitate you and your baby on your new journey as parent and child. Intellectual development can be promoted by permitting babies to be active, and to discover and invent on their own with your guidance. Select toys and activities for your baby that are appropriately matched to her developmental stage. A toy that's too challenging will either be frustrating or confusing to the baby, and something too simple will not stimulate his mind. Remember to give your baby toys that affirm her as a beautiful black child—right from the start. Our rich culture will be transmitted to your baby through your music, lullabies, stories, art, language, and what is and is not permitted.

Apart from potentially dangerous acts, it's okay to allow your infant to participate in what medical people call "developmental experimentation." Let her try something new if she shows an interest, even if you might think she's too young to do it. For example, if your baby is trying to stand, that means her legs are ready to attempt it. Don't discourage her in this by saying, "Oh, no, don't do that; you might fall."

By the same token, overstimulation can cause babies to become fussy, restless, and disinterested. They may even cry out of frustration. Watch for this and if it does occur, soothe her by holding and gently rocking her, or talking softly to her. Allow your baby to repeat activities and play with the same toy over and over. Practice and repetition give your child a way to "digest" newly acquired knowledge and to become skilled at the new activity.

Each month-by-month section of this chapter is divided into two parts: "This month your baby may be able to . . ." and "How you can stimulate your baby this month." Some months will have more information than others because there may be fewer major changes expected during a particular month.

The First Month

After the first 24 hours of life, your baby will be more alert and more willing to look around, as well as progressively more demanding. She is sensitive to touch all over and is sensitive to how she is being held. A young infant can actually sense if the person holding her is anxious or angry, and will react accordingly.

The senses of hearing and smelling are well developed at birth. Vision is not as well developed. At first, your baby's vision will be blurry, but not long after birth she will be able see your face while you hold her in your arms and can see distinct patterns and brightly colored objects up to about 8 inches away. They see most clearly at a distance of about 8 to 10 inches, so be certain to stay within this range when you want her to perceive an object or a face. Your newborn will stare at objects, faces, or into space, but he or she won't yet reach for anything, so don't be disappointed.

Your baby was born with a number of reflex actions, which, along with her five senses, are the sole ways she can experience the world around her. Reflexes form the basis for early mental development. At birth, these are isolated, underdeveloped, and uncoordinated. (See "Reflexes," in chapter 17, page 370, for more detail.) For example, if you step on a tack, you will automatically pick up your foot. If that happened to a newborn, she would feel pain, but would not be coordinated enough to know what to do in response to that pain.

Talk to your baby while she rests on your chest—she can feel the vibrations of your voice, which will be very comforting. Mothers are particularly satisfying to the baby because the baby knows the rhythm of her mother's breathing and heartbeat, and may actually recognize the tonality of voice. The best comfort you can give a baby is to try to reproduce the womb. Bundling snugly and rhythmic movements that reproduce the mother's heartbeat are very comforting.

The baby's muscles will be springlike until she is one month of age. If you straighten her arms or legs or open her clenched fists, they will quickly spring back to their original flexed position.

Although we can talk in generalities, every baby has his or her own personality. You can see some personality distinctions soon after birth. However, do not expect your baby's temperament during her first two weeks of life to stay the same as she ages. Your newborn baby still does not even understand that there are objects and people separate from herself and is struggling to figure things out. She doesn't know where she ends and where the rest of the world begins. For example, you'll notice that a baby might pull her hair so hard that it hurts, then cry as if someone else has hurt her. She doesn't realize that *she* hurt *herself.* Take comfort in this knowledge if you have a very fussy baby at this stage; she is just trying to adjust to life in a brand-new world.

This month your baby may be able to

◆ Briefly lift her head while lying on her stomach
◆ Mouth and suck her hands
◆ Squirm and kick
◆ Mimic your changing facial expressions
◆ Smile briefly when she's happy
◆ Focus on a face or object up to a foot away
◆ Grasp objects firmly
◆ Follow an object moved in an arc about 6 inches above her face
◆ Recognize and react to familiar voices by moving her arms and legs and vocalizing

How you can stimulate your baby this month

◆ Talk to your baby at every opportunity. This is a very important part of comforting your baby, and in promoting listening and talking skills—it's never too early to start. Although the baby cannot understand what you are saying, even at this early age your baby can pick up on the tone of your voice and your expressions. While you are doing housework and your baby is lying awake in her crib, talk or sing to your baby.
◆ Play music (try African or Caribbean rhythms) to stimulate baby's hearing.
◆ Make eye contact—very important to stimulate your baby's intellectual development. At this young age you will find that your baby will stare at your face for long moments and will also seemingly stare into space. She is curious about every little movement of your face when you are feeding her, for instance,

from your eyebrows to your lips. She is trying to identify you and identify *with* you.

◆ Select muted, yet contrasting patterns for your baby's crib sheets and crib toys. Did you know that even adults cannot focus on blue and red stripes at the same time? Our eyes have to move up and down, from one color to the other, in order to take them in. So imagine how easy it would be for a baby to become agitated by too many bright colors in the environment where she spends most of her time. Most African patterns make good choices for baby furnishings, giving her contrast and color without being overwhelming. Studies show that babies react to patterns with clearly defined edges and high contrast, so black-and-white-checked or -striped objects and items with contrasting shapes or human faces on them will be great for baby's mental stimulus.

◆ Stimulate her visually by pointing to a mobile or a moving toy.

WHY IS MY BABY CRYING?

It's the only way she can communicate

Here are some common reasons:

Wet, needs changing
Bored, wants to be played with
Hungry, needs to be fed
Has gas, needs to be burped
Uncomfortable, over- or underdressed
Tired, needs a wind-down to sleep
In pain, needs attention
Lonely, needs to be held close (try holding her over your heart)
Scared, senses tension in you or your husband
Frustrated, having difficulty adjusting to a new environment
Agitated, too much noise or excitement around her

The Second Month

Babies at this age begin to recognize their mother's voice and know their mother's touch and handling. They also begin to seek and respond to attention by smiling, making sounds, and actively moving their arms and legs. Your baby's personality should become evident now. Observe her and try to determine whether she is quiet or driven, enjoys gentle stimulation or screams for attention, sleeps lightly or long and deep. Making constant mental notations about your baby's personality will help you care for her better. Knowing and accepting your baby's temperament, body type, and other habits will also give you armor against the people who inevitably express that she isn't this or doesn't seem to be that.

This may also be the month you say good-bye to your baby for a while if you are returning to work. Make absolutely sure the sitter will do things for your baby *the way you do them.* Your sitter must continue to help her grow socially, physically, and mentally in your absence or the baby may suffer intellectually. Invest the time with the sitter to introduce the baby to this new person and to show the sitter how you'd like her cared for. Commit yourself to mothering your baby when you come home; offer her your undivided attention consistently each evening for a period of time. See chapter 6, "Getting Your 'House' In Order" for details.

This month your baby may be able to

◆ Lift his head farther up while lying on his stomach
◆ Turn his body from side to side
◆ While lying facedown, support himself with one arm straight out to his side and the other arm above his head
◆ Relate people with events (i.e., Dad with being held up high)
◆ Cycle his arms and legs
◆ Begin to follow some movements with his eyes
◆ Smile in response to your smile
◆ Follow an object with his eyes in a half-circle about 6 inches above his face
◆ Communicate in ways other than crying, such as cooing
◆ Have a more controlled grasp of objects
◆ Sleep through the night feeding

In partnership with Olmec, the pioneer in ethnically designed toys and dolls, PlaySkool has created the Kids of Color line of toys featuring brown faces and traditional African Kente patterns (1-800-PLAYSKL). Kids of Color Grabber Rattles shown here.

How you can stimulate your baby this month

◆ To develop visual tracking, try hanging a brightly colored red or yellow ring no more than 8 inches in front of your baby's eyes. In the first month or so, don't expect your baby to do anything more than glance at it briefly. Eventually, your baby will begin to follow the ring with her eyes as you slowly move it back and forth.

◆ Put a rattle in your baby's hand. She will quickly grasp it reflexively (the way she will grasp anything put in her hand) before dropping it. In the coming months, she will be able to grasp it for a period of time and actually take interest in it before she drops it.

◆ Hang a mobile over her crib. Choose one that looks interesting from the baby's angle, lying flat. Make sure it is securely attached so it won't fall on the baby.

◆ Take the baby outside for a stroll in her carriage. Make sure she is appropriately dressed for the weather. A gentle breeze on her face, birds chirping, tree leaves, and the motion of the carriage are all stimulating to the baby. And a nice walk will be good for you, too! This is a great way to incorporate your baby into a postpartum walking routine (for more, see chapter 9, "Your Physical Tank").

◆ Present your baby with various objects of different textures to hold and mouth. Make sure they are all nontoxic and are too big to choke on.

The Third Month

This month your baby may begin to coordinate various reflexes with one another. For example, she may grasp a rattle *and* suck on it. This is a big graduation for her; make sure you praise and encourage her. The three-month-old is more alert, active, and responsive than before. You may notice that his cries for a change, to be fed, or to be played with are now distinguishable (thank goodness!), though it may take longer for your husband to make the distinction if he does not spend as much time with the baby as you do. His pattern of sleeping has probably been established and he may sleep for stretches as long as 10 or 11 hours. How often you respond to him when he cries in the middle of the night will set the pace for many months to come.

Babies begin to recognize that their hands are a part of them and will amuse themselves just by watching them.

This month your baby may be able to

◆ While on her stomach, raise herself up on her forearms and hold her head up
◆ Hold a rattle for a longer period of time
◆ Smile spontaneously
◆ Sit with support for a few minutes
◆ Use both hands to grasp objects
◆ Put her fingers in her mouth, although at this age this behavior is usually accidental, not intentional
◆ Follow an object in an arc with her eyes; look toward a sound
◆ Show readiness for introduction of solid foods by being fussy after a feeding. Be sure to do this gradually, one food at a time; baby cereal is a good first choice.

How you can stimulate or soothe your baby this month

◆ Dangle colored toys about 8 inches away from the baby, moving them gently from left to right. Your baby will follow the toy with her eyes.
◆ Continue to place a rattle in your baby's hand. Watch each day for your baby to grasp the rattle longer and longer.

- ◆ Make efforts to have eye contact with her several times each day.
- ◆ Respond to her needs quickly, comfort her (instruct your sitter to do so also). This will help her handle the stress of growing. She will know that there is always protection and help nearby.

Solid Foods for Your Baby* (4 to 6 months)	Prepared Baby Food
5–8 tablespoons of cereal (rice, barley, oats, or mixed)	$\frac{1}{2}$ oz. (dry)
2 oz. of puréed fruit	$\frac{1}{2}$ jar
2 oz. fruit juice (fortified with vitamin C)	$\frac{1}{2}$ jar
2 oz. vegetable (yellow, green)	$\frac{1}{2}$ jar

*Amounts are general guidelines; respond to your baby's individual needs and consult with your pediatrician.

The Fourth Month

This month you may get exhausted pulling your baby's hand out of her mouth. Don't bother. Putting hand and toys to mouth is an important step in developing coordination and body awareness, and a natural way for babies at this age to explore the world. Besides, soon she may be putting her entire fist in her mouth! Just be sure to wash her hands when they get too dirty.

The baby is also becoming more agile. This is wonderful—but watch out. This also means she can work her way to the edge of the bed even when you leave only for a minute, and can fall off a changing table in an instant.

You may be overjoyed to see that some bottom teeth are budding out, though it's perfectly normal if they don't appear until much later (up to 12 months).

This month your baby may be able to

- ◆ Use both eyes together, giving her a better perception of depth; she will also see colors more brilliantly than before
- ◆ Follow an object moved in an arc for 180 degrees about 6 inches above face when dangled in front of her as she lies on her back
- ◆ Roll from back to side or from stomach to side or back

- Sit supported, with head steady, for 10 or 15 minutes
- Laugh aloud
- Lift her head up 90 degrees while lying on stomach
- Follow you with her eyes as you walk around the room
- Purposefully put her hand in her mouth, demonstrating increased coordination
- Respond to your interaction by smiling, cooing, or chuckling, as well as waving her arms and legs
- Look at and play with her hands
- Sleep through the night
- Reach for, grasp, hold, and release objects with her hand
- Skip the night feeding
- Splash when given a bath

How you can stimulate your baby this month

- While your baby is lying on her back, gently pull her up to a sitting position by the wrists. She should show ability to help pull herself up, controlling her head and neck.
- Exercise her by lifting her legs up and moving them from side to side at the hip and bending her legs at the knees to encourage range of motion.
- Offer simple toys that she can move around, bend, and otherwise manipulate.
- Show her her reflection in a mirror.
- Take her outside for strolls so she can get used to the world.

DID YOU KNOW ...

In some parts of Europe, babies are potty-trained at four months! They are fed while sitting on the potty. The theory is that the natural gastro-colic reflex—which gives us the urge to go when we eat—will encourage them to have a bowel movement. Don't try this at home, though—most pediatricians agree that it is a very compulsive and manipulative method that could have long-term negative effects on the baby. Approximately two years of age is the proper time to potty-train. Around this time, you will probably observe your baby instinctively assuming a squatting position when she has to "go." This is her way of telling you she's ready.

The Fifth Month

Get ready—this is usually a very active month. The baby will wake up early and be anxious to test out her new motor skills each day. She will not happily stay in her crib too long before wanting to be "rescued." She may also begin to show a disinterest in breastfeeding. You may feel some sadness at your baby's newfound physical competence. Don't worry—she still relies heavily on you and will for a while to come. Facilitate her new independence; it will really help her grow. Your baby's weight may plateau this month or she may lose a little weight due to her new mobility. If your baby is heavy for her age (16 pounds or more), encourage more vigorous activity—not more feeding.

If your baby has had steady, loving interaction with your mate since birth, she may show a strong desire to make physical contact with him now. Psychologists consider this attachment very important to the baby's healthy growth. Again, encourage and facilitate your husband's bond with the baby as much as possible.

Your baby now can reach for objects with two hands and may also roll over easily from the stomach to the back. Her eyes, fingers, mouth, and body are developing a coordination that she is delighted with—but one that may cause you some trepidation, especially because *everything* will be grabbed and put in that mouth! This is a good time to make certain that your home is child-safe. (See chapter 6 "Getting Your 'House' in Order," for details.)

The baby may begin to show attachment to one special doll, toy, blanket, or other object that brings comfort. Sometimes it is just a small piece of soft cloth or a length of satiny ribbon. She may carry the object everywhere and refuse to be detached from it, even for a moment. No need to be alarmed or embarrassed—in fact, you should be pleased. Your baby realizes that she must be separated from you occasionally and has found something to comfort her through those times. She has actually found a resourceful way to help herself cope with the frustrations of growing up.

This month your baby may be able to

- ◆ Hold his head and torso steady when sitting propped
- ◆ Smile in the mirror and realize that he is separate from his mirror image
- ◆ Roll over one way
- ◆ Be alert and ready to play and explore for longer stretches
- ◆ Reach for an object (like a ring) and grasp it quickly; has good aim
- ◆ Open his hands and eyes wide when trying to reach something
- ◆ Squeal in delight and whine if upset
- ◆ Babble and make vowel sounds such as "Ooh" and "Ee"
- ◆ Raise his chest with arms while lying on stomach
- ◆ Laugh when you play peek-a-boo
- ◆ Clutch you when you hold him

How you can stimulate your baby this month

- ◆ Starter blocks are good for this age to help him learn how to use his hands. Choose ones small enough to be picked up easily with one hand. This encourages thumb-and-forefinger grasping, which he will master later on. Colored blocks with contrast will hold your baby's attention longer.
- ◆ Expose him to different textures and shapes so he can learn concepts like "smooth," "rough," "furry," or "slippery."
- ◆ Help him learn to roll from his back to his stomach by practicing with him.
- ◆ Respond to his attempts at verbal expression. Feedback is important to early speech development.

Solid Foods for Your Baby* (6 to 9 months)	Prepared Baby Food
8–10 tablespoons of cooked cereal (rice, barley, oats, or mixed)	1 oz. (dry)
2–4 oz. of pureed fruit	½–1 jar
2–4 oz. fruit juice (fortified with vitamin C)	½–1 jar
2–4 oz. vegetable (yellow, green)	½–1 jar

*Amounts are general guidelines; respond to your baby's individual needs and consult with your pediatrician.

The Sixth Month

This can be an exciting month for parents, as some babies begin to enjoy "standing up" while supported by an adult (though they are not really ready to stand alone yet). Your baby's sense of direction is becoming more sophisticated. Changing and dressing her will become more of a fight as she learns to twist and roll all over the place. She will also be constantly experimenting with words, and may "call" you just for practice and to hear her own voice. This is a great sign of language growth and mental development. She will practice her hand-eye coordination by grasping for anything within her reach. She is learning that she can influence the objects in her environment and will practice this by throwing just about everything off her high chair. Through this experimentation, she is also understanding that things don't disappear forever once they fall on the ground. Pick up things for her as many times as you can tolerate; it is really helping her grow. At this age, she may show more interest in checking out her surroundings than in people or toys.

As the baby develops more physical prowess, she may want to stop breast-feeding and will push away the breast to tell you so. Don't feel rejected if this happens! This means that you've done your job well. Your baby will probably still need and desire the physical closeness that went along with nursing for a long while to come.

Hopefully, she will sleep through the night by this month, if she hasn't done so already (especially if you are helping, not hindering, her accomplishing this feat). Very active babies, however, may just need less sleep than quieter ones.

This month your baby may be able to

◆ Sit without much help
◆ Follow most objects with her eyes, even when they are fast-moving
◆ Play with a toy for an extended period of time
◆ Creep on her belly, using her feet and arms to move (usually backward)
◆ Make funny faces
◆ Begin to say some form of "Dada" or "Mama" and other vowel-consonant combinations.
◆ Play peek-a-boo with you, covering her eyes with her hands
◆ Transfer things from one hand to the other
◆ Bite you, if you're nursing
◆ Show likes and dislikes
◆ Hold and drink from a baby cup (with handles)
◆ Look at things upside down
◆ Sleep through the night

How you can stimulate your baby this month

◆ Encourage her to play peek-a-boo by asking, "Where's the baby?" This game is actually helping her learn how to develop humor and memory.
◆ If you are bottle-feeding, let her hold her own bottle if she wants to, but maintain physical contact; she will be soothed by your touch even if she seems to want to be independent.
◆ Support her with both hands as you put her in a standing position; this will later evolve into her standing while holding on to a table with both hands and eventually, with one hand.
◆ Talk to the baby using regular, clearly stated words, repeated again and again. She will usually babble after you talk to her, showing that she is listening and learning about sound.
◆ Give her pieces of paper (nontoxic) to play with. She will enjoy learning texture differences by bending and rolling the paper and learning the various sounds paper makes when it's crinkled.
◆ Encourage interaction with older children (supervised, of course). This is very valuable for her social development now.
◆ Continue to play different types of music for the baby. Encourage and praise her as she sways, bounces, and attempts to sing.

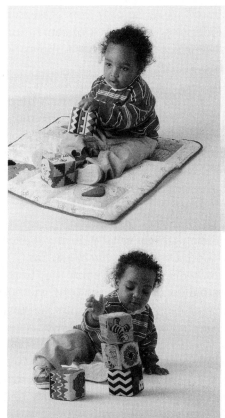

The Infant Activity Quilt, Soft Ice Cream Van and Soft Infant Blocks from Cultural Toys, (612) 339-1254, are boldly patterned, innovative toys that reflect our cultural richness and encourage baby to exercise her manual dexterity.

The Seventh Month

Motor development is the mark of this month. Your baby has discovered that there is a whole new world out there to explore now that he can sit up, twist, turn, and possibly stand up. You and your mate will need to keep a much closer eye on him than before.

Be very aware of your personal habits and what comes out of your mouth; your baby is watching much of what you say and do—and *how* you say and do things. She will imitate your behavior. Make sure she isn't picking up bad habits that you'll have to undo later.

Interestingly, just as she learns about and experiments with serious movement, she may begin to get clingy. Why? Because she now realizes that you can move away from her at a much faster pace than she can follow behind you and may be terrified at the idea of separation. Be aware of this and offer empathy. It is a sign of a healthy relationship that your baby wants to be near you. Research indicates that babies who don't undergo some degree of separation anxiety are indifferent about the absence of their parents and may be learning much too soon not to rely on them.

Don't be surprised if a baby who was standing up supported goes back to crawling for a while. It is an indication that she isn't quite ready for the stand-up world and needs the security of the ground a bit more before she ventures up again—as she definitely will. You may deal more with the baby's frustration at not being able to do everything she wants to this month. Comfort, assistance, and tolerance on your part will be particularly needed now.

Now that your baby is spending more time sitting up, he will probably discover his genitals. Girls may pull or poke their vaginas and boys may grab and play with their penises, usually during diaper changes, which may result in an erection. *Do not treat this like a crisis.* To your baby, genitals just seem like newly discovered toys that are always there to play with. It is perfectly normal behavior and the baby will not hurt herself or himself. If you get upset each time this occurs and say, "No!" you may be setting the stage for your child to have a skewed sense of her body in later years. Also, your negative reaction may only encourage the baby to do it more often. Babies who are in very dull, unstimulating environments may play with their genitals past the exploratory stage, as it may be the only fun or interesting thing they find to do. Make sure that you are providing your baby with enough interesting outlets for her to grow and experiment with all her new abilities.

Your baby may lose a little more weight now, especially if she's crawling. It's nothing to worry about—muscle tissue is being developed and fat is being burned. (Just what we'd like for ourselves, right?) Don't get bogged down with notions that fat babies equal healthy babies, and don't force-feed her. Avoid "tricking" the baby into opening her mouth to be fed—this is not only unkind but it can backfire when the baby catches on to the "trick" and rebels.

This month your baby may be able to

◆ Feed herself a cookie or cracker
◆ Eat strained, mashed, and other soft foods
◆ Begin trying to crawl, using mostly her arms and shoulders
◆ Get herself to stand
◆ Associate familiar sounds with occurrences that make her happy or sad. For example: (happy) the door opening means Daddy or Mommy has come home; the sound of dishes and silverware

means dinner is coming soon; (sad) when Daddy or Mommy puts on a coat, he or she is going to leave soon.

How you can stimulate and soothe your baby this month

◆ Place a favorite toy just out of reach of your baby to encourage her to move toward it. She may roll, creep, crawl, or do her own combination of the three—which is perfectly fine.
◆ Give her two things to hold, for instance a wooden spoon and a plastic bowl. The baby will enjoy exploring the possibilities of coordinated hand movement.
◆ Give her blocks of various sizes so she can learn the differences between them.
◆ Include her in conversations so she feels recognized.
◆ Comfort her by telling her you'll be back when you leave the room and communicate with her from the other room you're in. This will take practice as she may cry at first no matter what you do.
◆ Allow her to try to feed herself by giving her small bits of appropriate foods to experiment with (dry cereal; diced, cooked carrots; soft toast; etc.). Feeding may take a long time this way, but it's important that you let the baby explore, touch, look at, and smell her food so she learns more about her environment and experiences the joy of eating.

The Eighth Month

Your baby continues to improve her ability to move around and will need more room to move about now. Space is an important thing to provide now so she can further develop her motor skills. You don't have to have a big house with a sprawling backyard to have a well-developed baby, but confining her to a playpen or crib at this point will be unsuitable—and she will tell you so. She simply needs room to play around safely. It may mean moving some furniture or taking her outside to play more often.

Your baby will probably experiment with standing up and getting back down into a sitting position as her coordination is still being developed. You can help her by standing her up and guiding her back down several times. If feasible, putting down a rug will help cushion any body parts that may get banged during this learning process.

Diane Allford, Allford/Trotman Associates, Atlanta.

Baby is also distinguishing noises and the actions that produce them. For example, when she rattles a plastic jar with one object in it she notices that it sounds different than when the jar is full of objects.

Sleeping—or rather, getting her to sleep—can become a chore if you don't assertively establish a routine. If you haven't already, create "wind-down time" when you feed, change, and rock the baby for a while in a quiet setting to give her a nice transition into bed-time. Resist going to the baby after you've put her down to bed, even if she calls you. It will established a bad habit that puts the baby in control instead of you. Daytime naps may get shorter and your baby may naturally go from needing two naps to needing only one.

This month your baby may be able to

◆ Sit without support
◆ Look for a dropped object
◆ Crawl adeptly, possibly backwards and forwards
◆ Climb
◆ Hold two toys at a time, one in each hand
◆ Pass an object from one hand to the other
◆ Turn in the direction of a voice
◆ Take a step forward while standing supported
◆ Show keen interest in touching and examining your faces and possibly those of others

Solid Foods for Your Baby* **(9 to 12 months)**	**Prepared** **Baby Food**
8–10 tablespoons of cereal (rice, barley, oats, or mixed)	1 oz. (dry)
6–12 oz. of puréed fruit	1–2 jars
4–8 oz. fruit juice (fortified with vitamin C)	1–2 jars
2.5 oz. puréed meat or other iron-containing protein source (i.e., 1 egg)	1 jar
6 oz. vegetable (yellow, green)	1 jar

*Amounts are general guidelines; respond to your baby's individual needs and consult with your pediatrician.

How you can stimulate your baby this month

◆ Help her experiment with upside-down and right-side-up by turning pictures upside down and pointing them out to her.
◆ Let her explore your face with her hands and show her that she has a nose, too, by touching her nose, mouth, ears, etc., and saying the word to her.
◆ Encourage her interest in "putting things in" and "taking things out" by giving her household items like a plastic jar and several used thread spools (or buy a toy with a similar concept) so she can practice.
◆ Encourage her to get the toy she likes herself instead of bringing it to her. This will help her to enjoy her own accomplishments.
◆ Toys that involve simple cause-and-effect will be helpful now. For example: If I pull the string, I make the doggie walk.

The Ninth Month

There may not be much exciting new activity this month as compared to the two previous ones. The baby will continue to work on his motor skills, memory, and mental capabilities.

You may see what looks like regression in some areas. He may show signs of separation anxiety again, something you thought he got over months ago. He may cry uncontrollably when you have to go to work and suddenly dislike the baby-sitter he's had for months. Take heart in the fact that he is (a) likely to calm down and play happily shortly after you've left, and (b) may be actually less distressed than he led you to believe with his tantrum. However, know that the almost-walking stage is determined to be the worst phase to have to leave your baby for long stretches at a time. Some doctors have indicated that separation at this time may have a lasting negative effect on the child, making him anxious and overly demanding in the future. To counter any possible ill effects from separation, be sure to cuddle and talk softly to the baby for a little while before you leave; this can be similar to the "wind-down" you have at baby's bedtime. The closeness derived from this special routine will be a great comfort to him once you're gone, though he may still cry when you leave. Encourage the sitter not to approach the baby until you're finished, and even then it should not be done with overenthusiasm to distract him from your leaving.

Your baby may also become fearful of doing things you thought he mastered months ago, such as climbing on a chair, taking a bath, or playing with other children. Be quick to comfort and reinforce your baby as he goes through this awkward stage.

This month your baby may be able to

- ◆ Make an effort to retrieve a toy that is out of reach
- ◆ Point to things that he wants
- ◆ Pull himself up into a standing position (with the help of nearby furniture)
- ◆ Eat chunkier table foods
- ◆ Look for a dropped object
- ◆ Put one block on top of another
- ◆ Grasp a tiny object, like a marble, with thumb and finger (pincer grasp)

◆ Understand and respond to one or two words
◆ Pass an object from one hand to the other
◆ Crawl quickly

How you can stimulate your baby this month

◆ At this age your child will probably begin showing an interest in picture books, so be sure to have plenty on hand and read them through with her, discussing what is in the pictures.
◆ Praise her when she interacts well with a stranger; this is a big accomplishment for her social growth.
◆ When she points to something, tell her what it is; say the word over a few times. Soon you will need to interpret for her less and less as she grows her vocabulary.
◆ Continue to include her in your conversations with other adults by gesturing to her or talking to her when she babbles. Also, feed her at the dinner table when you and your husband eat, instead of feeding her earlier, so she feels like part of the family and can learn adaptive behavior.
◆ Introduce your baby to another baby her age or older to encourage her socially.
◆ Play games that involve her using her hands and fingers with dexterity, such as patty-cake and ball tossing.

DID YOU KNOW ...

Baby girls tend to be more attentive, talk or attempt to talk more, and show more advanced development and consistent behavior than baby boys.

The Tenth Month

This month you may observe whether the right or left will be your baby's dominant hand. You may notice that she will use one hand mainly for carrying things and the other for touching and exploring.

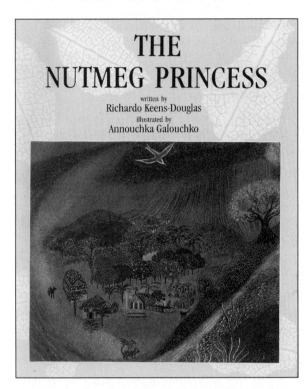

Culturally satisfying books will help build your child's self-esteem. She will begin to see herself reflected positively in books, pictures, and videos that feature black children. Grenada-born author Richardo Keens-Douglas's richly colored *The Nutmeg Princess* (Annick Press Ltd., Ontario, Canada, 1992). is a good choice. It is based on the folkloric "nancy stories" told in many parts of the West Indies. Golden Books in cooperation with Essence Communications, Inc., offer an entire series of beautiful books for black infants and children.

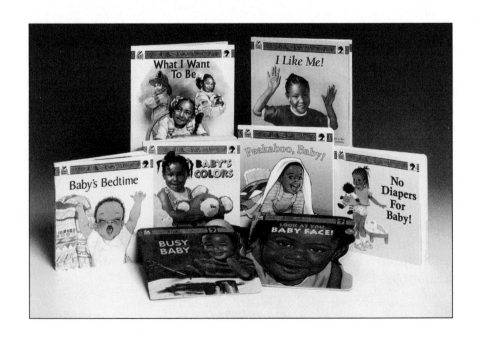

Your baby will begin to understand the "object concept," which refers to the belief that an object (person, place, or thing) will continue to exist even though she is not in direct perceptual contact with it. That is scientific terminology to explain that your baby now realizes that just because a toy fell off the edge of the table, it isn't gone forever. As a result, he will begin searching manually for hidden or fallen objects, knowing that the object continues to exist even when he can't see it, and that it can be retrieved. This applies to people, too. Babies will cry at the "loss" of a parent when he leaves the room, but as he keeps hearing his voice and seeing him return later, he realizes that people can, in fact, come back again. He is also learning how to gauge distance more accurately.

If you have a son, this is a great time for him to deepen his bond with his father, as he is beginning to identify himself as a male. Boys, and many girls, will love it when Daddy picks them up and plays rough-and-tumble. Boys really need the interaction with a male adult now, as they have probably spent most of their time with their mother or another female. Rough-housing—bouncing, jumping, spinning, rolling, and generally just having a lot of fun—is the key way that men bond with their babies, and is fine to do at this age. Be sure to encourage it!

This month your baby may be able to

◆ Repeat "Mama," "Dada," and one or two other words, indiscriminately
◆ Wave bye-bye
◆ Obey basic commands
◆ Help dress himself
◆ Pull himself up to a standing position from a sitting position
◆ Climb on chairs
◆ Walk with support; may walk sideways holding on to furniture with hands
◆ Understand and obey some simple commands (like "Go get the toy")
◆ Repeat the word *no*, without really knowing what he means
◆ Imitate your facial expressions—and your habits—good and bad
◆ Remember where hidden objects are and search for them
◆ Finger-feed himself a meal
◆ Drink from a cup, holding the handles
◆ Show dominance in one hand

◆ Push objects from side to side
◆ Show appreciation when music is played

How you can stimulate or soothe your baby this month

◆ Give your baby simple commands and see if he understands and obeys. For example, "Go get Mommy's shoe."
◆ Help your baby learn how to point to and how to recognize body parts using a favorite doll or animal. Point to the face of the doll and ask him, "Where is dolly's nose (eyes, teeth and so on)?" Then, when he understands this, ask him "Where is your nose?"
◆ Offer playthings that require baby to push a button, pull a cord, dial a play telephone, turn on a play switch, or other ways to use individual fingers or pincer grasp (index finger and thumb).
◆ Help your baby to learn tenderness by encouraging him when he shows sensitivity or attachment to a favorite doll or stuffed animal.

The Eleventh Month

By the eleventh month your baby will really be testing limits and resisting them as well. At the same time, she will be seeking your approval. Remember to be firm and consistent with the limits you impose. Your baby will be more active in helping herself get dressed by holding up her hands to take a top off or putting a foot in her shoe.

She may begin to associate qualities with things and behaviors with people. For instance, when you say, "What does the doggie do?" she might go, "Woof, woof"; when you ask, "Where does the birdie go?" she could point overhead. This makes for fun times spent playing such learning games with the baby.

Your precious baby will also develop her temper—and yours—to new heights right about now. She says no often and shakes her head, when she doesn't really mean no at all. She is also experimenting with the limits of *your* "No," not because she is a bad child, but because she is learning so many new capabilities at once that she needs to know where the boundaries are. She is unwittingly asking you to set the boundaries that *you* know are for her own safety and moral development. As her parent, it is your duty to train her in obedience. Experts agree that you should not give in to a temper tantrum by giving the child what she is whining for. One way to handle it is to simply ride it out, neither punishing nor comforting the child; the tantrum may very well cease as the child sees that he isn't able to manipulate you this way. Another method is to hold the screaming child during the tantrum, offering words of comfort but still refusing to give her what she wants. Diversion is often an effective way to quell a tantrum; the baby is taken away from the room where the thing she wants is and is introduced to something else.

Whatever your posture in these situations, stand firm in it: Babies can sense insecurity a mile away.

This month your baby may be able to

◆ Crawl well; don't be surprised if your baby crawls better backwards than forwards
◆ Stand much of the time, without assistance
◆ Squat or stoop
◆ Hold on to the edge of a crib, couch, or chair and walk along it
◆ Understand the meaning of "Mama" and "Dada"
◆ Understand the meaning of "Bye-bye," and may imitate a wave with her hand
◆ Drink from a cup when the parent holds it
◆ Pick up tiny objects with thumb and finger (pincer grasp)
◆ Understand the world *no* (looks sheepish when found guilty— or even before)
◆ Use two hands simultaneously to do different things, such as hold a cup and bring a spoon to her mouth
◆ Climb up the stairs (though it's harder to climb down)
◆ Get into a sitting position from lying on her stomach

How you can stimulate or soothe your baby this month

◆ Encourage her interest in climbing stairs by showing her how to come down: backwards on her bottom. You will probably have to model this for her many times before she gets it. Of course, always supervise your baby in a stairwell.
◆ Practice walking with her, holding both her hands; this may be better and safer than buying a walker, which can give her more mobility than she's ready to handle.
◆ Give her a toy that has some transparent part to it. This will help her learn the complexities of dealing with things that are "see-through."

- ◆ Talk her through the dressing process whenever you can so she'll get in the habit of picking up her leg to put pants on and holding up her arms to put on a top.
- ◆ Use facial expression, tone of voice, and hand gestures to help your baby understand more complex commands such as, "Go inside and give Daddy a hug."
- ◆ Help her walking efforts by making sure her shoes (soft-soled) fit properly; don't buy shoes a size larger thinking she will "grow into them."

HISTORICALLY SPEAKING . . .

 When families of the Ibo tribe in Nigeria hold a party for their newborn, it's quite an affair. All babies and toddlers in the village under three years old are included because they believe they are somehow psychically linked to the newborn. Interestingly, in the African Baganda tribe, a mother may hug, caress, or comfort a toddler when she is in distress, but kissing is unheard of. Sadly, there isn't a word that conveys love in the entire Baganda language. *What We Can Learn:* In America, the mother-child relationship is a primary importance, and in the black community it is often the closest relationship a child has. Yet, often the stress and strain of juggling the new role of parent (especially of a toddler) while trying to achieve personal and professional goals is overwhelming. One method that will help: Learn your child and learn about her expected behavior before it hits you full force. You'll be better prepared to meet the challenges your curious toddler will bring.

The Twelfth Month

This is the month when most babies are ready to walk. He may grab something to steady himself first, then will probably lurch forward with his arms extended in front for balance. Undaunted by constant falls, he will get up and practice again and again. It takes a lot of concentration for him to accomplish this new task, so he is not likely to perform it for strangers on demand. Don't subject him to command performances.

Your baby is now at the height of exploring the properties of space. He thinks it will be really great to find out what kind of sound a block hitting the TV screen will make, for instance. More often, he will choose to see how cool it is to throw things down from his high chair. Although this behavior may be annoying to parents, it should not be discouraged (when feasible) or punished, because it is an important stage in babies' developmental processes. Use the opportunity to teach your child the meaning of the words *up* and *down*. To make it easier on yourself, use covered cups at mealtimes and put only a small amount of food on his plate. Baby may not be as interested in eating as he once was and may only eat a few favorite foods. Getting in all the proper nutrition will be nearly impossible. *Don't sweat it.* Do your best to ensure that he is getting a reasonable amount of the recommended nutrients. You may consider adding an egg to his milk if he's not getting enough protein.

Getting him to sleep may become a task again. There is just too much excitement in the stay-up world for him to risk missing it by sleeping. Here's where "wind-down" routines come in handy again, though it may take longer than it did before. Naps, too, may not come easily. Expect the one-year-old to scale down to one nap each day. Nudge him gradually into an afternoon nap instead of a morning nap and you'll have an easier time putting him down for the night at a reasonable hour.

The baby may go through a "fear of strangers" period again, though he may play with new adults in the familiar setting of home. He may socialize better with babies and toddlers.

This month your baby may be able to

- ◆ Turn and reach for things in every direction while in a sitting position without losing her balance
- ◆ Recognize that it is his own reflection in the mirror and not another person
- ◆ Walk with support. Some babies walk quite well by the time they reach their first birthday, but others will need support. Don't worry if your baby is not yet walking; the average age for walking well without support is about 14 months. Each child has her own unique maturational timetable.
- ◆ Walk around in her crib by holding onto the rail

Photo courtesy Monique Greenwood.

- ◆ Pick up small objects with pincer grasp
- ◆ Speak three or more words; show traces of parents' accents, if any
- ◆ Imitate sounds that things make: i.e., train—"choo, choo'; dog—"bow-wow"
- ◆ Get to a standing position from a squat, and lower herself to a sitting position
- ◆ Hold and use a crayon
- ◆ Stack blocks
- ◆ Undress herself—constantly. (You may want to dress her in clothes that snap or button *in the back* to avert this.)

How you can stimulate or soothe your baby this month

- ◆ Give your baby a simple puzzle with large pieces. Initially the baby should be encouraged to remove the pieces. Eventually she will learn how to put the pieces in place.
- ◆ Show your child how to make a tower of blocks. Then watch as she tries to do the same. Let her practice this activity over and over and see the improvement.
- ◆ Stimulate your baby's speech and vocabulary by talking, singing, and reading to her.
- ◆ Appropriate birthday presents for one-year-olds include small, soft balls; small rag dolls and stuffed animals (just make sure

that eyes, noses, and other parts are sewed on securely enough so that your child can't chew them off); the tower toy with the rings of different sizes and colors, cloth and plastic books; and musical toys or toys with sound.

◆ Praise your baby constantly when she practices walking—this can make her walk farther before toppling.

◆ Take her to a pool. Many babies this age love water and may be naturally adept at swimming. Don't set your sights on the Olympics yet, though. Unless you plan to take her swimming consistently from now on, her enthusiasm for the water may be replaced by fear by age two or three.

CHAPTER 20

Baby-Related Medical Concerns

S kim over these typical baby-related medical concerns before you have to deal with them *for real* and you may save yourself some sleep when the time comes.

Supplies to Keep in Your Medicine Cabinet

Acetaminophen	Nasal aspirator
Adhesive tape	Rubbing alcohol
Alcohol swabs	Antibiotic ointment
Bandages	Ipecac syrup
Cotton balls	Thermometer (rectal)
Cotton swabs	Tweezers
Heating pad	Vaporizer
Hot-water bottle	Zinc oxide ointment
Antiseptic solution	Band-Aids
Cotton-tipped applicators	Flashlight
Gauze	Hydrogen peroxide
Instant ice packs	Calibrated dropper
Scissors with blunt ends	Tongue depressor

How to Take Your Baby's Temperature

When you were a child, there were only two types of thermometers: oral and rectal (and, of course, the back of your mother's hand). Today there are several additional choices, including an ear thermometer, a digital-display thermometer, and forehead tapes. A rectal thermometer is still often the best choice for infants and toddlers, though it has been found that mothers almost always accurately detect whether their child has a fever just by pressing their lips or back of the hand to the baby's forehead. Other signs of a fever include flushed cheeks, fast heartbeat, faster breathing, hotter breath, and sweating.

It's easy to tell the difference between a rectal and an oral thermometer. A rectal thermometer has a short, stubby bulb, while an oral thermometer has a long, thin end. Never use an oral thermometer in the rectum. Temperature readings from a rectal thermometer will be 1° higher than readings from other thermometers and are actually the most accurate.

If, for some reason, you can't or don't want to take your baby's temperature rectally, place the rectal thermometer under your baby's armpit for 3 minutes. This will give you a ballpark idea of your baby's temperature—it will be off by about 1 or 2 degrees.

A baby's normal body temperature varies from 98°F to 99.9°F, when taken rectally. The average oral temperature in babies is 98.6°, and under the armpit it may be ½ to 1 degree lower than oral. Rectal temperature may be ½ to 1 degree higher than oral. Every baby has his or her own normal body temperature within this range, and daily temperature can fluctuate somewhat in the course of a day. Learn your baby's normal temperature by taking it when he is healthy— once in the morning and once in the late afternoon. Any temperature greater than these numbers indicates a fever.

To take your baby's temperature rectally:

1. Wash thermometer with soap and warm water, then wipe with rubbing alcohol.
2. Thoroughly shake mercury level down to below 96°F using a wrist-snapping motion.
3. Lubricate bulb of thermometer with a generous amount of petroleum jelly.
4. Lay your child across your lap, stomach down, with legs dangling. You may want to keep her diaper half on in case she

urinates. An alternative position is to lay the baby on the floor or changing table on her back, grasping both ankles and flexing the legs toward the abdomen.

5. Spread the buttocks apart with one hand so you can see the anus, and gently insert the bulb 1 inch into the rectum with your other hand. With the same hand you used to spread the buttocks, press her bottom together so the thermometer stands firm. Hold the baby's legs down with your forearm to prevent her from kicking the thermometer with her heel.

6. Leave the thermometer in for about 3 minutes (a digital thermometer will give you an accurate reading in less than 30 seconds). Keep holding it and never leave your child's side while taking temperature.

7. Wipe off thermometer and read the level of the mercury.

8. Clean thermometer with soap and warm water, and then wipe with rubbing alcohol.

What to Do If Your Baby Has a Fever

Few conditions bring fear to parents more than their child's fever. Age is an important factor when deciding how to handle a baby with a fever. If your baby is less than two months old, a temperature of 100.3° or more (rectally) is considered to be a medical emergency and you should call your pediatrician. A temperature of 98° to 99.9°F rectally is the normal temperature range for infants. Very often, though, the cause of a fever in a baby this young is simply being overdressed. Doctors who treat infants brought into emergency rooms with fevers will often undress the baby, wait 15 minutes, and then take the temperature: It is often normal. You can do this at home. A fever also often turns out to be a symptom of a common cold. If, however, the temperature is still high after you undress her, call the pediatrician.

At the sign of fever, you may give your baby Tylenol drops or any brand of acetaminophen to reduce the fever and relieve body aches temporarily while her body heals itself. If your child is more than two months old, has a temperature of 102° or more, and is not responding to the Tylenol, you should call your pediatrician. Remember, pain relievers are not antibiotics; they are not cures. Once they wear off, the pain will probably return. A fever should last an average of 72 hours, going up and down, regardless of what pain reliever you give her. If it lasts longer than that, and is unresponsive to the Tylenol, call your pediatrician. If she's teething and has swollen gums, you can rub the Tylenol directly on the gums.

What to Do If Your Baby Has a Cold

Contrary to common belief, colds are not caused by cold weather or drafts. Colds are caused by germs. That means that someone gave the viral infection to your child. Sneezing, coughing, fever, and diarrhea with or without vomiting are the usual cold symptoms and are common to infancy and early childhood, especially where there are older children in the family. There is currently no cure for this condition, and the usual antihistamine/decongestants are not recommended for babies less than 12 months old. The treatment is simply to help her feel more comfortable while she heals herself. To help, put two to three saline (saltwater) drops to each of baby's nostrils followed by suctioning the nose with an ear syringe for young infants (birth to four to five months) or with the nasal aspirator for older infants who have larger nostrils. The secret to better suctioning of the nostrils is to close one nostril while suctioning the other. Be sure to squeeze the bulb *before* you put it in the nose to make sure you are drawing the mucus out, not blowing it farther in. This allows for better vacuum action of the syringe. Tylenol (acetaminophen) may be offered, but contact your pediatrician to verify. A steamy bathroom acts as a super sauna and helps open the nostrils. Run hot water in the tub until the bathroom steams up. Sit with the baby in your lap for about 20 to 30 minutes. This will open up her clogged sinuses and is usually enough to relieve much of the congestion.

Common Baby Health Concerns

Allergies

Allergies are an exaggerated immunologic response to a specific agent (allergens) or class of agents, which can cause anything from mild irritability to generalized swelling, shortness of breath, and shock. Common allergic responses are nasal congestion, diarrhea, rashes, and rectal bleeding. The first thing to do after observing the above signs is to determine what the cause of the allergic response is and, with the help of the pediatrician, eliminate that agent from your child's diet or environment.

Bronchiolitis

More life-threatening than bronchitis, bronchiolitis is an infection that occurs in the breathing tubes leading to the lungs (brionchial tree). It is associated with cough and shortness of breath and its symptoms resemble asthma. The RSV (respiratory syncytial virus) is responsible for this condition, which infects infants of less than 12 months of age. Very early in the infection an antiviral agent may be used successfully if your pediatrician feels it necessary. Most infants get through this condition with shortness of breath and low-grade fever and require only oral medication. Occasionally, hospital care may be required. This condition may last anywhere between two and six weeks.

Conjunctivitis (Pink Eye)

This is part of an upper-respiratory-tract infection or cold that has spread to the eye. The white of the eye becomes a faint to darker pink and is associated with itchiness and white to yellow discharge or mucus, which I've heard called "sleep" by some parents. Due to the itchiness the children will tend to rub the eyes with their hands, which causes germs on the skin to infect the eyes secondarily. An antibiotic instilled in the eyes four times a day for five days is usually enough to resolve the mucus production, and the pinkness should go away in two weeks along with the cold. This is a contagious condition, so don't be surprised if the rest of the family gets it too. By the way, I've found that children despise having eyedrops instilled in their eyes. A technique I've suggested to parents is to:

1. Wipe the eyelids with a damp cloth.
2. Have your child lie down on a sofa or bed with his face up.
3. Stand at his head and ask him to close his eyes.
4. Tell the child that you are going to put medicine on his eyes and it is going to be cold.
5. With the eyelids closed put 2 drops of the medicine on the eyelids where the lids come together.
6. Then ask your child to open his eyes.

The medicine will then flood into his eyes. Don't worry if some of it runs out. More of it will probably get in this way than with other methods.

Constipation

In the young infant this may present itself as hard, small balls of stool. Formula-fed infants may have an average of one bowel movement per day to one every three days. This is in part due to the iron in the formula and the lack of roughage in a young (less than four months of age) infant's diet. The first line of intervention I use is to increase the amount of water the infant gets. One ounce of water per week of life is added to the infant's diet, up to 8 ounces per day for the first four months of life. That is, if your infant is five weeks of age she would be given 5 ounces per day; at six weeks she would get 6 ounces per day, and so on, up to a maximum of 8 ounces per day for the first four months of life so as not to compromise the "food space" in her stomach.

The next line of intervention is to change the formula to a more easily digested preparation, such as soy-bean formula. If the infant is two months of age or older, a malt supex preparation (a barley malt extract that promotes softer stools) can be used to increase the roughage content of the diet. Available in drug stores.

Breast-fed infants can have as much as four to six movements per day to as little as one large movement per week. Constipation is rarely seen in breast-fed infants. Often when this occurs it is a transient situation, when breast milk is in short supply and the infant's intestines are not being stimulated well. This is corrected by persisting in the nursing until the milk comes in or supplementing the breast-feeding with formula or water.

In infants four months or older, juices will assist in loosening the stool.

Cough

Though it seems alarming coming out of such a little body, a cough is actually a protective reflex action that keeps foreign bodies from going down into the breathing tube. This happens when you clear your throat, for instance, or when you swallow something the wrong way and you cough a few times to get it out. If you have redness, swelling, and mucus production in the trachea, you will have a continuous cough because your body is trying to get rid of whatever is blocking the airway. If your baby has a persistent cough it will often be accompanied by cold symptoms. Coughs can be upper respiratory (throat) or lower respiratory (chest) and are distinguished by the sound of the cough. The best advice is to call your pediatrician if the cough is persistent. Often the doctor will ask a parent to let the baby cough into the phone so he or she can better determine what type of cough the baby has. Babies under 12 months of age should not be given cough medicines (antitussins), antihisthamines, or decongestants because these medicines can elevate their blood pressure and cause other difficulties. A cough preparation may be prescribed by a pediatrician for a young baby in certain cases.

Croup

This is one of the most strange-sounding coughs you'll probably ever hear. Croup can be caused by a viral infection or it can be spasmodic. Both types occur in the throat area and cause a characteristic barking cough (more like a seal barking than a dog's bark) or noisy sound on inhalation. Croup occurs in young children and is associated with relatively low fever of less than 101°F. Many parents have been so frightened by this cough that they bundle up their baby and set out to the hospital in the middle of the night, only to discover that the croup is gone by the time they get there. The mist in the moist night air often cures croup, though it will probably recur. Holding the child in a steam-filled bathroom can also calm croup. If it persists, call your pediatrician. If the baby has croup with a fever of 103°F, she will be x-rayed and tested for epiglotitis, a serious infection that can close off a baby's airways.

Dehydration

Approximately 60 to 70 percent of your infant's body is composed of water. If more than 1 or 2 percent of that fluid is lost, your infant is considered to be dehydrated. The signs of this condition are decreased activity, excessive sleepiness, a weak cry with the absence of tears, little or no urination, and a dry mouth. Situations leading to this condition are sores in the mouth or throat (for example, thrush and certain viral or bacterial infections); gastroenteritis with diarrhea and or vomiting. Rarely will an infant or child dehydrate by refusing to drink unless there is a physical reason. Even the most finicky eater will tend to drink. If your child has these signs of dehydration her pediatrician should be called for early intervention.

Ear Infections (Otitis Media)

Infections in the ear are very common in older infants and children (six months to about eight years). This is in part due to the relatively short eustachian tube (the tube that connects the back of the nose to the middle ear, where ear infections commonly occur) and the young, inexperienced immune system of children. The infections are suspected when your infant has fever associated with playing with the ear.

Having an idea of the anatomy of the ear is important to understanding ear infections. Behind the eardrum there is a space called the middle ear. It is in this space that most ear infections occur. That space would be all but closed if it were not for a very short and narrow tube (the eustachian tube) that connects the middle-ear space with the back of the nose and the throat. That tube allows for pressure equilibrium on both sides of the eardrum and for drainage of fluids from the middle ear. It doesn't take very much swelling of the nose and throat to close off that eustachian tube. The result is pressure, disequilibrium, and consequent pain in the middle ear. Germs can also move up that short tube and cause ear infections very easily. Consult your pediatrician.

Thrush

This is a yeast infection of the mouth, which is very common among infants and young children. It appears as white, raised patches that may look like milk on the inner part of the lips, mouth, and tongue. One can differentiate between milk and thrush by trying to wipe the white patch off with a piece of gauze. If it is easily removed then it is milk. Thrush will remain after attempts to remove it. This form of yeast (*Candida albicans*) lives in the mouth normally and causes infection after the mouth is constantly irritated by sucking. Nursing mothers can also get this infection on their breasts. Also interesting is that the yeast does not invade the bloodstream but goes straight through the intestines to the anus, where a yeast diaper rash can occur. This appears as a beefy, red rash noted at the anal area and spreading to the folds of skin in the groin area. The treatment for both areas will usually eradicate the infection over a two- to six-week period. We currently use an antifungal agent, but years ago gentian violet (a purple dye) was used so commonly that it was rare to find a child without a purple mouth. The duration of treatment can be extensive because the source of the infection (the yeast in the dark, damp, warm mouth, which is exposed to lactose daily) is persistent.

Vomiting

This is the forceful evacuation of the stomach and is often followed by dizziness. Usually, the reason is that the baby ate too much.

Most infants spit up, especially during the first few weeks. This often occurs after eating, accompanied by a burp, or may occur after a change in position. In infants the lower esophogeal sphincter, which holds the food and other gastric contents in place, is relatively ineffective, so they may need to expel. If your baby has vomited more than once, is feeding poorly, and seems to be in pain, call your pediatrician.

A NOTE ABOUT "GRIPE WATER"

This homespun mixture of salt, sugar, water, and alcohol has been given to babies for upset stomachs since the days of Great-Grandma. The sugary, salty solution will rehydrate the body *but* the alcohol in it is potentially very dangerous to a tiny baby's brain cells and liver—not to mention that you are introducing hard liquor to an infant!

Basic Baby Emergencies

Bleeding

Don't be overwhelmed by the sight of blood. Be as calm as you can and reassure the child. Take the baby away from whatever danger caused the puncture. Apply firm pressure to the site of the wound with a clean cloth for several minutes or until the bleeding stops. If it is a deep wound, or if the bleeding continues, call your pediatrician. If the bleeding seems under control, wash the area with soap and water and apply a small amount of antiseptic ointment. Place a bandage on the wound that would be hard for the baby to remove herself, otherwise she may take it off, put it in her mouth, and possibly choke.

Burns

A baby's delicate skin is very thin and burns more easily than an adult's. Take the heat out of the burn by sopping the area with a cool compress. Do *not* put butter on a burn; it only seals in the heat! First-degree burns or abrasions are brownish red and flat. Second-degree burns and abrasions blister (swell) and may bleed. Call your pediatrician if your baby has a second-degree burn or worse.

Make sure that only tepid water is used to bathe the baby to avoid scalding.

Choking

Imagine how many little items are lying around your house for a crawling baby to choke on. Probably hundreds. Infants can also choke on foods that are too "adult" for their immature digestive systems to handle. Whenever any substance other than air enters the airway (trachea) a natural reflex occurs to expel that substance. Very often, especially in infancy, saliva will enter the airway, causing choking periodically. This is a brief, tickle-type cough, which will sound more like clearing the throat than a bad cough. If your baby is coughing forcefully, allow him to do so for a minute or so before you panic. However, if the cough is accompanied by an inability to cry and a high-pitched noise, have someone call your local emergency number and proceed to give the baby back blows and chest thrusts to clear the airway (see illustration).

Give
5 back
blows . . .

and
5 chest
thrusts.
Repeat
until object
comes out.

When Baby Is Conscious and Choking: Position the infant facedown on your arm, with your hand supporting the infant's head. You can rest the arm on your thigh for support. With your other hand, strike the infant between the shoulder blades 5 times. Turn the infant onto his back, place 2 or 3 fingers in the center of the breastbone, and give 5 chest thrusts. Each thrust should be about 1 inch deep. Turn the infant facedown again and repeat back blows followed by chest thrusts. Stop as soon as the object is coughed up or the infant starts to breathe or cough. The infant should still be taken to the emergency room to be checked by a doctor.

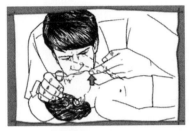

When Baby Stops Breathing: If the baby is not breathing, he will need you to breathe for him. To do this, tilt the baby's head back a bit and seal your mouth tightly over his mouth and nose. Start with 2 slow, gentle breaths and check to see if his chest is rising and falling as you do to make sure the breaths are going in. (If you are unable to breathe into an infant, his head may not be tilted properly or the airway may be blocked. Retilt infant's head and give breaths again. Give 1 slow breath about every 3 seconds until you've given 20 breaths. Check the baby's pulse on the inside of his upper arm. If the baby has a pulse but is still not breathing, continue giving the breaths until help arrives. *When Baby Has No Pulse and Is Not Breathing:* You will need to administer CPR. Place the infant on his back on the floor or table, preferably *near a telephone if you are alone.* Place two fingers on the center of the breastbone and compress the chest 5 times. Give 1 slow breath, then repeat the cycle of breaths and compressions again for about a minute.

Recheck the pulse. If you can't feel a pulse, continue with cycles of 5 compressions and 1 breath until help arrives. Check for pulse and breathing every few minutes. Be sure you or someone else has called your local emergency number.

The techniques described above will not do you much good if you haven't practiced them. Prepare yourself to care for your baby properly in a breathing emergency by taking a 1-day Infant & Child CPR course at your local American Red Cross. It's 1 day that can save your child's life.

Eye Injuries

Of most concern is the baby injuring herself by scratching her face and swiping her eye with her fingernail. Young babies often drag their fingers across their faces. Should they scratch their corneas, they could do permanent damage to their sight. Use an emery board on the baby's nails daily instead of a baby nail clipper.

Since an infant spends most of her time lying down, most other eye injuries will come from someone else or something else injuring the baby's eye. Extremely bright or fluorescent lights or flash bulbs from cameras can potentially injure a baby's eye. Try to bounce the flash off of a wall or ceiling if you are taking pictures, or take them outside in natural light. Keep the baby out of direct sunlight for more than a few minutes and use the stroller's canopy to shield the baby from the harshness of the sunlight.

There's very little you can do to help an eye injury except put a cool compress on the eye, try to assess the damage so you can explain it, and be sure to call your pediatrician.

Head Injuries

One of the first things a pediatrician will ask you if your child has a head injury is, "Did she cry right away?" If she did, this is a good sign. It means that she didn't lose consciousness, even for a short time. This minimizes the chances that she has a concussion (a bruise to the brain's surface). Console the child and ask her where it hurts. Comfort her and, if she is old enough, try to have her tell you how the accident happened. This will help you evaluate the severity of the head trauma. If she had a bad fall, for example, down the stairs, or off the bed onto a hard floor, contact your pediatrician. Check her eyes, mouth, nose, and ears for injury. Generally, a bump will emerge on the head and will grow from grape-size to golf-ball-size in a matter of minutes. Use a cool compress to reduce the swelling for about 48 hours. If the child did not cry instantly, she may have fallen unconscious for a moment, as her brain was literally shaken. Though this probably isn't permanently damaging, your doctor will evaluate her further if this is the case.

Insect Stings and Bites

Usually harmless. The sting or bite site will swell increasingly. Wash the area with soap and water to cleanse it of venom and/or insect saliva. One holistic treatment is to apply meat tenderizer and water to the sting or bite. This breaks up the protein molecules in the saliva and venom and renders them inactive. Apply .5 percent hydrocortisone cream to the area. If there is a stinger present, clean the area with peroxide and flick out the stinger with a credit card. Loosely bandage the bite site.

Call Animal Control in your area if your baby is bitten by a dog or another animal, even if it is domestic animal. You must be assured that the animal doesn't have rabies.

Mouth Injuries

Falling and biting the tongue, pushing a tooth up into the gums, damaging a tooth, or banging the outside of the mouth are common causes of mouth injuries among toddlers. If your baby falls and hurts his mouth, check for any gray or dark-colored teeth. This indicates that a tooth was injured and a blood vessel has ruptured. Broken teeth or teeth that fall out should be wrapped in a damp towel. Call your pediatrician or dentist immediately. The tooth may be able to be repaired or reinserted. Children also can fall with a protruding tongue, causing their tongue to be cut by their teeth. If the cut is deep, it may need to be sutured.

In younger babies, the most common problem in the mouth is thrush, caused by a yeast infection in the mouth (see "Thrush" earlier in this chapter). Sugar in baby formula or juice may cause this type of infection.

Avoid microwaving your baby's bottles because microwaves heat liquids unevenly. Feeling the outside of the bottle and even pouring a drop of milk on your hand can deceive you into thinking the milk isn't hot. The top could be hot, the middle warm, and the bottom cold. The result can be a baby with a scalded mouth. Also, microwaves can denature the milk—especially breast milk—so that the nutrients are killed.

Nose Injuries

Infants rarely have nose injuries. Nose-picking is a common cause of nosebleeds among toddlers. The amount of blood you think you see during a nosebleed will scare you, but it is less than what is actually there. The best thing you can do is to squeeze the front of the nose (the soft part) and lean the child's head forward, not backward as many people think. Hold it for a minute or two. How long the bleeding lasts depends on the size of the blood vessel that broke, but it shouldn't last very long.

Poisoning

Surprisingly, babies are often poisoned by things you wouldn't normally expect. They are usually too young to open jars or pill bottles, so they are often poisoned by houseplants, household cleaners, or even their own formula. Outdated cans of spoiled formula, and concentrated formula, which is meant to be mixed, are often fed to the baby by accident. Daddies, who may feed the baby less often than the mother, must watch for this. If a can of formula "hisses" and the liquid shoots out when you open it, bring it back to the store, it's spoiled. Make sure that jars of baby food are securely sealed.

Also, prevent toddlers or other small children from feeding the baby anything without your knowledge. Children want to be helpful and play grown-up like you, so they may use anything that looks like a baby bottle, such as a bottle of dish soap, to "help" feed the baby. Keep all soaps and chemicals out of the reach of a child. Make sure that your sitter's home is also reasonably child-proofed. Often grandparents don't child-proof their homes and tend to leave out pills and other items that can be harmful—even deadly—for a toddler. Paint chips, asbestos, fumes from a dry cleaner (especially if you live above one), and carbon monoxide from car fumes are all potential hazards for your baby. If you think your baby was poisoned, look around and try to assess what may have happened and call a poison control center immediately. Keep a bottle of syrup of ipecac in a locked cabinet or drawer in your home; use it to induce vomiting as your poison control center instructs by phone.

Sprains, Fractures, and Broken Bones

While broken bones in an infant may be more obvious to the eye, a sprain or fracture will be harder to detect. Generally, the baby will cry unconsolably for a long period, probably after a fall or hard knock. If this occurs, do a range-of-motion check on the baby, *very gently* moving or touching various places on the baby's body to see if something feels abnormal or if she intensifies her cry when you touch a certain part. Call your pediatrician immediately.

Resource Guide:
Places You May Want
to Know About

Pregnancy and Delivery

American College of Nurse-Midwives, 818 Connecticut Avenue NW, Suite 900, Washington, D.C. 20006, (202) 728-9860. Provides educational information about midwifery and can help locate certified nurse-midwives practicing in your area.

Depression after Delivery, P.O. Box 1282, Morrisville, PA 19067, 1-800-944-4773. Provides information on postpartum depression disorders, telephone counseling, and possesses a nationwide referral base of doctors experienced in treating the disorder.

National Association of Childbearing Centers, 3123 Gottschall Road, Perkiomenville, PA 18074-9546, (215) 234-8068. Provides information about childbearing centers across the country.

See also the YWCA, below.

Infant and Child Care

American SIDS Institute, 6065 Roswell Road, Suite 876, Atlanta, Georgia 30328, 1-800-232-7437, fax (404) 843-0577. Provides 24-hour crisis service, public awareness and prevention information, bereavement counseling referral services and research, and links families through a support network.

Auto Safety Hotline, 1-800-424-9393. Provides information about child auto safety as well as child car-seat recall information.

La Leche League (consult your phone book for the local chapter). Provides counseling, information, and support services for breast-feeding mothers.

National Organization of Single Mothers, P.O. Box 68, Midland, NC 28107, (704) 888-KIDS. Provides support and resource information for its members and issues a national newsletter.

National Organization of Mothers of Twins Clubs, P.O. Box 23188, Albuquerque, New Mexico 87192-1188, (505) 275-0955. Provides general and resource information about twins and multiple births. Maintains an ongoing list of books and periodicals about twins and multiple births.

National Women's Health Network, (202) 347-1140. Provides information on a wide range of women's health issues, including fibroids.

Poison Control Center (consult the front pages of your phone book for the local center). Provides prevention information and emergency services.

The American Red Cross, (703) 206-6000. Provides information and training on infant CPR.

United States Consumer Safety Products Commission, 1-800-638-2772. Provides information on baby safety, lead-poisoning hazards, and product-recall information. Also serves as a center for reporting unsafe products.

The YWCA (consult your phone book for the local chapter). Some chapters provide aquatics exercise programs for pregnant women.

Bibliography

Pregnancy and Birth

American College of Obstetricians and Gynecologists. *Planning for Pregnancy, Birth & Beyond* (Dutton).

Casey, Eileen. *Maternity Leave* (Avon).

Edeiken, Louise, and Johanna Antar. *Now that You're Pregnant* (Macmillan).

Evans, Debra. *The Complete Book on Childbirth* (Tyndale).

Henry, Dr. Lester, with Kirk Johnson. *The Black Health Library Guide to Diabetes* (Henry Holt).

Jones, Dr. Paul, with Angela Mitchell. *The Black Health Library Guide to Heart Disease and Hypertension* (Henry Holt).

Kitzinger, Sheila. *The Year after Childbirth: Surviving and Enjoying the First Year of Motherhood* (Scribner's).

Larson, Dr. David E., editor. *Mayo Clinic Family Health Book* (William Morrow).

Macnutt, Francis and Judith. *Praying for Your Unborn Child* (Doubleday).

Nilsson, Lennart. *A Child Is Born* (Dell).

Reuben, Carolyn. *The Healthy Baby Book* (Tarcher/Perigee).

Sears, Dr. William and Martha. *The Birth Book* (Little, Brown).

Smith, Dr. John M. *Women and Doctors* (Atlantic Monthly Press).

Smith, Pamela, and Carolyn Coats. *Perfectly Pregnant!* (Thomas Nelson).

Stoppard, Dr. Miriam. *Dr. Miriam Stoppard's Pregnancy and Birth Book* (Villard).

Thompson, Dr. Mavis, with Kirk Johnson. *The Black Health Library Guide to Obesity* (Henry Holt).

Verrilli, George E. *While Waiting: A Prenatal Guidebook* (St. Martin's).
Villarosa, Linda. *Body & Soul: The Black Women's Guide to Physical Health and Emotional Well-Being* (HarperCollins).

Baby Names

Abadie, M. J. *Multicultural Baby Names* (Longmeadow).
Faulkner, Benjamin. *What to Name Your African-American Baby* (St. Martin's).
Francis, Linda, John Hartzel, and Al Palmquist. *What's in a Name?* (Tyndale).

History of Birth

Campbell, Marie. *Folks Do Get Born* (Rinehard).
Diop, Cheikh Anta. *Cultural Unity in Black Africa* (Third World Press).
Mitford, Jessica. *The American Way of Birth* (Dutton).
Dunham, Carroll, and The Body Shop Team. *Mamatoto* (Penguin).
Logan, Onnie Lee. *Motherwit: An Alabama Midwife's Story* (Dutton).
Turner, Ann Warren. *Rituals of Birth: From Prehistory to the Present* (David McKay).

Baby Care

Brazelton, Dr. T. Berry. *Infants And Mothers*, (Dell).
Caplan, Frank, editor. *The First Twelve Months* (Grossett and Dunlap).
DeFrancis, Beth. *The Parent's Resource Almanac* (Bob Adams).
Eisenberg, Arlene, Heidi Murkoff, and Sandee Hathaway. *What to Expect the First Year* (Workman).
Jacob, Dr. S. H. *Your Baby's Mind* (Bob Adams).
Kelly, Paula, editor. *First-Year Baby Care* (Meadowbrook).

Index

· A NOTE ON THE TYPE ·

The typeface used in this book is a version of Janson, a seventeenth-century Dutch style revived by Merganthaler Linotype in 1937. Long attributed to one Anton Janson through a mistake by the owners of the originals, the typeface was actually designed by a Hungarian, Nicholas Kis (1650–1702), in his time considered the finest punchcutter in Europe. Kis took religious orders as a young man, gaining a reputation as a classical scholar. As was the custom, he then traveled; because knowledge of typography was sorely lacking in Hungary, Kis decided to go to Holland, where he quickly mastered the trade. He soon had offers from all over Europe—including one from Cosimo de' Medici—but kept to his original plan, returning to Hungary to help promote learning. Unfortunately, his last years were embittered by the frustration of his ambitions caused by the political upheavals of the 1690s.